D0084387

Religious Television

Controversies and Conclusions

COMMUNICATION AND INFORMATION SCIENCE

Edited by
BRENDA DERVIN
The Ohio State University

Recent Titles

Laurien Alexandre • The Voice of America: From Detente to the Reagan Doctrine
Bruce Austin • Current Research in Film Volume 4
Barbara Bate & Anita Taylor • Women Communicating: Studies of Women's Talk
Donal Carbaugh • Talking American: Cultural Discourses on Donahue
Kathryn Carter & Carole Spitzack • Doing Research on Women's Communication: Perspectives on Theory and Method
Fred L. Casmir • Communication in Development
Gladys Ganley & Oswald Ganley • To Inform or to Control Revised Edition
Robert Goldman & Arvind Rajagopal • Mapping Hegemony: Television News Coverage of Industrial Conflict
Enrique Gonzalez-Manet • The Hidden War of Information
Karen Joy Greenberg • Conversations on Communications Ethics
Gary Gumpert & Sandra Fish • Talking to Strangers: Mediated Therapeutic Communication
Robert Jacobson • An "Open" Approach to Information Policymaking
Manfred Kochen • The Small World
John Lawrence and Bernard Timberg • Fair Use and Free Inquiry Second Edition
Sven B. Lundstedt • Telecommunications, Values, and the Public Interest
Thomas Mandeville • Understanding Novelty: Information Technological Changes and the Patent System
Richard Morris & Peter Ehrenhaus • Cultural Legacies of Vietnam: Uses of the Past in the Present
Susan B. Neuman • Literacy in the Television Age
Eli M. Noam & Joel C. Millonzi • The International Market in Film and Television Programs
Eli M. Noam & Gerald Pogorel • Asymmetric Deregulation: The Dynamics of Telecommunication Policy
Gerald M. Phillips • Teaching How to Work in Groups
Carl Erik Rosengren & Sven Windahl • Media Matter: TV Use in Childhood and Adolescence
Michael Rogers Rubin • Private Rights, Public Wrongs: The Computer and Personal Privacy
Ramona R. Rush & Donna Allen • Communications at the Crossroads. The Gender Gap Connection
Majid Tehranian • Technologies of Power: Information Machines and Democratic Processes
Sari Thomas • Studies in Mass Media and Technology, Volumes 1–4
J.M. Wober • Fission and Diffusion: The Possibility of Public Power Over and Through the Machine

Religious Television

Controversies and Conclusions

edited by

Robert Abelman
Cleveland State University

Stewart M. Hoover
Temple University

Ablex Publishing Corporation
Norwood, New Jersey

Copyright © 1990 by Ablex Publishing Corporation

All rights reserved. No part of this publication may be reproduced, stored in a retrieval system, or transmitted, in any form or by any means, electronic, mechanical, photocopying, microfilming, recording, or otherwise, without permission of the publisher.

Printed in the United States of America.

Library of Congress Cataloging-in-Publication Data

Religious television : controversies and conclusions / edited by
  Robert Abelman, Stewart M. Hoover.
     p. cm. — (Communication and information science)
  Includes bibliographical references.
  ISBN 0-89391-643-9. — ISBN 0-89391-644-7 (pbk.)
  1. Television in religion—United States. 2. United States–
Religion—20th century. I. Abelman, Robert. II. Hoover, Stewart
M. III. Series.
BV656.3.R42 1990
269'.26'0973—dc20   89-78101
                                           CIP

Ablex Publishing Corporation
355 Chestnut Street
Norwood, New Jersey 07648

LIBRARY
ALMA COLLEGE
ALMA, MICHIGAN

To Our Families

Table of Contents

Introduction

With a new decade dawning, the structures of American electronic media are again in transition, against a backdrop of several decades of relative calm. The era of social quietude we know as "the 50s" was paralleled by a period of great stability in the form and structure of American broadcasting. From the introduction of comprehensive allocation and regulation of television in 1952, until the mid-1970s, a system of television broadcasting held sway which placed tremendous central power and programming authority in East- and West-coast-based commercial broadcasting.

Stability was the order of the day. The form and content of television programming of all kinds was largely dictated by the activities of a relatively small number of producers and advertisers. A television establishment which mirrored the social establishment exercised tremendous authority over all aspects of the medium as it grew and developed, including, most importantly, access to air time on it.

Technological change began to erode this authority in the 1970s. Cable television, long held at bay by the efforts of broadcasters and the Federal Communications Commission, grew and developed in rural and suburban areas, and eventually small national "ad-hoc networks" began to emerge which could provide some alternative programming based on these cable systems. Massive change came in the mid-1970s when domestic satellite transmission was deregulated, and true national real-time hookups became possible.

Broadcasting has not been the same since. Each year brings more and more change and realignment. Broadcasts of major sporting events have been the most recently affected, with many of them now going over to cable from their traditional place on "free TV." Before them, feature films found a most prominent place on cable, as did arts channels, music television, and extremely specialized channels (of which *The Weather Channel* is the best—and perhaps only real—example).

Systemic change came first, however, to what had been one of the "backwaters" of television in the establishment era: Religious broadcasting. Religious channels were the first, largest, and most prominent cable television networks, and continue to be important players in the business to this day. The television realities of the 1950s had enforced a certain form, structure, and system of access on religious broadcasting as they had done

1

with other types of broadcasting. The religious broadcasting that emerged with the new technologies, however, was unprecedented and unsettling.

Conventional churches found it threatening to have these sophisticated, national, real-time broadcasts available in homes throughout the country. Conventional religious denominations worried about the impact that this type of broadcasting (which was, after all, "paid-time" and which also appeared on a syndicated basis on over-the-air stations in many markets) would have on traditional relationships between religion and the media. Politicians began to take notice when some of these broadcasts took on political themes, and when they seemed to be playing a central role in the developing "new right." Theologians and other scholars began to decry the content of the broadcasts, most of which appeared to represent traditionalist and demodernist cultures at a time when modernism was the rule of the day. Media practitioners and scholars were fascinated with these developments because they seemed to represent the realization of a McLuhanesque vision of an age when the media and religion—centers of similar cultural power—would merge.

Simply put, most of these centers of cultural and intellectual authority began to realize that they lacked the theory or the tools to have anticipated—or understood—the emergence of the electronic church. What was it? Was it a new kind of religion? Was it really a new kind of broadcasting? Was it the emergence of a new reality which actually combined the power and prominence of mass media and religion? No one really knew.

The ministries of this new religious broadcasting seemed to grow and develop as the 1970s wore on. Coincident with the rise of the "new right," and culminating with the Reagan election in 1980, the religious broadcasting establishment seemed to be at least a symbol of—if not actually a cause of—much broader political and social realignment. Based on claims of massively large audiences (one estimate put the total audience for the electronic church at over 100 million) the political and social establishment took notice, and began to react.

Within a relatively short time-span, the "television preacher" or "televangelist" became a new cultural idiom. Jerry Falwell replaced Billy Graham as the most prominent and high-profile preacher in Washington. Robert Schuller was able to build a huge glass church from which to broadcast, and ran with the elite of Tinseltown. Oral Roberts, Pat Robertson, and Jimmy Swaggart opened universities and medical schools, funded by the Christian charity of their massive viewership.

A darker side of these ministries also emerged. James Robison, an evangelist from Dallas, became known for vitriolic attacks on gays and liberals. Jimmy Swaggart specialized in criticizing Catholicism. Jerry Falwell started an ominous organization called the Moral Majority. Falwell, and later Schuller, the Bakkers, and California Gene Scott fell into fiscal and legal difficulties.

The future seemed secure for most television ministries through the early 1980s, however, as audiences and income seemed to be growing fast enough to continue to support them. Some of them even began to develop internationally, with the major ministries all starting foreign distribution and fund raising to support it by 1985.

The phenomenon became front-page news again in 1987, when Oral Roberts announced a new fund raising initiative which seemed to be based on a threat by God to take Roberts to his eternal reward if a certain funding goal were not met. That same spring, Jim Bakker was revealed to have paid hush money to a former church secretary with whom he had had a sexual encounter. In 1988, the scandals continued with formerly-untouched Jimmy Swaggart also revealing a sexual impropriety—with a New Orleans prostitute. In 1989, Bakker's financial mismanagement of his PTL empire was revealed as he stood trial on 21 counts of fraud and conspiracy and faced 120 years in jail and a $5 million fine.

These controversies obscured what should have been the major electronic church story: Pat Robertson's candidacy for the Republican presidential nomination. Robertson had always positioned himself as the intellectual elite among religious broadcasters, devoting large segments of his program to lectures on national social and fiscal policy. His run for the presidency promised—at its beginning—to place him in the position of being the candidate of the conservative true believers—the "cultural conservatives"—at a time when post-Reagan realignment was dominating the Republican Party. His candidacy fizzled, and though he seemed to be contemplating a future run, he did not turn out to be the major force he expected to be. He *did* represent a new political power and sophistication on the part of the electronic church which *was* news, though.

Throughout these developments, observers continued to struggle with ways to analyze the new religious broadcasting. Theologians in the established churches continued to try to describe it in terms of its theology, which was largely fundamental or evangelical. Church leaders continued to search for and identify negative impacts on conventional churches. Political leaders of the left and the right looked for evidence of a new political force being formed. Scholars in the academic community continued to look for evidence of preexisting theories of religion and society in the phenomenon. Most of these initiatives have yet to fully account for the electronic church. It has defied simple description and has exhibited unexpected staying power.

For those of us who have been studying the electronic church for some time, the phenomenon has always had a curious, unpredictable character. When the first of the new religious broadcasts emerged nationally in the mid-1970s, they appeared to many to be just a curiosity and an anomaly. To others, they seemed to have more profound implications for contemporary assumptions about the roles and relationships of religious and media institutions.

No one, not even those of us who began to study the shows years before they appeared nationally, could have suspected at that time that they would continue to be "news" nearly 15 years later. Three developments, more than others, explain their continued public prominence.

First, their political implications. With a few notable exceptions, the roots of religious broadcasting were nonpolitical. Several of the new programs of the electronic church era seemed to change this tradition, with figures like Jerry Falwell, James Robison, Jimmy Swaggart, and Pat Robertson becoming increasingly involved in political issues and movements.

Second, the scandals. From its earliest days, religious use of the mass media had sometimes bordered on the inappropriate and scandalous. In the electronic church era, prominent religious broadcasters had been targets of accusations, legal investigations, and charges. But the 1980s opened a new chapter of major controversy and scandal, and the resultant public debate and dialogue.

And third, their entertainment value. Religious television programming has managed to attract and sustain a large and faithful audience because, in many instances, it has adopted the formats and techniques of popular, secular television. In addition, its placement in "fringe" time-slots has generated a substantial cult following among nonreligious viewers. It should also be noted that the recent scandals have provided fodder for commercial television news and entertainment programming, thereby generating greater interest and curiosity.

These 3 factors introduce different sets of emotions and issues into the debates about the phenomenon. The scandals have seemed to tap resentments and suspicions about these ministries and actually threaten their future health because the implication of hypocrisy is so potentially damaging to religious organizations. Concerns about the political implications of these programs are based in widespread fears and concerns about the proper role of religion in American society and politics. If the "media pulpit" confers on its figures a special power over the hearts and minds of viewers, then a political force of great potential will have been unleashed. The appearance and approach of religious television programming has generated concern that it has also changed the face of religion and religious expression.

These sensational implications of the electronic church have tended to mask a wide range of more subtle issues, however. Precisely what are the political potentials of these ministries? Are they a force pushing a conservative "social agenda" only? What is their role in government fiscal policy? At the state level? What affect might they have on education policy or on health policy in an era of AIDS? And what are their implications for religious institutions, religious belief, and religious behavior? What do they have to say about our received theories of the social and cultural role of the mass media?

Simply put, the electronic church raises a range of large, profound, and complex questions. It is a phenomenon which defies a simplistic or unitary explanation. Yet it has risen to prominence and demands whatever attention we are able to make at this point in time. The scandals and politics, in particular, have seemed to leave the electronic church on the social research agenda (probably permanently so), and are providing tantalizing new clues as to how people consume and make meaning of mass media in contemporary life.

The structure of this book has been dictated by the varied nature of the questions the electronic church raises. A view which hopes to be in any way comprehensive must address the topic from a variety of perspectives. Political science, sociology, anthropology, theology, ecclesiology, and communication studies all have something to contribute. Since it touches on many aspects of modern life, a range of such aspects is represented here. They are not exhaustive, but represent the best current thinking of those most directly involved in assessing the impact of the electronic church.

Inevitably, we must come around to the fact that the electronic church is, after all, a *religious* phenomenon. It is not like other media and it thus raises some unique characteristics and challenges for its observers. Religion has not been an easy thing for social science to study or understand. Received social theory has tended to relegate religion to a "tangential" or "residual" status in the social fabric. As derivative of the broader fields of sociology and social psychology, communication research has thus not been centrally interested in religion or religious phenomena.

Because of its appeals to transcendence, religion has always been able to hold part of its reality beyond scrutiny. Whatever tangible elements of it (belief, behavior, etc.) we might be able to study and account for, it can always claim to be something else, something beyond mere belief and behavior.

This fact has been daunting to some, but need not be, Social science has always only been able to describe what it can know empirically, and there is much about religion and the electronic church that can be and must be accounted for in this way.

Thus, this book is about phenomena, practices, and artifacts which have a self-conscious and self-absorbed religiosity as their basis, but it is not a book which claims to say very much about religion *qua* religion. It does not need to in order to document and enlighten us about these important current issues and trends.

It must, however, be comprehensive and multifaceted. Therefore, works by a variety of authors are presented. These writers have been chosen because they represent the best and most profound current thought and research on the electronic church. In a sense, they have selected *themselves* for inclusion in this volume because they have chosen to devote major attention to the new religious broadcasting through their professional or scholarly activities. They are a distinguished and notable group.

The author of every major recent book on the electronic church is here, presenting new and original work prepared for this volume. The investigators of the most important recent research projects are here, as are thoughtful people who have reviewed and critiqued those studies. Knowledgeable and reflective authorities from the world of religious broadcasting are here, presenting the cases for and against the electronic church approach in an incisive and clear way. The most prominent critics of the movement are here as well. The range of contributors to this volume ensures, in a way not possible otherwise, that the most current and profound thinking and research about religious broadcasting can be seen in contrast and in comparison.

The contributions of these authors have been organized around the major themes that have emerged in the last decade's debate about the electronic church. Part I gives overviews of the cultural and social significance of the movement, by presenting a range of the arguments and issues which have animated its defenders and critics. Part II looks at the history of religious television from 3 distinct perspectives—as a merging of urban revivalism and the Golden Age of Broadcasting, as an extension of religious expression, and the outgrowth of a changing regulatory environment. Part III presents the most recent research on the size and composition of the religious televiewing audience.

Parts IV through VI present perspectives on the most important areas of controversy surrounding the electronic church. In Part IV, the religious and theological bases and assumptions of religious broadcasting are discussed by representatives of the National Council of Churches, Judaic clergy, and secular humanism. Part V addresses the longstanding controversy over the fund-raising techniques employed by religious broadcasters. Part VI looks at the lack of division between electronic church and state.

Parts VII, VIII, and IX present some emerging issues and concerns about religious broadcasting as a subset of all broadcasting. In Part VII, authors examine the extent to which religion, religious themes, and religious values are, or can be, present in conventional, "secular" media. Part VIII looks at research on the extent to which the world presented in the content of religious broadcasting reflects its values or the values of wider society. Part IX presents 2 essays on the emerging issue of international religious broadcasting.

Essays from a variety of perspectives are presented in each chapter, providing the reader with the opportunity to compare and contrast the issues and arguments presented. Essays do not always therefore agree. Indeed, at times divergent perspectives are purposefully pitted against each other. Nor do they always disagree. They always, however, amplify and expand the terms of the debate by their breadth.

This volume comes at a specific point in the evolution of these phenomena. There has been over a decade of development and debate, yet no comprehensive assessment has yet appeared. It is our intention that this book be the first such assessment. It comes at a time when the political activities of the religious broadcasters have achieved a new focus, and at a time when the scandals have forced a reassessment and realignment by the movement. The essays here can help to explain these developments by presenting them in social, theological, and historical context. They also help us understand the past of the movement, and should provide keen insights into its future prospects and impacts.

It is an unavoidable fact that the recent scandals and the 1988 general election provide a common theme for many of these essays. They are not *about* the scandals, but must, necessarily, respond to the scandals and the politics. Both will no doubt continue, and some insights into their future are here. But there is more to the movement—and this volume—than the scandals and the politics.

This book is intended to be a complement to the other books which have appeared and will appear on this topic. None of them are, however, as comprehensive or multifaceted. Through these pages, we hope readers will be able to find the information and insights necessary to understand and evaluate the larger questions raised by the electronic church.

We believe strongly that this phenomenon and this book are important beyond the electronic church itself. We find ourselves, as a society, in a "media age" and cultural and anthropological studies are only now beginning to help us understand its implications. In the midst of this theoretical ferment, a phenomenon which seems to be significant of the use of modern media technology to serve traditional and deeply cultural ends, deserves serious scrutiny.

Indeed, there is a sense in which all television is "religious." That is, all television seems to be about *meaning*. It is an important conveyor of the social and cultural heritage, and provides its viewers with symbols and ideas which explain profound truths about the norms and values of the culture in which they live. A kind of television which claims for itself a special religious character is thus an important test of the extent to which the rest of television also contributes to cultural meaning for its audiences, and serves as a viable case study.

The electronic church also represents a new center of social and political power, one which is radically based in nothing more than its presence in the medium of television. The political figures of religious broadcasting are self-presented and self-designated. They have been accorded tremendous prominence and power due to the assumption that the forum provided by their television programs gives them power parallel to other national celebrities and politicians. They have effectively used the same direct-mail methods to gather large groups of constituents that have been used by political parties and instigators of social movements in recent years. An investigation of their actual political power and its implications thus is an important test of the utility of television as an independent base of social and political authority.

These are large and profound issues and questions, as we have said. The present volume, through its breadth and diversity, attempts to present the various ways scholars have chosen to look at the phenomenon of the electronic church. It is not the "last word" by any means. Instead, we hope it will be one of the "first words"—an important foundation for the long and complex task of understanding the evolution of religion and other cultural institutions in an age when the majority of Americans (and, increasingly, people throughout the world) turn to television for entertainment, enlightenment, and meaning.

Robert Abelman
Cleveland, OH

Stewart M. Hoover
Philadelphia, PA

I
Myths and Misperceptions

Religious broadcasting has become a major phenomenon on the American scene. The scandals, the politics, the controversies, the investigations, the flamboyant publicity—all of these things have contributed to a public picture of religious broadcasting which greatly differs from both its "received history" and its present reality. It has been accused of many things by its critics—both "religious" and "secular"—and many things have been claimed for it by its proponents and defenders. Much printer's ink and many hours of video and audio tape have been dedicated to analyzing it.

Yet the reality of the electronic church is as unclear after most of this debate as it was before it. The "new religious broadcasting," that which emerged in the mid-1970s as part of the broader revolution that was overtaking electronic entertainment technology, may well have been a revolution in religion and in television. We don't know just yet. What we do know is that the explanations for its rise, rapid spread, prominence, and (in some cases) its downfall, are probably simpler and more modest than is often claimed. It seems not to have emerged from a right-wing conspiracy to overwhelm modern public debate with reactionary propaganda. It seems not to be a major threat to conventional religiosity (writ large) though it certainly has implications for current trends in American Protestantism. Most importantly, it seems not to be a "new type of religion" as some technological determinists would have had it.

Its sources and its explanations are largely available to us the "old-fashioned" way—we must look for them in the historical, social, and cultural processes of the moment in which the electronic church emerged. It is, first of all, a kind of broadcasting, and its roots can be seen in the realities of that medium. It is also—of course—a "religious" activity, and we can learn much by considering its roots in American Protestant movements and in baseline American religiosity. It arose at a specific moment in history, in interaction with other developments, both "sacred" and "secular," and we must consider that history.

The greatest challenge facing any broadcaster is programming. Having several hours a day to program is one thing (and quite an expensive proposition in itself). Finding acceptable programming to fill those hours is another thing entirely. Television is very expensive to produce—exponentially more expensive than radio—and religious groups have traditionally been reluctant to exploit the potential of television, except on a basis where the production costs would be born by someone else. In the early days of television, those "someones" included local broadcasters and the networks themselves, who were eager to demonstrate that they had "public interest" motives at heart, and would be willing to pay for the production of programming that served public needs in addition to the commercial programming from which they derived much income.

Some religious organizations either could not or did not want to participate in such largesse. For them, television was therefore nearly out of reach due to its complexity and expense. The result was a kind of religious segmentation by medium. Independent, fundamentalist, "Bible Belt" preachers held sway on syndicated radio—often raising money on the air in order to pay the bills—and more establishment, mainstream, and ecumenical organizations were on local and network television.

Two broadcasts emerged which broke this mold. The first was Roman Catholic Bishop Fulton J. Sheen's which became a sensation on *commercial* television in the 1950s. Sheen's was such a popular prime-time program that he even became a ratings contender for a time. The second religious broadcaster who emerged to national prominence on television was Billy Graham, who was able initially to purchase air time from ABC, and later, when network time became more expensive, began to syndicate his crusades to independent stations.

The popular stereotype of religious broadcasting before 1975 (the beginning of the electronic church era) was then made up of these components. First, there were the national, industry-produced religious programs, typically produced by a dedicated "religion department" at each of the networks. These were usually aired in what came to be known as the religion "ghetto" on Sunday morning. Second, there were 1 or 2 nationally known religious figures who appeared more or less regularly (such as Graham and Sheen, the latter ending his program in the early 1960s). Finally, and most significantly for the average viewer or listener, there were the hundreds of religious *radio* programs which appeared all over the dial, especially at night. Many of these were more entertaining than enlightening to a typical listener, offering snake oil as well as salvation. Of course, a "hard core" of true believers listened to these shows regularly. For the majority, however, they continued to be a hackneyed, quaint, slightly amusing, but generally irrelevant backwater of the cultural environment.

These received stereotypes, however, masked changes that were already underway in religious broadcasting before 1975, changes which set the stage for the emergence of religious broadcasting as the major national institution it has become. Oral Roberts broadcast his tent-meeting healing services throughout the 1950s. Rex Humbard had been on television for years. Pat Robertson's ministry had owned a television station since 1961. Beginning in the early 1970s, more and more religious television stations had begun to go on the air (Armstrong, 1979).

The chapters in this section address the image and the reality of the religious broadcasting which emerged in the mid-1970s. It was not really as new as it seemed, but it was also not as easy to explain as most observers assumed. Each of the essays here comes at the phenomenon from a different direction. Sociologists and commentators Jeffrey Hadden and Anson Shupe present a thorough and incisive description of the ways in which prominent observers of the national scene—religious and secular—have "missed the boat" in their criticisms and analyses of the electronic church. They argue forcefully that the new religious broadcasting is in some ways more and in some ways less than "meets the eye," but that most observers have not understood it well, preferring to fall back on stereotypes and cultural myths about it—most notably that of Sinclair Lewis' *Elmer Gantry*. The best-known criticisms of religious broadcasting may tell us more about the biases of the critics than about the phenomenon itself.

Stewart Hoover presents a more comprehensive review of the 10 most popular and often-recounted "myths" about the electronic church. He suggests that the responsibility for spreading the most voluble of these myths needs to be shared by critics and supporters of the electronic church alike. Everyone's interests are often served by preserving some of these notions. He presents, for each myth, a historical or social analysis of it, and attempts to set each in a context from which the reader can, we hope, draw a more reasoned and durable conclusion.

Finally, communications professor Quentin Schultze reviews the phenomenon from a communication-theoretical perspective. The electronic church, he suggests, is a symbolic reality which has emerged out of the interaction between broadcast technology and evangelical social movements. Much of what we know and assume about it can be best understood if we look at the theological, social, and technological practices of the larger movements of which it is a part.

The overall message of this section is that, if we are to really understand the electronic church, we must look beneath its most durable and salient images. It is an important phenomenon, but one whose importance is in its very complexity, not in simplistic or stereotyped perceptions.

REFERENCES

Armstrong, B. (1979). *The electronic church*. Nashville, TN: Thomas Nelson.

1

Elmer Gantry: Exemplar of American Televangelism

Jeffrey K. Hadden
Anson Shupe

The first news of the televangelism scandals at Heritage USA had scarcely gone out over the wire services before an old name in the lore of evangelism found its way back into America's consciousness—Elmer Gantry. He was also a hypocrite and a slick-talking scoundrel. Gantry consumed great quantities of whiskey, seduced church secretaries, and removed the choir robes of countless virgins, all without the slightest qualm of conscience. He stole from little old ladies and lined his pockets with offerings from the collection plate.

Elmer Gantry was as loathsome a character as has ever been born in the mind of an American writer. Few Americans have actually read Sinclair Lewis's (1927) novel about the barn-storming tent evangelist. Still, millions know *Elmer Gantry* is a story about a preacher who personified all that is wrong with fundamentalist religion.

So magnificently and seductively does Lewis develop his conniving and lecherous evangelist that it is too easily forgotten that Elmer Gantry never existed. He is a composite caricature of all the worst features of evangelists, without the slightest hint that there were any redeeming features in any of them. The thought that some evangelists might have been honest men and women, doing the best they could by the means available to them to preach the gospel and do good, never emerges for even an instant.

Elmer Gantry cannot be understood outside the context of the man who created him. Sinclair Lewis was a social critic and satirist who not only rejected, but repudiated, his small-town Minnesota roots. Lewis hated everything that smacked of provincialism, conformity, or hypocrisy. He also hated lawyers and physicians, but most of all, Lewis hated religion. Lewis's life embodies the cultural struggle between the sophisticated secular urban world and the simpler life in the hinterland, a life which urban sophisticates presumed was rapidly dying out. Lewis was not content to merely walk away from his Midwestern roots; he spent his life attempting to hasten their passing.

Sinclair Lewis's caricature of an evangelist has survived. When the tele-vangelism scandals broke in 1988, the mass media wasted little time in invoking the name Elmer Gantry. But newspaper writers didn't have to pull the novel from a shelf or locate a videotape of the 1950s movie starring Burt Lancaster to become acquainted with Gantry. Lewis's character had long since left the tents with sawdust trails and taken up residence in plush television studios.

For most of this decade, made-for-television movies and dramatic series featuring a television preacher have been straight out of *Elmer Gantry*. An ABC television movie entitled "Pray TV" left viewers with little doubt that the message was about *preying* and not *praying*. Portrayals of televangelists in such series as *Murder, She Wrote, Mike Hammer,* and *Spencer for Hire,* among others, are vintage Gantryesque portraits.

Like Elmer Gantry, these fictionalized televangelists are obsessed with money and power. To protect their turf and hide their lecherous lifestyles, the characters portrayed have no qualms about living on the edge, even outside the law. Lying is not a defensive measure to save one's hide. It is, along with sweetness and slick talk, a means to whatever ends are desired. And, it is assumed, every high-rolling television preacher must have a carefully concealed Swiss bank account as insurance against the possible future discovery of his fraudulent religious racketeering. The legacy of Elmer Gantry which Sinclair Lewis bequeathed to American culture is a stereotype so mean and nasty that had he been portraying a black man we most certainly would have witnessed an outcry of protest demanding copies of the book be removed from libraries and that the movie version of the novel not be run on late night television.

Part of the success of any stereotype rests with a viewer's or reader's unfamiliarity with the person or group being portrayed. The negative image of contemporary televangelists is so powerful because it "fits" the legacy of the evangelist our culture has inherited from Sinclair Lewis. Millions of Americans who have never switched the dial on their television sets to a religious program are convinced, beyond any reasonable doubt, that the caricature they carry around in their head is quite literally true to life.

Occasionally academic scholars have published papers which, at least by inference, suggest that it might be inappropriate to tar and feather all religious broadcasters with the Gantryesque stereotype. But then came the dreadful televangelism scandals of 1987 and 1988. Oral Roberts, Jim Bak-ker, Jimmy Swaggart, and a lesser cast of luminaries, contributed to rein-forcing the Elmer Gantry stereotype.

The stormy month of March 1987 was a watershed in the history of religious broadcasting. It began when the press discovered that Oral Roberts was claiming to be held hostage by God Almighty. If Oral didn't raise $8 million in "ransom money" by the end of the month, God would surely call him home. The press descended upon Tulsa, Oklahoma for the bizarre countdown to April Fools Day, a donnybrook of extraordinary proportions. Would Oral emerge triumphant, cash in hand, from his Prayer Tower on the campus of Oral Roberts University? Or would he be snatched home by his Heavenly Father?

The media were having so much fun with the Roberts story that they missed the announcement that Tammy Faye Bakker, star of the PTL Network's *Jim and Tammy Show,* had entered the Betty Ford Center for drug rehabilitation. Then came the fateful announcement on March 19 that Pentacostal Jim Bakker was stepping down as head of PTL and Heritage USA, and that he would be replaced by fundamentalist Jerry Falwell. The precipitating event was the eminent disclosure of a sexual encounter Bakker had with a former church secretary seven years earlier. Bakker didn't deny that the tryst had happened, but he didn't go quietly or in shame. In his resignation statement, broadcast on the PTL Network, he claimed that he "was wickedly manipulated by treacherous former friends . . . who victimized me with the aid of a female confederate" (Bakker, 1987, p. A1). God and Tammy Faye had forgiven Jim for his brief sexual encounter with Jessica Hahn. He seemed perplexed that others could not forgive him as well. He was ready to get on with the business of building Heritage USA, Jim and Tammy Faye's own fantasy world, which they dreamed would one day be a veritable spiritual Disneyland.

Jim could only explain his unfortunate position in the context of years of "constant harassment and pressures by various groups and forces whose objective has been to undermine and to destroy us" (Bakker, 1987, p. A1). He admitted that paying blackmail was "poor judgment" but he only did it to "to protect and spare the ministry and my family."

With attention focused on the sordid details of the live soap opera unfolding at Heritage USA, Oral Roberts' give-or-I-die fund raising shenanigans might have been completely overlooked had it not been for his shameless acceptance of a $1.3 check from a Florida racetrack owner. The donor said he thought Oral ought to check in with a psychiatrist. But neither the putdown nor the thought that this might be Satan's money bothered Roberts in the slightest.

Even as America was learning the details of the blackmail paid for Bakker's brief encounter in a Florida motel, and trying to comprehend why a fundamentalist might encounter resistance to taking over a Pentecostal ministry, there came additional charges which drew yet another major televangelist into the conflict. From Norman Roy Grutman, attorney for PTL, came the accusation of "unmistakable evidence . . . that Jimmy Swaggart was attempting to orchestrate the ouster of Jim Bakker" (Frank & Grove, 1987, p. A14).

"I'm ashamed, I'm embarrassed," retorted Jimmy Swaggart, the thunderous pulpit pounder from Baton Rouge, Louisiana. Continued Swaggart:

The gospel of Jesus Christ has never sunk to such a level as it has today. We've got a dear brother in Tulsa, Oklahoma, perched up in a tower telling people that if they don't send money that God's going to kill him, then we got this soap opera being carried out live down in South Carolina all in the name of God. (Frank & Grove, 1987, p. A14)

But those who preached the gospel on the airwaves would sink lower still. There was a lot more embarrassment and shame to come: the sex, the bad taste, the details of the robbing of the PTL treasury, the rumors of an imminent return of the Bakkers.

Then there was the presidential candidacy of M.G. "Pat" Robertson, only months earlier the host of the *700 Club,* the most frequently watched religious broadcast in America (Clark & Virts, 1985). Robertson's campaign itself had some bizarre moments, but in April of 1988, just as it appeared that a former televangelist might be a serious player in the Republican presidential nomination sweepstakes, yet another scandal unfolded.

Jimmy Swaggart, the biggest and toughest and holiest of them all, tearfully confessed before television cameras that he too had fallen to the sins of the flesh. Unlike the indiscretion that Jim Bakker's former friends has lured him into, Jimmy Swaggart had, of his own volition, been hanging out with lowly prostitutes, in a New Orleans neighborhood. Marvin Gorman, once a rising televangelist whose career was wrecked when Jimmy Swaggart blew the whistle on his sexual misconduct, had trailed Swaggart to a seedy motel in New Orleans and photographed him with a prostitute.

While the fate of the Swaggart religious empire hung in doubt, Robertson's political aspirations did not. Robertson's claim that the timing of the disclosure of Swaggart's misconduct was a dirty trick staged by the Bush campaign helped seal his fate as an uncreditable candidate. He didn't drop out of the campaign immediately, but the enthusiasm of his "invisible army" was gone. And a financially troubled Christian Broadcasting Network brought him back to a co-host role on the *700 Club* in May, something he said would never ever happen.

Also in May, Rufus Reynolds, the judge presiding over the Chapter 11 bankruptcy reorganization of PTL, concluded that liquidation was inevitable. Jim Bakker returned to Charlotte claiming that "God has given us a plan how to pay for it and how to restore it" (Associated Press, 1988, p. A2). But arrangements fell through.

By midyear of 1988 it seemed that the saga of lurid revelations of sleaze and corruption in televangelism land would never end. And all of this was not Burt Lancaster portraying Elmer Gantry. It was life imitating art!

There have been scandals in American religion before. For more than 200 years, America's great evangelists have been colorful and controversial. And a few of them have been real rascals. So it should have come as no surprise that the development of radio and then television would only enhance the visibility of the controversial few. And indeed they did.

The scandals of 1987 and 1988 were not the first in broadcasting. Back in the 1920s, Aimee Semple McPherson, the beautiful and flamboyant radio evangelist, titillated America's prurient interests with her alleged love affairs. Father Charles E. Coughlin's bombastic demagoguery from his radical pulpit far exceeded any mixing of religion and politics that we have seen in more recent times. And in 1976, Billy James Hargis, whose program was carried on 140 television stations, became the first major televangelist to fall when he was accused of both homosexual and heterosexual affairs. Lesser figures of radio and television evangelism have fallen victims to booze, sex, and at least one was imprisoned for swindling his followers.

Nothing like the 1987–88 scandals had ever befallen religious broadcasting before. The scandals were a disaster to the broadcasting industry and a devastating blow to millions of listeners whose faith was shaken. To the secular mass media, it was "show time." "An irresistible spectacle," *Newsweek* called it on June 8, 1987 in its second cover story of the scandal in as many months (Watson, 1987). Cartoonists and satirists had a field day. Doug Marlette's nationally syndicated cartoon strip "Kudzu," for example, features in iconoclastic character named The Reverend Will B. Dunn. Transformed into a televangelist, Will's ministry was ruined when he got entangled with Tammy Faye in the "Mascarascam." But this did not destroy Marlette's ability to get Reverend Will entangled in every scrape faced by the whole world of televangelism. Perhaps no piece of videotape has been copied more times than the *Saturday Night Live* interview of the "Church Lady" with comedy troupe actors playing Jim and Tammy Faye Bakker discussing the infamous encounter with the church secretary at a Florida resort.

By any standard of soap opera sleaze, the televangelist scandals were spectacular first-class drama. For sheer entertainment, the unfolding sagas were better and juicier than any episode of *Dallas* or *Dynasty*. The mass media were accused, with some justification, of perpetuating a circus-like atmosphere. But if the mass media explicated the opportunity, and did not always exercise the best taste, it was the televangelists themselves who wrote the script.

Not all of the commentary was in fun. There was plenty of serious, sardonic satire, as a secular press discovered new heights of piety. "[B]eneath the little-girl sweetness and outrageous wigs and false eyelashes," wrote Jean Seligman in *Newsweek*, "Tammy Faye Bakker is as shrewd as Imelda Marcos—and probably just as unrepentant about her excesses" (1987, p. 69). And, wrote Tom Shales, *Washington Post* television critic, "The thrill of watching a *Jim and Tammy Show* is something comparable to the thrill of a Judy Garland show late in Garland's career, when some members of the audience showed up just to see if she'd make it through the night" (1987, p. B1).

With ratings soaring, ABC's *Nightline* devoted more than a dozen programs to the scandals. There was big money in the scandals, and no one made out better than the publishers of skin magazines. Hugh Hefner twice enticed Jessica Hahn to pose and tell all about her encounter with Bakker for the pages of *Playboy*. Later, *Penthouse* publisher Bob Guccione won the bidding rights to show all and send Debra Murphree, the prostitute that Jimmy Swaggart frequented on Airline Highway in New Orleans, on a promotion tour that included an appearance on the *Phil Donahue Show* to bolster sales of the July, 1988 issue of *Penthouse*. Seldom in the history of radio and television has there been such a blatant exploitation of a pathetic person for profit.

Before the scandals broke in 1987, large proportions of Americans were scarcely aware of the thriving religious broadcasting industry. But of those who were aware of the televangelists, large proportions of them held unfavorable opinions. In a national poll conducted for the *Los Angeles Times* in July, 1986, 59 percent of the public reported that they were "not aware" of Jim Bakker; 47 percent and 41 percent respectively said they were not aware of Pat Robertson and Jimmy Swaggart (Los Angeles Times, 1986). Only Billy Graham (by a margin of 3:1) and Robert Schuller (by a margin of 2:1) had net positive ratings. The scandals greatly increased name recognition and, predictably, negative ratings soared as well. The *LA Times* replicated their survey after the scandals broke and found that favorable ratings fell for everyone except Billy Graham (Los Angeles Times, 1987).

Had the scandals been limited to the Bakkers, America's heightened awareness of the religious broadcasters might have led to some sorting out of the cast of video vicarage. That is, Americans might have made discriminating judgments, sorting out the "good guys" from the "bad guys" as it were. But bombarded by the seemingly endless revelations of misconduct, it was inevitable that the negative imagery would spill over and taint the entire industry. How could America not come to the conclusion that the televangelists are scoundrels, all real-life Elmer Gantrys?

The high mass media visibility of religious broadcasters will pass. And most of them will consider that a blessing. The high visibility they received in 1987 and 1988 did not lead to a better understanding of who they are and why they are attractive to a rather substantial minority of Americans. Rather, it tended to reinforce the stereotypes that were already prevalent in our culture. These stereotypes, we have argued, are the legacy of an era of tension between religion and the emerging secular culture during the early part of this century. Sinclair Lewis' caricature of an unscrupulous evangelist is the conduit or carrier of that legacy. The unscrupulous televangelists have played their part in giving credence to the stereotype.

The myth of Elmer Gantry as exemplar of American televangelism will persist for a long time. It is a kind of variant on Gresham's Law: The dishonorable televangelists will not drive the honest ones from the airwaves, but the bad name they so deserve will tarnish the honest broadcasters as well and make it more difficult for the latter to do their work. And, in all likelihood, the myths enumerated by Stewart Hoover in the next chapter in this volume will also be with us.

An examination of information flow about religious broadcasters can readily provide an explanation of why the stereotypes and myths will persist. Production and distribution of information about religious broadcasting come from 4 groups: (a) the religious broadcasters themselves, (b) their adversaries, (c) scholars, and (d) the mass media.

Religious broadcasters. From the perspective of their adversaries, scholars, and the press, information that comes from broadcasters themselves is likely to be treated as propaganda. All organizations, of course, engage in some public relations efforts to create the best possible image of themselves. And only rarely have we witnessed examples of organizations voluntarily hanging their dirty linen out for public inspection. The press knows this and they expect organizations to hide information and put the best spin possible on that which they release. And given the legacy of highly negative images, televangelists and their spokespersons will be especially suspect of slick talk and hiding the truth.

Religious broadcasters have never had a very felicitous relationship with the secular media. They tend to view the media as unsympathetic, even hostile toward them. Most of them have sufficient anecdotal evidence to sustain continued suspicion and distrust of the media. And most of them have not brought in public relations specialists to deal with the mass media. For the immediate future, at least, broadcasters are likely to continue to view their audiences, and known sympathetic supporters, as the primary outlets for communications about their ministries. A few may develop more sophistication in dealing with the media, but most will continue to flounder, ducking communication as often as possible, and living in constant fear that reporters are really only present to "do a job" on them.

Religious broadcasters, thus, are essentially locked into a closed communications loop, maintaining positive images. As long as this remains the case, they are unlikely to have much input into what the mass media write about them.

Adversaries. Adversaries of religious broadcasting fall into 4 frequently overlapping groups: (a) theological, (b) competitors, (c) ideological, and (d) political. Theological diversity is at the heart of the religious vitality of American culture, and this diversity guarantees a large opposition. An overlapping, but distinct adversarial group are those who stand in competition for access to the airwaves. Liberal Protestants, who once had a virtual monopoly to the airwaves, are the principle but not the only group in direct competition. Ideological adversaries are committed to a secular world view and many in this group are opposed to any religious group having access to the airwaves (see, for example, Chapter 12). Finally, there are many who view the conservative political messages of the televangelists as a threat perception of "the American way." Norman Lear's People for the American Way, for example, was created for the explicit purpose of doing battle with the televangelists. In varying degrees, each of these 4 groups is engaged in the production and distribution of negative information about religious broadcasters.

Scholars. Scholars are the smallest group engaged in the production of consumable information about religious broadcasters. Indeed, a fair proportion of the scholarly community interested in religious broadcasting is represented in this volume. As often typifies scholarly groups, they are prone to communicate obtusely, elucidate *ad infinitum* alternative interpretations of the meaning of data, quarrel among themselves about matters that are imperceptible to the consumer public, and qualify conclusions to the point that consumers can't understand or don't care what they are saying.

To this should be added the simple observation that financial resources to conduct empirical studies of religion have long been scarce and this is unlikely to change. In the absence of large data bases, scholars are compelled to conduct small surveys and secondary analyses of resources like the Arbitron and Nielsen audience ratings, and to engage in creative speculation (see Chapter 3 for more information).

Scholars do play an important role as resource persons for print and broadcast journalists assigned to cover religious broadcasting. But given the diversity of interpretations among this group, and the absence of much authoritative data, scholars are not very significant players in the arena where the images, myths, and symbols about religious broadcasting are created.

Mass media. Most of what the general public knows about religious broadcasting is communicated through newspapers, radio and television news and documentaries, and radio talk shows. The messages from religious broadcasters, adversaries, and scholars are all filtered through the mass media.

The mass media collectively are not simply a conduit for communication of news and analysis. This was especially evident during the televangelism scandals of 1987 and 1988. Television personalities themselves became central players in the unholy wars. The guests they selected for their programs, the questions they asked and which answers they chose to probe, and analyses they offered made Ted Koppel, Larry King, and others as much a part of the spectacle as Jim and Tammy Faye Bakker, Jerry Falwell, Jessica Hahn, Oral Roberts, and Jimmy Swaggart.

The mass media were simultaneously makers, packagers, participants, and interpreters of the news. The images, analyses, and conclusions America received about the scandals and the broader world of religious broadcasting were essentially created by the mass media. The mass media shouldn't be criticized too severely for their role in keeping the story alive. But it is significant to note that during the 15-month period or so when the scandals were a regular part of the national news, not a single major news source devoted any time or space to investigative reporting about those televangelists who were not scandal-ridden. During the same time period, considerable investigative reporting resources were devoted to trying to uncover more dirt in other ministries.

It does seem curious that for all the attention devoted to the scandals editorial curiosity never brought forth any effort to learn and write about those ministries and personalities that were not scandal-ridden. One might assert that the mass media are biased against the televangelists, and there is some evidence to indicate that this is true. But the accusation of bias does not get to the heart of the problem. Rather than crying "bias," we can better understand the nature of the mass media coverage if we ask a simple and fundamental question: What are the presuppositions of those who decide what is newsworthy with respect to the subject they are investigating? If one assumes a priori that religion and the modern world don't mix, that religions belong properly in the private sphere, then it is highly likely that something as clamorous as televangelism will arouse suspicion from the onset. Nothing carries so well on visual-driven television as conflict. It follows that among the sources offering information about religious broadcasting, the adversaries of religious broadcasting are likely to gain a disproportionate amount of attention. That the critics share value presuppositions which are compatible with the presuppositions of the mass media is likely to result in their being viewed as "creditable" sources.

If the mass media had dug beneath the grotesque Gantryesque stereotype of the religious broadcasters, they would have discovered that most of the radio and television ministries are operated by men and women of good will and integrity. And they would have found that many of the broadcasters would readily admit that the scandals helped them to see themselves in a new light and forced them to reassess their own activities and accountability to supporters. Many now understand more clearly than they were earlier able to see how competition, the desire to grow, and, in some instances, how the sheer struggle to survive had drawn them into the use of fund-raising tactics that were questionable.

More importantly, in the past, religious broadcasters have jealously guarded their organizational autonomy. Scandals in someone else's ministry were not their problem. But the fraud, deception, and hypocrisy that became evident as details of the PTL scandal unfolded, and the hoax of a wrathful God holding his televangelist servant hostage to pay broadcasting bills were simply too much to ignore. The credibility of all broadcasters was profoundly challenged. Perhaps not so much out of an altruistic desire to be their brothers' keeper as a desire to protect their own hides, the National Religious Broadcasters created a regulatory agency (Ethics and Financial Integrity Commission) with real teeth to enforce standards of ethical conduct. Membership in EFICOM is *not* optional for NRB members. When Swaggart confessed his sexual misconduct, NRB Executive Committee wasted no time in recommending expulsion—even before the machinery of EFICOM was in place.

However reluctantly, the broadcasters have come to the conclusion that they cannot escape the negative stereotypes that a few of their brethren have helped create and sustain. If they don't become complacent once the storms of the scandals have blown over, the broadcasters would become a model of integrity for voluntary organizations in America. But this will not come easily. Even if there are no further scandals among NRB members for a sustained time, the most unscrupulous will remain outside of the organization's watchdog organization. And their excesses and misdeeds will continue to cast a shroud of doubt regarding the integrity of all broadcasters.

In the final analysis, the market test for those broadcasters who operate with integrity will be whether they are reaching an audience that finds inspiration in their message. And if they do, they will survive. But in the minds of the millions who are neither turned onto their programs nor attuned to their theology and world view, Elmer Gantry will remain alive and well as exemplar of American televangelism.

REFERENCES

Associated Press. (1988, June 9). Bakker says God has given him plan. *Charlottesville Daily Progress,* p. A2.

Bakker, J. (1987, March 20). Transcript of resignation statement. *Charlotte Observer,* p. A1.

Clark, D.W., & Virts, P.H. (1985, October 25). *Religious television audience: A new development in measuring audience size.* Paper presented at The Society for the Scientific Study of Religion Conference, Savanna, GA.

Frank, J.A., & Grove, L. (1987, March 24). The raging battles of the evangelicals. *Washington Post,* pp. A1, A14.

Lewis, S. (1927). *Elmer Gantry.* New York: Harcourt, Brace.

Los Angeles Times. (1986). Los Angeles Times poll: Religion and politics, LAT 108. Los Angeles, CA: Author.

Los Angeles Times. (1987). Los Angeles Times poll: Religion and politics, LAT 108C/Panelback. Los Angeles, CA: Author.

Seligman, J. (1987, June 8). The inimitable Tammy Faye. *Newsweek,* p. 69.

Shales, T. (1987, May 29). The "Nightline" coup. *Washington Post,* p. B1.

Watson, R. (1987, June 3). Heaven can wait. *Newsweek,* pp. 58–62, 65.

2

Ten Myths About Religious Broadcasting

Stewart M. Hoover

Religious broadcasting burst onto the national scene in the mid-1970s. Suddenly, it seemed, there was an endless and varied stream of religious programs on television, in places they had never been seen before (e.g., Chicago, New York, San Francisco). Perhaps more importantly, they were saying things and doing things religious broadcasters had never done before. They were not preaching all the time. They didn't look and sound like tent-meeting revivalists. Instead, a new, cool, smooth sophistication seemed to typify the personalities and programming of this "new-found" form of religious broadcasting.

All of this led to the widespread feeling that a major revolution in religious communication had taken place which, in part, amazed and confused many a casual viewer. Consequently, a mythology arose around the electronic church. A major watershed had been reached, many thought, and media religion had finally gone "big time." The image of the electronic church came to be made up of a number of "myths." The commonplace usage of this term implies falsehood. That is not what is meant here. Myth in the truest sense of the word implies a set of ideas and symbols surrounding social and cultural practice. These ideas and symbols may not be empirically verified or verifiable (the falsehood part) but by their nature they illustrate a greater or more abiding cultural or social truth. Thus, when we think of the mythology of the electronic church we must be aware that we are looking at a set of explanations and elaborations which tell us something profound about it, whether or not they can be independently verified as "true."

It is the purpose of this chapter to present, and discuss, 10 of the most common myths about modern religious broadcasting, and through them come to some more important underlying truths about the phenomenon. They are listed here not in order of importance so much as in order of their appearance in the debate about the phenomenon. Some of them arose out of the institutions and industries of the electronic church itself. Others come from critics of the movement. All of them, taken together, help us understand it better.

Myth Number I: The electronic church is what happens to religion when it goes on television. These new religious broadcasts seem, to many observers, to represent a type of religious expression which is troubling. The "show-biz" orientation (the sets, music, and "entertainment" value) of many of the programs seems to run counter to commonly-held assumptions regarding what is "appropriate" religious activity. Ministers of conventional churches are not usually thought to be selected because of their physical characteristics, yet the typical electronic church preacher is well-coiffed, well-dressed, smooth, and persuasive. They are even occasionally mistaken for regular television announcers, as one study found (Hoover, 1988).

More importantly, elements of the programs, which seem to mimic conventional (e.g., mainstream) television in form and style, seem to represent the bending and shaping of religion to fit the demands of a very secular medium. In the most comprehensive defense of the form, Armstrong (1979) addressed such criticisms by suggesting that the seeming sophistication of these programs is a natural consequence of having to compete on a medium where image is so important.

When seeing it for the first time, many people who are unfamiliar with American religious movements assume that the formats, technical sophistication, on-air fund raising, and general "hype" of the electronic church is an effect of the "medium" on the "message." While this may have been true with respect to some elements of these programs, by and large what the audience saw were tried and true formulas of the revival circuit, put to use in a new medium which was hospitable to them. In short, electronic church broadcasting springs from a religious tradition—frontier evangelicalism—which has always stressed a simple and straightforward message, carefully packaged for maximum effect (see, for example, Chapter 4 of this volume). Rather than being what happens "when religion goes on television," the electronic church is, instead, the use of the medium of television by a religious expression which simply "fits" especially well there.

Myth Number II: The electronic church has a huge and significant audience. The second myth stems from the roots of the phenomenon in rapid technological expansion. Many observers, broadcasters, and critics of the movement have too easily assumed that just because these programs are available in an unprecedented number of markets around the country, and because they have millions to spend on the purchase of transponder time on satellites and air time of local television stations, they must be supported by large audiences. This is an easy assumption to make. Commercial broadcasting is successful and indeed stays on the air *only* if it is attractive to large audiences. This is not necessarily the case with religious broadcasts. Because the money comes directly from donations, and not from the sale of advertising time, income is not really related to actual audience size. A commercial broadcaster must attract a large audience, confirm its size by purchasing audience research services from Nielsen or Arbitron, and then sell that audience to advertisers. A religious broadcaster only needs to raise money to purchase the air time on television stations or on a satellite, and he or she is in business.

Admittedly, there is some relationship between audience size and income to the electronic church. If no one watched, then there would be no one to call in, put their name on the mailing list, and be solicited for contributions. However, sophisticated modern fund-raising techniques such as those described by some studies of the phenomenon (Hadden, 1980; Hoover, 1982, 1988) need to rely on a much smaller audience than we might assume.

It has been important for religious broadcasters to be able to claim large audiences for a number of reasons. First, they have wanted to project a picture of momentum to the movement which would give it credibility and status in the "outside world." In an early book by a religious broadcasting spokesman, Ben Armstrong set this tone of looking to the outside for affirmation. Large overestimates have often been unquestioningly picked up by observers and critics alike. The largest audience claim of all, that there were 130 million regular viewers of religious television, came from such a secular source, *The Wall Street Journal* (Armstrong, 1979).

Second, the idea that the religious audience is a large one is almost more important *within* these ministries. All of them depend on donors to contribute funds based on some idea or measure of their success. The most obvious measure would be the number of people reached. A ministry which could claim a million viewers would have it over one which claimed 10 thousand.

The problem is that audience figures can rarely be accurately justified with respect to religious broadcasting. The audiences are simply so small that they are unreliably measured using standard audience ratings methodologies. One ratings point, for instance, represents over a million viewers. Typical ratings for electronic church broadcasts range from less than 1 point to about 6 points (Hadden & Swann, 1981; Horsfield, 1984; Martin, 1981). This is several million people, but because of the margin for error involved (approximately 3 points), such a spread could mean that anywhere from zero viewers to 9 million might be watching. We simply don't know. There is also a tendency for programs that are on more than one time a week in a given market to count viewers each time they tune in, thus duplicating viewers who watch more than once—a common occurrence.

One recent report commissioned by one of the religious broadcasting organizations (Clark & Virts, 1985) was widely touted to have found that nearly 40 percent of the television audience watches religious broadcasting. Upon closer examination, it was shown that that figure included everyone who watched *any* religious program for *6 minutes or more per month*—a trivial amount of viewing. The standard threshold used in commercial television ratings is 15 minutes or more *per week*—a more impressive criterion (Hoover, 1987).

The most reliable estimate of the actual size of the religious television audience continues to be that reached by the 1984 study done by Gerbner and his colleagues who were able, through a complex calculation, to account for many of the sources of error. Their estimate was that about 8.7 percent of the audience, or around 13.3 million viewers, at least occasionally watch at least one religious program (Gerbner et al., 1984).

Myth Number III: People use electronic church broadcasting as a substitute for going to church. The most common concern expressed by critics of the electronic church when it first emerged was the fear that it might be harming local churches. The thought was that if people could have access to this more attractive, sophisticated type of religious experience, they might forgo the trouble of actually going out to their own church. Research on religious radio had always found that the opposite tended to be true. That is, people who were attracted to religious broadcasting seemed to be people who were already religious, and that they were more likely than others to also be frequent attenders at and contributors to local churches (Johnstone, 1971; Parker, Barry, & Smythe, 1955). Further, most broadcasters of the electronic church have consistently maintained that audience members should go to church, that viewing their programs is no substitute (Armstrong, 1979).

Another element of the new religious broadcasting which made this question a bit more complex has been the fact that these broadcasts have tended to be fundamentalist or evangelical in orientation. A general resurgence and prominence of evangelicalism—called the rise of the "religious right"—coincided with the emergence of the electronic church and generated a fear among the mainline or establishment churches that these broadcasts might be either encouraging people to stay home from their "real" churches *or* that they might be encouraging people to go to evangelical or fundamentalist churches when and if they did attend.

The best available research suggests that it is still the case that religious television viewers are also religious in conventional ways—they are more likely than nonviewer of religion to also attend church regularly. So, overall, the electronic church does not harm the local church (Gaddy & Pritchard, 1985; Gerbner et al., 1984; Wuthnow, Chapter 7, this volume). However, there *is* evidence that among viewers of the electronic church in mainline, establishment, or liberal churches, and in the Roman Catholic church, there is a tendency for them to be drawn to more evangelical and fundamentalist directions (Bourgault, 1985; Hoover, 1988). The possibility therefore exists that the general trend for them to be active in church hides a tendency for them to be drawn away from their "home" church to more evangelical or fundamentalist ones.

Myth Number IV: The electronic church reaches "the needy out there." Religious broadcasting is an expensive endeavor. The major electronic church ministries need to raise between $150 and $200 million a year just to stay on the air. The scandals which have rocked the industry in recent years have highlighted the controversial nature of such activities. It is hard to justify the kind of money involved unless some pretty powerful effects can be claimed. Religious broadcasters have long said that a major justification for their activities is that there is a great mass of needy people in the world who need to be touched by their messages. The image projected is one of a society adrift, cut off from its traditional roots and values, and of people searching for stability and hope in the midst of this social and cultural confusion (Armstrong, 1979; Clark & Virts, 1985). In addition, many individuals face, on a daily basis, crises of health, family, work, and finance, which they often have to face alone.

Against this backdrop, modern religious broadcasting can propose a technological solution. By means of the anonymous mass medium of radio, and now television, such people can be reached, right in their homes, right in the midst of their crises. Religious broadcasters have many, many anecdotes to share of just such viewers' experiences. Many of these stories are striking. Some involve celebrities, such as Ephrem Zimbalist, Jr. and Charles Colson. Other stories involve more common people. All of them derive their momentum from the idea that this new technology—broadcasting—can cut directly through to people "who really need the message, right where they live," as proponents might put it.

We might say, then, that there are at least 2 types of viewers. First, we know from anecdotal evidence that there is a group of people for whom these programs have served the purpose of helping them in times of need. Their stories are shared with the broadcasters and recounted again and again—testimonies to the power and effect of these programs. Second, there seems to be a group of supporters of these broadcasts who do so in order to sustain ministry to the first group. Studies of viewers who are also members of major religious broadcasting ministries (Bourgault, 1980; Hoover, 1985) suggest that this latter group derives a good deal of its satisfaction with religious broadcasting from the sense that they are supporting them for "someone else." In their view, the potential that a given broadcast might reach out to people who have previously not been touched by the Christian or fundamentalist message more than justifies their support.

But which is the more important audience? The latter group may well be the majority. Remembering what we said earlier about the fact that the majority of religious viewers tend to be highly religious in other ways as well, we must conclude that most are people who were committed Christians, even committed evangelicals or fundamentalists long before they became involved in religious broadcasting. Research data have tended to confirm this (Gerbner et al., 1984). The former group, those who "need it," may be a smaller group, and one which serves to provide the anecdotal justification for the continuation of the ministries, paid for by the latter group (most of whom become "partners" or "members," but who may not actually *view* the programs regularly). Each "audience" thus has its purpose. Service to the few for whom the programs' *manifest* content is intended, is the major justification for these ministries' existence. The maintenance of such content serves a *latent* function for the group who support these ministries' outreach to others. The "supporters" group further see themselves to not be the target audience of these ministries, when in a way they are. The whole fund raising and support strategy of the typical major electronic church ministry is oriented toward providing these supporters with a program to support—one which claims a powerful impact on someone else—when a major impact is on the supporters themselves because they send money.

This may all sound mercenary, manipulative, and entirely too cold and calculating. In fact, no one involved in these ministries understands things in quite this way. All of them—broadcasters, supporters, and viewers alike—perceive things on the manifest level of first principles: Religious broadcasting is there to help those who really need it. The majority of members or contributors to these programs, however, and indeed the majority of their audience at any given time, is made up of people who see themselves to be on the "same side of the camera" as the programs' hosts and producers. They are partners in the ministry, not the targets of it, as they see it, when, in fact, they may well be what it is all about.

Myth Number V: The new religious broadcasting has more universal appeal than had traditional religious broadcasting. Consistent with the idea that electronic church broadcasts are intended to reach a group of people who really need their message—a group that has not been previously reached by the evangelical or fundamentalist gospel— is the idea that these programs must therefore be designed to reach audiences beyond the "traditional" audience for airwave religion. Before the advent of the new religious broadcasting, most people had accepted the findings of such studies as that of Parker et al. (1955) and Johnstone (1971) that religious broadcasts reach only those who are already religious. The typical viewer, according to research, is a middle-aged or older woman, who attends church regularly, and who is fairly conservative theologically and socially. In addition, religious viewers and listeners tend to come from lower-income brackets and to have had less education than their neighbors who do not view or listen.

The traditional form of religious broadcasting almost dictated that the audience would be a peculiar and already-convinced one. Pre-electronic church ministries were idiosyncratic, particularistic in orientation, and tied to the cultural, geographic, and social roots from which they sprang. Because the new religious broadcasting of the electronic church era was radically different, imitating the form and content of conventional television, it was assumed that it could reach out to a more universal audience. Men, younger people, ethnic groups, urban dwellers, and less self-consciously religious people could be reached, it was thought (Armstrong, 1979; Clark & Virts, 1985).

The claimed universal appeal of these broadcasts is vital to the continued support of the viewers discussed above. The myth that a great mass of needy people out there is being reached rests on an assumption about the utility of these broadcasts to attract "atypical" audiences (that is, to attract audiences not traditionally viewing religious broadcasting). The best research seems to indicate that if such atypical audiences are being reached, they are not watching in the great numbers often claimed. While there may be some tendency for younger or better educated or less "religious" viewers to be reached, that tendency does not equal a major surge in viewing by such audiences (Abelman, 1987; Hoover, 1987).

Myth Number VI: The electronic church is religion in the media age. There has been a persistent tendency, since McLuhan, to chart recent American history in terms of the gradual evolution of new forms of cultural and social expression—forms appropriate to a culture dominated by "the media." Observers such as McLuhan himself, and more recent popularizers such as Postman (1982, 1984) have looked for signs of the evolution of society along lines somehow defined by the pervasiveness of the instruments of the mass media.

Observers of religion have also sought such evidence. Cox (1973), for example, proposed that establishment religion seemed, in the period before 1975, to be singularly impervious to the "media age." Protestant theology, it was widely thought, is a culture of the written word, and is therefore potentially destabilized by a new system of cultural expression which is "postliterate."

More independent observers also wondered at the potential for the mass media to somehow affect the traditional turf of religion. Gerbner and Connaly (1978), for example, suggest that television might actually have usurped the traditional prerogatives of religion to help adherents define reality. Television, they said, might well be the "new religion" of the media age.

The new religious broadcasting emerged into this discourse. Some early observers of it suggested that it represented the evolution of a specifically "media-centered" religiosity. Critics of it from within the religious establishment suggested that it was a cynical and manipulative use of the new media for narrowly sectarian ends. The broad-based religious broadcasting of the "sustaining-time" era had been ecumenical and nonsectarian. This new religious broadcasting seemed to equate mass media religion with only one of the many streams which make up American Protestantism.

Such debates were entirely lost on regulators and the secular media industries. Cable television companies were thrilled to be able to present one or more channels devoted to religion—channels they did not have to pay for—and thus claim to represent, in their offerings, a wide range of tastes and interests within their communities. Cable's justification had always been that it could be the conduit of variety and choice. The fact that it could bring dedicated religious channels supported this ideology. The fact that these channels might not represent religion outside a very narrow, evangelical band, was not their concern.

Regulators were similarly blind to the implications of these developments. In a stinging indictment of FCC responsibility in this area, Lacy (1978) suggested that the Commission's *laissez-fair* approach to regulation of religion had put the Commission in the position of actually *violating* the First Amendment's "establishment" clause. They were, in her view, supporting the establishment of religion by refusing to consider whether these broadcasters actually served the public interest. A more recent analysis, by the Public Television *Frontline* documentary series (Public Broadcasting Service, 1988) came to a similar conclusion regarding Commission involvement in the continuing financial scandals at the ill-fated PTL Network.

The fact that the government was not too clear on the implications of the evolution of the electronic church was suggested by a conversation I had with members of the House of Representatives Communication Subcommittee Staff in 1978, soon after the religious cable networks had gone on the air. Mainline Protestant denominations have long been involved in the setting of social policy in communications. The court case which established for the first time that the public has "standing" in broadcast license-renewal proceedings was brought by the United Church of Christ, for instance. That case was *not* about the narrow interests of that church, or any church, in broadcasting, but was rather about the service of a station in Jackson, Mississippi to the black community of Jackson during the civil rights era in the 1960s.

I suggested to these congressional staffers that such religious organizations as the United Church of Christ might have some input into their efforts to modify regulation of cable television. Their response was surprise. "Why should religious groups be concerned about cable television?" One said, "Religious groups have been the first to introduce cable networks. They should be more satisfied than anyone else." The implication was that no distinction was made, for these staff people, between the longstanding institutional efforts of national denominations in media reform, and the emergence of independent, narrowly drawn, religious cable television programs. In short, the electronic church came to represent, for many people, the sum and substance of religion as a national presence.

The news media also came to see things this way. Due in part to the grandiose claims of audience size made by religious broadcasters (and discussed elsewhere in this volume) journalists assumed that the new figures of the electronic church must represent millions of people. Whereas in the 1960s Martin Luther King and the Berrigan brothers were major religious figures on the national scene, in the 1970s and 1980s, Jerry Falwell was looked to as a major spokesman for the interests of religious groups and people in the political environment.

In earlier times, spokespeople for religion emerged out of the institutional structures of formal religious groups, and rose to prominence because of a specific relationship to real constituencies. The superstars of the electronic church, by contrast, based their prominence entirely on their presence on the medium of television. The medium, in this case, did become the message, in a sense. Jerry Falwell was important because he was on television and could be presumed to have a large audience. The extent to which he actually spoke for that audience was not submitted to verification before he began to appear frequently in the "secular" media as a representative of American religion.

Myth Number VII: *The electronic church has created an "invisible army."* The political prominence of the electronic church is based in large measure on the perception that its audience is not only large, but also manipulable toward direct social action. Jerry Falwell's founding of the Moral Majority and other social action organizations such as the Coalition for Better Television created much publicity because of the assumption that such a move could mobilize many previously uninvolved people. The larger evolution of the "new right" also involved such organizations as the Religious Roundtable, which had as their objective the formation of a new, religiously based, political movement (Shriver, 1982).

Evangelicals and fundamentalists had traditionally been rather apolitical. Even though there was, within fundamentalism, a longstanding identification with conservative civic values, this conservatism rarely found itself moved to action. Further, there was evidence that these conservative Christians were not as likely to express their beliefs at the ballot box as were other groups. The evolution of a new means of reaching and politicizing this group—the electronic church—thus was thought to have potential for changing the nature of American politics.

The "new right" politics of the 1970s seemed to confirm that such changes were taking place. In 1976, *Time* magazine declared "The Year of the Evangelical," partly because for the first time a "born-again Christian" had been elected President of the United States (in fact, both candidates that year had claimed to have been "born again"). By 1980, the "new right" movement had found a champion of its social agenda in Ronald Reagan. The ideological power of the religious "new right" was confirmed by the fact that Reagan, a lukewarm churchgoer (who rarely attended even after his election) was also compelled to declare that he had been "born again" (Shriver, 1982).

All of this posturing was intended to play the assumed potential power of the newly political "religious right." The electronic church audience was seen as the core of this movement. Both Jimmy Carter and Ronald Reagan regularly appeared at the annual conference of the evangelical broadcasters, National Religious Broadcasters (NRB), eschewing opportunities to appear in person at conventions of mainstream religious communicators. The obvious calculation was that, while the latter group was only of marginal or particular significance, the evangelical electronic church broadcasters *also* represented a *political* constituency.

The political power of the electronic church was given a critical test in Pat Robertson's campaign for the Presidency in 1987–88. The social agenda of the "new right" had not received the attention in the Reagan years that many expected, and a dissatisfied constituency developed on Reagan's right, empowered and solidified by the centrist-leaning activities of Reagan's second term. Robertson, founder of one of the first, largest, and best-known electronic church ministries, was the logical person to test the power of the medium to mobilize a political electorate.

Robertson's father had been a U.S. Senator. He had a law degree from Yale, and had worked for awhile in Wall Street before a religious conversion led him to seminary and ultimately in ministry (Robertson, 1974). After over a decade of producing live television on his UHF station in Virginia, Robertson's move to a national cable audience in the mid-1970s also led to a change in the show's format and content. The *700 Club* in that period became a more intellectual program—one that covered "social" as well as "religious" issues (Abelman & Pettey, 1988; Hoover, 1988). Robertson himself came to be something of an expert in economics, periodically delivering diatribes on banking, economic policy, and a range of political issues. As a result, Robertson was better placed than most electronic church ministers to make a claim to be taken seriously as a candidate.

His candidacy was greeted with some apprehension by observers on the left *and* the right. It was basic to their assessments of him that he had a potential "invisible army" (a term he used himself) of supporters—people who had never before appeared in the political landscape, but who, if they did, would shift the turf in important ways (Ostling, 1986).

Of course Robertson had viewers who could potentially be political followers as well. As I noted earlier, anecdotal evidence exists that for some people, this was a transformation that fit well. But could they be described as an "army?" Were they a large enough number to justify the claims made as to their potential?

The test came as Robertson's candidacy moved through the primary season in the spring of 1988. The case made earlier in this essay was that there are probably 2 types of viewer of the *700 Club*. To review a bit, the most committed (and the most likely to believe in Robertson enough to support him *politically*) are those who support his broadcasts because they see themselves as *colleagues* with him in the provision of the ministry to others "who really need it." This first group, while it may be the majority of his actual audience, is relatively small in number. A larger group of less-involved or more loosely identified viewers might also exist; people who watch but do not necessarily contribute money or identify in a real way with Robertson as a champion of social and political causes. Even this latter group of viewers is smaller than most observers assume, but it is the extent of Robertson's potential "invisible army."

As Robertson moved through the primaries in 1988, a curious phenomenon seemed to occur. He did very well in those states (such as Michigan) where the primary was based on the *caucus* system. In a caucus, a candidate wins delegate votes by having people go out to local meetings and speak for him or her. These caucuses then vote, based on those in attendance, and their votes determine the number of delegates the various candidates receive. A small number of politicized and activist supporters can move on a caucus, and obtain delegates for candidates they support almost regardless of actual popular support in their communities.

Robertson's small but visible army *could* mobilize to work for him in these settings, where actual popular support was less important. The real test of the size of his "army" was in the states, however, where a popular referendum was the basis of delegate election. In those states, Robertson did rather poorly. His armies of newly politicized evangelical supporters turned out to be made up of "true believers" only. There was depth, but no breadth to his "invisible" armies. Even in the huge "super Tuesday" southern primary on March 8, 1988, he was unable to mobilize actual voters. Exit polls suggested that even voters who identified themselves as evangelicals did not support him in any real numbers.

What the Robertson candidacy confirmed was that to the extent the electronic church does entail an "invisible army," that "army" is a small one, and is not really "invisible" after all. It is made up almost exclusively of a small cadre of people who identified enough with Robertson to go out and work for him. The great, invisible, silent army assumed to be available to him via his television ministry seemed not to exist.

In a recent review of these events (written before Robertson's candidacy fizzled), Hadden and Shupe (1988) proposed that the last word is yet to be written on the political power of religious broadcasting and its role in the "new right." These authors contend that a long-term evolution is underway, and that subsequent elections will see more and more activity by Robertson and his political networks. Indeed, in the midst of the 1988 debacle,

Robertson himself began to couch his candidacy in terms of its being a "trial run" for subsequent races based on traditional grass-roots organizing (Los Angeles *Times,* Wednesday, March 9, 1988, p. C-21).

It may be the case that Pat Robertson or other electronic church ministers may yet come to be politically powerful and important. If they do so, it will only be through such traditionally "political" means. The campaign of 1988 clearly indicates that religious broadcasting holds no special power to mobilize an electorate, even in so politically charged an environment as the "new right" political era of the 1980s.

Myth Number VIII: Religious broadcasting has powerful "direct effects." All of the discussion up to this point has addressed this assumption, though from a number of different directions. Broadcasting has always been assumed to have direct power. We tend to think that, if one person can talk to many, without direct feedback—the essence of how we usually define "mass communication"—then effects must be forthcoming.

The consensus of research on "media effects" in fact suggests that their power is limited. They have effects, but those effects are often mediated by other social factors. Audiences do not behave like automatons. They think about and interpret what they see. This "obstinate audience," as Raymond Baur (1964) called it, has long since been found to be active in the process, and not likely to be easily swayed simply because something or someone appears on television or radio.

While many people understand this to be the case with regard to conventional broadcasting, it has somehow been easy to assume that with *religious* broadcasting, things are different. Religion, after all, makes powerful and direct claims on the loyalties and actions of its followers. Could we not then assume that religion could find in broadcasting a tool for motivating thought and action in a powerful way unknown to conventional broadcasting?

The fact is that religious broadcasting differs very little from non-religious broadcasting in terms of its ability to have a direct power over its viewers. Audiences tend to be self-selecting. They already believe, turning to religious broadcasting for confirmation of those beliefs. Available evidence suggests that those viewers who were not evangelical or otherwise religiously involved before they began to view—thus those for whom their involvement would seem to represent the greatest "effect"—tend to be somewhat skeptical and less convinced than would be the case if a "directly effective" power existed in the broadcasts themselves (Hoover, 1988).

In brief, audiences sizes tend to be small, and viewers of religious broadcasting are no more likely than viewers of conventional television to be persuaded by its messages. They choose to view because the broadcasts fit with beliefs they held long before they came to be members of the audience of the electronic church.

Myth Number IX: The electronic church robs from the poor to give to the rich. The most persistent criticism of the new religious broadcasting has been the suggestion that these ministries are nothing but exploitation. Critics usually cite fears that older people, in particular, are being manipulated to support these ministries at levels that far outstrip their ability to pay.

This is a legitimate fear when we take into consideration the amounts of money raised by some of these ministries, and the periodic scandals which have rocked the industry over fiscal irregularities at even the major electronic church organizations. Long before Jim Bakker's fall from power as a result of charges of a sexual encounter with a church secretary, the PTL empire was under scrutiny by the Internal Revenue Service. PTL even lost its nonprofit status in 1988 as the result of questionable financial arrangements.

There are many bizarre fund-raising anecdotes available. The popular image of the religious broadcaster has always involved a certain snide derogation of their capacity to appeal for money at the drop of a hat. The television era developed more sophisticated forms and techniques of this art, but the expense involved led to continuation of the practice, often through ingenious direct mail solicitations. Leading televangelists have sent mailings containing trinkets, photographs, handkerchiefs, and "prayer cloths," all intended to be the hook for financial and moral support from recipients.

These techniques work. Otherwise they would not continue to be used. Observers look on such things as a mailing from one broadcaster's mother asking the recipient to send her $100 so she could buy her son a new car for Christmas (Mailing, Jim Whittington Ministries, October, 1983) as signs of calumny and cynical manipulation by these ministries.

But are the poorest and most vulnerable the ones who support these ministries? Research indicates that it is not the poorer viewers who give the most money. Rather, the higher the income, the more people give. Average contributions are around $32 per month, with that amount given by the middle-income segment of the market. Poorer viewers give less (Gerbner et al., 1984; Hoover, Chapter 9 of this volume).

The stereotype of the electronic church, that it supports itself largely on the backs of gullible older people, is simply not borne out by the evidence. The 700 Club, for instance, raises half of its $150 million annual income from 5 percent of its donors, a group of extremely wealthy supporters, who may not actually be viewers at all (Hoover, 1988).

We might want to question whether a $20-per-month viewer, likely a retired person, might have better things to do with his or her money. The fact is that all charities, conventional churches among them, depend on income from a variety of people to support their ongoing ministries, and that such giving is considered to be basic to the Christian faith. The electronic church is not unique in its appeals for funds. We may question whether the money does any good, and we may note, in passing, that there is evidence that some ministries have actively *misused* funds, but the act of soliciting support from constituents—be they poor *or* rich—is nothing unique to religious broadcasting.

It further seems to be the case that the most committed of the supporters of the electronic church, even if told that their money goes for nothing more than the maintenance and continuation of the broadcasts so that more money can be raised to continue the broadcasts and so on (which *is* where most of the money goes) are not particularly bothered by that fact. Remember what was said earlier about the mindset of the basic supporter of these broadcasts. They have heard enough anecdotes about the powerful blessings of their favorite ministries to feel justified in continuing their support. The reactions of supporters of PTL to the allegations that so much of their contributions went to support a lavish lifestyle for Jim and Tammy Bakker tended to be that such a lifestyle was a sign of the blessing and success of the Bakkers' ministry (Fresno *Bee,* March 12, 1987, p. B-17).

Myth Number X: Religious broadcasting is an "Electronic Church." Religious broadcasting is *neither* entirely "electronic" nor is it really a "church." The major ministries of the new religious broadcasting are complex institutions which are only partially broadcasts. All of them have extensive publishing and direct-mail operations. Most have other activities, such as theme parks, and other ministries such as relief, counseling, and social service agencies.

Further, they are all embedded in a much larger network of organizations and ministries, which we might call the "parachurch." Americans seem to have a nearly insatiable desire to be religious and do religious things. American Protestantism has had a long history of church or parachurch agencies and activities (engaged in by laity as well as clergy), which have carried on a wide variety of activities. The best known of these have probably been publishing activities. David Noord (1984) has detailed the long and important history of religious parachurch organizations in American publishing from colonial times onward.

George Marsden (1982) has shown that evangelicalism, in particular, has moved in the middle third of this century to set up widespread and sophisticated agencies devoted to religious and social activities. Any observer of the religious scene since the 1960s has noted the large number of organizations and agencies, both not-for-profit and commercial, which have arisen to pursue these ends. There are independent overseas mission agencies, Bible translators, Christian mission aviators, counseling agencies, schools, colleges, textbook publishers, tract publishers, record companies, radio programming format syndicators, talent agencies, insurance companies, talent promoters, video and film producers, travel agencies, service clubs, and periodical publishers, among others.

The electronic church is only one of these activities; it is an important one, but one that is embedded in a much larger loosely connected network of activities. It is thus not merely a broadcasting phenomenon, but part of a much larger reality.

The electronic church is not really a "church," either. Most of these broadcasters specifically *avoid* calling themselves or being called "churches." Jerry Falwell's position is typical: "We tell them [viewers] to go find a Bible-believing church and join it" (Armstrong, 1979, p. 155). Telephone counselors who work for the *700 Club* are able to connect callers with a network of hundreds of hand-picked churches around the country where they are urged to go for personal, direct contact after their initial call to the "Club." This is consistent with the program's self-perception that it cannot be a substitute for a conventional church (Hoover, 1988).

One content analysis (Gerbner et al., 1984) found that out of the dozens of different programs analyzed, only *one* electronic church preacher referred to himself as "your TV pastor." The vast majority of these ministries instead project their role as a supporter of, not a competitor to, conventional church. Most research seems to support the view that few viewers turn to these broadcasts as such a substitute. They are a supplement instead (Abelman & Neuendorf, 1985; Gerbner et al., 1984; Hoover, 1985; Wuthnow, Chapter 7, this volume).

THE ELECTRONIC CHURCH: A COMPLEX PHENOMENON

A comprehensive picture of the electronic church emerges from this complex of images, symbols, myths, and data. The new religious broadcasting arose out of a long history of evangelicalism and evangelical broadcasting as a cultural form. From a background of particularism and marginality, there has arisen a phenomenon which has been able to project itself onto the center stage of American public life. Groups who once saw themselves at the margins of American culture have now been able to see the ideas and images they hold dear represented in the most national, cosmopolitan, secular setting of all: Television.

It should be obvious by now that this is a perception that is not necessarily supported by empirical evidence. Because of the way religious broadcasting derives its income, there is not a necessary relationship between their presence on television and the existence of a significant audience. In fact, most of these ministries seem to stay on the air with remarkably small audiences, and with a far less portentious reality at their core than is often assumed.

As these ministries have continued to command public attention, these and other myths have continued. The scandals which rocked the industry in 1987 and 1988 even added a new set of ideas to this mix. Where the myth of Elmer Gantry (see Chapter 1) had been vaguely at the heart of much public mistrust of the electronic church, after the scandals it has come center stage. On top of the perception that these ministries are about power and cultural ascendency has been added the very real idea that some of them may be just in it for the money, and may be hypocritical in other ways, to boot.

How will this evolving mythology affect the industry in the future? It is too early to say. Some ministries have faltered because of a loss of confidence on the part of their supporters. Others seem to be continuing. The fact that most of them rely not on a widely scattered and general audience, but, in fact, depend mostly on a "hard core" of close-by supporters, probably means that in the long term, most of them will continue.

The electronic church, in whatever form, will undoubtedly go on. Its greatest crisis is yet to be met—a crisis of establishment stability. Up to this point, these ministries have derived their momentum from a claim to be new, unique, powerful, and in ascendency. The phenomenon is now 10 years old, and we have yet to see unequivocal evidence that its programs have changed or reformed society in general. From the perspective of most viewers, things are probably not much better now than they were 10 years ago. How can the electronic church continue to claim legitimacy in an era where it cannot show major accomplishments, and in an era where it is rapidly ceasing to seem "new and different?"

As the electronic church fades into the humdrum of everyday life over the next few years, it may thus find itself fighting new myths. These myths will suggest that it—like the "establishment" churches and institutions it criticizes—has become *passé*, that it has ceased to be the dynamic force it seemed to be at its inception. Its maturation as a movement, and its future, depends on its being able to find new and unique claims and myths to which it can cling.

REFERENCES

Abelman, R. (1987). Religious television uses and gratifications. *Journal of Broadcasting & Electronic Media, 31*(3), 293–307.

Abelman, R.; & Neuendorf, K. (1985). How religious is religious television programming? *Journal of Communication, 35*(1), 98–110.

Abelman, R., & Pettey, G. (1988). How political is religious television programming? *Journalism Quarterly, 65*(2), 313–319.

Armstrong, B. (1979). *The electric church.* Nashville, TN: Thomas Nelson.

Baur, R. (1964). The obstinate audience: The influence process from the point of view of social communication. *American Psychologist, 19*, 319–328.

Bourgault, L. (1980). An ethnographic study of the "Praise the Lord Club." Unpublished doctoral dissertation, Ohio University, Athens, OH.

Bourgault, L. (1985). The "PTL Club" and Protestant viewers: An ethnographic study. *Journal of Communication 35*(1), 132–148.

Clark, D., & Virts, P. (1985, October 25). *Religious television audience: A new development in measuring audience size.* Paper presented at The Society for the Scientific Study of Religion Conference, Savannah, GA.

Cox, H. (1973). *The seduction of the spirit.* New York: Simon and Schuster.

Gaddy, G., & Pritchard, D. (1985). When watching religious TV is like attending church. *Journal of Communication, 35*(1), 123–131.

Gerbner, G., & Connaly, K. (1978, April). The new American religion. *New Catholic World,* pp. 52–56.

Gerbner, G., Gross, L., Hoover, S., Morgan, M., Signorielli, N., Cotugno, H., & Wuthnow, R. (1984). *Religion and television.* New York: Committee on Electronic Church Research.

Hadden, J. (1980, February). Presentation to the Electronic Church Consultation. New York University, New York, NY.

Hadden, J., & Swann, C. (1981). *Prime-time preachers.* Reading, MA: Addison-Wesley.

Hadden, J., & Shupe, A. (1988). *Televangelism: Power and politics on God's frontier.* New York: Henry Holt.

Hoover, S. M. (1982). *Religious group use and avoidance of television: A study of reasons and effects.* Unpublished thesis, The Annenberg School of Communications, University of Pennsylvania, Philadelphia, PA.

Hoover, S. M. (1985). *The "700 Club" as religion and as television.* Unpublished doctoral dissertation, University of Pennsylvania, Philadelphia, PA.

Hoover, S. M. (1987). The religious television audience: A question of significance, or size? *Review of Religious Research, 29*(2), 152–177.

Hoover, S. M. (1988). *Mass media religion: The social sources of the electronic church.* Beverly Hills, CA: Sage.

Horsfield, P. (1984). *Religious television: The American experience.* New York: Longman Press.

Johnstone, R. (1971). Who listens to religious radio broadcasts anymore? *Journal of Broadcasting, 16,* 91–102.

Lacey, L. (1978). The electric church: An FCC-"established" institution? *Federal Communications Law Journal, 31*(2), 235–75.

Marsden, G. (1982). Preachers of paradox: The religious new right in historial perspective. In M. Douglas & S. Tipton (Eds.), *Religion and America.* Boston, MA: Beacon Press.

Martin, W. (1981, June). The birth of a media myth. *The Atlantic,* pp. 17–21.

Noord, D. (1984). *The evangelical origins of mass media in America, 1815–1835.* Journalism Monographs No. 88. Association for Education in Journalism, Columbia, SC.

Ostling, R. (1986, January 17). Power, glory and politics. *Time,* pp. 62–69.

Parker, E., Barry, D., & Smythe, D. (1955). *The radio-television audience and religion.* New York: Harper and Bros.

Public Broadcasting Service. (1988, January). Frontline: Praise the Lord [telecast]. WGBH-TV, Boston, MA.

Postman, N. (1982). *The disappearance of childhood.* New York: The Free Press.

Postman, N. (1984). *Amusing ourselves to death.* New York: Viking.

Robertson, P. (1974). *Shout it from the housetops.* Plainfield, NJ: Logos Books.

Shriver, P. (1982). *The Bible vote.* New York: Pilgrim Press.

3

Defining the Electronic Church

Quentin J. Schultze

Religious broadcasting is one of the most widely discussed and frequently misunderstood manifestations of popular religion in the United States. Magazines and newspapers often write of the "electronic" or "electric church" as if it were a unified religious movement or a single type of broadcasting. Nothing could be further from the truth. Religious broadcasting is actually a farrago of preaching, personalities, promotions, and politics. Like soap operas and situation comedies, no 2 religious programs are exactly the same. In fact, the electronic church is neither a church nor a broadcast style. The great diversity of religious programming reflects the chaotic condition of American religion. It makes no more sense to speak loosely of the "electronic church" than it does to talk about the "American church."

Consider the wide variety of Protestant traditions represented on the airways. There have been old-fashioned Southern Pentecostals such as Jimmy Swaggart and new-style charismatics like former *PTL Club* host Jim Bakker. Robert Schuller shares Bakker's theology of positive thinking, which they both inherited from Norman Vincent Peale, but Calvinist Schuller rejects Bakker's emphasis on charismatic gifts of the spirit, such as speaking in tongues. Jerry Falwell and Charles Stanley are both conservative baptists with strong Southern roots, but Falwell's programs have centered on politics in recent years while Stanley's have generally emphasized personal piety. M.G. "Pat" Robertson, a former Southern Baptist turned charismatic who started the *700 Club,* created a program centered around God's miraculous power to heal and prosper; few Southern Baptists would support such theology. Oral Roberts was raised as a Pentecostal, joined the Methodist church in the 1960s, and went back to his faith-healing Pentecostalism in the 1980s. His programming reflected those personal changes during the same periods. It is impossible to characterize even 10 highest-rated religious broadcasts as a unified religious movement.

Consider as well the variety of program formats and styles in religious broadcasting. Swaggart's telecasts have been steeped heavily in old-fashioned, sawdust-trail revivalism, where evangelists shouted to the crowd from the front of a tent. Bakker and Robertson hosted talk shows. Schuller broadcasts the morning services at his Crystal Cathedral in suburban Los Angeles. Over the years Roberts has tried everything from films of his tent revivals to prime-time variety show specials. Falwell and Stanley continue to air their church services, although Falwell has taken far more liberty to develop special fund-raising appeals shot on location at Liberty University, in his private jet, and on the streets of New York. Clearly there is little unity in religious program format and style.

Nevertheless, it is possible to describe broadly the characteristics of the electronic church as distinct from other forms of religious broadcasting. Contemporary televangelism shares particular institutional values and organizational goals even though it represents a wide variety of theological traditions and programming formats. In this sense the electronic church is really nothing new; these values and goals have been part of religious broadcasting from the early days of radio (Schultze, 1989). The electronic church is characterized by (a) business values, (b) experiential theologies, (c) media-derived formats, (d) faith in technology, (e) charismatic leaders, and (f) spin-off ministries. Any television ministry which exemplifies all or most of these characteristics could safely be classified as part of the electronic church.

BUSINESS VALUES

Nothing is more significant for defining the electronic church than the fact that these ministries are governed partly by business and corporate values, including efficiency, productivity, and expansion. Unlike a local church, which is more likely to be animated by spiritual values, such as love, compassion, and sacrifice, broadcast ministries often thrive on the principles of professional marketing and management. This is not to say that televangelists are simply using the media for their own personal gain, although there are a few documented cases of such religious hucksterism (Randi, 1987). Most television ministries are driven by business values even though their founding goals are spiritual edification and evangelization. Television time is very expensive when multiplied by dozens and even hundreds of stations and markets. Every religious broadcasting ministry which depends upon the audience for financial support soon finds itself adopting the values of modern business.

The most fundamental distinction between the electronic church and other religious broadcasters is the extent to which a business ideology animates the organization. Independent ministries, lacking the regular support of a denomination or ecumenical council of churches, almost invariably turn to marketing specialists for advice on how to raise funds both on and off the air. Premium offers and direct-mail solicitations are carefully packaged.

They also consider their "success" in terms of ratings, market penetration, and especially financial contributions. For them, like most corporations, cash flow, product development, and market research are important considerations. When contributions drop, new marketing strategies might be tried, including changing the broadcast time, station, and program format. If audience ratings are especially low in a particular market, and few contributors emerge from that audience, the program will probably be taken off the air. Robertson based the *700 Club* format on audience research and ratings. Recognizing that viewers were attracted to personal healing testimonies, he built the show around the theme of God's healing power.

Over the years there have been various disputes among religious broadcasters over whether or not radio and television stations should provide free "sustaining" time to religious groups or individuals. In general, mainline Protestants and Roman Catholics have favored such sustaining time over paid broadcasts. Evangelicals and fundamentalists, on the other hand, have been very leery of such proposals out of fear that they will not receive such time or that stations providing sustaining time will be less inclined to sell additional air time for religious broadcasts (Saunders, 1969). The fact is that over the years religious broadcasting has become very profitable for many stations. That profitability has worked to the advantage of evangelicals and fundamentalists, who are far more likely to adopt the business values necessary for launching successful audience-supported television and radio ministries (Schultze, 1989).

In the 1980s, none of the 10 highest-rated weekly religious television broadcasts was supported primarily by a denomination or council of churches. Instead, the marketing experts ruled the religious television roost. From Swaggart to Roberts and Falwell, religious television was dominated largely by business-minded televangelists who successfully surrounded themselves with savvy management teams. These ministries were like corporations guided by the entrepreneurial spirit of charismatic leaders. Roberts, who had the most longevity of the group, spent decades cultivating business talent in his organization. As one historian has suggested, Roberts' longstanding ability to capture audiences and raise funds was due largely to his own ability to identify and hire business talent (Harrell, 1985).

The most telling sign of the intrusion of business values into contemporary religious broadcasting, however, was increasingly careful product development. In the 1980s it was no longer possible simply to purchase air time and broadcast the gospel. Hundreds of television and thousands of radio ministries were competing for a limited audience and increasingly scarce contributions (Horsfield, 1984). Only the most marketable versions of the gospel were easily sold to fickle and increasingly skeptical audiences. Financial survival required product research and development, especially product differentiation. Programs and preachers had to be distinctive and memorable. More than that, the gospel often had to be in tune with the wishes and desires of a consumer society. As Bruce Barron (1987) has documented, the "health-and-wealth" preaching of televangelists such as Kenneth and Gloria Copeland and Kenneth Hagin grew out of the demands of the audience for an optimistic gospel of financial prosperity and personal health. The electronic church was characterized by a sensitivity to the wants of the marketplace; it adopted the marketing concept, which was previously preached by business schools and now practiced by the preachers.

EXPERIENTIAL THEOLOGIES

In spite of the wide variety of theologies represented in the electronic church, there is a growing unity in the role of personal experience in validating such theologies. This is as true of the political sermons of Falwell as it is of the faith healing of Roberts and the possibility thinking of Schuller. Simply put, the experiential theologies of the electronic church are not taken from the historic creeds and confessions of the Christian church, from the writings of highly influential theologians, or even from the traditions of established denominations and churches. Instead, the electronic church stakes its theological claims on the experiences of its members as reported and interpreted in the broadcasts and writings of its charismatic leaders. This gives the electronic church an especially strong ahistorical quality; the gospel is usually interpreted in terms of the contemporary culture, rather than the culture being viewed through the eyes of the historic Christian gospel (Owen, 1980). As a result, the electronic church appears to some viewers to be without a theology, expressing its Biblical truths directly through personal experience. Swaggart championed this rhetoric in his condemnation of intellectuals, theologians, and non-Pentecostal Christian traditions, but many television evangelists offered their own experiential theologies.

The *700 Club* is an excellent example of the centrality of experiential theologies in the programming of the electronic church. Over the years the *700 Club* increasingly used viewer testimonies as evidence for the validity of its health-and-wealth gospel. Various production teams visited the homes and work places of viewers who claimed healing and prosperity as a result of following the faith principles of the show's hosts, especially Robertson. As Robertson himself proudly recalled, the emphasis on healing testimonies increased ratings dramatically (Buckingham, 1983). In other words, the experiences of viewers validated the claims of the televangelists; theology and programming were founded on the experiences and hopes of the viewers, not on particular doctrinal statements or creeds. In fact, Robertson's own writings are notable for their lack of theological references (Robertson, 1982). Robertson became his own theologian, establishing principles of the Christian faith out of his experiences and personal interpretations of scripture. He was even able to validate his theological assertions by claiming to heal individual viewers identified only by their ailments (Randi, 1987).

The *PTL Club,* under the leadership of Bakker, similarly created programming based on experiential theologies. In this case the show was a daily narrative tracking the lives of Jim and Tammy Bakker. Battles with the Federal Communications Commission and the *Charlotte Observer* were turned into spiritual warfare between the Kingdom of God and the army of Satan. Financial struggles to build the Heritage USA theme park were "victories" for the people of God. Like Robertson, Bakker's books created theology out of his own life experiences. Bakker's slogan, "You Can Make It," was his own theology of success for the common person. As Bakker writes in his book of that title, people should believe Bakker's theological claims precisely because his own life testified to their truthfulness (Bakker, 1983).

The electronic church is marked by this strong emphasis on experiential theologies. In answer to the question "Who says so?" the contemporary media evangelist is likely to reply: "I do, and my life and your life prove it." In part this trend toward experiential theologies is simply a reflection of trends in American charismatic and neo-Pentecostal religion, which is highly emotional and experiential. However, the electronic church extends experiential theology to other Christian traditions and churches. Falwell validated his political gospel by his own political involvement and his own Biblical interpretations of international politics (Halsell, 1986). Schuller's possibility thinking was validated by his rise from preaching on top of the snack shop of a drive-in theatre to preaching in the multimillion dollar Crystal Cathedral designed by architect Phillip Johnson (Voskuil, 1983). Experiential theologies link audience hopes to media proclamations. This is sound marketing and compelling programming for many people.

MEDIA-DERIVED FORMATS

The electronic church includes many different program formats which rely upon nonreligious program techniques and production standards. Unlike local church broadcasts, which merely film or tape community worship, the electronic church creates special formats for the camera. Sometimes traditional worship or revivals are simply adapted for the new media, but more likely the religious programs today are derived from successful secular programming fare. The electronic church increasingly mirrors the program techniques and production values of the secular television industry (Frankl, 1987). Televangelism is crouching toward Hollywood, the center of television production in the United States.

Few television evangelists can survive simply by introducing the camera and microphone to the revival tent or church liturgy. Tents and churches are being replaced with studios and stages. The sawdust trail has given way to direct-mail follow-ups and toll-free telephone numbers. Certainly the prime-time specials of Billy Graham are somewhat of an exception. Graham's organization still rents auditoriums and amphitheaters for local crusades; the television specials merely videotape the crusades. To this extent Graham is really not part of the electronic church, but a holdout to itinerant revivalism. However, even Swaggart's old-fashioned, Holy-Ghost revivals are steeped in modern television production values. Swaggart is an effective television performer who works for the camera more than for the live audience present in the amphitheater. Compared with turn-of-the-century American urban revivalists like Billy Sunday or Dwight L. Moody, Swaggart's stage histrionics are mild and unexciting. Swaggart plays to the camera, communicating with his face and arms. Stage space is relatively unimportant for Swaggart as the close-up camera shots closely follow his expressions and the microphone precisely tracks his vocal intonations. Although raised on the sawdust trail, Swaggart has created an effective telecast that alters the techniques of revival to more closely match the production values of modern television drama, where the face is king (Esslin, 1982).

The visual presentation of most electronic ministries is clearly based on secular formats. Rex Humbard was the Lawrence Welk of the electronic church, introducing his family to the stage and popularizing the music for his own gospel variety show. The *700 Club* and *PTL Club* have no religious precedents in the liturgies of churches or the programs of itinerant evangelists. Bakker's show was closer to the style of Merv Griffin, and Robertson's to that of Johnny Carson, but they were both religious versions of the late-night or afternoon talk/variety show. Oral Roberts long ago turned from the revival setting, experimenting with prime-time variety shows for a while, and more recently developing several different programs ranging from talk-show formats to stage preaching. John Ankerberg has created a version of Phil Donahue's daily talk program based on the conflict generated by members of opposing religious traditions. Although it is far more subdued than *Donahue* and *Oprah,* it cultivates the same production values of personal conflict and confrontation before a live audience. CBN created a religious soap opera, *Another Life,* patterned after the daytime soaps aired on the commercial networks, and produced by a soap opera writer from one of the commercial networks (Anderson, 1983).

FAITH IN TECHNOLOGY

Ministries of the electronic church share a faith in the redeeming power of communications technologies. These ministries see the mass media, especially the electronic media, as both mysterious and effective. They believe that cable and satellites, like God Himself, are able to break through the walls of religious unbelief and cross cultural and political boundaries that previously inhibited the spread of the gospel around the globe. God provided these media at this time in human history, says the electronic church, to accomplish worldwide evangelization before the Second Coming of Christ. Of course this technological faith is partly a rhetorical strategy that helps elicit funds from hopeful viewers and direct-mail supporters. But part of the faith in technology stems from a real belief in God's will to redeem the world through mass-media evangelism. In either case, the electronic church today links technology, theology, and faith (Schultze, 1987).

Ben Armstrong (1979), executive director of National Religious Broadcasters, captures the spirit of this faith in technology in his book *The Electric Church*. According to a vision Armstrong had while landing by plane in Chicago one night, the electronic media are creating a new form of worshipping and witnessing that approximate the early Christian church. In Armstrong's McLuhanesque imagery, satellites and cable television are bringing Christians together from around the world, creating a religious global village; radio and television are God's instruments for building an international community of believers. Armstrong even argues that the media represent a communications revolution as important as the development of the printing press and the start of the Reformation. Finally, he concludes that the angel prophesied in the Book of Revelation (14:6) might actually be a communications satellite: "Then I saw another angel flying in midair, and he had the eternal gospel to proclaim to those who live on the earth—to every nation, tribe, language and people."

Armstrong's sentiments and Biblical interpretations are exaggerated expressions of strong manifestations of technological faith among televangelists and their supporters. Falwell and Towns (1971, p. 75) have written that "the most effective medium for reaching people . . . is television." They speak of using the media for "saturation evangelism" where the gospel is preached "to every available person at every available time by every available means (p. 74). Television evangelist Swaggart (1984, p. 14) writes that his broadcast can "redirect a nation to the paths of righteousness. . . ." The electronic church is characterized by the faith that the electronic media are providentially redemptive—that these media were provided by God at this time in human history specifically to save souls before Christ returns. Seeing the hand of God in the power of the media, many televangelists join in the choruses of praise offered by Americans over the last 150 years for technological progress of all kinds (Schultze, 1987).

CHARISMATIC LEADERS

Nearly all highly successful electronic ministries have built on the name of an evangelist or religious leader. This, too, is nothing particularly new; Charles E. Fuller was popular in the 1930s and 1940s, Bishop Fulton J.

Sheen in the 1950s, and Billy Graham in the 1960s. However, there are still exceptions, such as *Day of Discovery,* which has been in the top 10 weekly broadcast television ratings for years. Started decades ago by Martin E. DeHaan, a medical doctor, the program is as popular as ever even without its founder (Adair, 1969). The drama show of the Lutheran Church—Missouri Synod, *This is the Life,* survived for years without persona (Ellens, 1974). But exceptions are few these days as televangelism emulates the successful techniques of Hollywood programs. It appears that the electronic church almost requires a strong-willed, charismatic leader for its own survival in the age of show business. As Neil Postman put it, "On these shows, the preacher is tops. God comes out as a second banana" (1985, p. 117).

As a media phenomenon, the electronic church is far more dependent upon charismatic leadership than is the local church. In most denominations there is considerable pastoral mobility, whether voluntary or dictated by ecclesiastical authority. The contrast with electronic ministries is stark; there is only a handful of radio and television ministries that have survived for long the deaths of their founders. Even the most successful media ministries have withered without charismatic leadership. This was true of Aimee Semple McPherson and Kathryn Kuhlman, for example, who were major media evangelists in the 1930s and 1950s, respectively. In fact, there is no case in the history of religious broadcasting of a successful succession to the throne after the passing of any major televangelist. Although numerous evangelists today have created positions for their sons in the ministry, the barrier between family and media personality remains nearly insurmountable. Members of the electronic church continue to plan for religious monarchy, but history suggests that the electronic revolution in American Protestantism will not pass along the throne without a loss in confidence among the congregants.

SPIN-OFF MINISTRIES

The electronic church is not only in the business of evangelism and entertainment. These broadcast ministries frequently turn into the fund-raising arms of large, multifaceted organizations. Programs usually become collection plates for the support of many other types of ministries and activities. It makes little sense to speak of the electronic church merely as a broadcast ministry. Religious programs today are likely to thrive on the symbolic and financial involvement of their supporters in a wide array of educational, social, and political activities. Although few televangelists establish exactly the same types of spin-off ministries, the drive to expand from broadcasting to other activities is an important characteristic of the electronic church.

Early radio evangelist, Charles E. Fuller, was one of the first religious broadcasters to establish an educational institution for training future pastors and preachers. Fuller Seminary has since become one of the most respected evangelical seminaries in North America. Not all religious broadcasters were so successful, but the electronic church continues to produce significant colleges, universities, and seminaries. In Tulsa, Oklahoma, Roberts started one of the largest Christian liberal arts colleges in the United States. Although affected by financial problems, Oral Roberts University (ORU) continues to attract thousands of students from a variety of Pentecostal Neo-Pentecostal and fundamentalist backgrounds. Falwell has similarly built Liberty University out of the support of thousands of followers of his ministry. His long-range plans call for a 50,000 student campus, the largest in the United States (Lee, 1983). Robertson established CBN University as a graduate school emphasizing the study of communications, public policy, and more recently law, which he inherited from ORU. Other televangelists, such as Swaggart and Hagin, started Bible colleges with the narrower goal of training people for the ministry. If most of these schools follow the trends of early American, church-related colleges and universities, they might grow in academic respect after the founding televangelists depart from the airways. This is true already of Fuller Seminary.

The electronic church also elicits viewer support for foreign and domestic missions. Some of them, such as CBN's Operation Blessing, emphasized privately funded social programs to aid the poor. In one of the most remarkable viewer-supported activities in the history of religious broadcasting, Robertson's CBN developed a literacy program and enlisted volunteers to administer it around the country. Bakker's PTL Network supported dozens of "People That Love" centers across the United States to help the poor and homeless. Swaggart emphasized world ministry through feeding the hungry in Third World countries, and he has raised millions of dollars for that cause. In recent years Falwell raised money for homes for unwed mothers and for urban ministries to homeless people, especially in New York City. Certainly some of the spin-off ministries, such as Bakker's Heritage USA theme park, were largely middle-class luxuries supported by those viewers who were likely to benefit from them. But the scope of spin-off ministries extends well beyond self-interest. The electronic church does far more than minister to itself over the airways.

Politically inspired spin-off "ministries" have clearly been the most controversial. From Father Coughlin in the 1930s, Billy James Hargis in the 1950s, and Falwell's Moral Majority in the early 1980s, political action has always been part of religious broadcasting. Robertson's 1988 presidential bid was little more than a well-organized variation on the theme of political salvation promised by hundreds of electronic ministries since the early days of radio. Television and radio evangelists have financed much political involvement over the years, although the desire to hold public office has not seduced them from the ministry. The political interests of particular electronic ministries has always waxed and waned with the vicissitudes of the national political spirit and the primary need to keep the broadcast on the air. Politics remains part of the electronic church, for good and bad, and there is little reason to expect things to change.

Spin-off ministries have usually served electronic ministries well as fund-raising appeals. It is not easy for many ministries to expand purely on the basis of their broadcasts. Spin-off projects often enable them to expand by continually involving contributors in additional causes and issues. Nevertheless, in recent years it has become clear that unsuccessful spin-off ministries can also tax the financial reserves and fund-raising abilities of even the largest electronic preachers. Roberts' City of Faith Medical Center attracted so few patients that it threatened the financial solvency of his broadcast operation, which cut back drastically on paid air time and shifted primarily to cable in early 1988. Falwell's political involvement eventually interfered with the evangelist's "religious" activities, and he resigned from leadership in political organizations. Before Bakker left PTL in 1987, the funding the People That Love centers was cut to keep the ministry afloat in the midst of enormous debts and a negative cash flow. Like expansionary nations or corporations, growing electronic ministries eventually find that size and diversification can lead to mismanagement and even decline.

CONCLUSION

Although religious broadcasting in America represents a hodgepodge of theologies and program formats, there are common characteristics which distinguish the so-called "electronic church" from other media ministries. The 6 characteristics described in this chapter go a long way toward defining the electronic church as a particular kind of social and cultural phenomenon. The electronic church cannot be defined simply in terms of its use of the electronic media. It is founded on shared values and institutional forms which transcend the theological and programmatic differences among these religious broadcasters. In spite of the simplistic media reports of recent years, the electronic church remains a diverse collection of media ministries held together not by tradition or even a common religious faith, but by ways of seeing and acting in the world. They sometimes fight among themselves, like cola manufacturers battle over market share and public image, but their institutional values and organizational strategies are remarkably similar.

REFERENCES

Adair, J.R. (1969). *M.R. DeHaan*. Grand Rapids, MI: Zondervan Publishing House.

Anderson, T. (1983, Summer). An interview with Jason Vinley. *Focus*, pp. 17–19.

Armstrong, B. (1979). *The electronic church*. Nashville, TN: Thomas Nelson Publishers.

Bakker, J. (1983). *You can make it!* Charlotte, NC: PTL Enterprises.

Barron, B. (1987). *The health and wealth gospel.* Downers Grove, IL: InterVarsity Press.

Buckingham, J. (1983, April). *Charisma,* pp. 25–30.

Ellens, J.H. (1974). *Models of religious broadcasting.* Grand Rapids, MI: William B. Eerdmans Publishing Company.

Esslin, M. (1982). *The age of television.* San Francisco, CA: Freeman.

Falwell, J., & Towns, E. (1971). *The church aflame.* Nashville, TN: Impact Books.

Frankl, R. (1987). *Televangelism.* Carbondale, IL: Southern Illinois University Press.

Halsell, G. (1986). *Prophecy and politics.* Westport, CT: Lawrence Hill & Co.

Harrell, D.E. (1985). *Oral Roberts.* New York: Harper & Row.

Horsfield, P.G. (1984). *Religious television: The American experience.* New York: Longman.

Lee, R. (1983, November 25). Falwell's college strives to become a fundamentalist university serving 50,000. *Christianity Today,* pp. 40–43.

Owen, V.S. (1980). *The total image.* Grand Rapids, MI: William B. Eerdmans Publishing Company.

Postman, N. (1985). *Amusing ourselves to death.* New York: Viking.

Randi, J. (1987). *The faith healers.* Buffalo, NY: Prometheus Books.

Robertson, P. (1982). *The secret kingdom.* Nashville, TN: Thomas Nelson Publishers.

Saunders, L.S. (1969). The national religious broadcasters and the availability of commercial radio time (Doctoral dissertation, University of Illinois, 1969). *Dissertation Abstracts International, 29,* 2663A–2664A.

Schultze, Q.J. (1987). The mythos of the electronic church. *Critical Studies in Mass Communication, 4,* 245–261.

Schultze, Q.J. (1989). Evangelical radio and the rise of the electronic church 1921–1948. *Journal of Broadcasting & the Electronic Media, 32*(3), 289–306.

Swaggart, J. (1984, November). Divine imperatives for broadcasting ministry. *Religious Broadcasting,* pp. 14–15.

Voskuil, D. (1983). *Mountains into goldmines.* Grand Rapids, MI: William B. Eerdmans Publishing Company.

II

The History of Religious Television

Religious broadcasting didn't emerge onto the national scene *de novo* in 1975. It has a long and complex past. Religious broadcasters were among the first broadcasters on the air in the years 1910–1930. The first remote broadcast by a commercial station was of a church service.

In their book on the electronic church, Jeffrey Hadden and Charles Swann (1981) report that the first religious broadcast probably dates from well before these developments, however. Reginald Fessenden was the pioneer of voice transmission via the new technology of radio. In an experiment on Christmas Eve, 1909, Fessenden wanted to demonstrate in a public way the utility of his device. Knowing that many ships at sea carried radiotelegraph receivers for safety reasons, he announced that he would do an experimental voice broadcast to these maritime stations. Searching for an appropriate text to read, he decided to read Bible passages.

As Quentin Schultze pointed out in Chapter 3, broadcasting has always held a fascination for certain religious groups. The mass, anonymous, "one-to-many" nature of broadcasting has often been seen as a particularly efficient way to propagate religious messages. Particularly for those groups, such as American Protestant evangelicals, who stress the conveyance of a simple message of salvation, such a medium can be seen to be ideal.

It is not a foregone conclusion that religious groups will easily fall into use of broadcasting, however. There are many religiously-based traditionalist cultures for whom broadcasting is inherently bad. Amish and separatist Hassidic communities in the United States proscribe even ownership of radios and television sets. Most streams of Islam are skeptical of film, television, and radio, particularly as these media might potentially be used to convey images of Mohammed himself, something that is prohibited in the Koran.

Even the same conservative Protestant sects which have seemed to be the source of most religious broadcasting have done so after a certain amount of controversy. In his history of Methodist broadcasting, William Fore (1972) pointed out that the Protestant faiths of the frontier—those we now know as fundamentalism and Pentecostalism, have always had a healthy dose of concern about the entertainment media. The realms from which film, radio, and television emanate are simple too close to the debased, secularized "entertainments" of the dancehall, the saloon, and the bordello for the liking of many such groups.

The tension between the traditionalist and skeptical past of conservative Protestantism and its present, which seems to have accepted broadcasting as an important and authentic carrier of the Gospel, has even provided some of the salience of these programs for certain of their viewers, according to a recent book by Stewart Hoover (1988). For some of them, the fact that a figure like Pat Robertson can appear on the national, secularized medium of television has given an added note of momentum to his message. He has captured this debased medium for "the good."

The institutional history of the electronic church has emerged from these roots and this past into a present where it is accepted as a foregone conclusion in both "secular" and "sectarian" realms. The chapters in this section address this history.

Razelle Frankl describes how the form and content of contemporary religious broadcasting is based in the "past" of the urban revival movement. The forebears of the electronic church preachers are not so much the country preachers of the frontier as they are the well-known revivalists of the cities. The cities were, after all, where Protestantism first had to come to grips with the rapidly increasing diversity of American society and culture. Contemporary religious television is also about the synthesis of such diversity with the homogeneity of traditionalist American evangelicalism (Hoover, 1988). This is no small task for the television evangelists, and Frankl's account illustrates the rhetorical, content, and formal strategies whereby the legacy of the past has informed the reality of present practice.

Sociologist and Billy Graham biographer William Martin describes the history of the electronic church in the context of its relationship to the broader evangelical movement and its denominations. Religious broadcasting is really nothing very new, in a way, and Martin authoritatively presents what *is* new and unique about the phenomenon. Most significantly, Martin outlines the unique role that Billy Graham has played in evangelicalism and in evangelical communication. Graham is, in many ways, the symbol of both the rise of neoevangelicalism (and subsequently the neo-evangelical "new right") *and* the rise of evangelical, parachurch broadcasting. The picture of religious broadcasting Martin paints places Graham in the central role he deserves, both as a pioneer broadcaster and as a *symbol* of these wider developments.

Finally, Kimberly Neuendorf sees the history of evangelical broadcasting to be integrally related to the history of nonevangelical religious broadcasting. Much of what we know of today as standard practice in fund raising and institutional organization in the electronic church, is based in the early development of federal and industry policy regarding religion. The half-century of rivalry between the mainline Protestant establishment and the independent, noninstitutional fundamentalist and evangelical religious broadcasters has left us with a legacy of policy, institutional organization, and institutional relationships which defines religious broadcasting in the electronic church era.

The history we see here is one which is long and complex. The purpose of these chapters is to integrate, from 3 perspectives, how it is that religious broadcasting has come to take the form we see it in today.

REFERENCES

Fore, W. (1972). *Broadcasting in the Methodist Church, 1950–1970.* Unpublished doctoral Dissertation, Columbia University, New York.

Hadden, J., & Swann, C. (1981). *Prime-time preachers.* Boston, MA: Addison-Wesley.

Hoover, S.M. (1988). *Mass media religion: The social sources of the electronic church.* Beverly Hills, CA: Sage.

4

A Hybrid Institution*

Razelle Frankl

Today's electronic church may best be described as a hybrid sociopolitical institution, made up of one part urban revivalism and one part Golden Age of Broadcasting. Its disparate parentage largely explains the roles, types of organizations, and effectiveness of this American institution. Urban revivalism assumes that the clergy influences an individual's choice of salvation, which previously rested with God only, and is responsible for the establishment of a message suitable for mass consumption. The economic and regulatory factors in the broadcast industry determined religious broadcasting's organizational structure, contributed to its prevalence, and stimulated its popularity (Frankl, 1984, 1987).

RELIGION ACCOMMODATES BROADCASTING

The true impact of urban revivalism can best be seen in an examination of the legacies of 3 great urban revivalists: Charles Grandison Finney, Dwight Moody, and Billy Sunday. Charles Finney (1792–1875) articulated the ethos of urban revivalism upon which contemporary televangelism is based. Finney's *Lectures: On Revivals of Religion* (1960) explained to the clergy how to conduct revivals or, given the primary calling of the revivalists, how to win souls. This text provided the ideological justification for making revivalism a planned event instead of the mystical, spirit-filled happening of the past. Furthermore, Finney exhorted ministers to use "any means" to produce powerful excitements and to play an active role as an agent of God.

Part of Finney's legacy was his preaching style, which relied on a sales strategy and the use of plain talk to appeal to audiences. Finney embedded Biblical literalism into the revivalists' preaching style, a tradition that continues today among the evangelical-fundamentalist preachers. Finney favored the direct Biblical words rather than sophisticated theological doc-

* This essay first appeared in *Critical Studies in Mass Communication*, September 1988, pp. 256–259. Reprinted here with permission.

trines, just as he favored the grammar and rhetoric of plain people. This practice, which combined emotion and intellect into structure and persuasion, is part of our broadcast religion heritage.

Under Finney's tutorage, the work and social relationships of the revivalist preacher were changed, as the preacher functioned as gatekeeper in the heavenly hierarchy. He became God's subcontractor, his tools being the Bible, a hymnal, and unique techniques to excite religious fervor. When Oral Roberts "speaks to God" and urges his viewers to contact him so that he can pray for them, for example, he is following Finney's precepts for being the "wise minister" whose special task is to kindle interest and enthusiasm for Jesus among sinners.

Today's televangelists are criticized in the press for their emotionalism, their fraudulent theology, and their flamboyant programs. All of these accusations are reminiscent of the charges against Finney and his style of religious expression. The underlying schism between revivalists and the churches came into the open when Finney withdrew his Broadway tabernacle in New York City from the Presbyterian Church and established an independent congregational form of governance. This parallels the situation between the independent organizations of the televangelists and the mainstream religious organizations that are part of larger denominations.

While Finney profoundly altered the ethos and preaching of revivalism, Dwight Moody (1837–1899) rationalized and routinized the organization of revivalism and some of its rituals about 30 years later. Overall, Moody's major contribution to urban revivalism was to introduce a businesslike organizational structure into the religious realm and to institute managerial techniques to improve the operation and effectiveness of revivals. Moody also contributed to the social milieu of revivalism through the creation of an infrastructure for Bible schools and institutes. These schools, in particular the Moody Bible Institute in Chicago, continue to educate and train students to carry on the work of Moody and other revivalists. When fundamentalism evolved as a social movement, some of these Bible schools became part of that movement. Today, these Christian schools are major building blocks for many televangelists (Oral Roberts, Pat Robertson, and Jerry Falwell in particular) in their attempts to evangelize and influence the non-Christian world. They also serve as successful vehicles for fund raising (Public Broadcasting Service, 1984).

Billy Sunday (1862–1935) characterized himself as a businessman for the Lord. According to Weisberger (1958) and McLoughlin (1955), Sunday transformed urban revivals into "professional amusements" by his showmanship and commercialism and played down much of the religious connotation associated with revival meetings. In his emphasis of large-scale entertainment and his streamlining of Moody's churches, schools, and missions into one single-minded revivalist corporation, Sunday developed urban revivalism into an ideal organizational structure for entering the business of broadcast programming upon its inception (Frankl, 1984).

By the time broadcasting came into its own, urban revivalism was a well-managed, routinized, and rationally planned religious phenomenon. It had become an institution dedicated to evangelism with its own ethos, thus allowing inspirational preachers such as Bishop Fulton J. Sheen, Norman Vincent Peale, and Billy Graham to grasp the new technology as a viable vehicle of expression. While these men were not interested in establishing teleministries, they clearly demonstrated the intimacy, power, and broad audiences of the new media, thereby serving as role models for more contemporary urban revivalists such as Oral Roberts and Rex Humbard. Urban revivalism had established distinctive values and beliefs suitable for mass broadcasting. Also, it had developed an entertaining style of presentation conducive to radio and television programming and capable of attracting and sustaining an audience. Instead of arguing about the suitability of television for religious expression, as have the liberal denominational Protestant and Catholic communities, the televangelists regard technology as God's gift for their work in spreading the gospel. Instead of arguing about the costs of producing and broadcasting religious programs, they have created effective fund-raising strategies through on-the-air solicitations.

BROADCASTING ACCOMMODATES RELIGION

Other factors contributing to the growth and expansion of the electronic church were changes in the regulatory environment and market conditions of the television industry during the 1960s and 1970s. For example, the Surgeon General's banning of tobacco and liquor advertisements from broadcasting, and the resultant loss of advertising revenues, forced stations to find new sources of income. As a result, many stations became more receptive to selling broadcast time to religious programmers than they had been in the past. This was enhanced by the modification of Federal Communications Commission policy that permitted commercial, as well as sustaining, religious programming to meet the public-interest obligations of licensees (Lacey, 1978). With this change, local stations could fulfill their licensing obligations and also generate income with one program.

It is important to note that, by the 1960s, local affiliates of the networks had acquired greater autonomy, a freedom that enabled them to sell to religious sponsors without jeopardizing either their network ties or their license renewals. This development, combined with economic pressure and the removal of policy barriers, created a new and much larger market environment for religious programmers. Programmers thus began to build a stronger audience base for future expansion. No longer having to confine their religious broadcasts to early Sunday mornings, independent stations sold evening time as well, including prime-time.

By the end of the 1970s, the electronic church included cable networks, radio and television stations, and over 65 nationally syndicated television programs. Within the electronic church, at least 8 televangelists dominated the market and had built expansive teleministries. The growth of the electronic church is supported by organizations, schools, political action committees, and Christian activities that perpetuate the televangelists. The television programs reinforce the Christian lifestyle, just as Pepsi commercials reinforce and remind the viewers to buy this particular brand of soda.

In recent years, evangelism continues as the dominant type of religious programming on both radio and television. The February 1987 issue of *Religious Broadcasting,* published by the National Religious Broadcasters (NRB), indicated that "20 religious radio and almost 2 religious TV stations are opened each month somewhere in America" (Nicholas, 1987, p. 20). There are currently 1,370 radio stations with a religious format. The expansion of religious television stations has been more rapid; NRB data indicate that there are now 221 religious television stations in this country. A corollary to the growth in television stations has been the increase in religious television program producers. In 1987, there were 414 religious program producers, compared to 280 in 1982. Dan Nicholas (1987, p. 22) suggests that this increase in the numbers of Christian broadcasting professionals occurred "in part because of the increased use of satellite delivery, which provides the opportunity for live, issue-oriented programming."

Clearly, revivalists have a long tradition as religious entrepreneurs. This tradition, along with the birth of broadcasting, a period of economic anxiety in the broadcast industry, and federal deregulation, has contributed to the rapid growth of religious broadcasting. What does the future hold? Overnight ratings from the A.C. Nielsen Company indicated that the April 28, 1987 airing of CNN's *Larry King Live* scored its highest rating ever, and the second highest for any CNN telecast, when it narrowcasted an interview with new PTL leader Jerry Falwell in the midst of the PTL controversy (Stilson, 1987). On May 27, 1987 ABC's *Nightline* presented a 72-minute interview with the Bakkers, which drew the most viewers in the 8-year history of the program (Abelman, 1988). This evidence suggests that televangelists have generated interest in a broader audience than ever anticipated. The fit between evangelism and broadcasting continues to be a good one.

REFERENCES

Abelman, R. (1988). Financial support for religious television: The impact of the PTL scandal. *Journal of Media Economics, 1*(1), 23–39.

Finney, C.G. (Ed.). (1960). *Lectures: On revivals of religion.* Cambridge, MA: The Belknap Press.

Frankl, R. (1984). *Popular religion and the imperatives of television: A study of the electronic church.* Ann Arbor, MI: University Microfilms International.

Frankl, R. (1987). *Televangelism: The marketing of popular religion.* Carbondale, IL: Southern Illinois University Press.

Lacey, L.J. (1978). The electronic church: An FCC established institution? *Federal Communication Law Journal, 31,* 235–275.

McLoughlin, W.G., Jr. (1955). *Billy Sunday was his real name*. Chicago, IL: University of Chicago Press.

Nicholas, D. (1987). The quiet revolution in Christian broadcasting. *Religious Broadcasting, 19*(2), 20, 22, 111.

Public Broadcasting Service. (1984, June). *Frontline: Give me that old time religion* [Television program]. Boston, MA: WGBH-TV.

Stilson, J. (1987, June 1). Ratings high: The Bakkers are a hot draw on TV interview programs. *Electronic Media*, pp. 1–39.

Weisberger, B.A. (1958). *They gathered at the river: The story of the great revivalists and their impact upon religion in America*. Boston, MA: Little, Brown, & Company.

5

Giving the Winds a Mighty Voice

William Martin

The electronic church, a phenomenon of secular concern for little more than a decade, had long been an integral aspect of American religion. Two months after KDKA in Pittsburgh became the nation's first licensed radio station in 1921, the Calvary Episcopal Church began broadcasting its Sunday evening service. Religious leaders quickly recognized radio's potential as a tool for teaching and evangelism and, by 1925, approximately one-tenth of the more than 600 radio stations in America were owned and operated by churches and other religious organizations. Almost from the start, the more liberal and "respectable" mainline denominations dominated broadcasting over the major networks, which gave them free time in return for nondenominational and, usually, noncontroversial programming. Shut out of this cozy arrangement, the more abrasive fundamentalists were forced to improvise. In keeping with their paradoxical penchant for using the latest technology and highly flexible organizational structures to confound those inclined to dismiss them as backwater rubes, they developed broadcasting strategies that not only worked at the time, but gave them the experience and outlook that have enabled them to dominate the field for the last 3 decades.

The key figure in this process was California evangelist Charles E. Fuller, founder of the *Old-Fashioned Revival Hour*. In the depths of the depression, Fuller attracted enough listener support to enable him to persuade the Mutual Broadcasting System to accept his program. By the middle of 1943, he was being heard on more than 1000 stations and his nonprofit ministry was buying 50 percent more air time than the secular company in second place. His success soon led him to found Fuller Theological Seminary, one of the most respected of all evangelical schools today. Fuller's preeminence gave him, without his having sought it, a central role in shaping the strategy virtually all electronic ministries would eventually use in getting their programs to the public. Pressure from secular advertisers, who coveted his choice time slots, and from the Federal Council of Churches, which opposed the practice of selling time for religious broadcasts, led Mutual to shift

63

Fuller's programs to less desirable hours and to cut their length. Rather than accept the switch, Fuller lined up a makeshift network of independent stations and sent them recordings of his programs, which they could play at whatever time was available.

This simple strategy became the standard method still used by virtually all religious broadcasters whose radio or television programs are aired over more than one station or cable network. It also facilitated the explosive growth in recent years in the number of religion-oriented radio stations. Since evangelists typically pay such stations a fee equivalent to the costs of air time plus the revenue the station would receive it if sold advertising, station owners do not have to bother with selling advertising or worry about whether anyone is listening. Further, the small staff required to play the evangelists' tapes and handle announcements can make these stations dependable and relatively trouble-free income producers. These factors have repeatedly made it possible to convert money-losing secular stations to a religious format and have them show a profit within a few months' time. Many stations, of course, operate on a nonprofit basis, and some provide programming comparable in range and cost to secular stations in the same markets.

As this severely abbreviated sketch suggests, the electronic church is not a new creature. On the contrary, it was a key element in an alternative institutional structure, erected during the 1920s and 1930s, that enabled evangelical Christianity to withstand intense social and intellectual pressures, overcome traumatic losses and humiliation (best symbolized by the Scopes trial), and emerge in the 1940s as a reasonably unified and powerful force in American life. Still, it is television that has made religious broadcasting a topic of wide discussion, and with which this essay is primarily concerned.

As had been the case with radio, television schedules included religious programming from the time it became a viable medium. As early as 1939, the Federal Council of Churches produced *I Believe,* a program in which prominent theologians discussed the relationship between religion and everyday life. It followed this with a children's puppet show and with other efforts that proved the new medium could be used for something more innovative than the traditional sermon. In 1950, soon after the major networks began extensive programming, the Seventh-Day Adventist Church produced *Faith for Today,* a series, made William A. Fagal the first television pastor. Missouri Synod Lutherans followed with *This Is the Life,* the first religious dramatic series, and Southern Baptists produced an impressive array of dramas, documentaries, biographies, cartoons, musical productions, and films designed especially for television. The Presbyterian Church in the United States produced a lively interview program and, during the 1960s, the United Church of Christ presented a provocative series of lectures relating Christian teaching to major social problems.

The most successful religious program of the early 1950s was the Roman Catholic program, *Life Is Worth Living,* which consisted of nothing but a half-hour address by Bishop Fulton J. Sheen. Making full use of his commanding physical presence and considerable dramatic ability, Sheen demonstrated once again what George Whitefield had proved in 1740: that a substantial proportion of the American population will respond enthusiastically to a charismatic and self-confident man who purports to speak for God. He also demonstrated that preachers are subject to the same uncertainties that bedevil other television performers. Apparently irritated by Sheen's prominence and widely recognized arrogance, Cardinal Spellman cancelled the program in 1957. When it was revived in 1959, Sheen had lost his hold on the public's attention.

Despite its obvious possibilities, fundamentalist and evangelical preachers of the sort who had been the mainstay of religious radio were slow to use television, largely because of the required leap in expense and expertise and the realistic recognition that members of their natural audience were underrepresented among set owners at the time. The first independent evangelist to use the new medium in a significant way was Rex Humbard, who began telecasting services from his church in Akron in 1952. "I saw this new thing called television," he recalled, "and I said, 'That's it.' God had given us that thing . . . the most powerful force of communication to take the Gospel into . . . every state in the union."

Three years later, Oral Roberts created a sensation when he sent the high-voltage excitement of his miracle healing services into the living-rooms of hundreds of thousands of people who had never been exposed to Pentecostal religion. Roberts used the tent-service format until 1967, when he abandoned the crusade circuit and the program to devote full attention to his fledgling university. When he returned to the small screen in 1969, he began using a variety show/interview/low-key preaching format that kept him at or near the top of the ratings for religious programs until 1979, when his audience began a decline that he has never been able to reverse.

Billy Graham's entry into electronic ministry vividly demonstrated both the possibilities for extending one's reach by means of radio and television and, equally significant, the changes that involvement in mass media inevitably force on a ministry that uses them. In 1950, a string of successful crusades in Los Angeles, Boston, Columbia, South Carolina, and Portland, Oregon, had brought Graham a spate of national publicity, but he was still conducting his campaigns with the assistance of a small group of associates who were paid out of love-offerings and were bound to him by nothing more formal than personal loyalty. The launching that year of the *Hour of Decision* radio broadcast required him to form the nonprofit Billy Graham Evangelistic Association (BGEA) and, for the first time, to lease office space, hire a secretary, and appoint a business manager. Within weeks after a modest beginning on 150 ABC stations, the program was being heard over more than 1000 stations and was posting the highest ratings the Nielsen service had ever recorded for a religious broadcast. When mail began to flood into Graham's Minneapolis office (over 178,000 letters in 1951, and twice that the following year), BGEA purchased a modest office building and its staff soon expanded from 2 people to well over 100. The mail brought in sufficient money to pay the bills, but it also contained so many requests for personal and spiritual advice that Graham began his "My Answer" newspaper column in an effort to deal with some of them on a wholesale basis. As requests for sermons, books, sheet music, and recordings aired on the programs mounted, he formed a tax-paying retail company to meet these needs. And, predictably, the weekly broadcasts enhanced the appeal of Graham's crusades, since they gave people the opportunity to see in person the dynamic young preacher they had heard on the radio.

On the strength of such success, Graham began to produce feature films with an evangelistic thrust and experimented for a time with a television program for children and a studio program that featured preaching and interviews. During a momentous 1954 crusade in London, he made 26 fifteen-minute "fireside chat" programs for the Independent Television network. But the real breakthrough for Graham came in 1957, when ABC set aside its policy against selling time to religious broadcasters and aired, on 17 successive Saturday nights, live services from his crusade in Madison Square Garden. The immediacy of the live service, their origin from New York and the Garden, and the prime-time slot combined to make the telecasts far more successful than the studio shows had ever been. The first broadcast posted a 8.1 Trendex rating (against Jackie Gleason's 12.5 and Perry Como's 20.0), which translated into approximately 6.5 million viewers, enough to fill the Garden to capacity every day for a whole year. The impact of taking viewers into a live service—the format Graham retains to this day—was explained by a contemporary observer:

> When the average, moral, reputable American sees Dr. Graham in a studio telling him he needs to be "born again," his first impulse will be to discredit him as a religious fanatic. But if the viewers sees thousands of respectable, normal people listening and consenting to all this he hears, and then sees hundreds voluntarily get up and walk to the front in response to a low-pressure request, he'll begin to consider the message and situation with some sincere, honest interest. It's much easier to say a single speaker is wrong than to discredit the conviction and decision of thousands. (Pollock, 1966, pp. 238–239)

Despite the success experienced by Humbard, Roberts, and Graham, other evangelists had difficulty breaking into television. The networks and major local stations preferred to donate time to religious organizations, as part of their FCC obligation to present public-service programming, and they seldom showed much interest in bestowing their favors on fundamentalist or Pentecostal preachers. The breakthrough came during the latter part of the 1960s, when agents for various ministries convinced the owners of struggling UHF stations that religious programming could furnish them with a solid, dependable source of income for Sunday morning time slots that were typically bringing in little or no revenue. A 1960 FCC ruling that permitted stations to meet their public-service obligations with paid religious broadcasts also favored evangelicals, since most "mainline" denominations were still refusing to pay for air time. This improved climate not only fostered the dramatic growth of evangelical programming on secular stations but led to the birth of television stations majoring in religion. With advances in cable and satellite technology, national networks of Christian broadcast facilities became technically and economically feasible

The most notable of these ventures has been Pat Robertson's Christian Broadcasting Network, which has grown from a single religiously oriented UHF station into the second largest cable operation in America, and produced a legitimate candidate for the presidency in the process. Before it was gutted by scandal, Jim Bakker's PTL network also had a substantial reach, and the Trinity Broadcasting Network, headed by Paul Crouch and headquartered in California, is rapidly expanding the number of its markets. Jerry Falwell's Liberty Broadcasting Network, the Southern Baptists' American Christian Television System, and the Roman Catholic External Word Television Network represent other hopeful attempts to extend the borders of the electronic church.

As the 1980s draw to a close, most religious broadcasting falls into 1 of 4 categories: (a) long-running ecumenical and denominational programs, which occupy an ever-diminishing amount of air time and reach an ever-smaller audience; (b) weekly worship services televised over local stations by individual congregations and varying widely in quality and impact, depending primarily on the effectiveness of the preacher; (c) the syndicated programs of Graham, Roberts, Falwell, Robert Schuller, Kenneth Copeland, James Kennedy, and their colleagues; and (d) the offerings of the cable and satellite networks. There is, of course, some overlap between these components, particularly in the placing of local and syndicated programs on the schedules of cable and satellite networks. Because of the increased cost of time on local secular stations, it seems likely that most of the new growth in religious telecasting will occur in the realm of cable and satellite technology.

One obvious possibility is the development of electronic churches whose reality would match the metaphor. Some denominations, such as the Assemblies of God and the Latter-Day Saints, already beam programs and special messages via satellite to dishes attached to individual church buildings, to enable congregations all over the nation to view the programs simultaneously. The same technology could easily be adapted to set up "franchise" churches in which the instruction, preaching, and special musical numbers could originate from a single source, and a man or woman approved by the ministry could serve as pastor and administrator in local churches. Such churches would obviously be vulnerable to the abuses inherent in a religion centered around a single person or small group of people, but it might be possible to create a policy that could avoid some of these problems. On this and other matters, the future of the electronic church is hard to predict, but it would probably be a mistake to believe that we have already seen all of the various ways in which religious broadcasters can use communications technology to expand their ministries and preach the gospel to the outer parts of the earth.

Billy Graham's experience illustrates well the kinds of expansions and elaborations that use of broadcast media can engender in the structure of a ministry. The intrinsic nature of television and its audience can also affect the content of religious programs. Television specializes in simple, arresting messages. Anyone who has tried to discuss his or her academic speciality for the *Six O'Clock News,* or even an hour-long talk show, has felt the frustration of trying to compress insights gleaned from years of study into a few terse "sound bites." One soon learns to lop off qualifications, to smooth rough edges, to lead with a "grabber," and, above all, not to sound "too academic." A full, satisfactory statement might lose an audience that can change channels from across the room. This characteristic of television fosters programs that emphasize excitement, celebrity, success, instant gratification, and easy solutions. This is no less true of religious than of secular television. Most of the top religious television programs either offer cornucopian this-worldly success or proclaim that present hard times will be supernaturally transformed at the imminent Second Coming of Christ. Both approaches imply that the promised result is only a phone call or letter or book or pamphlet away.

The television preachers insist, of course, that the essence of the Christian gospel is not difficult to comprehend, that its genius resides precisely in its simplicity. And certainly, one cannot require 20th century American preachers to travel from city to city by donkey or sandal, or expect that a person committed to using television to preach the gospel would not make some accomodation to its demands, but the emphasis of many programs on slickness, success, and celebrity stands in garish contrast to the Biblical picture and proclamations of the Old Testament prophets and of Jesus and his apostles. Long before television, of course, evangelists knew how to entertain their audiences with celebrities and heroes and vaudeville-type performers; Billy Sunday, for example, once livened up a revival service with a performance by Al Jolson's chorus girls. Still, the involvement of evangelists in a medium used primarily for entertainment and commercial purposes has inevitably exaggerated tendencies toward celebrity and consumer religion.

The inordinate financial demands of a large television ministry, coupled with the competition for viewers and money this necessarily entails, can easily have negative effects on a television minister's integrity. Despite the tumult generated by Jim and Tammy Bakker's Heritage Village hyper-drama and Jimmy Swaggart's motel madness, the ranks of television preachers probably contain fewer flat-out charlatans than one might suppose. There have been, of course, some notable gaps between preachment and practice, including adultery, incest, alcoholism and drug addiction, mail fraud, arson, embezzlement, and outrageous pandering to racism and bigotry. Faith healers have hired shills to fake cures and, as magician/fraud-investigator James Randi has demonstrated, sometimes use stage-mentalist techniques and electronic devices to obtain information they claim came directly from God (Randi, 1987). But most probably believe what they preach and have a sincere desire to serve God.

Still, the insatiable financial demands placed on them by the rising cost of television, the continuing expense of various projects they have undertaken in efforts to expand their ministries, and the high costs of fund raising itself has led some prominent ministers to do things they may not have done had they not been under such tremendous pressure. Oral Roberts may be so close to the edge that he genuinely believes God held him hostage to raise an $8-million ransom to cover expenses related to a medical school commissioned by a 900-foot Jesus, but when he looks into the camera and says, "You write me. I'll read your letter and I'll write you back," he knows he is not describing what happens to the hundreds of thousands of letters that pour into his Tulsa headquarters. Jerry Falwell and several other prominent preachers have sent letters in which they spent 3 pages pleading for money for orphans or disaster relief or foreign missions, then, on page 4, noted that anything over a certain sum—typically above 5 percent of what such a letter could reasonably be expected to bring—will go to regular expenses.

Another ploy used by some is to include a notice, in exceedingly tiny print, that "in good faith" the evangelist will feel free to use the money for purposes other than those described in the letter, or that it will be used "in accordance with Ezra 7:18," the text of which (not printed on the notice) reads as follows: "Whatever seems good to you and your brethren to do with the rest of the silver and gold, you may do, according to the will of your God." The ability of computers to personalize letters also leads easily to an abuse of trust, so that a naive supporter may actually believe that their favorite TV minister stayed up until 4:00 a.m., thinking specifically about "one of the most faithful friends I have had in my entire ministry." And, of course, some media ministers have repeatedly tried to pry open pocketbooks with palpably demagogic tactics, as when they characterized secular humanists and liberals as moral equivalents to robbers, rapists, murderers, communists, and perverts, and imply that a $20 contribution to their ministry is the only way to keep Oliver North free and Old Glory flying.

Compounding the problem is a tendency toward autocracy, reflected in boards of directors that consist of the evangelist, his wife, a son or brother-in-law, and 1 or 2 ciphers who can be counted on not to question God's servant on any matter of substance. In such a setting, a man whose chief talent is persuasion can easily persuade himself as well as others that whatever he wants—a Rolls Royce, a church secretary, a hospital, or political power and influence—is precisely what God wants him to have, that his will is God's will and beyond challenge, reproof, or correction.

Examples of such overreaching abound, from the cavalier refusal of Jim Bakker and Jimmy Swaggart to see any inconsistency between tearfully begging for funds while building million-dollar homes for themselves to Pat Robertson's claim, in a letter to a critic, that to oppose him is to oppose God, since he is "the anointed of God," the Hebrew translation of which is "Messiah." Popular evangelists are scarcely unique in their attractions to the triple temptations of money, sex, and power, but the combination of their particular talents and the structure of most of their organizations leaves them notably vulnerable to these temptations and the trouble they bring.

The 1988 decision by the National Religious Broadcasters to adopt a new code of ethics to which all its members must subscribe may help curb gross abuses of financial trust. To submit to its requirements means increased regulation, extra expense and effort, and, probably, aggravating scrutiny by the media and others playing an adversarial role. In light of the recent scandals, these seem a small price to pay for much-needed assistance in repairing the reputation and shoring up the integrity of electronic evangelism.

Pat Robertson's suggestion that the shaking-out precipitated by the Bakker scandal might well precede a widespread revival was probably a rosy reading of the signs. On the other hand, predictions that the electronic church will not recover from the scandals of 1987–88 are also unwarranted. Television religion is here to stay. It can be a force for demagoguery and an instrument to turn people from serious engagement to simplistic solutions, but it can also strengthen and deepen the faith of viewers by providing them with instruction, exhortation, inspiration, hope, encouragement, entertainment, example, and opportunity for service. As it gets better, and it is improving, it will probably serve these same functions for growing numbers of people. It also serves a symbolic function of great importance, in that it has been the chief means of serving notice to the nation that evangelical Christians are no longer content to be treated as a backwater minority, but are a force with which to reckon—socially, politically, and theologically. Folk to whom a medium has meant so much will not readily abandon it in times of trouble.

REFERENCES

Pollock, J. (1966). *Billy Graham*. New York: McGraw-Hill.
Randi, J. (1987). *The faith healers*. Buffalo, NY: Prometheus Press.

6

The Public Trust versus the Almighty Dollar

Kimberly A. Neuendorf

The history of broadcasting in America has been a continuing story of order arising out of disorder. Much legislation aimed at bringing structure to our communication environment has been instituted *post hoc,* after problems have been identified. For example, in 1988, legislation was considered that would monitor televangelists' pocketbooks; this proposal followed charges of fiscal and moral excess against several prominent religious broadcasters (*Religion in America,* 1987).

At the very outset of radio broadcasting, the unnecessary death of hundreds on the sinking Titanic signaled the need for law—the wireless operator on a nearby ship was not at his station, and did not hear the radioed pleas for assistance. Thus followed the Radio Act of 1912, and later the Communications Act of 1934, the law under which we presently operate. Indiscriminate use of the airwaves was brought to a stop. The limited spectrum space suitable for allocation to broadcast facilities makes the airwaves a limited commodity, and over the years, this valuable commodity has been carefully carved up among commercial channels, military and police use, CB, and other noncommercial uses. American broadcasting is viewed as a public trust, something that because of its great potential and because of the finite size of the electromagnetic spectrum carrying it[1] belongs to the populace at large.

In most countries, the manifestation of the airwaves as a public trust is direct—governments own and operate all broadcast stations, or license and closely monitor those entrusted with the broadcast task. In the United States, the execution of the public trust has been more complex, involving a rather loose governance of private-enterprise broadcast owners by the Federal Communications Commission. While the loss of a license to broadcast only rarely occurs (and such loss is usually due to violations of rules of a

---

[1] There are presently over 9,000 radio stations and more than 1,000 television stations broadcasting in the United States (Geller, 1985). In major broadcast markets, the airwaves are virtually filled—that is, there are few suitable frequencies left to allocate.

technical nature), through the process of granting licenses, the FCC does exercise indirect control over what content is broadcast.

The Communications Act of 1934 has as its major tenet the notion that broadcasters operate "in the public interest, convenience and necessity." Over the years, more specific guidelines have been developed to grant some predictability to broadcasters seeking license renewal. In 1960 the FCC issued a report reiterating the "major elements usually necessary to meet the public interest, needs and desires of the community" (FCC, 1960, p. 2314); "religious programs" was 1 of 14 entries.[2] Although the list was not intended to be a "fixed formula," it was routinely applied by the FCC to license renewal cases (Loevinger, 1964–65).

For many years, the attitude that religious programming was part of the broadcast station's public interest commitment held sway. As we shall see, changes in the regulatory environment have changed this view substantially. But the roots of religious broadcasting reach back to the earliest, experimental years of the medium of radio.

THE HISTORY OF RELIGIOUS BROADCASTING: FOUR ERAS

When viewed from a perspective of how those with a religious message are able to gain *access* to telecommunication channels, a history of religious broadcasting in America may be sectioned into 4 parts, determined by the regulatory environment in each era, and the corresponding methods by which the programming was produced and financed:

Era 1:   Precommercial religious radio (through about 1927)
Era 2:   Sustaining-time religious broadcasting (1927–1960)
Era 3:   Paid-time religious broadcasting and the growth of the Electric Church (1960–1980s)
Era 4:   Religious cablecasting—paid-time in a free marketplace (1980–on)

Each era has had its own unique set of assumptions about the role of broadcasting in American society, including official and popular beliefs about what constitute appropriate methods of funding. Era 1's notion that broadcasting was not even necessarily commercial gave way to Era 2's emphasis on organized business that had a public duty to "share the spoils" of lucrative broadcasting by underwriting noncommercial enterprises such

---

[2] The list of 14 follows: (a) opportunity for local self-expression, (b) the development and use of local talent, (c) programs for children, (d) religious programs, (e) educational programs, (f) public affairs programs, (g) editorialization by licensees, (h) political broadcasts, (i) agricultural programs, (j) news programs, (k) weather and market reports, (l) sports programs, (m) service to minority groups, and (n) entertainment programs.

as religion. Era 3 assumed that the business of broadcasting and the public duty of broadcasters were not at all at odds, in that broadcasters were allowed to meet their public commitment *and* charge money at the same time. A cause's commercial viability began to dictate its appropriateness for broadcast. The current cable-oriented Era 4 fulfills the dream of a rich marketplace of ideas, where commercial viability is more easily attainable.

Era 1: Precommercial Religious Radio

Commercial broadcasting as we know it did not emerge full-blown. Many of the first radio stations were owned by manufacturers or retailers hoping to sell radios. Others were first run on a common carrier basis, whereby individuals or groups would essentially rent the studio for an hour at a time and broadcast whatever they wished. In this experimental environment, religion was a common type of content for radio broadcasts. One of America's first broadcast facilities (KDKA in Pittsburgh, owned by Westinghouse) included an Episcopal church service in its first year's offerings—for the simple reason that a station engineer sang in the church choir (Hadden & Swann, 1981). The success of these broadcasts was emulated by new radio stations across the country. The first regular religious broadcasts were aired on WJBT ("Where Jesus Blesses Thousands") in Chicago in 1922 (Flake, 1982). The evangelist Paul Rader reconstructed a typical service on the air, bringing his high-spirited religion to listeners who otherwise would never have been exposed to it (Hadden & Swann, 1981).

These were the wild and wooly days of radio, and the most aggressive and innovative individuals grabbed the chance to use the new medium. The Radio Act of 1912 failed to give Secretary of Commerce Herbert Hoover the ability to *deny* licenses to broadcast, resulting in such pandemoniac phenomena as "renegade" radio—stations that kept changing broadcast frequency or power, despite Hoover's warnings. Such was the case of the station licensed to evangelist Aimee Semple McPherson, who responded to her station's temporary shutdown with a telegram to Hoover: "Please order your minions of Satan to leave my station alone. You cannot expect the almighty to abide by your wavelength nonsense. When I offer my prayers to him I must fit into his wave reception" (as cited by Head with Sterling, 1982, p. 139).

Not all early religious broadcasters were as colorful as McPherson, but many ran seat-of-the-pants operations on tiny budgets. As commercialism crept predictably into radio broadcasting, religious programming suffered—stations owned by religious groups were sold to commercial concerns, and as airtime became more valuable, access by religious groups to the airwaves became more restricted.

Era 1, then, was characterized by a general lack of telecommunication policy, with great freedom of access and no restrictions on how broadcasters might finance programming. Some time for religious broadcasting was donated, much of it was purchased, and no laws either required or prohibited access to the airwaves by religious communicators.

Era 2: Sustaining-time Religious Broadcasting

Contributing to early religious radio's decline was the Radio Act of 1927, which brought tighter technical standards and replaced makeshift broadcast facilities in the religious community with professional broadcast operations (Gentry, 1984). However, this same act laid the groundwork for the *donation* of airtime, and often of production costs, to religious groups. In establishing religious content as one mandate for broadcasters, the Act of 1927 assured access to the airwaves for religious organizations.

The model of religious broadcasting became one of *sustaining* time (i.e., time provided free-of-charge) for mainline church services with the development of network commercial radio (NBC, CBS, and Mutual Broadcasting System by 1934, with the split-off of ABC from NBC in 1943). All networks eventually instituted policies that prohibited or restricted the selling of airtime to religious groups or individuals. Figure 6.1 displays time-lines for the policies of the 4 major radio networks, as well as the main religious bodies with whom sustaining-time programming was arranged.

These policies against paid-time broadcasting were ostensibly an effort to simplify the process of providing the public service of religious broadcasting, but had the effect of restricting access to the "chosen"—national, largely Protestant organizations. Whereas the first era of religious broadcasting had favored individual, aggressive effort, this second era of sustaining time gave the advantage to well-organized, predictable efforts. The networks were fast becoming big, well-oiled machines. Since most stations were network affiliates, even local access by churches tended to follow a sustaining-time pattern that favored locally prominent churches. Broadcasting was seen by society at large as having a responsibility for meeting the spiritual needs of special people (e.g., "shut-ins") and for providing reinforcement of people's religion, *not* for presenting new or different religious doctrines or attempting to change audience members' religious convictions. Hence, mainline churches expected and got the lion's share of broadcast coverage.

Jennings (1968) has described in detail the role of some of the major religious organizations of the radio era (1920–50), largely formed in response to the broadcast challenge:

FCCC: Federal Council of Churches of Christ, founded in 1908, members included Baptist, Methodist, Episcopal, and Presbyterian sects.
JRRC: Joint Religious Radio Committee, founded 1944, members included Methodist, Presbyterian, and Congregational churches.

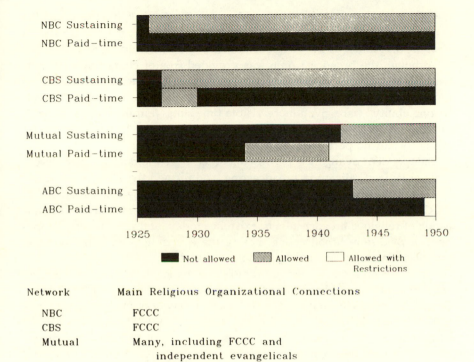

Network	Main Religious Organizational Connections
NBC	FCCC
CBS	FCCC
Mutual	Many, including FCCC and independent evangelicals
ABC	FCCC, NAE, ACCC

Figure 6.1. Radio Network Policies Toward Religious Broadcasting 1925–1950

PRC: Protestant Radio Commission, founded 1947, members included *organizations* such as the FCCC and the JRRC, as well as churches.

ACCC: American Council of Christian Churches, founded in 1941 in opposition to the FCCC.

NRB: National Religious Broadcasters, endorsed and joined by the National Association of Evangelicals (NAE) in 1945, in opposition to the FCCC. Currently active.

The single most powerful organization of this type was the Federal Council of Churches of Christ (FCCC), a coalition of 21 churches that was the major source of decision-making power for national religious radio programming. Although Jennings (1968) is critical of the FCCC's lack of interest in the power of radio as a "societal force" (p. 487),[3] he acknowledges its clear

---

[3] "The Federal Council's relationship with [networks] was almost entirely public-relations oriented . . . Even as the network found less and less time for religious programs, the Federal Council remained publicly silent, apparently accepting whatever periods it could come by as gifts gratefully received . . . If the Federal Council was considered a potential custodian of the public interest in broadcasting, its leadership must be judged wholly negative" (Jennings, 1968, pp. 486–87).

dominance for over 30 years of broadcasting. Each week, it determined the content of all NBC religious broadcasts, the content of the *CBS Church of the Air,* and much of the religious content on Mutual and ABC.

Although the broadcast *time* was provided free of charge by each network, funds for the *production* costs came mainly from donations by listeners. In order to fulfill these needs, better speakers with manifest "broadcasting ability" were given more visible time slots (Jennings, 1968, p. 486). During this era, religious broadcasters first recognized an advantage to airing those who performed in a more polished manner.

Independent evangelicals grew concerned over the dominance of large-scale organized religion in broadcasting, and formed the National Association of Evangelicals in 1942, and the National Religious Broadcasters (NRB) in 1944. The NRB has evolved into the largest, most active organization of religious broadcasters in existence today, and was an early proponent of *paid-time* broadcasting, noting the evangelical potential of radio that was seemingly ignored by mainline churches.

As television made inroads on radio's dominance, the trend for mainline religion continued. The National Council of Churches (the FCCC's successor) "successfully lobbied the [television] networks for a policy of sustaining time only" (Hadden & Frankl, 1987, p. 103). This continuation of sustaining time has been viewed by some as a threat to First Amendment guarantees, and most certainly a violation of the FCC's Fairness Doctrine, assuring the coverage of conflicting points of view.

Throughout the sustaining-time era, independent preachers (mainly evangelists) were largely excluded from the councils of churches that controlled programming. This was due in part to a theological separatism that was bilaterally desired, but may also have been the result of pressure on networks by mainline churches (Hadden & Shupe, 1987, p. 63). As Curtis (1978) notes, evangelists "had to purchase time to have a voice and presence in television. Most prestigious stations had a policy against 'commercial religion' and refused to sell them time" (p. 21).

Consequently, most religious programming was rather homogenous in focus and appearance. Ellens (1974) has characterized religious television of this era as falling into only 4 categories: (a) using the camera and microphone as an extended pulpit (e.g., the Roman Catholic Bishop Fulton Sheen); (b) creating a spectacle (e.g., Billy Graham specials); (c) teaching (e.g., the National Council of Churches' *Lamp Unto My Feet,* and the Lutheran Church-Missouri Synod's *This Is The Life*); and (d) provoking earnest thought in "spot" public service announcements (e.g., the Franciscans' series on saints).

Era 2 was a time of big-business broadcasting, epitomized by the development of powerful networks. The general view of broadcasting was one of a great protectorate and provider, *owing* the audience fair and decent programming. Religion was seen as just one of a number of essential services that broadcasting ought provide. In line with this thinking, religious broadcasting was carefully controlled and time was allocated to it in a strict manner; paid-time coverage was largely prohibited.

Era 3: Paid-time Religious Broadcasting and the Growth of the Electric Church

In 1960, the tradition of sustaining time was dealt a blow by a new interpretation of broadcast regulations by the FCC. The Federal Communications Commission decided that "there is no public interest basis for distinguishing between sustaining and commercially sponsored programs in evaluating station performance" (Federal Communications Commission Reports, 1960, p. 2315). Stations could meet their public interest requirements *and* reap profits by charging for air time. This action was followed by a precipitous drop in the proportion of religious programming that was sustaining-time, from 47 percent in 1959 to only 8 percent in 1977. As Figure 6.2 shows, however, this was due to an increase in paid-time re-

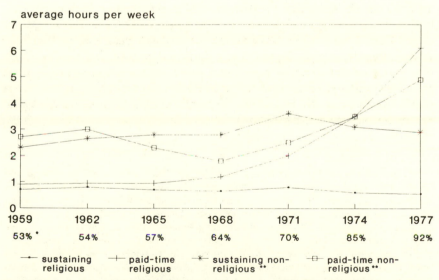

Figure 6.2.   Trends in Religious and Other Non-Entertainment Television Programming

Source: Federal Communications Commission, 1979, Figures I & II.
*this row shows the % of religious programming that was paid-time
**does not include entertainment, news, or sports programming

ligious programming, rather than a drop in sustaining-time programming, resulting in a net gain in religious broadcast time.[4]

The 1960 FCC decision effectively broke the broadcast oligopoly of mainline church organizations by opening religious broadcasting to all who could afford to pay. It encouraged the development of true "electric churches," congregations that exist only via broadcasting and are financially self-perpetuating. Radio had seen a few of these,[5] but television was to foster even more. Hadden and Shupe (1987) identify this phenomenon as the latest manifestation of the "parachurch," first seen in America in the 19th-century urban revivals.

Fund raising became a critical task for both affiliated and independent religious broadcasters. One source of funds has been the sale and rental of materials such as books, tapes, films, Bibles, and other religious artifacts; Robert Schuller, Jerry Falwell, and Billy Graham are prominent national religious broadcasters who have used this approach for years (Abelman & Neuendorf, 1985; *Christianity Today*, 1987). But the primary method of fund raising over the past 25 years of religious television has been direct solicitation of donations.

While in a few cases funds are raised irrespective of the broadcast process (e.g., *The World Tomorrow*'s self-proclaimed reliance on church members' tithing), most are clearly linked—a further development of electric churches. Abelman and Neuendorf (1985) found 42 percent of explicit money requests to be tied to some type of generalized ecumenical educational activity. Appeals aimed at the viewers' dependence on televangelism (e.g., "Don't forget, [your gift of twenty dollars] will mean that we'll be able to stay on your station. That gift is meaningful to both you and us"[6]) are less prevalent (Abelman & Neuendorf, 1985), but seem to have grown in frequency and explicitness. Other appeals include what Morris (1973) has called the "success and prosperity doctrine," promising material reward in return for monetary contribution.

---

[4] This figure is derived from data collected by the Communications Committee of the United States Catholic Conference, the Communications Commission of the National Council of Churches of Christ, the Office of Communication of the United Church of Christ, UNDA/USA and others (Federal Communications Commission, 1979). This coalition conducted a content analysis of the nonentertainment program offerings of local television stations in 36 U.S. markets from 1959 to 1978. The results were included in a petition to the FCC that argued against the 1960 interpretation, and claimed that the findings show increasing dominance by paid-time religious programming and a "sharp decline" in sustaining-time programming. It is unclear from the petitioners' presentation whether "average hours per week" is calculated by market or by television station.

[5] For example, the Omaha evangelist R.R. Brown invited listeners to join his World Radio Congregation, dispensing membership cards. The late Herbert W. Armstrong—later a prominent TV evangelist—launched his *Radio Church of God* in 1934 (Hadden & Swann, 1981).

[6] Jack Van Impe, broadcast of September 17, 1983.

A 1987 survey of the top televangelists by *Christianity Today* found most self-reporting that viewer donations are a prime source of funding. Robert Schuller, Jerry Falwell, Billy Graham, D. James Kennedy, Pat Robertson, George Vandeman, and James Robison all rely heavily on donor contributions and spend an average of 11.7 percent of their income on fund raising (*Christianity Today*, 1987).

In order to raise funds commensurate with the ever-rising costs of national broadcasting, religious broadcasters have had to aim at general rather than specialized, religiously devout audiences. And, they have needed to adapt to the growing secularism of American life during the past 25 years. Three general approaches have been taken to increase viewership (Neuendorf, Kalis, & Abelman, 1987):

1. An increase in *evangelistic presentations* has coincided with the latest religious revival—that period since 1945. Earlier revivalist periods had been characterized by entrepreneurial traveling preachers who achieved dramatic conversions, attaining high emotionalism in a camp meeting-style format. Seventy years ago, Billy Sunday, a former pro baseball player turned traveling evangelist, captured the imaginations and the purse strings of the crowds he drew with "ecclesiastical fireworks" that included jokes, flag waving, musical numbers, and occasional handsprings (McLoughlin, 1959). It is no wonder that this style, translated to the small but vibrant screen, is the most successful type of religious broadcasting to date—its visual activity and musical excitement are perfectly suited to television.

And the apparent commercialism of evangelism has been transplanted as well. Billy Sunday, drawing on the 1830's works of Charles Grandison Finney (father of American revivalism), explicitly and favorably compared his techniques to those of big business.[7] He went "so far as to calculate the cost of $2.00 a soul" (Frankl, 1987, p. 53). In 1983, the televangelists explicitly asked viewers for an average of $328 per hour (Abelman & Neuendorf, 1985).

2. A variety of religious *networks* have developed from the first syndicated programming (e.g., *The Lutheran Hour*) and isolated individual ownership of broadcast stations (Lacey, 1978; Religion in America, 1987). At first, these self-proclaimed "networks" were nothing more than well-publicized syndication agreements, resembling very little the massive, full-time operations of the "Big 3" television networks. But the seeds were planted with the careful building of per-program systems of syndicated coverage. For example, Rex Humbard began telecasting in Akron in 1953, and opened his specially-built Cathedral of Tomorrow in the 1960s. The introduction of videotape at about this time allowed him to send his mes-

---

[7] "'I am not only a preacher but [a] businessman. I endeavor [to] bring: 1. System [and] organization; 2. Business principles; 3. Common sense' into revival work" (McLoughlin, 1959, p. 420).

sage virtually anywhere, and by 1970 his program was carried by 115 stations (Fore, 1987; Hadden & Swann, 1981).

3. Many *secular television formats* have been adapted to religious goals. Early examples include the drama of the *Catholic Hour* and the Jewish *Eternal Light* on radio during the 1940s (Jennings, 1968), and the humor and warmth of the durable 1950s cartoon, *Davey and Goliath*. Later examples have included the sports show *Athletes in Action,* the children's game show *Junior Bible Bowl*, and the Roman Catholic news magazine *Real to Reel.*

Era 3, spanning the years from 1960 through the early 1980s, saw the systematic commercialization of religious broadcasting. The assumption during this time was that while broadcasting certainly has an obligation to provide fair coverage, it did not have to provide it free-of-charge (note how the Fairness Doctrine dictated that if one political candidate was sold commercial spot time, all other candidates for that race had to be free to *purchase* time as well).

Era 4: Religious Cablecasting—Paid-Time in a Free Marketplace

All 3 of these methods have found a strong foothold in the world of cable television. During the 1950s, CATV—community antenna television— developed as a means of getting television signals to remote communities. Cable was television's stepchild, and as such was largely ignored by business and government alike. But as its importance grew during the 1960s, and its purpose expanded to that of bringing greater *diversity* of programming to cities as well as rural areas, the FCC began regulating cable much as it had radio and television (Geller, 1985); in 1972, the FCC set up regulations that more closely resembled common carrier rules, however.[8] The FCC's ability to regulate cable was curtailed in a 1979 Supreme Court decision, but then some powers were reaffirmed in the 1984 Cable Act.

The Cable Act of 1984 specified a host of technical and bureaucratic procedures for local cable franchising and operation. The *content* of cable offerings, however, is not held up to FCC scrutiny. In fact, with the court-ordered elimination of the NAB Codes in 1983, such content-related criteria also have been largely eliminated from the broadcast license renewal process. With this trend of *deregulation,* the mass communication environment more and more resembles a free marketplace.

In 1978, Lacey identified religious broadcasting as the single case where (a) the specific type of content was encouraged (nay, mandated) by the FCC, but at the same time, (b) the programming was not evaluated or

---

[8] Requiring, for example, public access and educational/government access. For a full discussion, see Fogarty and Spielholz (1985).

scrutinized by the FCC for fairness (the FCC has assumed that religious matters are not controversial, and has not applied the Fairness Doctrine), educational value (the FCC has made no distinction between educational and evangelistic efforts), or appropriateness of fund-raising activities (the FCC has scrutinized other nonprofit organizations, but has shied away from passing judgment on religious bodies). Lacey concluded that since the FCC selectively failed to apply relevant rules and regulations to *religious* broadcasting, the FCC was in effect aiding in the establishment of religion, a violation of the First Amendment. However, many of these issues are quite irrelevant to the current religious *cable* environment—there is no concern with limited spectrum space, and therefore no mandate for the FCC to assure that facilities are operated in a generalized "public interest."

The religious cablecasting era dates from 1977, the year in which the Christian Broadcasting Network (CBN) became available for cable. Developed by the *700 Club's* Pat Robertson, CBN cablecasts to over 34 million viewers (Meyers, 1987), 24 hours a day. CBN has sold commercial time to advertisers such as Vicks, General Mills, and Kraft in order to fund programming that has included soap operas, early morning news, miniseries, and children's entertainment (Spring, 1982). In 1986, it was the fourth largest cable network in terms of viewership, with an average quarter-hour audience of 288,000 households (up 30.5% from the year before) (Meyers, 1987).[9]

CBN has estimated its 1987 advertising revenues at more than $3 million, with plans for co-op advertising with cable operators. Additionally, it has joined a consortium of 17 cable networks, CableOne, that will negotiate with clients for advertising across all networks. All of these revenue-producing plans are standard cable network operating procedure.

Other religious networks available on cable (e.g., the troubled PTL network, the Catholic Eternal Word Network, and Trinity Broadcast Network) generally seek substantial funding from the viewership and/or from commercial sponsors, but have not come close to matching CBN's dominance in viewership or business acumen. It should be noted that CBN's stated goals are a bit more generalized than those of most religious networks—to encourage "family" values and morality. CBN tends to define "Christian" in a sociological sense, not just a strictly religious sense.

While it was the foresight, persistence, and popularity of televangelists that launched religious cable, the use of secular formats has been integral to its long-range financial success. Another technique pioneered by CBN is the interspersing of religious and nonreligious "family" entertainment. The semireligious soap opera *Another Life* and the nonreligious *Dobie Gillis*

---

[9] It trailed WTBS Superstation (average quarter-hour audience of 620,000 households), Cable News Network (CNN; 326,000), and Nickelodeon (295,000).

have been popular parts of CBN's cablecast day, for example, used as lead-ins to programs with a more religious tone.

In Era 4, our society is an information-as-commodity environment. While the free marketplace of ideas is not always free of charge, the multiplicity of options for a religious communicator is growing. Cable television has no legal obligation to represent different points of view, the assumption being that there are enough channels available for all audience factions to achieve access.

FUTURE GLANCES

Recent scandals of televangelists have elevated public awareness of the structure of religious broadcasting and cablecasting in the 1980s. Although the current deregulatory climate would predict failure for such proposals, Congress has made moves toward instituting a mechanism by which financial accountability among televangelists may be assured (Frame, 1987a, 1987b; Spring, 1987; "TV preachers to testify," 1987).

At the same time, outrage in the religious community over televangelists' indiscretions may have resulted in the development of the cable era's FCCC—"Vision Interfaith Satellite Network" (VISN) "will shun soliciting money" (Cornell, 1988, p. 16A) and instead rely on commercial sponsorship. Approached by a major cable firm that had dropped the scandal-ridden PTL Network, VISN founder Rev. Daniel Paul Matthews enlisted the cooperation of 20 "faith groups," including Protestant, Eastern Orthodox, Jewish, evangelical, and Roman Catholic denominations. Objecting to the "personal pietism" model of the current top religious broadcasters, VISN created a standards and practices committee that has already set down content rules: "No material that denigrates or maligns any other faith or religion, no programs that proselytize to gain members at the expense of other churches and no use of time to solicit funds" (Cornell, 1988, p. 16A).

VISN began cablecasting in September 1988, and has affiliation agreements with MSOs (multisystem operators) that will make the network available on a full-time basis to 18.4 million homes by the end of 1989. VISN board of directors member, Nelson Price, notes that VISN is different from other religious networks in its pointed exploration of "faith and ethical issues," its appeal to "overlooked" audiences such as children and the aging, and its expressed goal of trying to "help support local congregations" (personal communication, October 3, 1988). The network's outlook on financial support resembles a cooperative. The network will be supported by a combination of producer-pay and advertising revenue, with about 40 percent of all programming provided by member faith groups and 60 percent acquired or produced by VISN.

While some have feared that the freedom of cable will lead to a host of Billy Sundays—showmen extraordinaire who are able to convince audiences to part with their money—it may also lead to the first real exercise of democracy in religious television, where the voting will be done in the ratings books. No longer a "public trust," religious telecommunication puts its trust in the public to determine which types of programming will survive and prevail.

REFERENCES

Abelman, R., & Neuendorf, K.A. (1983). Themes and topics in religious television programming. *Review of Religious Research, 29*(2), 152–174.

Abelman, R., & Neuendorf, K. (1985). The cost of membership in the electronic church. *Religious Communication Today, 8,* 63–67.

Christianity Today surveys the top TV preachers. (1987, October 16). *Christianity Today,* pp. 46, 48–49.

Cornell, G.W. (1988, March 12). Mainline faiths send signal, launch TV network. *The Plain Dealer,* p. 16A.

Curtis, A.K. (1978, September). A new apostasy? *Eternity,* p. 21.

Ellens, J.H. (1974). *Models of religious broadcasting.* New York: William Erdmans Publishing Co.

Federal Communications Commission Reports. (1960, July 29). *Report and statement of policy research: Commission en banc programming inquiry* (FCS 60-970 91874). Washington DC: Author.

Federal Communications Commission. (1979). *Submission by the Communications Committee of the U.S. Catholic Conference and others in the matter of amendment of the Commission's rules concerning program definitions for commercial broadcast stations by adding a new program type, "Community Service" and expanding the "Public Affairs" program category and other related matters* (BC Docket No. 78-335, RM-2709). Washington, DC: Author.

Flake, C. (1982, May 19). Sunday night live. The electronic kingdom. *The New Republic,* pp. 9–11.

Fogarty, J. R., & Spielholz, M. (1985). FCC cable jurisdiction: From zero to plenary in twenty-five years. *Federal Communications Law Journal, 37,* 113–129.

Fore, W.F. (1987). *Television and religion.* Minneapolis, MN: Augsburg Publishing House.

Frame, R. (1987a, March 20). The state of Christian broadcasting. *Christianity Today,* pp. 48–50.

Frame, R. (1987b, November 20). Trying tighten the belt of financial accountability. *Christianity Today,* pp. 50–51, 53.

Frankl, R. (1987). *Televangelism: The marketing of popular religion.* Carbondale, IL: Southern Illinois University Press.

Geller, H. (1985). Communications law—A half century later. *Federal Communication Law Journal, 37,* 73–83.

Gentry, R.H. (1984). Broadcast religion: When does it raise fairness doctrine issues? *Journal of Broadcasting, 28,* 259–270.

Hadden, J.K., & Frankl, R. (1987). Star Wars of a different kind: Reflections on the politics of the religion and television research project. *Review of Religious Research, 29*(2), 101–110.

Hadden, J.K., & Shupe, A. (1987). Televangelism in America. *Social Compass, 34,* 61–75.

Hadden, J.K., & Swann, C.E. (1981). *Prime time preachers: The rising power of televangelism.* Reading, MA: Addison-Wesley.

Head, S.W., with Sterling, C.H. (1982). *Broadcasting in America* (4th ed.). Boston, MA: Houghton Mifflin Company.

Jennings, R.M. (1968). *Policies and practices of selected national religious bodies as related to broadcasting in the public interest 1920–1950.* Doctoral dissertation, School of Education, New York University.

Lacey, L.J. (1978). The electric church: An FCC-"established" institution? *Federal Communications Law Journal, 31,* 235–275.

Loevinger, L. (1964–65). Broadcasting and religious liberty. *Journal of Broadcasting, 9,* 3–23.

McLoughlin, W.G., Jr. (1959). *Modern revivalism.* New York: The Ronald Press Company.

Morris, J. (1973). *The preachers.* New York: St. Martins Press.

Neuendorf, K.A., Kalis, P., & Abelman, R.I. (1987). *The history and social impact of religious broadcasting.* Paper presented to the Mass Communication and Society Division at the annual meeting of the Association for Education in Journalism and Mass Communication, San Antonio, TX.

Religion in America: Praise the Lord and pass the loot. (1987, May 16). *The Economist,* pp. 23–24, 27–28.

Spring. B. (1982, January 1). Pat Robertson's network breaks out of the Christian ghetto. *Christianity Today,* pp. 36–37.

Spring, B. (1987, November 6). TV ministries and taxation. *Christianity Today,* pp. 36, 38, 40, 42.

TV preachers to testify. (1987, August 31). *Newsweek,* p. 64.

III
The Viewers of Religious Programming

As with any form of broadcasting, the survival of religious television programming is dependent on the size and support of its viewership. Indeed, the very success of this fare is often reflected in terms of sheer quantity of audience. Spokespersons such as Ben Armstrong, the executive director of the religious broadcasters trade association, National Religious Broadcasters, have claimed the audience to be as large as 100 million during the recent growth stage of religious television (Armstrong, 1979). Televangelists themselves have laid claim to substantial audiences: Jim Bakker figured his PTL audience to be over 20 million; Jerry Falwell estimated his television audience at 15 million; James Robison boasted a viewership of 10 million strong (Hoover, 1988).

Similarly, the failure of religious television is measured by audience decline. A recent *Newsweek* article (Martz, 1988) reported the potential demise of religious broadcasters by noting that Pat Robertson lost 45 percent of his audience, that Swaggart—once the unchallenged leader in the field—"lost half his flock and dropped to third place" (p. 26), and that Robert Schuller—the new ratings leader—lost more than 500,000 as a result of the recent scandals.

What has received considerably less media attention, but is the basis for a true understanding of the success, failure, and impact of religious television, is *who is* the religious television audience? One needs to understand the motivations behind consumption, whether and in what ways viewership can be a means of religious expression, and what the audience takes away from the viewing experience. Only then, when the superficiality of head counting is replaced by a more robust understanding of audience, can the significance of this religious mass communication phenomenon be understood. Furthermore, to best understand the various controversies surrounding religious broadcasting, one needs to go beyond sheer quantity and examine the significance of audience size from the perspective of religious broadcasters, clergy, and media critics.

The purpose of this section is to provide information, insight, and perspective on the religious television audience. In order to do so, 3 essays report findings from 3 investigations conducted simultaneously, but without affiliation, at the height of religious broadcasting in the early 1980s. The first, by Robert Wuthnow, draws primarily on the results of a Gallup survey from the Annenberg/Gallup Study of Religious Broadcasting, on which he served as primary researcher. Wuthnow offers his views on whether or not religious television furthers the privatization—that is, the declining public, corporate, and communal quality—allegedly characteristic of American religion. He addresses the concern that religious broadcasting may be a cornerstone of a trend toward a highly subjective and idiosyncratic expression of faith by a good portion of the American population. His data suggests that religious television viewing falls along the lines of "broad cleavages in American religion" and reinforces the strength of these divisions in religious expression.

Based largely on research conducted for Unda-USA as part of the Religion in Broadcasting (RIB) project, principal investigator Robert Abelman examines the viewership of religious fare from the audience's perspective. Reporting on empirical examinations of viewer motivations and gratifications, he introduces the notion that religious television viewers are not homogeneous in terms of religious faith, church involvement, or involvement with the medium. Rather, religious television programming attracts a variety of viewers for a diversity of reasons consistent with existing uses and gratifications research on soap opera and news program viewship. While Wuthnow places the responsibility of the "privatization" of religion through television on television, Abelman gives the audience full credit.

Comparing data from the Annenberg/Gallup study (on which he served) and a proprietary study conducted for CBN by the A.C. Nielsen Company (Clark & Virts, 1985), Stewart Hoover explores the significance of audience size from the vantage point of religious broadcasting professionals and religion practitioners. He concludes that, in contradiction to reports of audience size and significance by religious broadcasters, religious television viewing continues today to be what it has always been—a relatively infrequent behavior which is seen to be socially desirable by most Americans, and a behavior largely engaged in insectors of society that have traditionally been the most "religious." Taken together, these chapters reveal the intimate, spiritual, and interactive relationship between the medium, its unique message, and people that comprise the mass audience.

REFERENCE

Armstrong, B. (1979). *The electric church.* Nashville, TN: Thomas Nelson.

Clark, D., & Virts, P. (1985). *Religious television audience: A new development in measuring audience size.* Paper presented at The Society for the Scientific Study of Religion Conference, Savannah, GA.

Hoover, S. (1988). Audience size: Some questions. *Critical Studies in Mass Communication, 5*(3), 265–271.

Martz, L. (1988, July 11). TV preachers on the rocks. *Newsweek,* pp. 26–28.

7

The Social Significance of Religious Television*

Robert Wuthnow

Other than the new religions and the political upsurge of the "religious right," few developments in American religion illustrate so effectively the full impact of the state, technology, and education on matters of faith as the rise of religious television. Bred of favorable changes in FCC regulations, succored by the latest advances in telecommunications technology, and deeply conditioned by the rising influence of higher education, religious television provides a vivid example of the social processes that have restructured American religion since World War II.

To many, the advent and rapid growth of religious television exemplifies the continuing vitality of evangelical religion in American society. To suggest that religious television may instead be linked to some of the most thoroughly secularized forces currently operating, therefore, is likely to seem either farfetched or hopelessly naive. Nevertheless, it is this relationship that deserves attention, not in order to cast any doubt on the sincerity of televangelists or their audiences, but as a means of illuminating the deep extent to which social conditions have influenced the character of American religion. Framed in perhaps a less provocative way, the question at issue is not one of scrutinizing the message of the television preachers for some hidden-agenda—as many in the theological establishment have been prone to do—but of utilizing the development of religious television as a case study for testing some popular conceptions concerning the processes of secularization.

THE PRIVATIZATION OF AMERICAN FAITH?

One of the most frequently advanced characterizations of American religion is that it is becoming increasingly "privatized" (e.g., Luckmann, 1967). That is, the public, corporate, communal quality of religion is said to

* This essay first appeared in *Review of Religious Research, 29*(2), December 1987. Reprinted here with permission.

be declining, leaving individuals with their own highly subjective and idiosyncratic expressions of faith. The terms "private" or "privatized" actually carry several connotations in this context. One suggests that the religion practiced by an increasing number of Americans may be entirely of their own manufacture—a kind of eclectic synthesis of Christianity, popular psychology, *Readers Digest* folklore, and personal superstitions, all wrapped up in the anecdotes of the individual's biography (Bellah, Madsen, Sullivan, Swidler, & Tipton, 1985). A different connotation suggests that religious practices remain subject to much more orthodox influences, namely the churches and synagogues; they merely have no influence on public affairs in the world of business and politics. According to this conception, religion has withdrawn into the "private sphere" to function much in the same manner as leisure activities, voluntary gatherings, and family relations (Habermas, 1975). Still a different connotation focuses on the possibility that even within the private sector religious expression may have become less public, less organized, less relational, leaving individuals radically alone in their experience of the divine. All 3 of these connotations bear some resemblance to popular images of American religion.

The idea that religious expression is becoming increasingly the product of individual biographies is supported by the very fact of America's pluralistic religious culture. With several hundred different denominations, sects, and cults to choose from, every individual can pretty much tailor his or her religious views to personal taste. As individuals are increasingly exposed to the teachings of different faiths through books, television, travel, and geographic mobility, eclecticism becomes the likely result. This tendency is also reinforced by the highly individualistic ethos in American culture which asserts the individual's freedom of conscience in matters of religion. We believe that individuals should make up their own minds about what they believe, drawing on whatever sources of inspiration they may find. Thus, it is not uncommon to find public expressions—President Eisenhower's famous remark uttered in the 1950s, for example—that faith is important, but we do not care what that faith is.

The second meaning of privatization—that religion has no influence in the public sphere—seems on the surface to be contradicted by the voracious appetite that American politics has shown for religious influences. From the civil rights movement to the antiabortion campaign, examples of religion playing a direct role in public affairs are scarcely difficult to identify. Yet these examples fail to contradict the deeper insights of this version of the privatization argument. The question is not so much whether clergy lead sit-ins or presidents draw support from religious groups, but whether any of these activities matter on as broad a scale as they once did. The argument of theorists who have advanced the idea of privatization is that a greater and greater share of the decisions affecting public life are made strictly on grounds of economic profitability, technical feasibility, and political control. Indeed, even this formulation may be an understatement since it suggests greater exercise of conscious decision-making capacities than may be the case, given the tremendous complexity of economic forces, bureaucracies, and vested interests that shape social life. For the individual the effect of these impersonal forces is seen increasingly in a withdrawal from active participation in political life, other than voting, in evidence of psychological alienation from government and business, and in actual retreat into the private pleasures of consumerism, personal hobbies, and the nuclear isolated family. Religion, it is claimed, has accommodated itself to this broader retreat from public life. Apart from obvious exceptions such as religious organizations against nuclear warfare or abortion, the evidence suggests that churches focus the bulk of their resources in areas dealing with personal spirituality, moral behavior, child-rearing, marital relations, and emotional care, rather than delving into the implications of religious values for issues of community planning, capital investment, business conduct, social justice, or public policy (e.g., Hunter, 1983). Many religious leaders will, of course, defend these preferences on grounds of scriptural or theological insight as well as pragmatic considerations of church unity and growth. Nevertheless, the removal of religious priorities from the public sphere merely supports the allegation that it is becoming more deeply privatized.

The third connotation of privatization—that even within the religious sphere communal ties are breaking down—draws support from arguments about the increasing anonymity and isolation of modern society in general. The terms in which this discussion has been cast are household phrases— "lonely crowd," "mass society," "secular city." As cities have grown, as geographic mobility has increased, as small neighborhoods and villages have been replaced with shopping malls and football stadiums, the argument goes, fewer and fewer people participate intimately in primary support groups. Instead, they exist as nameless faces in the crowd, associating mainly with strangers with whom they have only fleeting and highly instrumental relations. The religious realm may provide one of the few refuges from this anonymous existence, providing opportunities for fellowship, sharing of common interests, and first-hand relations free of instrumental calculations. Yet the question has been raised as to whether these activities may also be eroding in the face of broader societal tendencies. If, for example, the typical American moves at least once every 5 years, can religious groups provide the kind of intimate fellowship that may have once existed in rural or small town churches with more stable memberships? And if the typical church finds it necessary to hold worship services for 500 to 1,000 members in order to achieve competitive economies of scale, do religious communities eventually come to resemble audiences and spectator sports rather than supportive groups?

The widening appeal of religious television adds new considerations to the discussion of privatization in all 3 of its current usages. Does it lead to greater eclecticism in individual religious styles? Does it reinforce the tendency for religion to become a purely private leisure-time activity? And does it further weaken the relational bonds of religious communities?

The question of eclecticism is raised chiefly by the fact that switching television channels is a good bit easier than switching churches. In other words, one can "shop around" until one finds just the television preacher who suits one's own personal tastes without ever leaving the comforts of home. In addition, the opportunity to watch dozens of different programs enhances the likelihood of developing a purely idiosyncratic version of faith—a little self-help doctrine from Robert Schuller, some political views from Jerry Falwell, and a sense of liturgy from the local parish's broadcast. Furthermore, the lack of feedback and interaction that characterizes mass media communication may reinforce eclecticism: Lacking opportunities to ask questions, not having to confront others' views in open discussion, and not having to accept any doctrines or creeds for "membership," the religious television viewer is essentially free to derive his or her own interpretations.

Over the long run, any of these possibilities seem likely, especially if cable television programming were to enhance the menu of religious broadcasts to the point of having, say, Mormon preaching, yoga exercises, and home meditation all available in addition to more standard offerings. At present, however, the prospects of increasing eclecticism are severely limited by the fact that little diversity exists in the bulk of religious programming. Of the top 10 programs (based on total viewership as reported in Gallup surveys), only one—Baptist programs—is associated with a mainline denomination (Gallup Organization, 1984). All of the others are sponsored by personalities who tend to take an evangelical or conservative approach to religion; for example, Billy Graham, Jimmy Swaggart, Oral Roberts, Pat Robertson, and Jim Bakker. The message of these programs largely reflects the theological orientation of traditional Protestant fundamentalism. Thus, it seems unlikely that viewers of these programs will be led toward greater eclecticism in expressing their faith; if anything they will become more uniform in their views, as is suggested in Annenberg's "religious mainstreaming" interpretation of the effect of heavy religious television viewing (Gerbner et al., 1984).

The question of religious television reinforcing withdrawal of religion into the private sector also seems to have a mixed answer. On the one hand, religious television viewing, like regular television viewing, is a private leisure activity. And studies demonstrate that heavy viewers of religious programming tend to be heavy viewers of television in general. Evidence also suggests that the gratification viewers receive from watching religious programs mainly concern their private lives rather than their knowledge or awareness of broader social issues. For example, the Religious Television

Survey (the national survey conducted by the Gallup Organization as part of the Religion and Television project) found that the reasons given most often for watching religious programs focused on entertainment, inspiration, music, worship, and spiritual growth. On the other hand, religious television has scarcely been limited to the private sphere, as is most amply attested to by the involvement of televangelists such as Jerry Falwell, Jimmy Swaggart, and James Robison in "new right" politics. Religious television has been used to raise funds and to develop mailing lists for political campaigns; it has also played a major role in aggregating the resources needed to build alternative educational institutions, such as Liberty Baptist College, CBN University, and Oral Roberts University. At the grass-roots level, viewers are also aware of the more public uses of religious television; for example, about one quarter of the viewers in the Religious Television Survey said they liked to watch in order to "know more about what's happening in the world" and an equal number said they appreciated getting "information about important moral or social issues."

More than either of these 2 kinds of privatization, however, the idea of declining relational bonds has been raised by the growth of religious television. If an increasing number of people fulfill their religious needs by watching religious programs on television, is it not likely that they will cease participating actively in local churches and fellowship groups? And if these viewers direct an increasing share of their charitable giving toward religious television, will the churches be able to maintain their clergy and local programs at accustomed levels? These were, in fact, among the more pressing questions addressed in the Religious Television Survey.

The results of the study provide little support for the idea that religious television viewing is associated with declining participation in organized religious activities. Viewers were in fact more likely—by a margin of 48 percent to 33 percent—to attend church at least once a week than were nonviewers. Partly, of course, this difference reflects merely a greater interest in religion in general among viewers than among nonviewers. A more accurate estimate of the relation between viewing and church attendance requires taking into account differences in the general importance people attach to religion. Nevertheless, when this was done, the results still failed to provide any evidence that viewing is negatively associated with church attendance. A multiple regression analysis which controlled for differences in self-perceived religiosity, age, and education, for example, showed a slight positive relation still existing between religious television viewing and church attendance. A discriminant factor analysis which controlled for evangelical beliefs, age, race, region, education, religiosity, and several other factors also showed a weak positive relationship between church attendance and religious viewing (Gallup Organization, 1984).

As with any statistical analysis, these results are not absolute. There were a few people for whom religious television provided a substitute for personal religious participation. Indeed, one religious viewer in 7 said they watched religious programs instead of attending services regularly. And about one viewer in 5 watched programs between 10 a.m. and noon on Sundays, suggesting a possible tradeoff between viewing and attending church. But a more detailed analysis of the data revealed that negative relations between viewing and church attendance were limited to small segments of the public with highly special characteristics: Persons requiring assistance in going places, the elderly, and those with the lowest education levels. None of these groups was sufficiently large to affect the overall results.

Other types of religious involvement also appeared to have held up well against the intrusions of religious television. Again taking into account differences between persons who said religion was very important to them, fairly important, or not very important, viewers at each of these levels tended to be just as likely as nonviewers—if not more so—to have done volunteer work at their churches. They were also as likely as nonviewers to have donated time to help others, to have done volunteer work in other community agencies, and to be members of voluntary organizations in their community.

As for financial contributions, the study also documented no clear evidence for the fear that religious television might be undermining the financial base of local churches. Clearly, churches might be stronger if the millions of dollars sent to televangelists were instead put in local offering plates. But the study cast doubt on the realism of this hypothetical assumption. The money given to religious television programs appears to result from extra donations that would not likely be given at all were it not for these programs. Thus, with levels of religiosity taken into account, viewers gave just as much to their churches as did nonviewers. This conclusion was also confirmed by multiple regression results which controlled for religiosity, age, education, and dollar amounts given to religious television programs.

Another set of results from the Religious Television Survey that, with one exception, challenged the idea that religious television is associated with an erosion of organized religion focused on the role of dissatisfaction and other barriers to local religious involvement. Part of the idea of privatization is that people turn inward because they become disenchanted with public institutions. They may continue to participate in these institutions, but psychologically they withdraw. In the case of religion, they may continue to attend church, perhaps to keep up social appearances, but fewer of their religious needs are gratified in church; hence, they turn to more private pursuits such as watching religious programs on television. This notion has much to recommend it: The numerous religious movements, cults, the rapid growth of religious publishing, quasireligious and occult teachings all suggest a degree of restlessness with the churches.

But the empirical evidence reveals that this restlessness should not be exaggerated, nor does it seem to be much of a factor in the growth of religious television. Of those polled in the Religious Television Survey only 15 percent of the viewers and 14 percent of the nonviewers said they were dissatisfied with "the way things have been going lately in your local church or synagogue." On more specific issues, the only complaint that was voiced by more than a small minority had to do with "too much emphasis on money at my local church or synagogue"—about 1 in 5 (viewers and nonviewers alike) said this applied to them.

Or the whole, viewers were no more likely to express dissatisfaction with their churches than were nonviewers. For example, 12 percent of the viewers said they objected to some of the things their church was teaching, but the comparable number among nonviewers was 18 percent. Only 9 percent and 8 percent respectively said their local church failed to meet their spiritual needs; the same proportions admitted feeling uncomfortable with the people at their church; and even fewer—5 percent and 6 percent, respectively—were dissatisfied with their pastor.

The study also found that, despite whatever reservations people may have about their churches, they still overwhelmingly look to the churches instead of religious television for spiritual guidance. This was true even among relatively serious viewers of religious television, that is, those who said they had watched an hour or more during the previous week. Among this group church still outranked religious television by a 2 : 1 margin on a question that asked respondents to say whether they felt the church or religious television was contributing more to their spiritual life.

The one exception to this general pattern of findings was that the small subgroup in the study who were both extremely dissatisfied with their local church and also watched religious television did show a tendency to withdraw from participation in their local church. More precisely, church attendance was lower among viewers than among nonviewers within this dissatisfied segment of the public. Again, however, this segment was sufficiently small that it did not affect the overall results.

Thus, little evidence seems to exist on balance from which to argue that religious television is producing a more privatized substitute for involvement in organized religion. The vast majority of those who watch religious television simply do so in addition to taking part in religious services personally. The reason why this is so seems to reflect chiefly the fact that the 2 modes of religious expression produce different kinds of gratifications. According to the respondents in the study, religious television provided them with inspiration, information, and music, in addition to preaching at times when it was not available at church. Church, on the other hand, even for viewers, continued to be liked for preaching and inspiration, but it was liked considerably more than religious television for such experiences as worship, feeling close to God, and companionship or fellowship. In other words, the communal and ritual aspect of religion continued to be highly valued and it was fulfilled, as should be expected, mainly by the churches rather than television.

One final bit of evidence which warrants consideration in assessing religious television in relation to the idea of privatization is that even religious television viewing is not as private an activity as might be thought. To be sure, watching Rex Humbard in the privacy of one's living room can scarcely be a social activity in the same sense as going to church or participating in a discussion group. But there are social dimensions of religious television viewing that should not be overlooked. Religious television viewing takes place not so much in the strict isolation of individuals' relations to their television sets, but as part of a rich network of social interaction. In the Religion Television Survey, more than half of all viewers (52%) said they usually watched with someone else rather than watching alone. In addition, 5 out of 6 said they discussed these programs with other people. Not surprisingly, these discussions were most often with family members. But about 4 viewers in 10 said they sometimes had discussions with friends, 1 in 4 sometimes discussed programs with other people from their church, and 1 in 5 indicated they sometimes discussed them with their pastor.

For the most part, then, the privatization thesis turns up empty-handed in attempting to grasp the broader significance of religious television. This is not to suggest the absence of privatization as a force in American religion. Many indications point clearly to the pressures leading toward more private, subjectivistic, isolated expressions of faith. But religious television seems to be neither a response to privatization in any specific or direct sense for the majority of its viewers nor a phenomenon that is significantly contributing to this process. In some global sense the advent of religious television, even apart from its dependence on modern technology, is probably more compatible with the privatized lifestyles and religious leanings of contemporary Americans than it might have been in most historical periods, of course. But the fit between this phenomenon and contemporary culture is scarcely a hand-in-glove relation. The content of religious television tends to be more uniformly orthodox than diverse or idiosyncratic; it provides information about public issues of political and social interest as well as private inspiration; its viewers continue to be actively involved in local churches and other community organizations; they maintain their financial commitment to the churches; they show little evidence of shifting loyalties to the televangelists because of disenchantment with their own churches; and even viewing takes place in the context of families and discussion networks instead of happening in lonely isolation. In short, the privatization thesis, while compelling on the surface, fails to be of much assistance in trying to understand the social characteristics of religious television and its audience.

THE EFFECTS OF SOCIAL RESTRUCTURING

As an alternative framework, what of the effects on religious television of social restructuring? How have the broader changes which have taken place in American society since World War II—the growth of the state, educational expansion, and the culture of technology—shaped the character of religious television? Can the social aspects of religious television be understood within the same matrix of developments that have restructured American religion more generally?

The direct effect of the state on religious television can be seen in the FCC and IRS regulations to which television programming is subject. Because television is subject to federal regulations and because religious programs raise millions of dollars from nationwide audiences, the televangelists stand in a much more vulnerable position relative to the state than most clergy ever have. Local churches may feel the effects of zoning laws and local clergy may be active in community politics, but seldom are they as likely as the televangelists to run up against direct federal restrictions.

The direct effects of technology on religious television can also be seen not only in its usage of satellite hook-ups, cable channels. WATS lines, and computerized direct-mailing services, but also in the content of its message. As Marshal McLuhan taught us to recognize, television is a "cool medium" in which intimate conversation, relaxed discussion, and humor play a more effective role than fiery rhetoric and a loud voice. Fulton Sheen became the master of this new style in the 1950s. One would wonder how much the televangelists have learned about this style when considering the traditional tent-meeting approach of a Jimmy Swaggart or Rex Humbard. Nevertheless, it is evident from even a casual viewing of religious television that a number of the leading televangelists—Pat Robertson and Jim Bakker, for example, have succeeded by abandoning the hot rhetoric of a Billy Sunday for the cool demeanor of a Johnny Carson. Even Jerry Falwell, still the angry preacher arousing the masses from damnation, has learned the value of an intimate heart-to-heart chat taped in his private office.

It is, however, not so much the effect of such social factors on the religious broadcasters as the effect of these factors on the religious television audience that seems most worthy of attention. Viewers of religious television are not located simply at random with respect to the broader society. They exhibit distinctive social attributes which are revealing of the changes that have been taking place in American religion.

It is well to recognize in the first instance that religious television viewers are extremely diverse both socially and religiously. For example, despite the fact that many of the leading broadcasts come from southern states, almost 2 out of every 3 viewers—as found in the Religious Television Survey—live in other parts of the country. Many viewers are white Protestants, but about 1 in 5 is black and an equal number are Roman Catholics.

Many are evangelicals, according to the way Gallup surveys operationalize this concept (Gallup, 1978), but by the same standards 63 percent do not qualify as evangelicals and as many as a third are associated with mainline Protestant denominations, such as Methodists, Lutherans, Presbyterians, or Episcopalians. Nevertheless, in comparison with the social characteristics of nonviewers there are some distinct differences.

As might be expected, viewers are much more likely than nonviewers to share evangelical or conservative religious convictions. In the Religious Television Survey the belief that "the Bible is the actual word of God and is to be taken literally, word for word," for example, was held by 58 percent of the viewers, compared with only 28 percent of the nonviewers. Similarly, more than half of the viewers (55%) compared with only a quarter (24%) of the nonviewers described themselves as having been "born again." Since the largest religious broadcasting organizations emphasize evangelical themes, this characteristic of the religious television audience should come as no surprise.

Predictably, religious television viewers were also distinguished from nonviewers by virtue of being heavy viewers of conventional television. Within each level of religiosity, respondents who watched 4 or more hours of conventional television a day were at least 5 percentage points more likely to have watched a religious program in the past 30 days than were persons who watched conventional television less than 2 hours a day. The former were also more likely to have watched religious programs at least 2 hours during the past week than were the latter.

These characteristics are interesting less in themselves than for what they suggest about the social strata from which religious viewers are likely to be recruited. Persons who watch conventional television in high amounts, most studies find, tend to be older than average and less well educated. Persons who hold evangelical beliefs tend to be drawn from the same social strata. The religious television audience thus reflects the combination of both these effects.

In the Religious Television Survey, 48 percent of the viewers were age 50 or older, compared with only 31 percent of the nonviewers. And only 23 percent of the viewers had even been to college, compared with 34 percent of the nonviewers. Despite the fact that age is associated with lower probabilities of having been to college, both factors were significantly related to religious viewing. For example, 52 percent of the persons in the study who were age 50 or over and who had no more than a grade school education had watched religious television in the past month, compared with only a quarter of those in the same age group with college degrees. In the age bracket comprised of 30- to 49-year-olds, half of the grade school educated had watched, compared with 22 percent of the college graduates. And in the 18- to 30-year-old category, where too few had only grade school educations to make valid comparisons possible, 21 percent of the high school graduates had watched compared with only 13 percent of the college graduates.

In terms of broader social restructuring, then, in which education becomes an increasingly important measure of standing and social resources, religious television viewers tend relatively to be recruited from among the dispossessed. Very few are young people with college educations; most are older people with lower levels of education.

The study also demonstrated an important connection between religious viewing and being dissatisfied with the moral climate of the nation. Among nonviewers, for example, only 31 percent said they were very dissatisfied with "the way moral standards have been changing in America," but among viewers this proportion rose to 50 percent—and most of the remainder said they were somewhat dissatisfied.

Piecing the various findings together, it seems clear that religious television has come to occupy a distinct niche in American society that in turn reflects some of the broader changes that have been shaping social relations over the past several decades. Its audience is located among relatively less advantaged segments of the population who also identify with conservative religious ideas and who feel unhappy with the moral direction in which they believe the culture to be heading. All of these characteristics, it might be noted, reinforce one another, but each contributes somewhat independently to the likelihood of being a religious viewer as well. The same characteristics, it should also be noted, distinguish those who watch religious programs frequently from those who watch less frequently, and those who donate money to these programs from those who do not.

THE REINFORCEMENT OF RELIGIOUS CLEAVAGE

The growth of religious television has led critics to worry vocally about its potentially negative effects on the local church. Those fears for the most part have proved to be unwarranted. But the critics have failed to foresee a deeper ramification of televangelism. It was, perhaps inevitably, destined to attract the widest audiences among those who already spent unusual amounts of time watching television and whose devout commitment to traditional religion was sufficient to motivate their time, energy, and financial contributions toward the televangelists. This was the natural audience—the niche of convenience—to which religious television became tailored. And there were plenty of funds, plenty of preachers, and plenty of viewers to make it work.

But the natural audience for religious television was also a socially dispossessed segment of the society. Despite its more visible aspirants among the national elite, it was relatively concentrated among the elderly and the less educated. If for no other reason than the fact that television and evangelical religion intersected to form this audience, it was largely devoid of representation among the better educated sector of the secular elite. Thus, an additional element found its way increasingly into the message of the televangelists.

That was the message of moral reconstruction. The dispossessed provided a sufficiently large pool of religious viewers that their sense of moral erosion came to be expressed in the appeals of religious programming. Not surprisingly, the programs appealed to those who felt the moral order was on the skids.

At the same time, this selective process drove an ever larger wedge between religious television and those with other religious convictions, and between the morally concerned "religious right" and those among the secular elite.

Religious television was clearly an important resource for the disadvantaged evangelical. It not only provided personal religious gratifications in a world that seemed otherwise awry, but it also created a sense that one was participating in something broader—that perhaps the moral order could be saved. Religious television did not replace the local church. It merely created an umbrella under which the remnant of God's people could come together, if only symbolically, for renewal and strength.

The shelter provided by that umbrella was no less genuine to those who experienced it because it was transmitted via communication satellite than if it had been created in a local revival meeting. It was, however, a shelter that failed to convey meaning for most who looked across the cultural chasm from their position in the liberal churches, the universities, and high-tech institutions of the secular society. For them, religious television was not so much a shelter but a stumbling block. It was simply yet another cultural barrier which divided American religion.

REFERENCES

Bellah, R., Madsen, R., Sullivan, W., Swidler, A., & Tipton, S. (1985). *Habits of the heart*. Berkeley, CA: University of California Press.

Gallup, G. (1978). *Religion in America, 1977–78*. Princeton, NJ: Princeton Religion Research Center.

Gallup Organization. (1984). *Religious television survey*. Princeton, NJ: The Gallup Organization.

Gerbner, G., Gross, L., Hoover, S., Morgan, M., Signorielli, N., Cotugno, H., & Wuthnow, R. (1984). *Religion and television*. New York: Committee on Electronic Church Research.

Habermas, J. (1975). *Legitimation crisis*. Boston, MA: Beacon Press.

Hunter, J. (1983). *American evangelicalism*. New Brunswick, NJ: Rutgers University Press.

Luckman, T. (1967). *The invisible religion*. New York: Macmillan.

8

Who's Watching, For What Reasons?

Robert Abelman

For years, Jim and Tammy Faye Bakker rode out crisis after crisis from their set at the Praise the Lord (PTL) Network television studio. The Bakkers asked for viewers' sympathy during federal government investigations of misappropriated funds in 1979 and revelations of their luxury homes and exuberant salaries in 1984 (Gordon, 1986; Schulz, 1986). They asked for viewers' financial support when the PTL Network claimed bankruptcy in 1986 (Simpson, 1987a). In early March 1987, they asked viewers for prayers when it was revealed that Tammy Bakker was being treated for drug addiction (Ostling, 1987a; Simpson, 1987b). And in late March 1987, they asked for viewer forgiveness as allegations of a sexual encounter between Jim Bakker and a PTL secretary became public and the stuff national headlines are made of (Associated Press, 1987a, 1987b; Public Broadcasting Service, 1988; United Press International, 1987a, 1987b).

Clearly, scandal is nothing new for the PTL network. Similarly, controversy has been a way of life for religious broadcasters in general. Much discussion and debate over the apparent lack of division between electronic church and state (e.g., Barrett, 1986; Johnson & Tamney, 1985; Mann & Petersen, 1980; Mashek, 1986; Mayer, 1980; Pierand, 1985), the exercise of social power by the preachers with a nationally televised pulpit (Gaddy, 1984; Horsfield, 1984; Tarr, 1983), and the misappropriation of funds from on-air solicitations (e.g., Public Broadcasting Service, 1984; Simpson, 1987a; Traub, 1985) has been raised, time and time again, by media critics.

Throughout these controversies and ordeals which, according to the evangelical community, tarnish the image of the nation's most high-profile televangelists and their ministries (see American Broadcasting Company, 1987a, 1987b, 1987c), the viewers have remained faithful. Indeed, research suggests that the viewership of and donations to religious programming have increased rather than decreased during the most recent crises (Abelman, 1988a, 1988b; Hadden, 1986a, 1986b). Even secular news and informational programs focusing on the PTL scandal have generated great interest and boosted viewership (Stilson, 1987).

While the various controversies and scandals surrounding religious television raise clerical concern about the propriety and potentially negative impact of on-the-air worship (see Fore, 1979; Marty, 1967), consistently high ratings and the national media attention religious television has recently received serve to focus our attention on more basic issues. In particular, just who is watching religious television? In light of the nearly perpetual state of controversy, what are identified by viewers as their paramount reasons for consuming televised religion? Regarding the recent PTL scandal, has it had any significant impact on viewers' perceptions of religious programming and its leadership?

Of the limited amount of research that has been conducted on the religious television audience, the general consensus is that it can be characterized succinctly as demographically downscale and religious (Buddenbaum, 1981; Gaddy, 1984; Gaddy & Pritchard, 1985); that is, typically older, poorer, less educated, and more likely to be blue-collar workers or unemployed than the average American television viewer. Other reports suggest that key variables likely to identify a viewer over a nonviewer include being female and urban (Fore, 1987; Horsfield, 1984).

However, the most precursury examination of the breadth and scope of nationally distributed religious programming suggests a much broader appeal. Nearly half of the programming carried by religious broadcasting and narrowcasting networks and independent stations is comprised of fire-and-brimstone sermons and religious services conducted by a host of fundamentalist and charismatic televangelists. However, in order to best compete with secular programming, religious fare also consists of just about every popular secular programming genre, including talk shows (*700 Club*), game shows (*Bible Bowl*), children's shows (*Davy and Goliath*), soap operas (*Another Life*), news/magazine shows (*Reel to Real*), sports programming (*Athletes in Action*), and music/variety shows (*The Jim and Tammy Bakker Show*).

It becomes evident, then, that today's religious programming has the capacity of being many things to many people. According to Horsfield (1984, p. 120), this is actually the intention of religious broadcasters, for they "choose their audience by the content, format, and marketing of their programs . . . (and) maintain the specific structure of their audience because it is the most financially supportive." Recent research suggests that this strategy is quite effective, for there are actually 3 distinctive types of religious television viewers who are attracted to this highly diversified programming for highly divergent reasons.

RELIGIOUS TELEVISION VIEWERS

Over the years, uses and gratifications researchers have identified different types of television-viewing behavior among viewers of secular programming. Rubin (1983, 1984) and Windahl (1981) interrelated viewing motives of the commercial television viewing audience and found 2 primary types of television viewing—ritualized and instrumental. According to Rubin (1984, p. 69), ritualized viewing consists of more habitual use of television for diversionary reasons (e.g., time consumption, companionship, relaxation), and a greater affinity with the medium itself. Instrumental viewing reflects a more goal-oriented use of television content to gratify informational needs or motives. These 2 patterns of television use have been found among audiences for secular crime/adventure programs and cartoons (Hawkins & Pingree, 1981), news programming (Kippax & Murray, 1977, 1980; Rubin, 1981) and soap operas (Carveth & Alexander, 1985; Compesi, 1980; Rubin, 1985).

Recent research (Abelman, 1987, 1988c, 1989) has provided evidence that these distinctive types of viewers can also be found in the religious television audience. However, there are important differences in religious and secular programming that challenge existing uses and gratifications research. Although much of religious fare appears to be quite similar in format to its secular counterpart, the majority of religious programs explicitly call for viewer action on and response to various political and ideological issues (Abelman & Pettey, 1988; Ostling, 1986), offer spiritual guidance (Horsfield, 1984; O'Brien-Steinfels & Steinfels, 1983), and seek viewer involvement in the form of financial support for humanitarian causes, international ministries, and to help pay the cost of program production and distribution (see Chapters 15 and 16, respectively). Consequently, unique dimensions of ritualized and instrumental viewing have surfaced, as has a third distinctive type of viewer unique to religious television—the curiosity seeker.

Ritualized Viewers [faith reinforced, not "born again"]

The largest contingency of audience members for religious television, comprising approximately 65 percent of the religious televiewing audience, is the ritualized viewer. These consumers best fit the demographically downscale profile described above. They are also more likely to be religious and church members, to participate in other religious activities, to be Protestant and evangelical, and to be more conservative in a wide range of religious beliefs, values, and attitudes. Ritualized use of religious television encompasses the habitual nature of using the medium itself, a preference for televised church services and evangelical programming, and a high level of television consumption. These viewers are not "born again" via this programming but, rather, have their faith reinforced and strengthened through viewership.

This reinforces Fore's (1987, pp. 104–106) suggestion that religious programming is "not necessarily effective evangelism. It rarely speaks to people outside their natural constituency . . . (and) serves primarily to express and cultivate, rather than extend or broaden, existing religious beliefs." Along the same lines, it is the ritualized viewer that provides approximately 95 percent of all financial contributions to evangelical programming (Abelman, 1988b). In other words, while the rationale behind these broadcasts is to increase the flock by bringing the Gospel to the "unchurched," it is the already "born again" viewer that is its primary audience and the one paying the bill for program production and distribution.

According to Hadden and Swann (1981, p. 19), the main impetus for making donations and the primary allure of these programs to this audience is the televangelists themselves and the fact that they offer a whole new way of experiencing religion:

> The logic of television is simply that if you want people to watch a program, you must entertain them—visually, aurally, totally. Today the [television] evangelists realize full well that they are in hot competition, not only with a lot of secular and a few mainstream religious programs, but with each other as well. And they realize that the sophistication and slickness of their productions—in effect, their Hollywood quotient—can determine their success or failure.

Neuendorf and Abelman (1987, p. 53) confirm this observation in their analysis of communicator style of televangelists, suggesting that each televangelist, in his own unique way, has merged religiosity with entertainment to attract and maintain viewers:

> It appears that the evangelists found in the traditional preaching/revival programs are highly divergent; employing a wide range of communication types and television techniques to relay their messages. Some are creatures of the medium in which they appear, complete with dynamic personality, telegenic good looks, and an educated eye for the TV camera. Others are as they were when their programs originally aired on radio, full of poignant verbal content and void of visual display. Still others lack presence in front of the camera but have the presence of mind to manipulate the camera to amplify the visual effect.

Perhaps the strongest allure of this form of programming for ritualized viewers, particularly in the face of recent adversity, can be found in the foundation of Christian charity. According to a viewer survey implemented immediately before and after the PTL scandal, ritualized viewers readily forgave the sins of Jim Bakker and became stronger supporters of his ministry. Abelman (1988a) found that ritualized viewers maintained their faith in the perceived personal and social importance of religious television, and in their perceptions of the credibility of televangelists in general. Their viewership has not faultered.

Apparently some religious broadcasters and narrowcasters do not believe that the allure of religious programming for these viewers—whether it be the nature of presentation or blind faith—is strong enough to maintain viewership. Tele-Communications, Inc., the nation's largest cable television company, was the first to abandon the Bakker's PTL ministry. This amounted to 500,000 PTL network subscribers; nearly 4 percent of PTL's total viewing households (Goeken, 1987). Although no conclusions can be drawn about the true impact of the scandal on viewership until the recent controversy has subsided, the abandonment of the PTL network appears to be premature at this time, particularly when considering ritualized viewers of this fare.

 ## Instrumental Viewers

While most of the audience for religious fare is highly religious, over one-third are "unchurched" or express little interest in religion in general. Over half of these viewers, comprising 20 percent of the total religious televiewing audience, are best classified as instrumental viewers. Instrumental use of religious television reflects the viewing of informational programming, which includes religious programming that has adopted commercial television formats (e.g., news, talk shows) and informational programming indigenous to religious broadcasting (e.g., Bible studies, sermons). These viewers are significantly less religious and more educated than ritualized viewers, and watch religious programming for its unique presentation of and perspective on world news and events and information regarding moral and philosophical issues.

Recent reports suggest that there is sufficient nonreligious informational content in religious programming to attract and satisfy this type of viewer, above and beyond that of other alternative forms of programming. For instance, the close association between televangelist Jerry Falwell and President Ronald Reagan has been the most often cited example of the growth of political content in religious fare (see Mann & Petersen, 1980; Mayer, 1980). According to several learned observers, this relationship was the result of "concerted efforts by Republican conservatives to enlist the aid of fundamentalist ministers and televangelists" (Pierand, 1985, p. 100) in order to "energize the Christian right and siphon votes from other candidates" for major elections (Ostling, 1986, p. 62).

Others believe that it is the televangelists who are initiating entrance into the political arena, as exemplified by Pat Robertson's candidacy for the 1988 presidential election. Ostling (1986, p. 62) suggested that the fact that Robertson was even a potential candidate reinforces "the extraordinary power and influence amassed in the past decade by the shrewd, colorful headliners of Gospel TV." According to Horsfield (1984, p. xiii), some journalists have observed that the television preachers, by unifying and motivating these information seekers, could hold the key to elections:

Table 8.1.   Program Themes by Televangelist.

	Social		Religious		Political	
	1983	1986	1983	1986	1983	1986
Swaggart	4%	13%	96%	70%	—%	17%
Bakker	14	26	86	69	—	5
Robertson	35	37	46	34	19	29
Falwell	11	21	89	67	—	12
Schuller	6	12	94	88	—	—
Roberts	6	5	94	95	—	—
Copeland	—	2	100	98	—	—
Angley	—	5	100	93	—	2
Kennedy	6	6	94	94	—	—
Robison	—	—	100	100	—	—

From Abelman and Pettey, 1988, p. 319.

For some fearful observers, the growth of evangelical broadcasting represented a massive takeover by the political and moral right and a plot to establish a religious republic with the evangelical and fundamental broadcasters as major spokespersons.

A recent outburst by Jimmy Swaggart, who declared that the Supreme Court was "an institution damned by God Almighty" for allowing abortions (Ostling, 1986, p. 69), adds fuel to these accusations and provides no shortage of fodder for the instrumental viewer. In addition, there is further evidence (see Abelman & Pettey, 1988) that instrumental viewers need not limit their viewing to Falwell, Robertson, and Swaggart. A well-balanced combination of political, social, and religious information has been found within the most widely available and highly rated religious programs. As can be seen in Table 8.1, the quantity of nonreligious fare has also increased and become more wide-spread across the televangelical community in recent years.

Nonetheless, there is every indication that religious broadcasting has lost its allure for instrumental viewers, the result of the most recent controversies. According to Abelman (1988a, p. 50), "the PTL scandal has apparently quenched the primary motivation for watching religious fare for the instrumental viewer—the search for accurate information presented by a reliable source." The article reports that the scandal, which involved the withholding, distortion, and manufacturing of information by the Bakkers, the PTL organization, and other televangelists diminished viewers' belief that these people were viable sources of information. Similarly, revelations regarding Swaggart's elicit sexual encounters while chastising the Bakker's for immoral conduct further reduces the credibility of televangelicals. Popular reports that the viewership of religious programming has diminished over the past year may have tapped into this segment of the televiewing audience.

Reactionary Viewers

The possibility of a third type of religious broadcasting consumer was intimated by Parker, Barry, and Smythe (1955, p. 408) when they suggested that:

> There are logical reasons for listening or nonlistening that go deep into the personal and personal-social situation of audience members, far deeper than their simple identification with Catholics or Presbyterians, or nonparticipants in any church.

Similarly, Dennis (1962) found that people viewed particular religious programs for other than religious reasons. He identified moral, informational, and entertainment concerns as motives for viewing, but also found that people viewed religious fare as a substitution for church and commercial, secular programming.

Indeed, departing from existing uses and gratifications literature, a third type of religious television usage can be found. Seeking neither religion nor information from religious programming, this type of viewer is primarily a manifestation of the national media attention religious television has received in recent years. Best classified as a "curiosity seeker," these viewers apparently consume religious programming for 1 of 2 related reasons. The first is in reaction to a general dissatisfaction with secular television programming. These viewers do not watch large quantities of religious television, nor do they necessarily perceive the medium as being overly important in their lives. They have chosen, however, to seek an alternative to the plethora of available commercial programming as a response to their general dissatisfaction.

The second reason is in reaction to the well publicized controversies that have surrounded religious broadcasting since its resurrection in the 1970s. In light of the recent scandal facing the PTL network, Falwell admitted that PTL and religious television in general are fighting for their lives: "I would be lying to you if I said that members of this board are not concerned about the future of this ministry." He declared that "arrogance and lack of accountability among TV ministries had damaged the Christian cause" (Ostling, 1987b, p. 60). To the contrary, it appears as if a segment of the viewership of religious programming, albeit comparatively smaller (15%) than ritualized and instrumental viewers, are attracted to the same phenomenon that Falwell fears will diminish the viewing audience (Abelman, 1988c).

Although religious television is currently in a state of flux, due to recent controversies involving Bakker, Swaggart, and others, it is clear that it has attracted such a diversified viewership that its future remains quite solid. While the names of the prominent televangelists may change, the credibility of the electronic church may waver, and scandal may come and go, the allure of this fare is so diverse that it will never be want of a substantial viewership. The allure of religious television, after all, lies in its many faces.

REFERENCES

Abelman, R. (1987). Religious television uses and gratifications. *Journal of Broadcasting & Electronic Media, 31*(3), 293–307.

Abelman, R. (1988a). The impact of the PTL scandal on religious television viewers. *Journal of Communication and Religion, 11*(1), 41–51.

Abelman, R. (1988b). The impact of the PTL scandal on viewers' financial contributions. *Journal of Media Economics, 1*(1), 23–38.

Abelman, R. (1988c). Motivations for viewing the "700 Club." *Journalism Quarterly, 65*(1), 112–118, 164.

Abelman, R. (1989). "PTL Club" viewer uses and gratifications. *Communication Quarterly, 37*(1), 54–66.

Abelman, R., & Pettey, G. (1988). How political is religious television programming? *Journalism Quarterly, 65*(2), 313–319.

American Broadcasting Company. (1987a, March 23). Transcripts of "Nightline" Show #1520. New York: Journal Graphics.

American Broadcasting Company. (1987b, March 24). Transcripts of "Nightline" Show #1521. New York: Journal Graphics.

American Broadcasting Company. (1987c, April 24). Transcripts of "Nightline" Show #1544. New York: Journal Graphics.

Associated Press. (1987a, March 26). Falwell presides at PTL. *The Plain Dealer*, p. 2a.

Associated Press, (1987b, March 27). Bakkers to get PTL pay, but will not participate. *The Plain Dealer*, p. 21a.

Barrett, L.I. (1986, September 29). The patrician and the preacher. *Time*, p. 30.

Buddenbaum, J.M. (1981). Characteristics and media related needs of the audience of religious TV. *Journalism Quarterly, 51*, 266–272.

Carveth, R.A., & Alexander, A. (1985). Soap opera viewing motivations and the cultivation process. *Journal of Broadcasting & Electronic Media, 29*(3), 259–273.

Compesi, R.J. (1980). Gratifications of daytime TV seriel viewers. *Journalism Quarterly, 57*, 155–158.

Dennis, J.L. (1962). *An analysis of the audience of religious radio and television programs in the Detroit metropolitan area*. Unpublished doctoral dissertation, University of Michigan, Ann Arbor, MI.

Fore, W.F. (1979, January). The electronic church. *Ministry*, p. 5.

Fore, W.F. (1987). *Television and religion*. Minneapolis, MN: Augsburg Publishing.

Gaddy, G.D. (1984). The power of the religious media: Religious broadcast use and the role of religious organizations in public affairs. *Review of Religious Research, 25*(4), 289–301.

Gaddy, G.D., & Pritchard, D. (1985). When watching religious TV is like attending church. *Journal of Communication, 35*(1), 123–131.

Goeken, D. (1987, June 2). PTL network dropped by biggest cable firm. *The Plain Dealer*, p. 21a.

Gordon, R. (1986, April). Video vicars: How they tune out the press. *Washington Journalism Review,* pp. 39–47.

Hadden, J. (1986a, January). The great audience size debate. *Religious Broadcasting,* pp. 20–22.

Hadden, J. (1986b, February). Getting to the bottom of the audience size debate. *Religious Broadcasting,* pp. 88, 116, 122, 124, 126, 128.

Hadden, J., & Swann, C.E. (1981). *Prime time preachers.* Reading, MA: Addison-Wesley.

Hawkins, R.P., & Pingree, S. (1981). Uniform messages and habitual viewing: Unnecessary assumptions in social reality effects. *Human Communication Research, 7,* 291–301.

Horsfield, P.G. (1984). *Religious television: The American experience.* New York: Longman.

Johnson, S.D., & Tamney, J.G. (1985). The Christian right and the 1984 presidential election. *Review of Religious Research, 27*(2), 124–133.

Kippax, S., & Murray, J.P. (1977). Using television: Programme content and need gratification. *Politics, 12,* 56–69.

Kippax, S., & Murray, J.P. (1980). Using the media: Need gratification and perceived reality. *Communication Research, 7,* 335–360.

Mann, J., & Petersen, S. (1980, September 15). Preachers in politics: Decisive force in 1980? *U.S. News & World Report,* pp. 24–26.

Marty, M. (1967). *The improper opinion: Mass media and the Christian faith.* Philadelphia, PA: Westminster.

Mashsek, J.W. (1986, July 14). From pulpit to podium, a forceful presence. *U.S. News & World Report,* pp. 24–25.

Mayer, A.J. (1980, September 15). A tide of born again politics? *Newsweek,* pp. 28–36.

Neuendorf, K., & Abelman, R. (1987). Televangelism: A look at communicator style. *Journal of Religious Studies, 13*(1), 41–59.

O'Brien-Steinfels, M., & Steinfels, P. (1983, January/February). The new awakening: Getting religion in the video age. *Channels, 2*(5), 24–62.

Ostling, R.N. (1986, February 12). Power, glory-and politics. *Time,* pp. 62–69.

Ostling, R.N. (1987a, March 30). A really bad day at Fort Mill. *Time,* pp. 62–69.

Ostling, R.N. (1987b, May 11). Taking command at Fort Mill. *Time,* p. 60.

Parker, E.C., Barry, D.W., & Smythe, D.W. (1955). *The television-radio audience and religion.* New York: Harper and Row.

Pierand, R.V. (1985). Religion and the 1984 election campaign. *Review of Religious Research, 27*(2), 98–114.

Public Broadcasting Service. (1984, June). Frontline: Give me that big time religion (telecast). WGBH-TV, Boston, MA.

Public Broadcasting Service. (1988, January). Frontline: Praise the Lord (telecast). WGBH-TV, Boston, MA.

Rubin, A.M. (1981). A multivariate analysis of "60 Minutes" viewing motivations. *Journalism Quarterly, 58,* 529–534.

Rubin, A.M. (1983). Television uses and gratifications: The interactions of viewing patterns and motivations. *Journal of Broadcasting, 27,* 37–51.

Rubin, A.M. (1984). Ritualized and instrumental television viewing. *Journal of Communication, 34*(3), 67–77.

Rubin, A.M. (1985). Uses of daytime television soap operas by college students. *Journal of Broadcasting & Electronic Media, 29*(3), 241–258.

Schulz, W.F. (1986, April 2). Contributor's misled. *The Christian Century,* pp. 321–322.

Simpson, E. (1987a, March 22). Park's success is questionable after Bakker's latest scandal. Cox News Service (syndication).

Simpson, E. (1987b, March 23). Paying the price for saving souls. Cox News Service (Syndication).

Stilson, J. (1987, June 1). Rating high: The Bakkers are a hot draw on TV interview programs. *Electronic Media,* pp. *1,* 39.

Tarr, L.K. (1983, October 21). Are some electronic preachers social Darwinists? *Christianity Today,* p. 50.

Traub, J. (1985, May/June). CBN counts its blessings. *Channels, 5*(1), 28–34.

United Press International. (1987a, March 24). Bakker claims plotting for "Hostile Takeover." *Tyler Morning Telegraph,* p. 2.

United Press International. (1987b, March 25). TV evangelists cast stones: Swaggart named PTL "Judas." *Tyler Morning Telegraph,* p. 1.

Windahl, S. (1981). Uses and gratifications at the crossroads. In G.C. Wilhoit & H. deBock (Eds.), *Mass communication review yearbook* (Vol. 2, pp. 174–185). Beverly Hills, CA: Sage Publications.

9

The Religious Television Audience: A Matter of Significance or Size?*

Stewart M. Hoover

For the past 10 years, the phenomenon of the electronic church has become increasingly prominent, controversial, and devisive in the field of mass communications, and to an even greater degree, in the public political sphere. The "evangelical right," in which several of these broadcasters and broadcast organizations have played a part, has been claimed a significant factor in several recent general elections. One such broadcaster, the Rev. Jerry Falwell, has gained international attention as a spokesperson for what he calls "traditional values" in national politics, and even foreign policy. And, as political fortunes begin to take shape for the 1988 Presidential race, another of these broadcasters, Pat Robertson of the Christian Broadcasting Network (CBN) Inc., has decided to run for that office.

In the midst of these developments, one issue has continued to raise controversy about these programs both within the field of broadcasting and in the broader political context: The actual power and impact of the programs themselves, and specifically the actually size of their audiences. That is, how many people watch this type of programming?

Widely differing estimates of the size of the electronic church audience have been offered by sources such as the executive director of the Religious Broadcasters' trade association, Dr. Ben Armstrong (1979) who has claimed over 100 million, and leading critics of the movement, notably Dr. William Fore (1975) of the National Council of Churches, who asserts the number of viewers is less than 10 million. The popular press have contributed to the confusion of the issue, often accepting unquestioningly either high or low estimates. The *Wall Street Journal,* for instance, is credited with being the source of the highest estimate of all, 130 million (Hadden & Swann, 1981).

There are only 2 reliable sources of empirical data on this question, and each is not without error and bias. The source of the largest estimates have

---

* This essay first appeared in *Review of Religious Research, 29*(2), December 1987. Reprinted here with permission.

been a number of national polls conducted over the last decade by firms such as the Gallup Organization, where estimates that 30 to 40 percent of Americans view these programs have not been uncommon (Gerbner et al., 1984). More conservative (and more reliable) estimates have come from the national audience ratings firms, where individual syndicated religious programs have rarely been found to achieve ratings representing more than 5 percent of television households nationally, or in individual markets (Hadden & Swann, 1981; Martin, 1981).

Two analyses based on actual ratings data emerged early in this debate. In a study of national ratings for the most popular programs at the time, Martin (1981) estimated the total audience to be 9.7 million households and 13.7 million actual viewers, not accounting for (that is, including) multiple viewing by individual viewers. When adjusting for multiple ("duplicated") viewing, he suggested that "a figure of 7 to 10 million seems fair." Noting that the ratings figures only report viewing frequencies of at least once a week, he went on to speculate that occasional viewers (those viewing less than once a week) would swell the total audience to perhaps 23 million, a figure which would square with some earlier data from the national polling firms (Martin, 1981).

Hadden and Swann (1981) carried out a similar analysis of all 66 syndicated religious programs included in the Arbitron Corporation's *Syndicated Program Analysis* at that time. Their estimate was very near to that of Martin, 20.5 million viewers (Hadden & Swann, 1981).

Aside from further polling data, only 2 investigations have cast additional light on this issue, both based on more carefully controlled access to and analysis of ratings data. The Annenberg-Gallup Study of Religious Broadcasting (Gerbner et al., 1984) contained 2 separate estimates of total religious television audience. One was yet another survey "self-report" based estimate obtained by the Gallup Organization (40% of the population). The other, based on examination of Arbitron ratings data and on a ratings-derived sample of confirmed viewers of religion (that is, those who actually viewed during their diary-keeping as Arbitron ratings households), estimated the total *weekly* audience to be 13.3 million viewers, or about 6 percent of the total national audience.

The Gerbner et al. study has been the target of criticism, some well-taken, some superficial, even disingenuous in tone (cf. Engel, 1984; Frankl & Hadden, 1987; Schultze, 1985). These criticisms have not, however, questioned the central feature of that study, its unprecedented data base of "confirmed" religious television viewers. As such, Gerbner et al. obtained the only reliable data to date on *duplicated* viewing by individuals, allowing for gross measures of viewing such as aggregate audiences of all religious programs in a given week, to be weighted to account for viewing of more than one program by viewers.

More recently, 2 researchers at the Christian Broadcasting Network released data from a proprietary study conducted for CBN by the A.C.

Nielsen Co. (Clark & Virts, 1985). Amid much fanfare, no doubt fueled by the speculation that CBN's president, Pat Robertson, was contemplating a run for President, prominent popular journals reported the overall finding of this study that the top 10 religious programs, between them, attract over 40 percent of American households. A closer examination of this study reveals that while it contains some significant advances over earlier estimates, the widely-reported total-viewing figure was based on viewers' watching 6 minutes or more *per month,* where the Martin, Hadden and Swann, and Gerbner et al. findings had used the cutoff of 15 minutes *per week* (the threshold normally used in reporting audiences for commercial broadcasts.) Clark and Virts note that their *weekly* viewing figure (again with the threshold of 6 minutes, not 15, as with the other studies) is lower than the monthly by about half, or 21.1 percent of households.

Clark and Virts shed no new light on other issues, however, including no new, more reliable estimate of viewers-per-household in religious viewing households, nor additional information on the frequency distribution of numbers of different programs viewed by each viewer (both issues important to accurate estimation of overall audience size). While the assertion is not specifically addressed or supported in the publicly-released version of the Clark and Virts work, their figure is assumed to be a nonduplicated figure representing all viewers who watch at least 1 of the 10 programs in their study (6 minutes or more per month), each of these viewers being counted only *once* for the overall audience figure. There is no methodological statement to support this assumption other than a general statement that Nielsen methodology enables the estimation of a *cumulative* figure which is nonduplicated. Such an estimate, when contemplating a phenomenon as infrequent as religious viewing, could be prone to rather significant levels of error, as shall be seen.

Each of these latter 2 studies has addressed an additional feature of this issue which has been claimed to be significant. This is the effect that distribution of these programs via religious-oriented *cable networks* has had on total audience figures. The Gerbner et al. Arbitron data included an unequivocal measure of Cable Television subscription, and enabled an assessment of the relationship between subscribing to cable and overall religious viewing (see Hoover et al., 1986, for a complete discussion of these findings). Clark and Virts were able to obtain some cable data from the Nielsen Homevideo Index, but were unable to come to conclusive results other than to speculate that cable television might be one of the factors contributing to unmeasured additional viewing of religion (beyond their 40% figure).

Disagreement Over Ratings-Based Estimates

There are several ways to account for the discrepancy between the Gerbner et al. and the Clark and Virts figures, the 2 most recent and presumably most reliable estimates. The greatest amount of difference is seemingly due to the analysis frames chosen. The aggregate figure for Clark and Virts is for *monthly* viewing of at least 6 minutes, and for Gerbner et al., 15 minutes *weekly*. Some seasonal fluctuation or overall increase in viewing in the period between the studies might account for some of the difference as well, though there is no reason to expect large maturation differences.

Other sources of error in one or both of these estimates will be discussed presently, but all of these issues are related to the primary fact that when measuring religious television viewing, we are analyzing relatively *insignificant* portions of *total* television viewing. The tools we have at our disposal to analyze viewing are gauged to the demands of dominant commercial programming. They are necessarily less precise at assessing such small segments of the total audience.

DATA THROUGH TWO LENSES

The debate over the size of the religious television audience converges from 2 directions. The first is the technical or methodological realm, where the problems of assessing a unique phenomenon which is a relatively infrequent activity strain the common tools and assumptions of audience research techniques aimed at commercial broadcasting with its large numbers and massive audience flows. The second context is the wider social policy and political realm, which asks some fairly direct and specific questions of these data. How significant (in a social sense) is Jerry Falwell's audience? How potentially powerful a force would a Pat Robertson campaign for the Presidency be? How important a political force is the Moral Majority, or conversely, People for the American Way (the most vocal of the anti-"new religious right" organizations)? How significant an alternative to "conventional" television (with its oft-noted "secularism") is the electronic church?

The particular concern of the latter context often informs the approach taken in the former. To the critics of the electronic church in the mainline church, a different level of social significance is assigned to 6 minutes of viewing per month than would be the case with a religious broadcaster concerned with "total aggregate" audience figures which might be used in promotion and fund raising. A secular critic of the political implications of these institutions might look with apprehension on seemingly large audience figures, while another analyst might wish to look beyond amorphous measures of audience membership to concrete measures of "membership" in (or even "commitment" to) a given broadcaster's organization, or financial support of it.

One of the implications of audience figures—the impact that such viewing has on more "conventional" religious behaviors—is far less threatening to conventional churches than was at first feared, according to research (see, in particular, Gerbner et al., 1984). Such viewing does not seem to be associated with decreased levels of local-church attendance or financial support in *aggregate*. Other questions still deserve attention, and each of them would have slightly different implications for definitions of viewing and audience membership which might undergird further analysis.

It is part of our common "received history" of revivalism and evangelicalism that the question of what constitutes "an adherent" or "a believer" or "a convert" has always been a matter of debate. William Martin notes that there is a fairly common suspicion among observers of broadcast and nonbroadcast preachers alike that they sometimes "count arms and legs instead of heads" (1981, p. 10). It is part of the grand tradition of revivalism to take "on faith" each new profession of salvation by a participant in a rally, service, or meeting. Each such convert adds to the total fold of the saved, *and* to each evangelist's reputation, adding to his or her credibility and overall audience appeal and power to continue the good work of pursuing Christ's "Great Commission." Thus, there never has been any great incentive to accurately account for numbers of individuals reached. Each new profession by an individual may well represent the *true* turning point in his or her faith, and thus could reasonably be imputed to the work of the ministry through which it happened. It has thus been the case that there has been, dating from the prebroadcast era of evangelicalism, an incentive to actively report "duplicated audience figures" of a kind.

This tradition certainly pervades the broadcast ministries, begging the question from astute observers, "what, then is *significant* viewing, the *critical* point where mere participation in the audience (which could occur by chance or error by a given viewer) yields to a greater level of commitment or participation?" This question, in itself, reveals some misapprehension of the guiding ideology of evangelical broadcasting. Among the stories which seem to carry the most power for viewers are those where such "incidental" or "accidental" viewing leads inexorably to a profession of faith or to personal salvation (see, in particular, Bourgault, 1980, and Hoover, 1985, for accounts of the importance of such mythology to the overall influence of the experience of audience membership). Under these circumstances, the counting of even the most inconsequential-seeming encounter with the programming as "audience membership" makes some sense.

SOURCES OF ERROR IN ESTIMATING RELIGIOUS AUDIENCE SIZE

The above issues aside, the availability of the public report and data archive of the Annenberg-Gallup study, and the recent release of findings from the Clark and Virts study, provides an opportunity for an assessment of what is known about the audience size and composition of the electronic church. A purely methodological approach to these issues must take into account the variety of ways that an accurate audience estimate will always be elusive, given current research tools.

Self-Report Bias

It has been widely observed that national opinion surveys have consistently reported much larger audiences for religious broadcasts than would seem to be the case from ratings data (cf. Clark & Virts, 1985; Gerbner et al., 1984; Hadden & Swann, 1981). The differences between the 2 measures have largely been explained by the "demand characteristics" of the polling situation, where a respondent is likely to choose a "socially desirable" answer regardless of actual behavior. In a nation where a much larger percentage of the public report being religious and report attending church regularly than actual attendance figures reflect, such a thing as listening to or viewing religious broadcasting can be assumed to be a more "desirable" response than to deny viewing or listening.

This "self-report bias" has been thought to be ameliorated somewhat by measures of viewing taken by the commercial ratings firms, Nielsen and Arbitron, which have as their goal measurement of actual viewing *behavior*. Clark and Virts note, however, that there is a consistent tendency for ratings based on viewer-kept "diaries" of viewing (which are, after all, "self-reports" themselves) to *under-report* viewing of independent, non-network stations. Since the majority of airings of religious broadcasts take place on such stations, this error may result in an underreporting of religious viewing. Clark and Virts base the significance of their findings on the assertion that *metered* ratings overcome this bias by removing the role of the respondent in having to reliably report his or her behavior. The meter or "black box" is affixed to the respondent's television set, and automatically records which channel is being viewed, and for how long (it does not, however, report who, if anyone, is watching—an important source of error in itself).

While the-meter-is-better-than-self-report argument has some attraction, it fails to account for what can be presumed to be a countertendency, that is, for those who *view* religious programs, and presumably feel some affinity and commitment to them, to be scrupulous (or even overscrupulous) in their diary keeping about such viewing. The anecdote of the upwardly mobile viewers who overreport their viewing of Public Broadcasting leads to an equally plausible assertion regarding this "specialty" subset of programming. It is commonly observed that the ratings services themselves encourage this sort of "demand behavior," to a degree, by assuring participants in diary and meter samples that this is their opportunity to help establish what America will see on television (while cautioning them *not* to change their viewing habits intentionally with such "steering" in mind).

If it is true that the more committed/attracted are more prone to over-report, then a comparison of metered and self-reports could provide a test of the quality and appeal of this programming. If it is powerful and attractive programming, appealing to a loyal audience (which is what we would expect if it were the sort of significant phenomenon often feared and touted) then self-reports should be *higher* than metered reports (or, at least, the bias *against* independent or specialty stations should be mediated by the desire of adherents to report or over-report that they view). The finding that metered ratings are more favorable toward religious television therefore could be construed as reflecting *negatively* on the power and appeal of these programs for their viewers.

The argument that a meter-based rating of religious audience size is preferable, is also confounded by a potential error of a different kind. Self-reports, whether in national surveys or on ratings diaries, involve a self-classification as a "religious viewer" or as a person who is somehow attracted to such programs. Included in a metered rating figure would be a group of persons, an unknown percentage, who for some reason may view these programs, but would be reluctant to classify themselves as "viewers of religion." Among these would no doubt be those persons who watch such programs for "entertainment" of a very secular kind, attracted to the uniqueness and oddity of the programs. There is much anecdotal evidence that a great number of people who are, in fact, *hostile* to these programs, watch them. While they would be reluctant to identify this viewing either in a poll or a diary, some of them may appear in metered rating figures. Also appearing in such figures presumably would be many cases where the set is simply left on, unattended—also an unknown portion of the total.

Construct Problems

Aside from the problem of establishing what constitutes a meaningful type or *level* of viewing, there is the further problem of defining or specifying precisely what a religious program *is,* a problem which leads to both conceptual and methodological consequences.

Self-reports in opinion surveys invariably rely on respondents' own definitions of what constitutes a "religious program." Thus the viewers' self-classification as a "religious viewer" may be based on a widely different interpretation than the a priori assumptions of investigators. The investigators in the Annenberg-Gallup study, for instance, found that one measure of viewing, the self-report of programs "regularly viewed," elicited a wide range of responses when respondents were asked to "name" programs. These included theatrical films such as *The Ten Commandments,* as well as vague and undefined exposures, such as "The Pope whenever he's on" or "anything produced by the Vatican," and seemingly irrelevant entertainment fare such as *The Thorn Birds,* a contemporary network potboiler in which a priest is the main character. In all, that study encountered over 150 such "unclassified" responses among the 1300 respondents.

A second type of construct difficulty relates to the *specification* of religious programs used in the technical sampling process, with either the self-report based diaries, or the "cleaner" meters. In both cases, investigators must specify for the ratings firms precisely which day-parts and channels are to be counted as "religious programs." The ratings firms accept this a priori specification, with no systematic check on its reliability. Religious programs, which often appear in so-called "ghetto-ized" time slots, are frequently pre-empted, or shift their time, day, and station of appearance. Error thus enters when the ratings firm samples audience viewing based on a time slot which no longer contains a religious program, and misses that program in its "new" slot.

This is a difficulty with both the Annenberg-Gallup and the Clark and Virts studies. The former study contains fairly reliable data for the nationally-syndicated religious programs (based on Arbitron's own classification in its *Syndicated Program Analysis*). However, viewing of *local* programs had to be specified by day-part based on a systematic analysis of listings information from *TV Guide*. The latter study did not deal with local programming at all, and with only 10 of the 66 nationally-syndicated programs, but all day-parts surveyed had to be specified by the investigators themselves.

There is also the conceptual construct problem—as noted earlier in this paper—of defining "a religious viewer." What is "religious viewing?" Is it viewing regularly, occasionally (how are these measured?), the full program? Fifteen minutes of it? Six minutes? Weekly? Monthly? Is is ancillary behavior, such as "joining" the *700 Club* or the *PTL Club?* Is it becoming a "Prayer Partner?" Is it contributing regularly? Infrequently? Traveling to the center where the program is produced to be in the "live audience?"

In his analysis of some members of the *700 Club*, Hoover (1985) found that there is not necessarily a connection between viewing, joining, and contributing. Several of his respondents viewed rarely, if at all, but were significant financial contributors to the program. In another study of the Christian Broadcasting Network, the same author found that a relatively small number of contributors accounted for half the income to the ministry (not an uncommon pattern for a not-for-profit corporation) (Hoover, 1982). Are these major donors "just" viewers of CBN?

Significance of Duplicated vs. Non-Duplicated Viewing and Program Sampling

The earliest analyses of these issues (Hadden & Swann, 1981; Martin, 1981) addressed the obvious error introduced by duplicative counting of a viewer each time he or she views a religious program, achieving massive total audience estimates. The Gerbner et al. analysis accounted for this phenomenon by establishing a weighting factor which would discount viewing of multiple programs, so as to arrive at an estimate of the number if different viewers represented by aggregate ratings for all religious programs. Clark and Virts based their claim on nonduplication on the Nielsen company's methodology of establishing cumulative nonduplicated audience estimates.

Surveys or polls, which rely on a self-classification to condition, have one great advantage over ratings measures: They are inherently nonduplicated measures of overall viewing (their limitations due to demand characteristics and construct problems have already been discussed).

But, there is a related issue, again having to do with *analysis frame*. On a conceptual level, the significance of an audience of a given size is in part based on the analyst's assessment of religious viewing compared to general viewing behavior. This comparison is, after all, the only standard available. Intuitive logic suggests that the measure of attraction of a program is somehow a function of its likelihood of being selected by a given viewer out of a fixed set of viewing opportunities in a given week. A rating for a program (particularly for a specialty program with a small audience, such as a religious one) is therefore a measure of preference for that program *beyond* mere chance. Any program has a given probability of being selected at random. A rating, viewed from this perspective, should be a measure of preference beyond that level of probability. Some programs have a better chance than others of being selected through such random processes. A program which is on at a time when more rather than fewer viewers are in the audience has an increased chance of being selected, and thus its "intuitive significance threshold" should be higher. Such would also be the case with a program which is on 5 days a week, or 6, or 7.

Clark and Virts (1985) address this issue, pointing out that in their results, the daily programs (the *700 Club* and the *PTL Club*) do not register as much of an aggregate ratings advantage over weekly shows as they would have expected.

These issues do not concern conventional broadcasting. *Individual programs* are the focus of most ratings attention, individual programs which are vying for relatively large shares of the total audience available in their time-slots. The question put to the data by research such as that discussed here is far different. It is, really, "out of the total number of viewing opportunities available in a given week, how many of those opportunities result in viewing of *any* religious program?" Thus an aggregate weekly rating figure for "religious viewing" (nonduplicated *or* duplicated) is a percentage not only of the total audience available (not just "viewing at that time"—i.e., not the "share") at that slot, but of all possible audiences available during that week. Seen in that light, the figures often reported represent a minuscule percentage of total viewing opportunities by all television households. To further compound the conceptual error by suggesting that such a figure can be compared to the weekly rating or share of any given commercial program is a comparison of apples and oranges which is quite misleading.

Once it has been established that a certain set of programs have a certain audience size, how is that to be compared to other activities, and to viewing of television in general? The most common assumption is that such aggregate ratings figures are comparable to conventional television viewing. For instance, in its story on the Clark and Virts study, *Variety* noted:

> It is the first time viewership of religious programs has been analyzed with the same methods used for network ratings. Actual figures showed that out of more than 33,000,000 [sic], 40.2 percent watched the evangelists. William Behanna [of Nielsen] said most top-rated network prime time shows also reach about 40 percent of U.S. Viewers. (1985, p. 30)

Such a comparison is seductive and misleading. It compares the total number of viewers who viewed at least 6 minutes, in a given month, of a *genre,* with the weekly audience of *one program.* A far more useful comparison (though still slightly misleading) would be to compare the Clark and Virts figure with the total percentage of the U.S. television audience which watches "situation comedies" or "crime dramas" (*at least 1* installment of either of these) for 6 minutes or more per month. The latter figure would undoubtedly be nearly 100 percent of the total audience. However, even this comparison is misleading because it assumes a similar base in terms of total opportunities to view each of these genres in a given month. The base figure out of which comparative percentage would need to be derived, in order to actually be comparable, would be the base of total viewing opportunities available across the entire national television market, in 6 minute segments. The comparison between the percentage of those opportunities taken to tune to the religious *genre* would need to be compared to the percentage taken to view any of the other *genres.* Even with the impressive exposure the 66 syndicated religious programs get in program schedules nationally, their performance in this sort of a test would obviously be less impressive than suggested by *Variety.*

None of this is to argue that an aggregate audience (household) rating of 40.1 nationwide is not impressive for what it is, it is rather to say that when we ask the question of the total size of the religious audience, we are asking a qualitatively different question than is normally tested using ratings methodology.

The issue of *sampling* introduces one additional source of error in estimation into the projections made by all earlier ratings-based studies of these issues. In the discussion so far, the inadequacy of ratings measures of viewing of religious television have been noted. The "numbers," the accrual rating and share figures for most religious programs, are so small so as to be massively affected by the sampling error of the methodologies used. For example, Clark and Virts report that the sampling error for the overall ratings measures in their analysis is ±1.3 percent. At the same time, they report ratings for the various programs in their analysis at from 0.6 (*Day of Discovery*) to 3.1 (*Jimmy Swaggart*). In all cases with such small audience size, a much larger portion of the actual variance *could be error* than is the case with programs with larger audiences.

This error is further compounded, in most reports of the "national audience" of religious broadcasting, by the fact that to achieve such a national estimate, ratings firms must first gather ratings data from each of the several hundred markets surveyed in the country as the basis of syndicated program ratings (syndicated programs *cannot* be rated nationally by a single, national survey since they are on in differing patterns from market to market). Then, the various market ratings are *added* to achieve a national figure. Clark and Virts point out that one source of *underreporting* of religious viewing is that below a certain cutoff point in each market (usually around a rating of 1, or 1% of the total audience in the market) religious programs simply are not counted or reported at all. It should be remembered that such a low figure is so near or so far below the margin for error in the sampling technique used, that reporting of such results would be of questionable scientific judgement. The judgement of taking great stock by figures *nearly as small* also deserves careful consideration.

THE RELIGIOUS AUDIENCE: CHANGING OR STABLE?

The social significance of the debate over the size of the religious television audience is based on the issue of whether or not the new phenomenon of the electronic church represents a new reality in the history of religious broadcasting, as has been claimed by its supporters and critics alike, or whether it is somehow firmly based in what had been traditionally understood to be the "natural" audience for religious programs. From the earliest serious analysis of religious broadcasting, the landmark Parker, Barry, and Smythe study (1955), it has been assumed that the audience for religion was fairly consistently made up of older, lower income, less educated, and more "religious" (in a conventional sense) viewers. A variety of studies since Parker, Barry, and Smythe have confirmed these findings, adding that women seem more likely to view or listen than men, nonwhites are somewhat more likely to view or listen than whites, and that viewers seem to be more likely to live in rural areas then in cities, and in the south than in the northeast (Buddenbaum, 1979, 1981; Gaddy & Pritchard, 1985; Hadden & Swann, 1981; Horsfield, 1984; Johnstone, 1971; Lester & Romjue, 1981; Martin, 1981).

The Annenberg-Gallup study found that these characteristics still hold

Table 9.1. Demographic Characteristics of Viewers of Two or More Hours of Religious Television Weekly.

		Viewers Viewing 2 Hours or More	Total Sample Frequency[1]	Mean Religious Hours in Sample[2]
Age	18–29	7.3	22.4	.47
	30–49	31.0	43.4	.43
	50–65	34.9	24.5	.35
	Over 65	26.7	9.7	.35
	Total	(232)	(1,493)	
Sex	Male	31.9	41.2	.38
	Female	68.1	58.8	.40
	Total	(232)	(1,493)	
Race	White	73.9	87.7	.39
	Nonwhite	26.1	12.3	.38
	Total	(199)	(1,342)	
Education	Less than High School	40.9	19.9	.37
	High School Graduate	33.9	38.2	.41
	Some College or More	25.1	41.9	.43
	Total	(232)	(1,435)	
Household Income	Under 15,000	48.0	29.5	.37
	15,000 to 24,999	31.5	29.4	.42
	25,000 to 35,000	8.0	7.3	.39
	Over 35,000	12.5	23.7	.45
	Total	(200)	(1,280)	

[1]This column presents overall demographics for the sample (weighted).
[2]This column presents mean *hours* of weekly viewing by religious viewers in the sample.
From Gerbner et al., 1984, p. 22.

true for this audience, generally, though there is some evidence that slight differences exist among the various programs (Gerbner et al., 1984) (see Table 9.1). Clark and Virts (1985) reported some variation between programs, as well.

These questions are significant because much of the debate over the size of the religious television audience is actually a debate over its *composition*. It is logical to assume that a certain percentage of any population of television viewers (a percentage contingent on the demographic characteristics described by most credible research) could be expected to be viewers of religious television. The debate over the significance of this "new" phenomenon of religious broadcasting, the so-called electronic church, is a debate over the extent to which *these* programs reach beyond this "basic," or "natural" audience, reaching other demographic groups, attracting "atypical" viewers. These broadcasters, *and* their critics, share the assumption that this is happening to some degree, that modern religious broadcasting is stretching beyond its "basic" audience, and through scheduling and format strategies, reaching a more diverse (and therefore, also larger) audience. Promotion literature, books written by religious broadcasting industry leaders (see, in particular, Armstrong, 1979), and the trade magazine, *Religious Broadcasting,* are full of attention to this matter of attracting younger, more upscale, less "religious" viewers.

Even research studies done by the broadcasters themselves indicate a consciousness of the centrality of this issue. Clark and Virts, for example, describe their demographic findings entirely in terms of the assumed generalizability of the religious television audience. They note, for instance, the finding that while the majority of viewers for all programs are over 55 years of age:

> The spread between the two age groups [for women] is more nearly equal for *The 700 Club* [the flagship CBN program] (55% to 45%) and the *Old Time Gospel Hour* [Jerry Falwell's program] (56% to 44%) than for the other programs where there is a *two-or three to one ratio in favor of older women.* [emphasis added]. (1985, p. 21)

They conclude, "the data raise questions about the accuracy of the generalization that the audience of religious television consists primarily of older females." Without appearing to quibble on this point, it should be pointed out that the data would seem to confirm, not disconfirm the generalization, even when compared to the demographic distribution of conventional television viewing, where older women also predominate.

POSSIBLE SOURCES OF INCREASE IN AUDIENCE

Promoters and critics alike point to three specific dimensions of modern religious broadcasting which are claimed to contribute to an increase in the size and expansion of the composition (and therefore, the significance) of the religious television audience.

Availability

There is a great deal of logic to the argument that the actual audience size (irrespective of its demographic characteristics) should increase as programs become more widely available. Before 1975 (when satellite distribution became technically and legally possible for the first time), the number of persons who actually had *access* to religious programs was somewhat smaller than it is now (though such programs as Jerry Falwell's *The Old Time Gospel Hour* were widely syndicated before then).

Availability in recent years has also been affected by the twin phenomena of dedicated "religious" UHF-TV stations (which increased in numbers in the mid-1970s, moving into major markets for the first time, according to Armstrong, 1979, and Hadden & Swann, 1981) and dedicated religious-only cable television networks (of which there are at least four at this writing).

These developments cannot necessarily be assumed to increase audience size due to access alone, however. In most cases where religious stations and cable networks have been made available (at least in major cities) many of the programs carried by them (such as Oral Roberts' and Jerry Falwell's programs) were already on conventional television stations in those markets through "bicycle" syndication (the most economical method of syndicating a program—videotapes are mailed, returned and reused). Instead, the emergence of the dedicated religious programming services (cable channels and religious over-the-air stations) has probably led to an increase in the *diversity* of programs available (less well-known programs with lower syndication budgets could afford the lower rates on these services), and in *scheduling* flexibility.

It has been widely noted that the most prominent of the electronic church programs have been intentionally designed to no longer "look like" the stereotypic "television preacher." Christian Broadcasting Network and the PTL Network (the former both an over-the-air broadcaster and a cable network operator, the latter a syndicator and cable network operator) have been widely noted for their formats, which generally conform to the talk show genre familiar to most Americans from their commercial television viewing.

In addition, both of these producers (and to an extent, others) have from time to time experimented with additional program offerings of quite different formats yet. In the 1981–82 season, for instance, CBN gained national attention for producing *Another Life,* a Christian soap opera. More recently, CBN has introduced, and then cancelled, a news program (there had always been a news segment on CBN's *700 Club*) and PTL had been experimenting with a cooking and homemaking program called *Tammy's House Party.*

Several studies have found some variation in the demographic make-up of the various religious programs. (Clark & Virts, 1985; Gaddy & Pritchard, 1985; Gerbner et al., 1984), but their relationship to such format and appeal variations is as yet dubious and not clearly articulated. For example, Clark and Virts note that the slight advantage (in terms of real numbers) *The 700 Club* and Jerry Falwell's *Old Time Gospel Hour* have over their competition in attracting men under 55 is related to their formats. However, their explanation of the commonality between these 2 programs which would tie them together in this way is less than convincing. They describe the latter program as having "an educational emphasis," when both anecdotal assessment and a more empirical one (the content analysis performed as part of the Gerbner et al. study) would suggest that, to the contrary, this program is primarily a conventional church service (albeit one where there is a "social gospel" of a kind preached from the pulpit).

In his study of *700 Club* audience members, Hoover (1985) found little evidence that those who were "atypical" in demographic characteristics (younger, better educated, nonevangelicals) were attracted by that program's "atypical" format. These viewers instead seemed to be the ones most "reached" by the program's traditional elements (prayer, Bible teaching).

Scheduling

With the new and different format and "appeal" experiments typical of some electronic church broadcasters, and with their new potential reach via cable and independent-TV distribution, has come the ability to experiment with scheduling options outside the traditional "religious ghetto" of Sunday morning, late nights, and early mornings.

Clark and Virts report, however, that the programs with the greatest flexibility in scheduling and/or audience accessibility, the weekday programs of CBN, PTL, and Jimmy Swaggart, actually register loyalty figures (measured by the number of times each is viewed in a given period) which are not that much higher than those of prominent ghetto-ized weekly shows, such as Kenneth Copeland's and Robert Schuller's. In addition, the top-rated show in their analysis overall was a weekly one, Jimmy Swaggart's (Swaggart produces and syndicates *both* a weekly and a weekday version).

Clark has noted (1984) that scheduling can contribute the greatest amount to overall audience size when religious programming can break into prime-time hours, something that has been prohibitively expensive, except for occasional special programs. In fact, the much-noted cable networks have allowed for prime-time airing of religious programs, though not on over-the-air stations, where admittedly, the majority of viewing takes place. Whatever unique contribution scheduling might make, *should* be evident in *religious-cable* viewing figures. If accessibility of religious programs at convenient times is the *only* impediment to the viewing of them by large percentages of the population, viewing of religious programs in cable television households should reflect this. This does not turn out to be the case. In a recent analysis of their data on cable television, the Annenberg-Gallup researchers (Hoover et al., 1986) could find no evidence that viewing of any type of religious television was higher in cable than in noncable households (see Tables 9.2–9.4).

Table 9.2.   Cable Subscription in Religious-Viewing and Nonviewing Households.

	Religious Viewing Households (%)	Non-viewing Households (%)
Subscribe to Cable	32.7	36.1
Do Not Sub-scribe	67.3	63.9
Total	(1,263)	(1,333)

[Not significant at $p<.05$]
From Hoover et al., 1986, p. 10.

Table 9.3.   Religious Viewing as Contingent on Cable Television Subscription (Weighted Data).

	No Cable TV (%)	Cable TV (%)
Religious TV Household	10.6	9.9
Non-religious TV Household	89.4	90.1
Total	(953)	(534)

[Not significant at $p<.05$]
From Hoover et al., 1986, p. 13.

Table 9.4.   Percentage of Viewers Reporting Change in Religious Viewing Among Cable and Non-Cable Households.

Percentage Who Report Viewing Has:	Cable HH's	Non-Cable HH's
Increased	21.7	16.8
Stayed the Same	69.4	73.9
Decreased	8.9	9.3
Total N	(236)	(465)

[Not significant at $p<.05$]
From Hoover et al., 1986, p. 16.

Clark and Virts make one additional suggestion supporting a larger rather than a smaller estimate of audience size. They point out that their aggregate figure includes only viewers of the "top 10" programs, and that including viewers of other programs, including local ones, would increase the total audience somewhat. The Gerbner et al. regional sample contains several measures which could shed some light in this issue. They report (1984) that the preponderant pattern is for viewers to concentrate in the syndicated programming, with very little viewing of local programs. For instance, only 17 percent of viewers of the daily programs (all 3 of which are included in Clark and Virts' "top 10") view any local religious programs at all, and only 15 percent of those who watch nationally-syndicated *weekly* programs watch any local programs. In addition, the Gerbner et al. regional sample included one measure of the 10 most popular programs on the air at that time, and an analysis reveals that only 14 percent of viewers of those programs report viewing any local programming in addition.

These findings suggest that the overall availability of a variety of programs of new and different formats, and at convenient and flexible times outside the Sunday Morning "ghetto," *regardless of its source* (Cable or Religious UHF-TV) would *not* appear to increase its viewing outside its "basic" or "typical" audience.

Both Clark and Virts and Gerbner et al. include some attention to the question of attractiveness of various *formats* to "atypical" audiences. As was noted before, the Clark and Virts findings are less than convincing on this score. Gerbner et al. (1984), note that in their analyses, the demographic differences among various formats were so slight as to be uninterpretable.

A SIGNIFICANT AUDIENCE?

The overall significance of the size of the religious audience is, as has been said, related to broader issues of policy, politics, society, and culture. What do we mean by "religious television?" Do we mean only programs intentionally produced with self-consciously "religious" motives by religious organizations? Can we include a broader range of programs which might have some religious meaning or significance for viewers, even if not produced for explicitly "religious" purposes? If what we wish to assess is the overall consumption of religious meaning by the television audience, we must certainly include the latter in our definition.

It is even the case that we might wish to include all television as "religious" television, if we are concerned with the traditional social functions of religion (for a complete discussion, see Gerbner et al., 1984).

The debate, as we have encountered it, is somewhat more narrow and proprietary, however. Electronic church broadcasters themselves have a certain interest in focusing on broadcasting of a certain kind, as do their critics. This is a distinction which is lost on viewers, however, who choose their own ways of articulating what is and is not "religious" about television (see Bourgault, 1980, and Hoover, 1985, for accounts of these processes with regard to audiences of explicitly religious programming).

The act of viewing itself is far from clearly articulated in most assessments of these issues. What does it mean to view six minutes of *any* religious programming in a month, or 15 minutes a week? What is a significant *level* or *type* of viewing? Demand characteristics introduce an unmeasurable level of error into self-report assessments, but such effects of "social desirability" are, in fact, a measure of *something*, establishing that, overall, religious television viewing is seen by "average" Americans as a desirable, positive behavior. What is unclear, of course, is whether they actually participate in that behavior. Clark and Virts make a claim regarding demand characteristics which, as previously noted, reflects negatively on the importance of these programs for their viewers. By claiming that ratings diaries underrepresent viewing of religion, they assert, by implication that these programs are *less* important to their viewers than we would expect if they were to be a credible and powerful *alternative* for them.

The *quality* of viewing and participation is a further matter of some disagreement. Gerbner et al. found that viewers of religious programs reported contributing to them in surprisingly large amounts (the mean contribution among regular contributors was over $35 per month). Hoover (1982, 1985) has found that involvement in these programs is constituted, for viewers, out of more than the simple act of *viewing*. Some contributors and "members" seem not to view much at all, but can also articulate their sense of identification by contributing, subscribing to publications, attending local meetings of support groups for the broadcasters, travelling to the center where the program is produced, and participating in allied ministries and activities promoted by the broadcasts. Such involvements are so accessible and so involving for viewers who are interested in them, that they can be said to constitute an alternative, "para-church," which extends the ministry of broadcasters *and* the conventional church in a multitude of informal religious activities and settings (Hoover, 1985). Simply put, the measures of viewing most often used to assess the "audience" of the electronic church are totally inadequate to assess the depth and quality of the viewing experience, and are thus poorly fitted to the task of explaining the overall "impact" of religious broadcasting in any detail. Claims of Armstrong (1979), Clark and Virts (1985), and others that these programs constitute an important new service with important effects related to their audience size and composition (Clark and Virts refer to these broadcasts as the "sixth estate") are not supportable by the data. The data do not tell us much about the religious significance of these programs; *neither* do they tell us much about their political significance.

We know, with some certainty, that viewers of religion are more politically conservative than their nonviewing cohorts. We know also that they are more "religious" in a conventional sense. Aside from these gross measures, however, attempts to estimate the overall size of the religious audience have little prospect of teaching us anything significant about the phenomenon. The debate over size seems to have taken on a momentum of its own, driven by the proprietary interests of the broadcasters themselves on the one hand, and the vague fears and apprehensions of their critics on the other. Only through careful and continued analysis of data only now becoming more available can we make important contributions to understanding of this phenomenon.

CONCLUSIONS

The analyses and discussions here do not definitively answer all questions about the size and composition of the religious television audience. However, there are some general conclusions possible, based on what has been said.

First, religious television viewing appears to be both an infrequent behavior, and one which is engaged in for very short periods of time. For instance, Clark and Virts' impressive national aggregate audience figure included all viewers who had viewed any one religious television program for as little as *6 minutes* in a *month*. In the Arbitron-based data obtained by Gerbner et al., mean *weekly* viewing was just over one-half hour. Further, there is evidence that Americans tend to treat viewing as a socially desirable behavior when responding to opinion polls, but they do not go out of their way to ensure that they accurately represent their viewing of these programs when they participate in ratings diary surveys.

Second, the size of the audience is actually quite small, if any reasonable threshold for weekly viewing is chosen. It is unlikely that the overall, unduplicated *weekly* (the frame used by commercial ratings firms) audience is any larger than the 13.3 million estimated by Gerbner et al. The discrepancy between the audience-size estimates of Clark and Virts and earlier studies can be largely explained by means of differences in threshold criteria. This resolution, however, obscures larger questions of the social significance of viewing and quality of viewing, issues which cannot be addressed through viewing estimates alone.

Third, the often-cited capability of cable television and other alternative channels to *increase* the overall size of the religious audience can be tested using Gerbner et al. data. It appears that cable television does *nothing* to increase the audience size or affect its composition. If anything, these data seem to suggest that cable households actually watch *less* religious television than noncable households (for a complete discussion, see Hoover et al., 1986).

Finally, the argument over the size of the religious audience is actually an argument about the *composition* of that audience. It appears that the most-cited features of the electronic church, its "new" formats and scheduling flexibility, have had little effect on the composition of the audience. Religious television viewing continues today to be what it has always been—a relatively infrequent behavior which is seen to be socially desirable by most Americans, and a behavior largely engaged in in sectors of society that have traditionally been the most "religious."

The electronic church is indeed a new, important phenomenon. There is little evidence available from the most-cited data that its importance is related to a new surge in the size of its audience or a change in the composition of that audience outside categories of viewers which have come to be "typical" of the phenomenon of religious broadcasting in the 6 decades since its beginning.

REFERENCES

Armstrong, B. (1979). *The electric church.* Nashville, TN: Thomas Nelson.

Bourgault, L. (1980). *An ethnographic study of the "Praise the Lord Club."* Unpublished doctoral Dissertation, Ohio University, Athens, OH.

Buddenbaum, J. (1979). *The audience for religious television programs.* Master's thesis, University of Indiana, Bloomington, IN.

Buddenbaum, J. (1981). Characteristics of media-related needs of the audience for religious TV. *Journalism Quarterly, 58,* 121–131.

Clark, D. (1984). Personal interview with the author, New York.

Clark, D., & Virts, P. (1985, October 25). *Religious television audience: A new development in measuring audience size.* Paper presented at The Society for the Scientific Study of Religion Conference, Savannah, GA.

Engel, J. (1984, June). Caution: Findings subject to interpretation. *Religious Broadcasting,* pp. 26–27.

Fore, W. (1975, September 17). Religion on the airwaves: In the public interest. *Christian Century, 92,* 26–33.

Frankl, R., & Hadden, J. (1987). A critical review of the religion and television research report. *Review of Religious Research, 29*(2).

Gaddy, G., & Pritchard, D. (1985). When watching TV is like attending church. *Journal of Communication, 35*(1), 123–131.

Gerbner, G., Gross, L., Hoover, S., Morgan, M., Signorielli, N., Cotugno, H., & Wuthnow R. (1984). *Religion and television.* New York: Committee on Electronic Church Research.

Hadaway, C. (1978). Denominational switching and membership growth: In search of a relationship. *Sociological Analysis, 39*(4), 330–339.

Hadden, J., & Swann, C. (1981). *Prime-time preachers.* Reading, MA: Addison-Wesley.

Hoover, S.M. (1982). *Religious group use and avoidance of television: A study of reasons and effects.* Unpublished thesis, The Annenberg School of Communications, University of Pennsylvania, Philadelphia, PA.

Hoover, S.M. (1985). *The "700 Club" as religion and as television.* Unpublished doctoral Dissertation, University of Pennsylvania, Philadelphia, PA.

Hoover, S.M., Gerbner, G., Gross, L., Morgan, M., & Signorielli, N. (1986). *The size of the electronic church: An analysis of data on cable television.* Unpublished paper, The Annenberg School of Communications, University of Pennsylvania, Philadelphia, PA.

Horsfield, P. (1984). *Religious television: The American experience.* New York: Longman Press.

Johnstone, R. (1971). Who listens to religious radio broadcasts anymore? *Journal of Broadcasting, 16,* 91–102.

Lester, B., & Romjue, A. (1981). *Correlates of conservatism: A consideration of the electronic church.* Paper presented to the Society for the Scientific Study of Religion, Toronto, Canada.

Martin, W. (1981, June). The birth of a media myth. *The Atlantic,* pp. 17–21.

Marty, M. (1970). *The righteous empire.* New York: Dial Press.

Parker, E., Barry, D., & Smythe, D. (1955). *The radio-television audience and religion.* New York: Harper and Bros.

Schultze, Q. (1985, Fall). Vindicating the electronic church?: An assessment of the Annenberg-Gallup study. *Critical Studies in Mass Communication, 2*(3), 283–290.

IV

How Religious is Religious Television?

The electronic church raises many issues for observers, defenders, and critics. At the base of much of the controversy surrounding it, however, lies one important issue of judgment: The extent to which these broadcasts are or are not authentic religious expression. Critics form conventional churches look on the use of television as a means of religious expression with some suspicion. Critics from the secular world question the "bully pulpit" provided by access to valuable, public air time nationwide. Critics from the world of politics express concern about the activism of many of these broadcasts, questioning whether such a national, political face is a proper role for religion, anyway.

There is controversy over whether the Christian faith is amenable to communication via television. This is even so within the evangelical community, out of which the electronic church emerged. A prominent evangelical writer, Malcom Muggeridge, noted in *Christ and the Media* (1977), that much of modern television is, in fact, inimical to authentic Christian faith, and that television shows limited promise as a conveyor of its truths. In contrast, the most prominent apologist for the medium, Ben Armstrong of National Religious Broadcasters, in his book *The Electric Church* (1979), claims that the new technologies of television and satellites are endowed with an unprecedented power to spread Christianity.

There are really 2 issues involved in most of these debates. First is the question of whether television can be an authentic, substantive, "religious" experience. That is, can it replace, or support, the type of religious experience and consciousness typically experienced in conventional places or means of worship? An extension of this question is whether it can or should be an authentic "parachurch" activity, one that, while it is not substantively religious, is nonetheless authentically supportive of the work of conventional churches and conventional religious expression.

The second issue is one of the role of religion in contemporary society. Because of its prominence, the electronic church has forced the issue of how religious figures and religious institutions are to be involved in the working out of contemporary social, political, and cultural life. For many years, religion had appeared to be on the wane. Even given the prominence of religious leaders in the antiwar and civil rights movements of the 1960s, the emergence of the electronic church introduced what seemed to be an unprecedented role for religion in the political life of the country. This emergence has raised the question in the minds of many observers, of whether it is appropriate for religion to be as active in politics as Jerry Falwell, Pat Robertson, and other figures of the electronic church and the religious "new right" have been.

At the base of the electronic church's activism is a claim that it is involved in the rebirth of America's authentic religious roots. After a period of modernism and secularism, the argument goes, we are in the midst of a realignment in which the religious basis of the "founding fathers" is once more being asserted. Religious television is a powerful tool in this realignment, because it has allowed direct access to the homes and minds of many people in the country, who share belief that such change and reform is necessary.

It is not surprising that such an appeal to traditionalism and conservatism should concern a wide variety of interests. Particularly those who have been involved in, or supportive of, the progressive and liberal initiatives of the past 2 decades in law and social policy find this call to return to the roots one which may undo much progress.

More basically, the problem is one of diversity versus homogeneity. The United States is now a culturally, religiously, and socially diverse nation. Many of the changes which have concerned conservative and traditionalist interests are direct consequences of this diversity. There is thus a sense in which it may not be possible to actually realize the reform and realignment advocated by the "new right" and its allies in the electronic church, without confronting this diversity directly.

The lines are thus drawn, and the debate rages on, finding one particular focus in the question of how and whether the electronic church is an authentic religious, and not just a social or political, expression.

The chapters in this section address the issue of authenticity from very different vantage points. William F. Fore, a prominent commentator on the phenomenon of the electronic church who comes from the liberal, mainline perspective, raises important questions about the social and theological roots of the new religious broadcasting. In the process, he presents a cogent argument for the traditional position of the mainstream church with regard to religious broadcasting.

Rabbi Bruce Abrams presents a critique of some of the theological assumptions underlying the electronic church, In doing so, he identifies the rationale for why religious broadcasting has not been embraced by the Jewish community and why the Jewish community is often the topic of discussion in religious broadcasts.

Finally, we present a conversation with Paul Kurtz. Kurtz is a leading American Humanist, and a prominent and widely published spokesperson for humanist ideas. Humanism has become a major target of the religious right, and Kurtz responds to some of those attacks, as well as bringing some unique insights into the electronic church's role in the new right movement.

These perspectives, in contrast with those of the advocates for evangelical religious broadcasting, suggest that many of the ready assumptions about it have been too easily "taken on faith" by observers and critics. There is more to religion than the electronic church, and there are more perspectives on the place of religious media in American life, than we often hear.

REFERENCES

Armstrong, B. (1979). *The electric church*. Nashville, TN: Thomas Nelson.
Muggeridge, M. (1977). *Christ and the media*. Grand Rapids, MI: Eerdmans.

10

"Living Church" and "Electronic Church" Compared

William F. Fore

It is ironic that the electronic church, which both the press and public have tied closely to the evangelical churches, is in fact a source of considerable embarrassment to most evangelicals. When the National Association of Evangelicals met shortly after Jimmy Swaggart confessed to sexual misdeed, the *New York Times* (1988) reported not only their "chagrin" over that scandal, but also their rejection of Pat Robertson, a former top television evangelist, in a straw poll of presidential candidates.

The term "evangelicals" in America has come to mean those who stress fidelity to the traditional doctrines of the Protestant Reformation, but who also stress the importance of the experiential over the intellectual, and religious fervor over liturgy—a group comprising some 10 to 35 percent of the population.

But fundamentalists, such as Jerry Falwell, generally reject inclusion in this group, preferring to comprise a tiny minority even within conservative Christianity. Charismatics, who stress speaking in tongues and other dramatic indications of direct experience with the divine, stand somewhere between the 2 in terms of inclusiveness; Pat Robertson, Jim and Tammy Bakker, and Jimmy Swaggart are part of this relatively small charismatic group. And both Robert Schuller and James Kennedy, 2 of the top 10 electronic church preachers, are members of mainline churches and might reject identification with some evangelicals.

One important implication of this diversity is that the rapid increase in evangelical church membership, such as in the Southern Baptist Convention, should not be confused with participation or even a relationship with the electronic church groups.

Actually, the electronic church has not been growing. A recent A.C. Neilsen report (1986) indicates that viewership for the electronic church programs probably peaked around 1978, and has been holding steady or even decreasing ever since. The Annenberg-Gallup study revealed that the total number of viewers who watch as little as 15 minutes per week is about 13.3 million, if it is assumed that 2.4 persons on average are watching each television set (Gerbner et al., 1984). However, if one assumes the much more likely figure of 1.8 persons per household (since these programs are most often found in fringe time), then the same Annenberg-Gallup data reveal that the number of persons watching *one hour* of more per week (a more reasonable definition of a regular viewer than a mere 15 minutes) is 4.84 million persons, or 2.17 percent of the total population.

While there is considerable diversity in doctrine and style, the major televangelists—the 10 or so who attract the lion's share of public attention—have many characteristics in common. All depend upon a single highly charismatic leader. All produce weekly, and in some cases, daily, television programs which feature expensive, high-quality production. All utilize a combination of television-satellite-cable delivery services which are paid on a commercial basis. All employ sophisticated WATTS-line telephone referral-computerized newsletter contact and follow-up.

It is these whom I define here as the electronic church, while cautioning that many parts of religious broadcasting are not included in such a definition. The mainline churches have produced programming in cooperation with local stations and national networks since the very beginning of radio and television, and these programs continue today at a reduced level as broadcasters have discovered the financial rewards of selling time to the electronic church rather than to churches as a public service. Also there are literally thousands of local radio and television religious programs which are not related to the electronic church phenomenon but which continue to be broadcast every week.

HISTORICAL ROOTS

I have described elsewhere how the electronic church phenomenon may be understood in the historical context of the Great Awakenings and revivals of America (Fore, 1987). Briefly, there have been 4 of these periods of intense religious activity in America. The first, from 1730 to 1760, helped to create a cohesive unity out of the colonialists and to inspire them to press for their freedom from Great Britain. The second, from 1800 to 1830, further clarified the "manifest destiny" of America and its expansion. The third, from 1890 to 1920, helped people come to terms with the challenge of the science and technology and inspired them to attempt "to make the world safe for democracy." We currently are in the midst of a fourth "awakening," which began about 1960 and may last for another decade, this time in response to the disillusionment which followed the Vietnam War and the gradual decline of American hegemony worldwide.[1]

---

[1] For a more detailed analysis of the Great Awakenings, see McLoughlin (1978).

Each awakening has been characterized at first by a national feeling of disillusionment and despair, a lack of clear guidance and sense of direction. In each cycle the first response has been an admonition to return to the past, a call back to the fundamentals, expressed by such preachers as Jonathan Edwards, Timothy Dwight, and Billy Sunday. It requires no great leap of imagination to understand the preaching of Jerry Falwell and Jimmy Swaggart in this context. But in each cycle, there eventually developed a reaction against this call to the past, and instead a new integration of faith and values within the society helped move it forward to tackle the pressing issues of the day.

It remains to be seen how our current Great Awakening plays out in history. But the electronic church phenomenon is almost certainly a significant expression of the first stage in the present cycle.

The electronic church has its roots in 2 additional social factors. One was the political cooptation of televangelists in the late 1970s. When Paul Weyrich began to develop the concept of the Moral Majority, he realized the political movement needed a religious component. He chose Jerry Falwell, then the relatively obscure preacher of one of the nation's fastest growing churches and an experienced television personality. Falwell seized the opportunity and was catapulted by the press into national prominence. His success resulted in many other evangelists, including Rex Humbard, Jimmy Swaggart, Jim Bakker, and James Robison, becoming politicized despite the historical aversion most conservative preachers have toward politics. By 1986 it was clear that Falwell's group was not able to develop decisive clout at the ballot box. Falwell was not even able to elect a Republican to Congress in his own district, and the Republican party ceased to take Falwell seriously.

The other social factor was the emergence of broadcast deregulation which emerged tentatively in the 1970s and became full-blown in 1980. At the very time that televangelists had discovered the possibilities of the computer-generated direct mail technique for fund raising, the FCC, led by the new Reagan administration, removed virtually all public service obligations from radio and television broadcasters. Rather than being obliged, in exchange for their license, to ascertain the public needs and interests and provide programs which met those needs and interests regardless of whether or not the programs were revenue producing, stations were now free to sell "their" time to the highest bidder. Soon Sunday mornings became a new source of income for stations, and a new opportunity for those televangelists who knew how to raise the necessary income to pay the bills.

THE MESSAGE

In the context of the Great Awakening cycle with its call to return to the authority and certainty of the past, the message of the electronic church

preachers is fairly predictable. Peter Horsfield (1981) identifies the themes
of the program as follows:

1. The programs are authoritative, in an era when authority in general
   seems to be in question. The hosts of these programs tend to embody
   this ideal of authority.
2. The programs stress the individual as the basic social unit. The individual is thus encouraged to take action, either by supporting the program, being "born again," or both.
3. The programs stress mainstream American social values. Effort is re-
   warded, the free enterprise system is valued, and there is equal opportunity for all to succeed. Horsfield contrasts this view of the evangelists
   with the mainline network programs which more frequently are critical
   of these values.
4. They reinforce belief systems of their viewers by presenting attractive
   and socially recognized personalities who add credence to them.
5. They see the faith struggle to be one of competition between God and
   the Devil.
6. They are grounded in an eschatology which is meaningful for viewers
   who may see their own circumstances to be hopeless. The programs
   proclaim the end of the world, but yet feature guests and a worldview
   that endorses success in the here and now.

The basic values expressed in the electronic church are found not so
much in its rhetoric as in the overall image of its programs. These values
are: Winning, being Number One, getting your just due, wealth, power,
prestige, and beauty—in other words, the essence of the American Dream.
The televangelists tend to reinforce the secular culture's worldview in their
program style, role models, and selection of content, while at the same time
attacking it in their use of traditional religious rhetoric. Behind the "God
bless you" and "the Lord loves you" lies a dominant visual environment
that reinforces the basic values of American secularism.

We are dealing here with a total cultural situation. The role of the
electronic church in society, and the assumptions and worldview that it
represents, greatly influence its message and methods. Sociologist Wade
Clark Roof (1984) points out that there are two streams in American religious thought. One is traditional Christian conservatism, which deals with
the Bible literally, accepts a supernatural world, and worships a God who
acts in an anthropomorphic way in response to human appeals. The other is
traditional Christian liberalism, which accepts the findings of science, looks
at the world in terms of observable data and cause and effect, rejects a
supernatural reality, and worships a God who transcends reality but is
constantly revealed through it.

These 2 streams run in tandem within the mainline churches, with many parishioners adhering more to one view or the other. But the mainline churches have failed to unify these streams into a single and meaningful whole, and this resulted in a crisis of confidence. People who are essentially supernatural in their worldview find the mainline church too worldly and concerned with the here and now; they are moving out of the mainline churches into the growing evangelical churches. At the same time, many people who are essentially informed by the scientific worldview reject the supernatural and find the mainline churches too otherworldly; they too are leaving these churches in favor of even more liberal expressions, or else are rejecting institutional church affiliation altogether.

This scenario accounts for both the phenomenal increase in evangelical church membership as well as the decrease in mainline membership. According to this analysis, the mainline churches will continue to dwindle until such time as they can put together a view which makes sense to people living in an age that is informed by scientific methodology, but who at the same time believe in an immanent and transcendent God. While a few mainline churches have managed to bridge this gap, most have failed to do so. In communication terms, these mainline churches don't know what their message is, don't know who their audience is, and don't know what methods to use to communicate.

On the other hand, the conservative churches know exactly what their message is, because it is circumscribed in a clear, explicit, and closed system. The message is something written down, diagramed, a *thing*. The only communication question for this group is how to transfer that information into people's awareness most effectively. They call it "reaching people with the Gospel"—the hypodermic needle approach, long rejected by communication theorists. The issue for these conservative Christians is not whether people are asking the right questions, or how their message relates to the felt needs and interests of the audience, or even what meanings are conveyed by the messages in the mind of the recipient. The task of the televangelist is infinitely simpler than the task of the mainline churches, because they know exactly who they are, what they stand for, what their worldview is. They need only find the most "persuasive" medium to communicate it.

Thus evangelists seized on radio at a very early date, then audiovisuals, later television, and now satellite and cable television. We can depend on the conservative religious groups always to be in the forefront of the latest communication technology, because their only question is how to fashion the largest hammer to drive their particular nail.

Of course, such an approach violates not only the canons of good communication theory, but also good education methodology and community theory. Communication which respects the individual must take into account what the listener-viewer brings to the situation, what views are already held, what questions are asked, what needs are unmet. It requires feedback which takes into account people's perceptions. It takes into account the dialogical growth process. The televangelist's approach is bad theology as well, because it reduces the Almighty to a closed set of propositions and formulas, violates the integrity of the individual, and rejects the possibilities for novelty and growth.

But while the approach of the electronic church may be unsatisfactory in terms of good communication, education, and theology, it is very attractive to those who crave a simple and precise solution to life's complex and bewildering problems. The point is that once one accepts either the conservative or liberal religious worldview, one must also accept the consequences in terms of the constraints as to what media, messages, techniques, and processes can and cannot be employed by the communicator.

PROS AND CONS

We can identify 3 areas where the electronic church has made a positive contribution to religious outreach. One is that it has recognized the needs of a segment of the population, probably between 2 percent and 4 percent, who feel especially threatened and uneasy about what is going on around them. These people believe that their personal and family lives are threatened by outside forces over which they have very little control. They have considerable self-doubt about their own worth, but do not trust authority figures such as doctors, lawyers, politicians, or the clergy. They feel that they have not received their just due in society, that they are unrecognized, unappreciated, unloved. This sense of malaise and alienation has been clearly identified by the televangelists. The mainline churches, on the other hand, have neither identified this problem nor have they attempted to speak to it.

Therefore, these same people are in many cases intensely bitter about the failures of the local churches. They characterize the mainline churches as dull, unfriendly, insensitive, dying, dead, unscriptural, not Gospel-filled, agents of the Devil—in other words, not meeting their needs.[2]

One can conclude that there are many people, living right next door to the mainline churches, whose needs have neither been identified nor met by those churches. Clearly the mainline churches need to recognize that the electronic churches are a judgement on their own failure to recognize and meet a need. Indeed, the case can be made that if the mainline churches were doing their job in meeting the needs of these alienated people, there would be much less receptivity for the electronic church.

Second, at its best, the electronic church is effectively meeting the specialized needs of some people, particularly the ill, the shut-ins, the el-

---

[2] For a detailed analysis of 500 letters in response to an article on the electronic church written for *TV Guide* see Fore (1981).

derly—those who cannot relate to their community in other ways. The programs of some of the televangelists bring a new kind of community to these people and undoubtedly are helping some of them. For example, Robert Schuller's *Hour of Power* brings a sense of drama, worship, and church to some people who get it no other way. The *700 Club* provides assistance to persons through program elements which teach nutrition and family budgeting and other aids to coping in an increasingly complex world.

Third, again at its best, the electronic church makes contact with people whom the mainline church have no way of contacting, people who, for a variety of reasons, simply feel uncomfortable in a middle-class church environment. The televangelists are identifying these people and referring them to counseling and to community groups which in some cases can provide significant help. Some suicidal people have been helped back from the brink by telephone calls and referrals. Pat Robertson claims that more than 25,000 persons are counseled each year by the *700 Club,* and the mainline churches need to take this as another valid criticism of their own failure to create communication systems to reach the people in their own local community. Instead, people have to dial an 800 number and reach someone in a cubicle in Virginia Beach, Virginia, in order to find an available and compassionate listener.

But while the electronic church has some positive elements, it has negative elements as well, and these negative elements considerably outweigh the positive. For while the televangelists are able to identify the sense of alienation in people with remarkable accuracy, they are all too ready to take advantage of this alienation and to use it to their own advantage. Many of the televangelists systematically exacerbate and build on self-doubt in precisely the same manner as commercial broadcasting.

The tactics of these preachers in many ways are psychologically ingenious. They are "religious" expressions of the secular utilitarian culture which tends to use people as things. In the long run many of their techniques have serious harmful effects.

A favorite electronic church technique can be called the "successful people" syndrome. Almost every popular evangelical program includes interviews with persons who have succeeded in business and life in general— a singer or a well-known businessman who describes how bad things were until God was brought into the picture, but how now all is wonderful, give God the glory. The message is simple: Believe in God and all will be wonderful for you, too.

There is a serious problem with this tactic. When hopeful converts begin to realize that they are *not* becoming especially wealthy, are *not* getting all the money or things they want, what can they do? Their religion prevents them from blaming God, or even from blaming the preacher who claims to represent God. They can only blame themselves, and this tends to push them into even more self-doubt and alienation. The "successful people" approach is bad psychology as well as bad theology.

Another favorite technique is the "give-to-get ploy," used in one way or another by every major televangelist. The message is: "If you give—really give—to God (which means to that evangelist), then God will return that gift to you and much more." The evangelists are not talking about spiritual gifts; they parade before the television screen those who have Made It Big, who asked for a car and got it, who wanted money for the down payment on a house and got it, who asked, and gave—and got.

Oral Roberts calls this the "Seed Faith" concept. You say you haven't gotten something back from God? Then you just haven't given enough! And so this "heavenly lottery" attracts countless thousands who even borrow money to support their evangelist and thus increase the chance of hitting it big like the folks they see on television. But as in any other lottery, the losers outnumber the winners a thousand to one.

The electronic church surely meets the needs of some people. When one is talking about an aggregate of several millions, there must be some people in the group whose needs are being met in adequate and genuine ways. However, on balance the electronic church has tended to mislead people and to provide them with a message that has every little relationship to the Gospel of Jesus Christ which they claim to serve.

Heresies

The messages of the televangelists embody 3 of the classic heresies which have dogged our Christian tradition almost from its beginning. One is *Manichaeism,* which in the third century proposed a dualistic world that separates everything into light and darkness, spirit and matter, good and evil. The electronic church preachers tend to pose very issue this way: Either you are good or bad; America is God's while Russia is the devil's; accept Jesus and be saved or expect the hellfires of the damned on judgment day. Manichaeism was rejected by Augustine as intellectually and morally inadequate, but it has persisted in many forms throughout Christian history, and is evident today in most television religion.

A second electronic evangelist heresy is *Palagianism,* a distortion of Christian dogma that promises considerable earthly rewards for the faithful. Palagianism denies that original sin exists, affirms that "If I ought, I can," and holds that everyone has the power within themselves to not sin but to do whatever they truly desire, so long as they have faith. Palagianism is a particularly popular American distortion of historic Christianity. It was popularized in the 1950s by Norman Vincent Peale, and more recently by his spiritual descendant, Robert Schuller, though it is evident to some degree in all of the electronic church evangelists.

A third heresy among the televangelists is *Nominalism* ("Speak the name of the Lord Jesus Christ and you will be saved"), which fits nicely into the electronic church's emphasis that the individual need merely "name the name" or "accept the Lord Jesus Christ" to be saved.

Perhaps the strongest appeal of the electronic church, and its greatest heresy, is that is gives religious sanction to the American tradition of utilitarian self-interest. Robert Bellah (1980) has shown that American culture from its early beginnings has held 2 views in tension: On the one hand, the Biblical understanding of community based on the notion of charity for all members, a community supported by public and private virtue; and, on the other hand, the utilitarian understanding that community is a neutral state which allows individuals to pursue the maximization of their self-interest— the Spencer/Locke tradition.

The electronic church actually harmonizes these conflicting traditions by corrupting the Biblical tradition so that religion itself becomes the key to maximizing self-interest, and there is no effective linkage to virtue, charity, or community. This corruption of the fundamental Biblical concept of conscience into self-interest is one of the most serious of all the electronic church's distortions.

What the Churches Can Do

How should mainline churches respond to this new media-religion? What positive steps can they take to be involved in the mass media while recognizing the dangers of being coopted by it?

The first positive response of the churches must be to continue to work in the area of programming. Just because there are dangers does not mean the churches should abandon the enormous potential for good that television represents. But the solution does not lie in the directions taken by the electronic church.

Attempts by the mainline churches to examine the moral and spiritual views of Biblical Christianity in relation to society today reveals an area of great moral ambiguity. Transcendent religious values are so much at odds with society's values that it is difficult and often impossible to deal seriously with significant issues on radio and television. Some sensitization through mass media is possible, of course. But the dangers of being taken in by the media are so subtle and so powerful that it is incumbent upon religious communicators to approach all programming in television and radio with the greatest caution and theological sensitivity.

The objective in using radio and television should be *pre-evangelism*. You cannot *be* the church on radio and television. I doubt that you can even give the answers to serious religious questions satisfactorily on radio and television. *But you can raise the right questions,* help people ask who they are and what they are here for and whether they have any worth and if so why.

The church, therefore, should use the mass media as *preparation for the gospel*. This involves 3 steps. First, it requires exploring with people what Paul Tillich calls the "boundary situations," those places where modern men and women reach the limits of their human existence, where they sense a lack of personal meaning, a fear of being useless and of not having worth. Second, it requires affirming through the media those persons and events that have been able to deal with these "boundary situations" creatively and with faith: News stories from Manila and South Africa; biographies of Gandhi, Martin Luther King, Mother Teresa, and Archbishop Tutu. And third, it requires pointing to the churches as the place where people can go to begin to work out their salvation, find community, and discover the power of confession and forgiveness.

Religious broadcasting can help lead people to understand what the gospel message is, and can encourage them to go where they can get more answers and possibly, to use a decidedly nonmedia term, become saved. That place is, simply, the church. Television should be a signpost, *a servant of the local church—and never the other way around*.

Believers should not be asked to support television ministries because television is the church. Television must be used as a tool, but used very critically, making certain never succumbing to the temptations of the power that the medium tends to confer, never allowing church leaders to become media celebrities, never allowing programs to become caught up in the demands of television so that the gospel becomes debased to the point where it ceases to be the Gospel at all.

The second positive response of the churches should be *media education*. Parishioners must be systematically exposed to the cultural biases and distorted values systems of our culture in the light of the prophetic visions of the Old Testament and the harsh demands of the New.

Unfortunately, church leaders, both nationally and locally, still tend to view television as if it were merely a major entertainment diversion which keeps people away from church, rather than as an alternative religious force which is wooing people into a whole new way of thinking about, and living in, our world. Real media education will not become effective until it has penetrated the thinking of every theologian, pastor, and parishioner- and among other things, this calls for a change in approach to the training in every theological school.

Finally, the churches must continue to work for *media reform*. Television creates images of such power and such appeal that in fact it functions as though it were a religion. But in addition, it functions with such centralized economic and political power that genuine competition of ideas in our society is becoming suppressed. One talk of the Christian churches is to challenge this power and principality, to work toward ways of opening up the communication process in society for the widest possible exchange of views and ideas.

There will be no remedial action to counter the overdose of violence on television, or to achieve a thorough airing of all positions on matters of public importance, or an opportunity for the public to hear "fringe" positions, or the broadcasting of quality programming for children, so long as the television industry is able to neutralize regulation through its political and economic power. The freedom of mass media without corresponding responsibility is the freedom of the "free fox in the free henhouse," an intolerable social situation of media domination and repression that could be fatal to religious freedom of expression, and even fatal to the democratic process itself.

In summary, the electronic church aspect of religious television today is driven primarily by considerations of economics and power. Expecting to use the enormous power of television for their own purposes, the televangelists have instead been used by it. They have had to conform their messages to meet the demands of TV—demands to get larger audiences to get more money to get more stations to get even larger audiences. In order to get larger audiences, their messages had to please the audience, and never offend them, and that requirement becomes fatal to any authentic proclamation of the Christian faith.

It is an open question as to whether the televangelists were corrupted by the power of the media, or whether they simply found in the media a comfortable fit for their kind of religious evangelism. Undoubtedly both factors have been at work. The evangelists wittingly bought into the world of commercial television, certainly in order to reap its rewards of vast audience reach, and also perhaps to benefit from its other rewards of money, power, and prestige. In any case, they used one of the most powerful institutions in our culture, and, inevitably, that power began to corrupt them. The scandals of Oral Roberts, Jim and Tammy Bakker, and Jimmy Swaggart are only the surface manifestations of this corruption; far more serious are their programs which denigrate authentic Christianity in the name of Christianity and make use of God in the name of God, misleading millions of persons about the nature of genuine religious experience.

As the television ministries turned into show business, and the ministers into celebrities, the Gospel became no Gospel at all, but a parody which, in religious terms, was heretical and idolatrous. Unfortunately, as in the case of most heresies and idolatries, their messages actually conformed to many of the deeply rooted values of the secular society, and so gathered and greatly pleased an audience. Fortunately, this audience is small, and is not growing.

One can hope that the experience of the electronic church will afford a useful object lesson for both mainline and evangelical churches as they consider how to relate their own understanding of religion to television and other mass media in the years ahead.

REFERENCES

Bellah, R. (1980). *Varieties of civil religion*. New York: Harper.

Fore, W. (1981). Beyond the electronic church. *The Christian Century, 2*, 29–30.

Fore, W. (1987). *Television and religion: The shaping of faith, values and culture*. Minneapolis, MN: Augsburg.

Gerbner, G., Gross, L., Hoover, S., Morgan, M., Signorielli, N., Cotugno, H., & Wuthnow, R. (1984). *Religion and television*. New York: Committee on Electric Church Research.

Horsfield, P. (1981, October). And now a word from our sponsor: Religious programs on American television. *Review Francaise D'Etudes Americaines, 12*, 260-274.

McLoughlin, W. (1978). *Revivals, awakenings, and reform*. Chicago, IL: University of Chicago Press.

News of the Week Section. (1988, March 13). *New York Times*, p. B1.

Nielsen, A.C. (1986, November). Report on devotional programs, November 1986. *Neilsen Station Index*. New York: Author.

Roof, W. (1984). *Community and commitment: Religious plausibility in a liberal Protestant church*. New Haven, CT: Elsevier.

11

Why Televangelists are Bad for Judaism and Why Judaism is Bad Televangelism

Bruce Abrams

In the early days of television, the networks made free air time available to all the major religious groups. It became a major vehicle for the evangelists. The Jews, however, have never had a national religious broadcast. I believe they never will. There are 2 related reasons. First, Jews do not believe that one must be Jewish to be saved. This removes the compulsive theological need to rescue a sinner from the flames of hell. Second, Jews do not actively seek converts. We believe that all good monotheists, be they Christian, Moslem, or Jew, have an equal place in the world to come. Since there is no theological need to be Jewish to be saved, there is no practical need for the masses to convert to become Jewish. Consequently, the Jews will never embrace a television ministry as the major purpose of religious television is conversion. It is just not the Jewish way, and never will be. That is not to say that Jews are adverse to television publicity.

Preachers and Rabbis and Imams are all in the news today. It seems that the future of religion belongs to wild-eyed mystical fanatics not only in Christianity, but also in Judaism and Islam. But let's take a moment to examine their beliefs and their history, for if we are to understand the future we had better understand the past.

Judaism is the unquestioned founder and father of all Western religions. Abraham is the father and Jesus and Mohammed are his 2 sons. Abraham began a long journey of monotheistic faith in the Twelfth Chapter of the Book of *Genesis*. "Now the Lord said, 'Get thee out of thy country, and from thy kindred, and from thy father's house, into the land that I will show thee'" (Genesis 12:1). God promised further, "I will bless them that bless thee and him that curseth thee will I curse" (Genesis 12:3).

The lesson of the father was not lost on the sons. Judaism became central to both Christianity and Islam. Said Jesus, the rabbi, "I come not to destroy the Torah, but to fulfill it." Said Mohammed, the desert leader who patterned himself after Moses, "the Jews are the People of the Book."

The mystical apocalyptic strains in Islam are reshaping our world today in the blood and fire of *Jihad*—"holy war." But, for now, we will leave this youngest child aside because he is beyond the scope of this essay on Christian fundamentalism. I only bring him in to point out the rise of similar phenomenon throughout our world today; namely, the emergence of a vindictive, vengeful, fanatical right wing populism that cloaks itself in the mantle of falsely pious self-righteous religious mysticism. The leading proponents of such an ideology in America are the television preachers Jimmy Swaggart and Pat Robertson and Jerry Falwell. There are major differences between the fundamentalists like Falwell and Pentecostalists like Robertson and Swaggart. The Pentecostalists believe in the "gift of tongues," and the fundamentalists believe such gifts come not from God, but from the devil.

One thing they do share, however, is an obsessive fascination with the Jews. The voice of God speaking to Abraham reverberates deeply within their theology: "In thee shall all the families of the earth be blessed" (Genesis 12:3). Indeed, they think they are blessing us with the pivotal role in which they place the Jews. But as one wise soul put it, "With such friends, who needs enemies?"

There was no small measure of disappointment on the part of Christiandom when Jews did not convert *en masse* to the new religion. They come to call the Christian Scriptures the New Testament and the Jewish Scriptures the Old Testament, with the idea that Christianity "a religion of love" had replaced Judaism, "a religion of law." This was despite the fact that Jesus said he came to replace nothing. Even Luther, who during the early phases of the Reformation condemned the "passion preachers who do nothing else but exaggerate the Jews' misdeeds against Christ and thus embitter the hearts of the faithful against them" came to heap violent fury on the head of the Jew. In 1542 he wrote a pamphlet called the "Jews and Their Lies" in which he referred to the Jews as disgusting vermin and called for 8 specific anti-Jewish actions: (a) Burn all synagogues; (b) destroy Jewish dwellings; (c) confiscate Jewish holy books; (d) forbid rabbis to teach; (e) forbid Jews to travel; (f) forbid Jews to charge interest on loans and confiscate Jewish property; (g) force Jews into slave labor; and (h) expulsion. Sadly, all 8 of the actions that Luther suggested be taken against the Jews have occurred. And throughout the centuries Luther's ferocious anti-Semitic language has provided fuel for hatred and prejudice.

Charismatic, passionate Christian preachers from Luther to Swaggart have always put the Jews on center stage and have always been disappointed when we did not convert. That is why the Jews do not trust the television preachers. In spite of their seemingly strong support for Israel, we are suspicious of an underlying anti-Semitism particularly when we examine their beliefs carefully. As Irving Kirstol has said, "It is their theology, but our Israel" (see Silberman, 1985, p. 352).

Their Armaggedon theology calls for an eschatalogical scene that goes like this. According to the book of Revelation, an anti-Christ will emerge and unite the world under his rule. (Throughout history, the faithful have claimed such people as Henry Kissinger, the Pope, and Peter the Great—among many others—to be the anti-Christ.) When the anti-Christ appears, 144,000 Jews will convert to Christianity. They will be like super Jimmy Swaggarts converting millions. Then Russia will invade Israel. During the nuclear holocaust that follows, the faithful will ascend to Heaven to watch the final war—the Armaggedon between the Christ and the anti-Christ. This ascension is called "the rapture." After the Armaggedon, the Messiah will begin his 1,000 year reign on earth. During these 1,000 years, all who did not believe in the Messiah and survive the Armageddon will have a final opportunity to convert. If they do not, they will burn forever in Hell.

And thus the Jews will fade from history. The television preachers believe we will have fulfilled our role when we either convert, are nuked, or burn forever in Hell. Thanks, but no thanks.

Some questions: (a) Is the flamboyant theology of televangelists really "religious?" and (b) Why is there no parallel phenomenon among the Jews? In other words, why is there no Jewish Jimmy Swaggart?

Are these programs really religious? I have a bit of theological advice for the televangelical community. You see, like Pat Robertson, I get requests every now and then to do a miracle. The guys will be going out to play golf and they'll say, "Gee, Rabbi, can't you do something about the weather?" To which I always replay, "I'd like to, but I'm just in sales—not in management."

That is the problem with these television preachers. They forget who's boss. And because they have a block of the faithful, because they can raise hundreds of millions of dollars, because they can fool some of the people all of the time—they think of God as another employee of the electronic church. They become "management" able to change the weather and find hostages in Lebanon and locate nonexistent missiles in Cuba. Sadly, God becomes reduced to the salesman.

Can there be a greater sin? Can there be a greater perversion of religion? Are they really "religious?" In a word—No!

Where have they gone wrong? And why is their electronic church so profoundly and absolutely not Jewish? Why is Jimmy Swaggart not a Jew?

This is not to say that rabbis have not sinned. Rabbis, ministers, priests, imams, all clergy persons are imperfect servants of a perfect God. And, as imperfect beings, clergy of all faith have sinned. Jimmy Swaggart is not the only clergyman to commit a sexual indiscretion. Jim and Tammy Bakker are not the first to steal money from the collection plate.

Judaism teaches us to hate the sin, but to love the sinner. We must forgive Swaggart and the Bakkers as people. In other words, if they repent of their sins, Judaism teaches us to forgive their deeds, but not the twisted theology that caused the deeds.

Television preachers believe 2 things that put them completely outside of religion as understood by the Jews. First, they say *act now, convert now, be saved now*. In Judaism, we believe talk is cheap and deeds are essential. We believe the world is saved by your hands, by *mitzvoth*, good deeds—and not by the so called good intentions in your head. But we do not believe in impulsive action, particularly when it comes to conversion. When they asked Rabbi Akiba in the Talmud which is more important, deeds or study, he answered study, "For without study, we will not know what to do." In Judaism, study comes first. Our synagogue is called a *schul*, which is the yiddish word for school. When ranking relative importance, we say you can sell a synagogue to become a school, but not vice versa. The house of study—school—comes even before the house of prayer. And fully one-third of every Jewish religious service is given over to the study of Torah.

The television preacher may tell you to act now before it is too late, but Judaism teaches study before you act. Open your mind before you make a decision.

Why do they insist we act now? It is because their second belief is the gates of Hell are waiting to consume you in the eternal fires of damnation if you are not saved now. There is nothing comparable in Judaism.

Compare Brother Jimmy whose unforgiving and unloving theology includes the eternal suffering and damnation even of infants to Rabbi Akiba. Rabbi Akiba lived during the time of the Roman persecution of the Jews in the first and second century of the Common Era. He himself became a martyr when the Romans stripped the very flesh from his body. And, yet, his theology included only love and forgiveness for all sinners, even for his enemies, the Romans, and their dreaded tax collectors.

It is said that Rabbi Akiba once walked through a graveyard and saw a charcoal burner who was scurrying around like a frantic beast of burden carrying an unbearably heavy load of wood. Akiba turned to him and said, "Why do you carry such a heavy burden upon your shoulders? If you are a slave, I shall appeal to your master. I shall redeem you, and set you free. If you are poor, I shall give you charity. Please let me help you."

The man, however, replied, "I'm not of the living, but of the dead. And my punishment throughout eternity is day after day, I am fated to gather an overwhelming burden of wood. And then all through the night I set the wood on fire so that I might burn in its flames. I burn and feel pain, but I am never consumed. And so it goes, day after day, night after night. I am the only one ever to receive such eternal hell."

"My son," asked Akiba, "What have you done to receive such a cruel punishment?"

"I was a tax collector for the Romans," replied the suffering soul. "I favored the rich and I was a scourge to the poor, breaking their backs with unfair taxes just as my back is breaking now from the wood. Truly I am reaping what I sowed. I even stooped so low as to seduce an affianced virgin on the Day of Atonement. I ruined her wedding day and defiled the holiest day of the Jewish calendar. And worse yet, I paid no attention to my bastard son born of the virgin. I don't even know where he is today."

"Is there no relief from your punishment?" asked Rabbi Akiba. At first the man replied, "no," but on second thought he said, "I did hear them say my punishment would be relaxed if my son would stand up in the congregation and recite 'Blessed is His Glorious Kingdom forever and ever.' But how will we ever find my son?"

"I will try," said Akiba, "give me the virgin's name." So Akiba sought high and low, went from town to town. He found the son, an uneducated ruffian like the father. Together they fasted for 40 days and 40 nights. They studied together. And the son stood up in the Congregation and said "Blessed is His Glorious Kingdom forever and ever." And, that night the poor soul came to Rabbi Akiba in a dream and told him: "I have been rescued from eternal hell." And from that moment on, even the lowest sinner is always ultimately forgiven. There is no devil. There is no eternal Hell. There is no real religious foundation as defined by Judaism for the outrageous claims of the television preachers.

Nonetheless, there is a future for television preachers. The recent scandals will destroy the periphery but not the central core of believers. However, this core is clearly non-Jewish; they will never draw Jews into their fold. And while there are right-wing Jewish fanatics like Meir Kahane, there will never be a Jewish Jimmy Swaggart.

But Jimmy and Pat and the Bakkers will not just go away, because you really can fool some of the people all of the time.

REFERENCES

Silberman, C.E. (1985). *A certain people—American Jews and their lives today.* New York: Summit.

12

In Conversation: Paul Kurtz, International Humanist and Ethical Union

with Robert Abelman

Q. *Rev. Donald Wildmon, president of the American Family Association (formerly the National Federation for Decency), has suggested in this volume (see Chapter 23) that the commercial television industry is dominated by secular humanists, especially within the creative ranks. This, according to Wildmon, has resulted in a humanist theology infiltrating prime-time programming which is undermining the Christian fabric of this country. As co-president of the International Humanist and Ethical Union, would you agree with this view? Has your organization taken a stand regarding these and similar accusations?*

A. I categorically deny these charges. Secular humanism involves at least 3 defining characteristics: (a) It is committed to a method of inquiry, namely the use of reason and scientific methods for establishing truth claims. Humanists wish to develop critical thinking in the schools, that is, to teach students to evaluate ideas by reference to reason and evidence. Given the nature of the medium, television is hardly a promoter of this basic approach, for it emphasizes visual imagery, color, and sound, rather than the development of cognitive skills; (b) Secular humanism draws upon the sciences for its cosmic outlook. But aside from a few programs on public television such as *Nova, Cosmos,* and *National Geographic,* television does not contribute very much to the public understanding of science. Secular humanism is highly skeptical of the supernatural view of reality, belief in the afterlife, and other Biblical claims, but there are almost no careful critiques of religious faith on commercial television. Instead the televangelists pour forth *probiblical* propaganda that is virtually unchallenged and; (c) Secular humanism is deeply committed to a set of humanistic values— such as the realization of human potential, the development of reason, and creativity in individuals. And it wishes to cultivate individual human growth, autonomy, freedom of choice, tolerance, and responsibility. Yet insofar as television focuses on consumer-oriented values and panders to taste, it hardly contributes to the evaluation and cultivation of qualitative appreciation, so vital to the full actualization of human powers. The charge that the outlook of secular humanism dominates the commercial television industry is simply false.

Q.   *Briefly define religion, as proposed in your book* Eupraxophy: Living Without Religion *(1989). Is secular humanism a religion?*

A.   Fundamentalist televangelists maintain that secular humanism is a religion and hence it should be banned from the public schools and other areas of social life. Religion in my view postulates the belief in a deity or dieties to which it owes prayer and obedience. But it is possible to lead a meaningful life without this faith. Secular humanism is not a religion. It is a philosophical, scientific, and ethical outlook, a *eupraxophy*, as I have defined it. This word is derived from Greek roots: *eu*—good, *praxis*—conduct or practice, *sophia*—philosophic and scientific wisdom. What it means is that one can live the good life, contribute to society, be a good citizen, develop moral values in one's children without formal identification with religion or a belief in God. Millions of Americans are secularists, and many famous Americans have experienced humanist values today and in the past: Jefferson, Paine, Madison, Franklin, Mark Twain, Robert Ingersoll, Margaret Sanger, Clarence Darrow, John Dewey, Sidney Hook, Carl Sagan, Isaac Asimov, and others.

Q.   *Based on this definition, how religious is commercial television programming?*

A.   Commercial TV hardly espouses or defends eupraxophy. It almost never criticizes the basic religious faith in God. Although it has of late criticized the moral excesses of some televangelists it has not defended a thoroughly secular and humanist outlook.

Q.   *How religious is evangelical television programming?*

A.   Such programming is much like commercial television in the sense that its main emphasis seems to be on hucksterism, that is, the selling of products and the raising of money. Sincere commitment and religious devotion to a creed have been overshadowed by vitriolic attacks on others in our pluralistic society. Instead of piety and virtue one hears political and moralistic sermonizing "in the name of God." It is a betrayal of the best of religion for its most vulgar excesses. It has abandoned tolerance, a basic humanistic virtue, so essential to a democratic society.

Q. *Clearly, there is no programming that explicitly claims to be purposefully supporting secular humanism or which is produced by secular humanist organizations. Why have secular humanists not taken
their theology to the airwaves?*

A. Secular humanists have been guests on television programs, but other
than 2 TV series that I moderated in the mid-1970s, which were
offered free of charge to stations and public service, we have not
sponsored our own programs per se. Perhaps we should. But it is more
difficult to "sell" reason, critical intelligence, and moderation to a
public instead of promises of instant salvation or by arousing fear of
hell and damnation. Commercial advertisers are sometimes reluctant
to advertize on programs that may offend the religious sensibilities of
some of their viewers.

Q. *Given the breadth and scope of evangelical broadcasting in this country, which often condemns secular humanism, is there no desire for
"equal time?"*

A. This is a good question. At one time I took the lead in asking the
commercial networks to provide some kind of balanced programming,
particularly in regard to the prominence of paranormal claims without
adequate scientific criticism. We even requested to the FCC to apply
the Fairness Doctrine, but were unsuccessful. Given the power of
television I think that where one side to a controversy is unfairly
attacked, it ought to be given the opportunity to respond. Given the
First Amendment there had been some reluctance to ask religious
programmers equal time. Now that the Fairness Doctrine has been
weakened the question is at present moot. I think that the Fairness
Doctrine ought to be brought back, and that it should be applied to
controversial issues including religion.

Q. *What do you believe to be the impact of the Bakker and Swaggart
scandals on religious belief and expression in this country?*

A. I hope that it demonstrates to the public loud and clear that not all of
the saints in the country are in the churches and the sinners outside;
and that belief in God or religious observance is no guarantee of
morality and virtue. The point is that there are millions of people who
do not belong to any religious denomination and yet are really decent
folks. Until the recent sex and money scandals televangelists were
largely immune to public criticism, though they feel free to indict
everyone else. Actually, *Free Inquiry,* published by the Council for
Democratic and Secular Humanism, was the first national magazine to
expose the shenanigans of the faith healers: Oral Roberts, Pat

Robertson, W.V. Grant, Peter Popoff, Ernest Angley, and others. We found that they were using the airwaves to deceive sick and gullible people who were promised miraculous cures. We exposed their efforts and showed that the claims of instantaneous cures could not be sustained by the evidence. Since then the media have been somewhat bolder in criticizing the gross indiscretions of televangelists. Still, religion is basically immune to open debate and critical examination. In a free and democratic society there should be far more give and take. If religious televangelists can proclaim their beliefs and espouse their values with impunity—as they are entitled to—then the public at least ought to have an opportunity to hear skeptical scientific and philosophical criticism of their claims. The television networks have in my judgment an obligation to present the alternative dissenting scientific and secular outlook.

REFERENCES

Kurtz, P. (1989). *Eupraxophy: Living without religion*. New York: Prometheus.

V

The Electronic
Collection Plate

Is there any American citizen who has not been caught in the wave of national attention given the sex-and-money scandal that rocked the PTL empire? The *Charlotte Observer* article (Shepard, 1987, p. 1A) that announced the combined $1.9 million salaries and bonuses of the Bakkers caught many casual observers of religious broadcasting by surprise . . . dumbfounded by the breadth and scope of the misappropriation of electronic church funds.

Interestingly, rumors of fatted calves within the evangelical community have circulated since the birth of broadcasting. Famed Pentacostal Preacher Aimee Semple McPherson was accused of faking her own kidnapping and ransom in the "Roaring Twenties." In the 1950s, Billy Graham first came under fire from the *Atlanta Constitution* regarding the handling of collections from his crusades. In response, he sought the advice of the National Council of Churches and subsequently placed himself on a salary paid by the Billy Graham Evangelistic Association. In the 1970s, the Evangelical Council for Financial Accountability was founded by several high-profile televangelists for the primary purpose of publically addressing the growing controversy regarding electronic church funds. More recently, the broadcast that God would "take Oral Roberts home" unless by March 21, 1987 believers came up with $4.5 million for missionary work became part of the tarnished heritage that is electronic religion.

Actually, Andrew Greeley (a noted Catholic priest and sociologist) has gone so far as to suggest that financial problems are not unique to the electronic church, but generalize to the living church and are inseparable from the business of religion itself. He argues: "I don't think the Catholics ought to throw too many stones, because what Jim and Tammy Bakker did was small potatoes indeed compared to the $2 billion Vatican banking scandal" (Barnhart, 1988, p. 110). Although Greeley further contends that "it ought not to be assumed implicitly that all electronic preachers are corrupt, money-grubbing hypocrites" (Greeley, 1988, p. 6), it is quite clear that recent escapades by Oral Roberts and the Bakkers have heightened criticism and concern. Clearly, the business of religion and religion as business are among the most talked about and longstanding controversies facing the electronic church.

In the chapters that follow, Joe Barnhart, Carl Henry, Robert Abelman, and Arthur Borden examine these controversies from highly divergent perspectives. Barnhart discusses the notion of the "New Folk Theology"—that is, how broadcasting has transformed the Gospel into the Gospel of Prosperity. He suggests that, when ministers appear on television day after day to deliver what they regard as the views of the deity, an occupational hazard develops: They risk identifying an increasing number of their own desires, ideas, and plans as devine promptings. Henry offers a theologian's perspective on evangelical fund raising, noting when and where the Gospel of Prosperity fails to take the Gospel into consideration. Abelman examines whether the controversies surrounding on-air solicitations are well-founded based on the frequency and quantities of monies requested by televangelists, the success of these solicitations, and the impact of the PTL scandal on contributions. Borden, president of the Evangelical Council for Financial Accountability, offers a perspective from the vantage point of the industry itself. Based on his experience with the volunteer membership of his organization, Borden defines the financial boundaries of the electronic church, dispels some age-old myths, and discusses the recent unpleasantness at PTL.

REFERENCES

Barnhart, J.E. (1988). *Jim and Tammy: Charismatic intrigue inside PTL*. Buffalo, NY: Prometheus Books.
Greeley, A.M. (1988, July 9). In defense of TV evangelism. *TV Guide*, pp. 4–7.
Shepard, C.E. (1987, April 18). PTL '86 payments to Bakkers: $1.6 million. *Charlotte Observer*, p. 1A.

13

Prosperity Gospel: A New Folk Theology

Joe E. Barnhart

In November 1988, Judge Reynolds closed the bankruptcy case of PTL and ruled that Jim and Tammy Bakker had taken excessive income from the PTL ministry. Bakker was ordered to return $4.9 million and Tammy over a half million. In addition, they were required to return together still another million. Jim Bakker's close assistant, David Taggart, must return $1 million as well. The question naturally arises as to how the PTL opulence and conspicuous consumption emerged within a tradition that had self-consciously sought to distinguish itself by denouncing "worldliness" and stressing "holiness?" The answer is that the "TV Preachers of the Golden Fleece" also subscribe to a second tradition, entrepreneurship, grounded in folk theology.

THE NEW FOLK THEOLOGY

Folk theology has always played a major role in religious movements because it is communicated directly to the laypeople in their own language. One of the most successful folk theologies was developed by John Wesley, 18th-century founder of the Methodist movement. In the 16th century a leading voice of the Protestant Reformation, Martin Luther, preached and penned a folk theology that has survived 5 centuries. Folk theology distinguished itself by responding to practical crises in the faith of a great portion of the populace. It is neither systematic nor intended to be scholarly theology. It is deliberately devotional, motivational, and inspirational. It may also function to communicate a moral challenge or to make sense of a social and moral crisis that many laypeople have been thrown into because of historical circumstances.

There is little question that Jim Bakker, Pat Robertson, and Oral Roberts have contributed to the emergence of a new folk theology. It goes under several names: The Gospel of Health and Wealth, Prosperity Theology, Deliverance Theology, or the Gospel of Success. Its principal 20th-century roots trace back to the swashbuckling faith healers of the big tent

159

and to popular God-wants-you-to-get-to-the-top sermons that reflect the theme of Norman Vincent Peale's best seller, *The Power of Positive Thinking*.

There is one key difference between the major modern proponents of the Gospel of Health and Wealth, on the one hand, and Martin Luther and John Wesley, on the other hand. Whereas Wesley and Luther had training in historical theology, Bakker and Roberts have none. Pat Robertson attended a seminary, but there is little indication that he has a great knowledge of the world of Biblical scholarship. Whereas Wesley and Luther could engage the theologians and Biblical scholars of their time in meaningful exchange, the big-time television charismatics appear to have avoided testing out their new theology in scholarly give-and-take exchanges.

The Prosperity Gospel of Bakker, Robertson, and Roberts is based on the following chain of arguments or premises from the faith healing tradition: First, God has supreme power over everything, including Satan, who plays a major role in the thinking of Pentecostals. Second, God does not want anyone to be sick. In only rare cases, God may cause someone to be ill, but only for the purpose of demonstrating his healing power. Third, Satan and his underworld sycophants are the prime cause of disease and illness. Fourth, God can overcome the power of the demons *if* the diseased and afflicted develop a proper relationship with God. Fifth, the gift of healing that Roberts, Robertson, and Bakker claim to have is double-barreled. It allows them (a) to make war on Satan and demons (even exorcising them when they have possessed someone), and (b) to inspire and instruct the infirm and diseased so that they may establish a "right relationship" with God and thereby open up the channels of healing.

As simple as it may seem, at least on the surface, Prosperity Theology takes the points above and inserts the phrase *economic hardship* or its equivalent in the place of *disease and illness*. In the place of *wholeness* or *health,* it substitutes *economic prosperity* and even *wealth*. In short, God can heal both the body and the bank account. According to this gospel, Jesus' death on the cross gained at least 3 victories for true believers: Deliverance of the soul from sin and hell, deliverance of the body from Satan and disease, and deliverance from poverty and economic hardship in this life.

The modern advocates of this new Prosperity Theology turn to Scripture for supportive proof texts. In John 10:10, Jesus is quoted as saying, "I am come that they might have life, and that they might have it more abundantly." In his books and on television, Pat Robertson relates stories of how believers set failing businesses back on the mountaintop of abundance and success by exercising great faith in Jesus and by contributing to Robertson's ministry. Oral and Richard Roberts are also fond of such testimonials. For Jim Bakker, Pat Robertson, and Oral and Richard Roberts, God has infallibly laid out steps that, if taken by Christian believers, will lead them to certain financial prosperity. A favorite scriptural text of the Bakkers is

Philippians 4:19: "But my God shall supply all your needs according to His riches in glory by Jesus Christ." Among the most successful television prophets of profit is the hard-selling Bob Tilton, who prays into the camera and loves to quote Deuteronomy 8:18: "But thou shalt remember the Lord thy God: For it is He that giveth thee power to get wealth." For people like Tilton, God intends wealth to go directly to Christian believers, not to sinners and unbelievers. And to reinforce this belief, he quotes again a Biblical text: "A good man leaves an inheritance to his children's children, but the sinner's wealth is laid up for the righteous" (Proverbs 13:22).

Similarly, A. A. Allen—an old-time Pentecostal evangelist, faith healer, and exorcist—is accredited with being the "John the Baptist" of the new folk theology. In 1962 he made the astounding proclamation that God had bestowed on him a "new anointing and new power to lay hands on the believers who gave $100 toward the support of our missionary outreach and bestow on each of them "POWER TO GET WEALTH" (Allen, 1963, p. i). He printed what he insisted was a verbatim report of the divine revelation to him:

> I am a wealthy God! Yea, I am not poor . . .
> But I say unto thee, claim my wealth in thy
> hand, yea, in thy purse and in thy substance.
> For behold I plan to do *a new thing in the
> earth!* . . . Yea, yea, yea, obey ye the
> servant of the Lord, for I have placed him in
> this place. Indeed, I did call him forth
> from his mother's womb. And I have kept my
> hand upon my servant. (pp. i–viii)

PROMISES AND HOW TO CLAIM THEM

Jet-set charismatic materialists look upon the Bible largely as a repository of promises, each of which has the Creator to back it up. As the new apostles of the "Name It, Claim It" religion, they name the blessing they want from God and then claim it as their rightful inheritance. When a fundamentalist oilman assured Pat Robertson that his drillers were on the verge of tapping into "the largest oil field ever discovered," Robertson grew very excited and said "it could revolutionize the fulfillment of Bible prophecy," since the oil was proclaimed to be in the land of Abraham ready to be claimed by those prepared to believe his promise as recorded in Scripture.

The Reverend Jim Spellman had no need to hustle snake oil or sink his money into Holy Land oil itself, for he found a slicker way to pump money straight out of the believers. Speaking at a 3-day Bible Prophecy Conference in Lakeland, Florida, Spellman sold copies of *The Great Treasure Hunt,* offering whiz-bang, scripture-riddled evidence that treasures lie in the sacred lands of Asher, Zebulan, Issachar, Ephraim, and Manasseh (Barnhart, 1986, 1988).

In his book *You Can Make It,* Jim Bakker (1988, p. 37) insists that the Creator has guaranteed prosperity on earth for every believer prepared to accept the guarantee. It is, of course, a practical question of exactly how one goes about claiming the putative promises. Bakker, as well as Oral and Richard Roberts, draw upon an agriculture model to reveal that many of the promises come into being only if the believers plant seed-faith. God will supply an abundant harvest if believers will take seed-faith from their wallets, purses, and checkbooks and plant them in God's vineyard or fertile ground.

The new folk theology teaches that the money planted in the hands of the God-appointed televangelists will not only benefit someone other than the giver, but *materially* benefit the *giver* himself or herself.

THE MEDIA AND THE MESSAGE

When televangelists elect to go on television daily, they wittingly or unwittingly commit themselves to becoming disciples of the Gospel of Prosperity. The financial needs of the daily program virtually require that they embrace the new folk-theology. Gifts of seed-faith are the late 20th-century indulgences essential to maintaining the structure of daily television ministry. Unlike the system of indulgences in the days of Martin Luther (which were designed to maintain the Roman hierarchy's superstructure), the modern Prosperity Gospel does not promise that the gifts will transfer a soul from purgatory to heaven. Rather, the promise entails a transfer from failure, sickness, and financial defeat to health and prosperity in the here-and-now.

Martin Luther spoke of "justification by faith." By "faith" he meant trust in the grace of God. He regarded salvation, not as the reward for good works, but as the supreme unmerited gift of God received through the believer's accepting trust. By contrast, the new folk theology defines seed-faith as the believer's overt work or deed. This "faith" is literally a financial investment in a putative program of guaranteed high-yield returns in the present life and for the benefit of at least oneself.

The Gospel of Prosperity, far from being a ministry to the poor, is aimed at a segment of those who have moved from across the tracks into the land of relative prosperity. This ministry has a twofold function. First, it provides a service or product tailored primarily for these newly affluent believers. Second, it takes their money and invests it in the ministry and the minister.

THE NEW CHRISTIAN HEDONISTS

Christianity in America has taken a sharp "this-worldly" turn. The Protestant Reformation sought to give all a chance to read the Bible for themselves, assuming they could read in the first place. The new Christian hedonism advances another democratic step forward to give everyone a justification for strongly desiring the material things of this world. No longer is money an evil that true believers must abhor or pretend to abhor, for capitalism is itself portrayed as belonging to the divine economy and scheme of things. The God of the Gospel of Prosperity wants His children to think mink! The new democratic Christian hedonism tells those who have made it across the tracks that they are okay if they accumulate filthy lucre. Indeed, it is no longer filthy when in the hands of the righteous.

But how do affluent believers know they are truly among the righteous? The televangelists step in with an answer: Professing Christians demonstrate that they are among the righteous by planting their seed-faith in the proper fields and vineyards. To prove that they are free from the love of money and have not bowed down to the golden calf, believers are urged to give a healthy portion of their earnings to television ministries. Indeed, such a deed of faith is portrayed as not a mere gift, but an investment in the fierce battle against Satan and the relentless forces of wickedness.

There is a powerful psychological thrust in this message. The faithful television viewers for whom the new folk theology has been created know that their prosperity can crumble. Playing on this anxiety, Jim Bakker looks into the cameras and talks the language of crisis. If the money does not come in, he tells them, the ministry that together they launched into uncharted waters could sink. The new Pentecostal and charismatic venture is a kind of Titanic, making its way in the high seas in high winds. The band is playing in the ship's ballroom, and all the activities offer both excitement and structure to the lives of those aboard. But now and then the ship's captain, Jim Bakker, reminds the passengers that it is quite possible that they could all sink. Before long, the money pours in to save the ship.

PTL's emotionalism and willingness to provide entertainment have caused some outside observers to overlook the intellectual aspect of PTL. The intellectual factor comes in story form. Every religion offers a story or narrative to "explain" what is going on in the lives of the participants and in their world. It is not imperative that their belief system be true; in fact, it could be largely fictional. What is imperative, however, is that those aboard the ship *believe* that it is true in some profound and significant way. Until this intellectual or cognitive aspect is understood to be absolutely essential to any religious movement, the fierce loyalty of its adherents will appear to outsiders to be scarcely more than groundless, pointless fanaticism.

Thus the Bakkers moved from the Garden of Success to the Garden of Excess. Their Prosperity Gospel actually encouraged social climbing and climbing to the top economically—merging gospel with entrepreneurship. What it failed to provide was an indication of the limits of wealth for the successful Christian.

THE THREAT

Daily television ministries create their own financial crises and the drama that goes with it. When the money fails to flow in and the promises of abundant blessings fail to generate the required money to fuel the ministry, the TV evangelist can sometimes take off the velvet gloves and the resort to unmitigated threats. Jim Bakker wrote, "When you rob God, it's going to come out of your hide! . . . Withholding from the Lord will place you under a curse of misfortune" (Bakker, 1983, p. 86). Bakker went on to specify troubles, bills, and emergencies that will befall those who fail to plant their money in the proper ministry.

The formula is simple: "Whatever you give to God, He will give back to you many times over. That's the secret of financial success—you can't outgive God" (Bakker, 1983, p. 88). But if you neglect to give, you will be a loser. God will see to that.

SUPERSTARDOM

Television ministers and rock stars have in common a vulnerability created by being thrust into fame and fortune with little training for handling either. There is enough evidence to suggest that to come into fame or fortune is to take a quantum leap psychologically. Some program of "basic training" would doubtless prove beneficial to those approaching this quantum leap. Jim and Tammy Bakker moved from the Garden of Success to the Garden of Excess in part as victims of their own inability to become self-critical after taking the leap. Indeed, the Prosperity Gospel tends to undermine common sense and the ancient Aristotelian principle of moderation. By speaking of the availability of Heavenly Father's infinite resources, the Prosperity Gospel preachers become almost oblivious to the possibility that the children of the putative rich Heavenly Daddy will become spoiled children with notions of miracles indistinguishable from childish magical thinking.

When ministers appear on television day after day to deliver what they regard as the views of the deity, an occupational hazard develops. They risk identifying an increasing number of their own desires, ideas, and plans as divine promptings. And since God is not to be doubted and disputed, his spokesman is not to be disputed.

REFERENCES

Allen, A.A. (1963). *Power to get wealth*. Miracle Valley, AZ: A.A. Allen Revivals.

Bakker, J. (1983). *You can make it*. Charlotte, NC: PTL Television Network.

Barnhart, J.E. (1986). *The Southern Baptist holy war*. Austin, TX: Texas Monthly Press.

Barnhart, J.E. (1988). *Jim and Tammy: Charismatic intrigue inside PTL*. Buffalo, NY: Prometheus Books.

14

Heresies in Evangelical Fund Raising*

Carl F.H. Henry

Heresy is a powerful word that must be used cautiously—particularly by theologians. To apply it unwittingly to certain issues can be presumptuous and problematic. I believe, however, the term is appropriate when it relates to certain policies and procedures that are, unfortunately, typical of some evangelical fund raising. Christians need to be alert to such distortions or deficiencies in the apprehension and application of Biblical truths and to the overall impact of these heresies on our Ministry and witness for Christ.

My observation is that evangelical fund-raising practices, unfortunately, are sometimes more shoddy than those of nonreligious agencies. Some secular agencies maintain a level of integrity in the use of funding techniques which even religious enterprises may well emulate. Fortunately, however, evangelical scams are relatively few. A religion that prizes truth more than feelings inevitably turns the searchlight on flim-flam.

Money—at least a certain amount of it—is indispensable. And raising money to establish, preserve, and enlarge legitimate Christian enterprises is not evil. Yet the danger is ever present that fund raising will encroach on the spiritual vitality and moral integrity of evangelical efforts. This is true of educational, of evangelistic, and of eleemosynary agencies.

Therefore, some soliciting practices need to be examined and then avoided. Jesus called Satan "the father of lies" (John 8:44). If a fund raiser thinks the way to promote the Lord's work is by deception, however subtle, he is in the service of false gods. I cite here examples of various approaches—some questionable, some downright unscriptural—and I have placed them under 7 general categories. These I call "heresies," original orthodoxies that have been twisted by some evangelical fund raisers in their struggle to reach a monetary goal. I don't want to depict fund raisers as villains; some current funding strategies and practices are carefully and thoughtfully handled. Many fund raisers are credible religious lobbyists. A few are irreligious ones.

---

* This material first appeared in *Fund Raising Management,* November 1988. Reprinted with permission.

But all run the risk of watching the bottom line more than God's highest priority.

I want to challenge the supposedly Biblical rationale behind some evangelical fund raising and to suggest potential heresies that need to be avoided.

SUBSTITUTING SLOGANS FOR SCRIPTURES

At the top of my list of concerns is that evangelical fund raisers need to reaffirm the Bible as their all-sufficient guide to faith and practice and to honestly submit every campaign principle and slogan to Biblical scrutiny.

An example is "God's work done in God's way will never lack God's supply." This is an acceptable enough statement, *if* it is honestly understood in the light of Jesus' awesome and fearsome warning in Matthew 7:21–23:

> Not everyone who says to me, "Lord, Lord," will enter the kingdom of heaven, but only he who does the will of my Father who is in heaven. Many will say to me on that day, "Lord, Lord, did we not prophesy in your name and in your name drive out demons and perform many miracles?" Then I will tell them plainly, "I never knew you. Away from me, you evildoers!"

He repudiates those who call him "Lord," who do works like His own and even give Him the credit. "God's supply" (or blessing) is therefore not based on orthodoxy of profession or an altruism or magnanimity of service but on obedience to His word and will. Anyone soliciting funds for Christian work must be fully persuaded that the ministry he represents not only is a response to human need or to opportunity, but preeminently is a response to God's divine mandate.

SUBSTITUTING SUPPOSED PROOF TEXTS FOR INTRINSIC PRINCIPLES

Some evangelical fund raisers base their principles on isolated Scripture texts, invoking them without regard to other Biblical references and molding Scripture to fit a preconceived warped view.

Fund appeals are almost routinely cloaked with some aura of Biblical legitimacy and passages on stewardship are used as bases for unrelated solicitations. Malachi 3:8–10 is frequently invoked to support "storehouse giving." In view of this passage, many pastors encourage channeling all one's contributions through the local church, whereas others no less energetically promote support of parachurch organizations. Yet complex hermeneutical presuppositions underly an extension of this passage to any and all modern giving. If we evade sound exegesis and open such texts to allegorical meanings, what are the overall implications for Scripture?

Often an appeal letter will begin with a Bible text such as, "Thanks be to

God for His indescribable gift!" (2 Cor. 9:15), and, having enlisted Jesus Christ merely as a transitional theme, will then conclude by soliciting funds for some current project and promising donors the promoter's latest book brimful of unprecedented spiritual blessing. Seldom is the fund seeker content to mention a need for which he is "looking to the Lord in faith" without the further suggestion that the Lord in turn is looking to the letter's recipient to handle the matter in His absence.

SUBSTITUTING A MOTIVATION OF GIVING FOR A MOTIVATION OF GETTING

Most evangelical agencies, though not all, avoid adducing a "prosperity theology" as a motivation for giving: The more you give, the wealthier you become. Some invoke Luke 6:38 ("Give, and it will be given to you") as a reciprocity guarantee, thus obscuring Jesus' teaching cited by the Apostle Paul: "It is more blessed to give than to receive" (Acts 20:35). The spiritual rewards of stewardship are thereby subordinated to material blessing. Successful entrepreneurs who stress that God has been instrumental in the growth of their businesses wittingly or unwittingly reinforce such prosperity theology. The error of the prosperity theme is not its emphasis that God blesses commercial integrity and sacrificial stewardship, nor that business success is attributable to divine providence, but rather is conversion of stewardship into a material prosperity tool, its attachment of giving to the expectation of personal financial benefit, and its correlation of spirituality with material gain. This approach fails to see stewardship first and foremost as a spiritual exercise for the glory of God and the advancement of His goals, one that when the giving is sacrificial, yields distinctive compensation of character to the donor.

What the Lord pours out on givers is blessedness, or happiness, and treasures of the spirit (cf. Matt. 7:11). There is no implication in Jesus' commendation of the widow who made the biggest contribution (two mites) at the Temple that she would from that moment prosper materially. But she did receive a blessing from the Lord that the "major donors" present that day in the Temple would never have (Mark 12:42–44).

Sometimes the appeal for "seed faith" or "seed money" is simply a variation of prosperity theology: Funds are solicited with the assurance that God not only will repay the gift materially but will also multiply the donor's cash reserves. Apart from such distortion, however, the notion of seed money has much to commend it as a launchpad for pilot projects.

SUBSTITUTING SECULAR SOURCES FOR SPIRITUAL RESOURCES

The growing evangelical pursuit of funds from nonevangelical or secular foundations, or unbelieving philanthropists, raises vexing problems. Some administrators at evangelical organizations or institutions are inclined to "take all the devil's money" one can get, and put it to godly uses. Others balk at drafting proposals that deliberately downplay specifically Biblical convictions in order to shape programs that non-Christian philanthropies are most likely to approve.

There may be, to be sure, overlapping moral and scientific concerns of interest to both an evangelical college and a secular foundation. No objection can be mounted if available funding does not oblige the receiving institution to compromise its own principles and does not encourage reliance on secular sources that in time may deviate that institution from its distinctive commitments. Yet it is not unthinkable that trustees may moderate an institution's commitments in order to secure outside funding that removes personal financial pressure from themselves. Additionally, the question of acceptance or nonacceptance of federal funds, a subject that falls outside the purview of this discussion, raises many of the same issues and introduces still others. But in any event, evangelical colleges, along with all other evangelical causes and organizations, must be supremely concerned that nothing shall erode their loyalty to God, their devotion to charter objectives, the goodwill of their constituency, and their dependence on prayer for faithful survival.

The miracle of feeding the 5,000 with one boy's loaves and fishes was divine multiplication of limited resources and not—as some imaginative liberals have explained it—a prodding of the crowd's nobler impulses to share their own lunches with each other.

As budgets spiral ever upward, ministries often look for leadership skilled in public relations and in raising funds from large foundations. Sophistication is required in preparing grant proposals, and personal contacts in the financial world are important. All of this tends to treat God as a peeping Tom in economic affairs, except when deficits so threaten survival that no earthly hope remains but to return to the prayer meeting.

The notion that gifts may be advantageously solicited from wealthy persons irrespective of their basic convictions often leads fund raisers to conform proposals to the special interest of one or another monied prospect. Helen Bergan's *Where the Money Is: A Fund Raiser's Guide to the Rich* (Alexandria, VA: VioGuide Press) then becomes the solicitor's main source book. The *Chicago Tribune*'s biweekly newsletter *Donor Briefing* alerts him to who is giving what to whom and why. Yet the fund raiser may be quite unaware that buying into nonevangelical or subevangelical funding may in the long run do as much harm to a ministry's theological and spiritual orientation as it does good to its present fiscal condition. As a compensation for their gifts, some large donors have expected personal or proxy representation on a board or governing body or other preferences and favors.

Not a few enterprises take their promotional cue from Madison Avenue, and eagerly taper their appeals to secular approaches. Evangelical ministries need constantly to investigate such dependency on the philosophy of secular professionals. It is understandable that some evangelical administrators readily enlist the expertise of secular fund raisers and investment agencies. But this practice brings with it great risks. Promotion built on philosophies of the secular world must always be carefully scrutinized; Madison Avenue's most successful commercials, it is said, are those that stretch the truth but do it subtly. In transferring financial activities to professional managers, administrators may unwittingly lose control of an organization's destiny. No less important are the convictions and character of any outside staff that is contracted to tap financial sources.

SUBSTITUTING MATERIAL INCENTIVE FOR SPIRIT-LED GENEROSITY

The prophet motive and the profit motive are often on a collision course; the prophet offers a free salvation, the profiteer wants to add a commission charge. Some fund raisers use radio and direct mail to peddle contribution premiums that vary in quality in ratio to the dollars given. They are hucksters of merchandise, indulging in such jargon as "No Christian home should be without one," using valuable air time or expensive brochures to tout the virtues of the "product" which will be sent in return for a donation.

Fund-raising premiums raise serious ethical problems. For one thing, the monetary value of such premiums is often exaggerated. At worst, a special spiritual benefit is attributed to floral sprigs or tiny twigs from the Holy Land, mother-of-pearl crosses from Bethlehem, olive wood amulets from Jerusalem, or cheap jade charms from Hong Kong or Taiwan. Such relics may not carry all the implications of the medieval indulgences, but they are nonetheless reminiscent of them insofar as they are depicted as laden with blessing if not with miracle power because they have been prayed over or are thought to protect the recipient against evil. If this were merely a religious extension of the cosmetic industry's "free bonus with purchase," it would be bad enough; far worse is the promise not merely of physical enhancement but of spiritual benefits that the almost worthless trinkets are presumed to convey.

Books, magazines, or cassettes are frequently sent as premiums. Donors must deduct their value from any IRS claim for a tax-exempt contribution. The hawker often puts their value not at actual cost but at the publisher's or producer's inflated price. IRS requirements are more murky when gift books are provided by an independent source to help stimulate support for a program. Publishers' closeouts, now and then distributed by evangelical agencies, often do little to enhance organizational goals. Some tax-exempt groups are careful to distribute books that reflect an organization's creative interests and achievements, thereby stimulating larger long-term support.

Doctrinally responsible ventures will distribute books of theological integrity that truly promote spiritual life. "Health and wealth" solicitations are often somewhat more ambiguous than the theologically articulate ministries and are sometimes less precise about how contributions will be used. Some theologically indefinite efforts focus constantly on world emergency needs, and alter their appeal goals and even modify their doctrinal tenets when they shift to new crisis concerns.

Much fund raising links generosity in making charitable gifts primarily to the tax break such gifts bestow on donors. In 1986 many charities advised U.S. citizens how they could benefit taxwise by giving before year-end when the new tax law became effective. The accounting firm of Arthur Andersen & Co. advised nonprofit institutions that opportunity was vanishing for wealthy donors to "get the government to pay as much as one-half the cost of lifetime charitable giving."

Fortunately evangelical appeals seem to have escaped the misleading secular offers of "something for nothing." No evangelical college has yet promoted an alumni lottery offering free tuition for a child or grandchild, or offered the second prize winner an all-expense paid trip to homecoming weekend for a class reunion.

Peter and John at the gate of the Temple (Acts 3) did not offer a "premium;" they offered to the lame beggar the power of the name of Jesus. What they themselves got in return was not dollars but a dungeon (Acts 4:3).

SUBSTITUTING METHODOLOGY FOR MINISTRY

Evangelical organizations do not wholly escape the temptation to post fake mailgrams or to dress up "junk mail" to look like first-class personal correspondence. Evangelistic enterprises and humanitarian agencies routinely imprint their envelopes with "Urgent—Immediate Reply Requested" or "Priority Mail" so that gullible recipients may think the correspondence is selective and private.

A more blatantly offensive device is the first-class letter sent by a stranger who addresses the prospect by first name and signs off on a first name basis. The correspondence shares supposedly confidential information (usually so intangible that its release could harm no one), and charts new evangelistic opportunities that promise certain success.

A special public relations feature of evangelicals is a vaunted personal interest in the individual as a person uniquely fashioned in God's image and created for distinctive service in the world. But in reality this personal touch is continually jeopardized. Obviously movements with large supportive constituencies cannot maintain personal relationships with all donors, and overstatement readily becomes the first step toward manipulating and exploiting the donors. Computer-generated correspondence that gives the impression of a personal exchange is bad enough. But when the person whose mechanical signature ends the letter guarantees that he will personally pray for all who write expressing their needs—and conveys the impression of a truly significant prayer burden for each respondent—the pitch is unconscionable.

One recent solicitation letter from a religious magazine began with the sender's personal assurance that "Today I have your name before me in prayer." But even the most determined correspondent would never manage 10,000 three-second sound blips like "Oh God, remember Carl Henry wherever he is, whatever his need," even if he prayed for 8 solid hours without stopping for breath. The writer adds that I am "deeply and strongly on (his) heart" because the American economy may suddenly plummet and seed gifts are needed. The letter proceeds to invert apostolic priorities by saying far more about money than about ministry.

The temptation also arises, on the basis of an evangelical entrepreneur's private faith, to exceed budget prospects by anticipating support which is not really in hand or in view of new and enlarged programs. Some such funding appeals have even blamed God for unfortunate overextension of enterprises: "The Lord has blessed this work so abundantly that now we are really in trouble trying to keep it going." Or again, "Without additional help we must cut back critical programs, but I know that is not God's will for us."

Financially faltering enterprises may suggest a need for Christian cooperation and merger. Personality-cult movements run a great risk when leaders become, as Mel Lorentzen, associate director of the Billy Graham Center, phrases it, "builders of personal empires 'in His name';" rather than serving as "commissioned agents of the heavenly kingdom," they compete with each other for cash from a common constituency. Just as lamentable is the sale and exchange of donor lists by some evangelical or fundamentalist agencies.

The fact that a cause is good does not of itself justify telephone intrusion at any hour of the day or evening. The year-end phonathon is an unpleasant tactic; the caller is not personally known, often interrupts something the responder considers more important, usually solicits a larger contribution than the responder is disposed to make, and demeans the prospect list into a series of technological statistics. Even worse is the long-distance supposedly person-to-person call in which the "operator" asks if one has just a minute to listen to an important personal message from Big Name Evangelical, and then is subjected to the insult of a recorded tape. Such an approach is an invasion of a person's time under false pretenses.

Other fund raisers suggest asking a "volunteer" to make a pitch to someone in his particular peer group. If the potential donor is personally unable or indisposed to give, fund raisers then invite the recalcitrant prospect to address the most vulnerable of his well-to-do acquaintances. The appeal to donor ego nullifies the ethical and spiritual gratification that donors ought to experience in giving. Another questionable device is that of publishing lists of donors and their gifts, thus making public what ought to be a private matter, namely, the extent of a donor's contribution. This practice exposes contributors to solicitation by still other fund raisers. Moreover, if such tactics are used to send smaller donors on a "guilt trip," they may alienate an important and perhaps even the largest segment of supporters.

SUBSTITUTING FEAR FOR FAITH AS THE MOTIVATION FOR GIVING

Direct-mail experts who advise Christian agencies, and in many cases devise their funding campaigns, say: Create a crisis, press the panic button—people will not give to something successful but only to a salvage operation. How does this cynical philosophy square with Jesus' teaching in Matthew 16:18, "I will build my church?" Nowhere does the Bible hint that the Lord needs our finite efforts to bail Him out of a budget crunch. To assume so maligns the faithfulness of God to His servants and His adequacy to run His business.

Yet some direct-mail strategists suggest playing on emotions. Conservatively worded direct mail that deals with substantive issues is said to be financially unrewarding; only by feeding the constituency "raw meat"— anxieties over homosexuality, pornography, sexual delinquency, drugs, and so on—will the recipient feel sufficiently moved to respond.

Even when prospective donors are told that the first $15,000 received will go to meet some dire need, what is often not mentioned is that the first contributions by radio and television audiences usually go toward meeting program overhead expenses. Unless an independent source has underwritten the salaries of an institution's development or stewardship staff, a substantial part of the money raised goes to pay salaries and travel costs, even where solicitation is done on commission. No fund raising can be done without administrative costs, and few organizations are in a position to devote every cent that is given to the cause for which contributions are intended. Hence, the percentage of funds that remain to advance an institution's spiritual and moral vision is crucially important.

Few factors permanently motivate the giving of believers more than a clear, unambiguous definition of objectives enunciated by a leader perceived to be trustworthy. A touch of charisma is an asset, but it will not compensate for a lack of personal integrity or for imprecise formulation of goals or for uncertainty over the intended use of funds. The risk of concentrating the promotion of an enterprise on a single personality is evident, however, not only does such a policy create problems of succession but the leader is sometimes also conceived as being more important than the work; consequently, the temptation arises to perpetuate family dynasties.

15
The Selling of Salvation in the Electronic Church

Robert Abelman

As was demonstrated in Chapter 6, the relationship between the growth of religious television and the financial contributions of its viewers has been intimate, integral, and long term. Indeed, religious programs were available from the beginning of television in the late 1940s in 3 distinctive forms: Network sustaining-time programs, syndicated sustaining-time programs, programs produced by local television stations, and paid-time religious programs—that is, programs produced by largely independent, evangelical organizations, syndicated nationally on air time purchased from local stations, and financed primarily by audience contributions. As television's popularity grew and the commercial networks became less charitable with their donation of air time to religious organizations, programming made available by mainline churches dramatically diminished while paid-time, viewer-supported programming by evangelicals managed to flourish.

By 1959, 53 percent of all religious fare on television was occupied by paid-time programming. Starting in 1960, independent evangelical organizations also began to purchase their own television stations and, in the 1970s, began acquiring failing UHF-TV stations in major markets. At the same time, deregulation of cable television was opening up unused channel capacity and deregulation of domestic satellite communications provided an inexpensive and efficient means of networking between newly acquired UHF outlets (Hoover, 1988; Neuendorf, Kalis, & Abelman, 1987). By 1977, the televangelists occupied 92 percent of air time containing religious fare, virtually eliminating local religious programming (Horsfield, 1984).

The willingness to buy air time and purchase facilities allowed these religious broadcasters to gain access to larger audiences which, in turn, led to greater contributions to and further expansion of their electronic ministries. Since that time, one of the paramount concerns of local clergy has been whether the television ministries are causing or at least contributing to the erosion of financial contributions to the mainline church (Armstrong, 1979; Horsfield, 1985). From the perspective of religious television critic William Martin (Public Broadcasting Service, 1984), "It is hard to tell whether they [televangelists] stay on television to raise money or raise money to stay on television." According to Hadden and Swann (1981), it appears as if the business of religious television has evolved into a "fiscal Catch 22" situation—the logic of the evangelical success formula demands reaching as many people as possible, but in order to pay for the increased production costs of reaching larger audiences, one needs an even larger audience.

The controversy regarding on-the-air solicitations is additionally fostered by the recent PTL scandal. It has always been clear, by the transformation of locally aired tent-revival programs of the 1950s into the professional, often elaborate nationally syndicated productions of today, that money obtained through broadcast solicitations has been placed back into programming and program distribution. However, as we have recently learned in the popular press (Hackett, 1987; Martz, 1987; Ostling, 1987a, 1987b, 1987c; Press, 1987; Watson, 1987a, 1987b), much of this money has also lined the pockets of Jim and Tammy Faye Bakker, who founded and headed the Praise The Lord (PTL) television network. More recent reports (Associated Press, 1988; Public Broadcasting Service, 1988) suggest that the Bakker's use of viewer contributions for personal gain has been going on for at least 5 years prior to the breaking of the story to the general public.

All of this has raised 3 primary issues regarding the nature of on-the-air solicitations. The first concerns the extent of these requests for money. What is the frequency and quantity of monies typically requested by the various televangelists, and are some televangelists more active solicitors than others? Second, what is the success of these solicitations in terms of actual contributions by the televiewing audience? And third, have the events surrounding the recent PTL scandal influenced the frequency and quantity of contributions by viewers? Each will be addressed in the following sections.

THE REQUESTS

In recent years, several content analyses have been conducted that specifically addressed the frequency and quantity of on-the-air solicitations in religious television programming. Gerbner, Gross, Hoover, Morgan, Signorielli, Cotugno, and Wuthnow (1984) examined the widest range of programs ($N = 101$), including nationally syndicated and locally distributed religious programs in the Philadelphia and Atlanta areas. According to the authors (p. 42), half of the total sample of programs made some explicit request for money. It was also noted that:

> The television ministries were considerably more likely than mainline church programs to make such requests: 55 percent of the former, compared to 20 percent of the latter, requested funds. The most prominent television minis-

Table 15.1. Amount of Air Time Used by Television Ministries for Financial Appeals

TV Ministry Relative Market Rank, 1981	Airtime Minutes	Average Minutes	Percentage Actual Airtime
1. Roberts	30	9.3	31.0
2. Schuller	60	7.2	12.0
3. Humbard	30	12.8	42.6
4. Swaggart	60	6.9	11.5
5. Falwell	60	13.8	23.0
6. Bakker	60	13.8	23.0
7. Robertson	90	14.2	15.7
8. Robison	30	10.8	36.0

From Frankl, 1987, p. 134.

tries were the most likely group of programs to make requests for money (63%), and these requests were likely to be numerous—four out of 10 of these programs made 3 or more requests during the course of the program.

Three other investigations confirm these findings. Abelman and Neuendorf (1985a, p. 108) found that "preaching/revival programs request the most money per hour, with talk shows a distant second. Religious dramas, typically produced by mainline church organizations, make no financial requests." Abelman and Neuendorf (1985b) suggested that only 9 of the 14 nationally available televangelists examined in their investigation made explicit appeals for money in their programs, with the most prominent ministries well represented among this group of solicitors. Frankl (1987) examined the 8 most prominent ministries specifically, and found that "passing the plate" was clearly a popular activity within these programs. She found that none of these televangelists used less than 10 percent of their air time for financial appeals and that, on the average, approximately 8.8 minutes per 30-minute program were employed for fund raising. As can be seen in Table 15.1, Frankl demonstrates that even among a sample of very active solicitors, some televangelists spend more time on fund raising than others. In particular, Rex Humbard, James Robison, and Oral Roberts engaged in the most on-the-air solicitations.

Regarding the nature of these requests for funds, Gerbner et al. (1984) suggested that specific amounts of money were not usually requested. Rather, items were usually offered for sale or as gifts in exchange for contributions. Magazines/newsletters and display items were offered very infrequently, while tapes, records, and books were more frequently solicited. Similarly, Abelman and Neuendorf (1985b) found that of the 14 televangelists examined in their study, 8 offered items for purchase during the course of their program; only 6 made explicit appeals for contributions.

Table 15.2.   Total Requests for Money by Televangelist

	Dollars in Purchase Items	Appeals for Money	Total Money Requested	Money Requested Per Hour
Swaggart	$ —	$ 90	$ 90	$ 36.00
Falwell	5013	2820	7833	2611.00
Schuller	175	75	250	83.33
Roberts	240	240	480	320.00
Armstrong	—	—	—	—
Humbard	—	—	—	—
Copeland	40	—	40	13.33
DeHaan	—	—	—	—
Van Impe	109	1030	1139	759.33
Angley	107	—	107	35.67
Kennedy	—	—	—	—
Robison	15	—	15	10.00
Price	—	—	—	—
Gottier	24	30	54	36.00
Totals	$5723	$4285	$10,008	$ 328.13 per hour

From Abelman & Neuendorf, 1985b, p. 66.

While Abelman and Neuendorf also found that tapes, records, and books were the most widely offered items, those costing the most money included Bibles and various display items (e.g., pins, plaques). Overall, an average of $187.64 worth of merchandise was offered on these programs per hour. The average cost of a Bible was $200.00. Although infrequent, explicit requests for money with no product in return averaged $140.49 per hour. Table 15.2 provides a summary of the findings from this report, across 3 sample programs from each televangelist. As can be seen, a total of $328.13 per hour was requested of the viewer across the sample of programs, with Jerry Falwell, Jack Van Impe, and Oral Roberts being the primary solicitors. If the "typical" viewer of religious fare watches approximately 2 hours of these programs per week, as has been suggested in recent research (see Clark & Virts, 1985; Gerbner et al., 1984; Hoover, 1987), then the average viewer is exposed to approximately $31,000 in requests a year.

Clearly, simple requests for funds may not be sufficient to actually merit financial contributions. Indeed, it has been noted that many religious broadcasters employ sophisticated letter-writing campaigns as a follow-up to and reinforcement of on-the-air requests (see Hadden & Swann, 1981; Horsfield, 1985). However, there is evidence that viewers are primarily motivated to contribute by the televangelists themselves (Neuendorf & Abelman, 1985), the result of information regarding where donated dollars are going and how they are being used. Before examining the effectiveness of requests for funds, it is important to first address the nature of the appeals used by televangelists that result in contributions.

Abelman and Neuendorf (1985b) found that the use of money for educational activities (56.8%) and to help defray the cost of program production and distribution (24.0%) were the most often employed appeals. Jerry Falwell's solicitations, accounting for approximately 66 percent of direct appeals for money across all televangelists, indicated that the money was going toward educational activities with the rest going toward various building projects. Jack Van Impe requested money from his viewers for the sole purpose of buying air time for his program. Oral Roberts and Fred Gottier also had specific and singular purposes for funds—health care for others and spreading the gospel, respectively. Although Jimmy Swaggart did not request as much money as some of his colleagues, he did offer the greatest variety of reasons for needing funds, among them spreading the gospel, helping and providing health care for the needy, building projects, and educational activities. Frankl (1987, p. 138) adds that Jim Bakker frequently engaged in a plea for help for a special crisis, including "a financial crisis because of tax problems."

THE RESPONSE

The controversy surrounding the financial relationship between religious broadcasters and their audience lies not so much in the fact that these programs make explicit requests for money as it does in the overwhelming success of these solicitations. Although the exact amount of money taken in by the various evangelical organizations is known only to them, due to their tax exempt status (see Chapter 6), it is clear by the recent growth of religious broadcasting that the previously discussed appeals for financial contributions have been quite successful. Hadden and Swann (1981) have suggested that, in 1980, the top 4 programs collectively took in over a quarter of a billion dollars. The next 5 largest took in more than $100 million; most of which came in $5, $10, and $15 contributions. In a public television investigation of religious broadcasting, it was revealed that the Jimmy Swaggart Ministry alone collected over $60 million in 1982 (PBS, 1984).

These reports are, of course, suspect due to their reliance on hearsay and information from the evangelical organizations themselves. Gerbner et al. (1984) and Abelman (1988a) chose to go directly to the source of these contributions. Among their research findings is that approximately 25 percent of the viewers of religious programs reported giving money to the electronic church. The former report noted that nearly one-third of these contributors earned a salary of less than $15,000 a year, and that 40 percent of the regular contributors gave to 3 or more programs. The latter investigation reported that it was the ritualized viewers—those who are highly religious, actively involved in church activities, and consume re-

Table 15.3.   "Average" Contribution (in dollars) to
Religious Programming

| | Giving | | |
Overall	Regular $35.17	Special $15.22	Infrequent $19.38
Income:			
< $15,000	32.77	14.73	18.26
$15–25,000	34.11	13.28	16.98
$25–35,000	34.38	33.25	21.82
> $35,000	48.27	15.60	23.80
Denomination:			
Protestants	36.05	15.32	19.86
Catholics	32.42	14.61	16.55
Others	18.00	16.50	17.14
Education			
< High School	35.72	13.73	20.72
High School Graduate	35.14	17.19	15.81
> High School	34.80	13.66	21.93

From Gerbner et al., 1984, p. 81.

ligious broadcasting largely out of faith and religious conviction—that were the primary financial contributors within the televiewing audience.

As can be seen in Table 15.3, which was extracted from Gerbner et al. (1984), those that contributed regularly to their favorite program(s) averaged $35.17 per contribution. Those that contributed "only for special appeals" average $15.22, while those that gave "only once and a while" did so at an average of $19.38 per contribution. The highest level of contribution was among those regular contributors who earned over $35,000 annually. Even among the less frequent contributors, those with high incomes gave the largest amounts of money. Interestingly, however, the researchers note that "although less than 10 percent of the 'special' givers have medium-high incomes, this group gives much larger amounts than the other groups of special givers" (p. 81). The report goes on to suggest that the average contribution for viewers of the "most prominent" programs was $22.41; for viewers of mainline programs, $18.13.

THE REACTION

According to the evangelical community, the misappropriation of PTL funds by the Bakkers, along with allegations of Jim Bakker's heterosexual and homosexual affairs, Tammy Bakker's drug addiction, and the well-publicized in-fighting among the PTL hierarchy has tarnished the image of the nation's most high-profile televangelists and their respective ministries (American Broadcasting Company, 1987a, 1987b, 1987c, 1987d, 1987e).

A recent Gallup poll of 1,026 Americans found that "some" or "very little" of evangelical programming was said to be trustworthy. The survey concluded that "there have been extravagances and questionable tactics, and surely this has soured people's attitudes toward giving [contributions] and toward Christianity" (Ostling, 1986, p. 70).

Evidence to this effect can be found in the televangelists' declaration of diminished offerings from the televiewing audience. Popular televangelist Jimmy Swaggart reported a $1.5 million decline in the April following the scandal. Robert Schuller, whose *Hour of Power* is carried by 172 stations, showed a 3 percent dip in donations in 1987. Pat Robertson, former Republican presidential candidate and host of religious television's top-rated program the *700 Club,* reported that April donations were down 33 percent and, as a result, laid off 500 employees in June (Ostling, 1987a).

Interestingly, however, observers of evangelicalism predict that, in the short run at least, "PTL supporters will rally around their beleaguered organization. The television ministries like PTL occupy powerful positions because they meet the spiritual and emotional needs of millions of viewers" (Ostling, 1987b, p. 67). Indeed, Heritage USA—PTL's religious theme park in South Carolina—has had more visitors than any time since Christmas following reports of the PTL scandal (Associated Press, 1987). In contrast to reports by Swaggart, Schuller, and Robertson, there is evidence that the viewership of and donations to religious programming has increased rather than decreased in the aftermath of the scandal. According to Arthur Borden (1987), president of the Evangelical Council for Financial Accountability, televangelists Billy Graham, Fred Price, Richard DeHaan, and others have actually declared record profits.

These contradictory reports of the impact of the PTL scandal on the religious televiewing audience were addressed in Abelman (1988b). According to this research, the PTL scandal impacted on different segments of the audience in significantly different ways. The reactionary consumer, for example—those who watch religious broadcasting largely out of curiosity and as an alternative to secular broadcasting—had their prescandal perceptions of low credibility of televangelists and poor money management of their organizations confirmed. Information-seeking instrumental viewers' perceptions of credibility and financial accountability diminished. "From a purely economic perspective," suggests Abelman, "it is clear these viewers are expendable. They are not likely to make financial contributions and play no role in the financial future of religious broadcasting" (p. 34).

Interestingly, the largest contingency of viewers—the highly religious ritualized uses of religious fare—maintained their faith in religious broadcasters, but their pattern of financial contributions has altered since the scandal. Table 15.4 suggests that the difference in the frequency of contributions before and after the scandal is highly significant, with the greatest changes occuring among those "regularly" contributing to religious televi-

Table 15.4.   Contribution Frequency by Wave

	Prescandal		Postscandal	
	N	%	N	%
Regularly	254	85.52	173	58.24
Frequently	23	7.74	23	7.74
Infrequently	8	2.69	—	0.00
Special Occasion	4	1.35	19	6.40
Not At All	8	2.69	82	27.61

$(X^2[4, N = 297] = 24.33, p < .0001)$

From Abelman, 1988b, p. 32.

Table 15.5.   Distribution of Contribution by Wave

	Prescandal		Postscandal	
	N	%	N	%
One Program	169	58.48	244	84.43
Two Programs	26	8.99	26	8.99
Three Programs	49	16.96	11	3.91
Four or More	45	15.57	8	2.77

$(X^2[3, N = 289] = 17.01, p < .0007)$

From Abelman, 1988b, p. 33.

Table 15.6.   Contribution Size (Contributors Only) by Wave

	Prescandal		Postscandal	
	N	%	N	%
Small	22	7.61	3	1.38
Average	219	75.78	202	69.89
Large	48	16.61	83	28.72

$(X^2[2, N = 289] = 6.18, p < .0415)$

From Abelman, 1988b, p. 32.

sion (85.52% to 58.24%) and those "not contributing at all" (2.69% to 27.61%). The decrease in the frequency of contributions is matched by the range of distribution of these funds. As Table 15.5 suggests, fewer viewers are giving to more than one program (41.52% to 15.57%). Interestingly, however, Table 15.6 suggests that the size of contributions has significantly increased. In particular, more viewers (16.61% to 28.72%) are making "large" (over $30) contributions. All of this suggests that "viewers have become more selective in regard to the recipient of their 'gifts,' but are demonstrating their faith [in religious broadcasting] through an increase in the size of contributions" (Abelman, 1988b, pp. 33–34).

SUMMARY

Clearly, explicit requests for funds are not as widespread among the tele-vangelical population as has been previously assumed by the popular press or feared by local clergy. Rather, there is a strong concentration of requests among a handful of televangelists. It should be noted, however, that these requests are frequent and the handful of solicitors is comprised of the most popular and well-known personalities in religious television. Consequently, they have been quite successful in having their requests answered by their viewers.

Research suggests that the 25 percent of the viewers of religious pro-grams reported giving money to the electronic church were highly religious and earning a moderate-to-low income. Prior to the PTL scandal, most contributors gave regularly to 3 or more programs. As a consequence of the scandal, however, the frequency of contributions and the number of pro-grams receiving contributions has decreased. The size of these contribu-tions has nonetheless increased. While "Charity shall cover the multitude of sins" (I Peter 4:8), charity in the form of financial contributions to re-ligious broadcasters has been influenced by the well publicized sins of PTL's Bakkers. With popular televangelists competing for a smaller popu-lation of contributors in the viewing audience, it is likely that the usurption of religious air time from local and mainline churches by evangelicals in the 1960s and 1970s will be repeated. This time, however, it will be evan-gelicals fighting each other for survival.

REFERENCES

Abelman, R. (1988a). The impact of the PTL scandal on religious television view-ers. *Journal of Communication and Religion, 11*(1), 41–51.

Abelman, R. (1988b). Financial support for religious television: The impact of the PTL scandal. *Journal of Media Economics, 1*(1), 23–38.

Abelman, R., & Neuendorf, K. (1985a). How religious is religious television? *Journal of Communication, 35*(1), 98–110.

Abelman, R., & Neuendorf, K. (1985b). The cost of membership in the electronic church. *Religious Communication Today, 8,* 63–67.

American Broadcasting Company. (1987a, March 23). *Transcripts of "Nightline" show #1520.* New York: Journal Graphics.

American Broadcasting Company. (1987b, March 24). *Transcripts of "Nightline" show #1521.* New York: Journal Graphics.

American Broadcasting Company. (1987c, March 26). *Transcripts of "Nightline" show #1523.* New York: Journal Graphics.

American Broadcasting Company. (1987d, April 24). *Transcripts of "Nightline" show #1544.* New York: Journal Graphics.

American Broadcasting Company. (1987e, April 28). *Transcripts of "Nightline" show #1546.* New York: Journal Graphics.

Armstrong, B. (1979, June/July). Does the electric church hurt the local church? *Religious Broadcasting, 19,* 40–43.

Associated Press. (1987, March). Falwell presides at PTL. *The Plain Dealer,* p. 2a.

Associated Press. (1988, January). U.S. knew of PTL lies 6 years ago, FCC investigator said. *The Plain Dealer,* p. 2a.

Borden, A. (1987, June 5). Interview [broadcast]. WAUB-FM, Washington, DC.

Clark, D.W., & Virts, P.H. (1985, October 25). *Religious television audience: A new development in measuring audience size.* Paper presented at For the Scientific Study of Religion Conference, Savannah, GA.

Frankl, R. (1987). *Televangelism: The marketing of popular religion.* Carbondale, IL: Southern Illinois University Press.

Gerbner, G., Gross, L., Hoover, S., Morgan, M., Signorielli, N., Cotugno, H., & Wuthnow, R. (1984). *Religion and television.* New York: Committee on Electronic Church Research.

Hackett, G. (1987, April 6). It isn't the first time. *Newsweek,* p. 23.

Hadden, J.K., & Swann, C.E. (1981). *Primetime preachers: The rising power of televangelism.* Reading, MA: Addison-Wesley.

Hoover, S. (1987). The religious television audience: A matter of significance or size? *Review of Religious Research, 29*(2), 135–151.

Hoover, S. (1988). Audience size: Some questions. *Critical Studies in Mass Communication, 5*(3), 265–271.

Horsfield, P. (1984). *Religious television: An American experience.* New York: Longman.

Horsfield, P. (1985). Evangelism by mail. *Journal of Communication, 35*(1), 89–97.

Martz, L. (1987, April 6). God and money. *Newsweek,* pp. 16–22.

Neuendorf, K., & Abelman, R. (1985). Televangelism: A look at communicator style. *Journal of Religious Studies, 13*(1), 41–59.

Neuendorf, K., Kalis, P., & Abelman, R. (1987, August). *The history and availability of religious television programming.* Paper presented at the Association of Education in Journalism and Mass Communication Conference, San Antonio, TX.

Ostling, R. (1986, February 12). Power, glory—and politics. *Time,* pp. 62–69.

Ostling, R. (1987a, March 30). A really bad day at Fort Mill. *Time,* pp. 62–69.

Ostling, R. (1987b, April 6). TV's unholy row. *Time,* pp. 60–67.

Ostling, R. (1987c, June 8). Of God and greed. *Time,* pp. 70–74.

Press, A. (1987, May 11). Will those cards and letters keep coming? *Newsweek*, p. 72.

Public Broadcasting Service. (1984, June). Frontline: Give me that big time religion [telecast]. WGBH-TV, Boston, MA.

Public Broadcasting Service. (1988, January). Frontline: Praise the Lord [telecast]. WGBH-TV, Boston, MA.

Watson, R. (1987a, May 11). Fresh out of miracles. *Newsweek*, pp. 70–72.

Watson, R. (1987b, June 8). Heaven can wait. *Newsweek*, pp. 58–65.

16

In Conversation: Arthur C. Borden, Evangelical Council for Financial Accountability

with Robert Abelman

Q. *Why and in what context was the Evangelical Council for Financial Accountability (ECFA) originally created? Was it generated as a solution to a pending accountability problem? As a result of the growth of paid-time religious broadcasting? As a vehicle for tax exempt organizations to document and make public their financial status?*

A. Concern over the fund-raising practices of religious organizations is not something new to the 1980s. Periodically, beginning with the church in New Testament times, there have been questions about the raising, handling, and dispensing of money. There has always been uneasiness about the church and money. One of the notorious abuses which led to the Protestant Reformation was the fund-raising practices being used in the 16th century.

The ECFA came into existence before the current crises. There were at least 3 concurrent events or movements that led to the formation of the ECFA. One was financial. During the 1970s there was a scandal in a Catholic missionary order, the Pallotine Fathers. Another was political. It was the introduction of legislation in Congress to require extensive and expensive reporting requirements by all charities with an income of more than $10,000 annually. The third was social. There was an increasing awareness of the rights of the consumer. The donor was viewed, in some ways, as a consumer with rights that had to be recognized and respected. These converging influences prompted the leaders of the Billy Graham Evangelistic Association and World Vision to take the leadership in the formation of the ECFA. These individuals were strongly encouraged by Senator Mark Hatfield, who told the leaders of Christian organizations to find a way to police themselves before the government intervened.

From the beginning, the strong tenants of the ECFA were proper accounting, an independent and responsible volunteer board of directors, and full disclosure of finances. In today's society, financial disclosure is not an option, but an obligation. The laws of the land grant certain privileges to religious and charitable institutions. These privileges require accountability, and there can be no proper accountability without adequate disclosure. The charity that refuses to disclose its finances is short-changing the public from which it derives its support, giving rise to suspicions as to how it is using the financial resources at its disposal.

9.   *Has the function of the ECFA changed from its origin to now? In what ways has its membership changed, particularly in terms of the top religious broadcasters?*

A.   Very soon after its formation, the ECFA found that there was a need for better and more precise fund-raising standards. The general standard on fund raising lacked precision and was expanded. These additions to the standards were very well received by the members of the ECFA, donors, and the media. Since there is no other organization in the charitable field dedicated solely to setting and enforcing financial standards for a membership organization, the ECFA had to develop the compliance and enforcement procedures as it went along. Over the years these practices have been refined so that it is easier to identify a problem and to decide whether there is a remedy or a need for the ministry to have its membership terminated.

Regarding the composition of the ECFA's membership, all kinds of Christian ministries are members. There are denominations, individual churches, foreign mission agencies, rescue missions, colleges, seminaries, elementary and secondary schools, evangelistic ministries, literary agencies, adoption agencies, counciling agencies, prison ministries, camps, associations, relief and development agencies, radio and television stations, radio and television programs, youth organizations, campus student ministries, retirement homes, drug treatment centers, community social welfare agencies, and Christian publishers.

The ECFA grew over 60 percent during the last 2 years (1987 and 1988). There are over 535 member organizations. The combined annual income of the members of the ECFA exceeds $2.1 billion. Most of the new organizations that have joined the ECFA are smaller ministries. Over 100 of the ECFA members receive less than $250,000 annually in donated income. There are 4 very large member organizations with donated income in excess of $50 million.

The most prominent religious television broadcasters that are members of the Council are James Kennedy (Coral Ridge Ministries), Richard DeHaan (Day of Discovery, Radio Bible Class), and Charles Stanley (First Baptist Church, Atlanta). The Billy Graham Evangelistic Association periodically buys time for the presentation of the

Billy Graham crusades. James Dobson (Focus on the Family), Chuck Swindoll (Insight for Living), Radio Bible Class, and Back to the Bible are large radio ministries that also belong to the Council.

Q. *What does your organization perceive to be the benefits of financial accountability . . . for the religious broadcaster, for the media consumer, for the government?*

A. When an organization is accepted for membership in the ECFA, it is subscribing to a set of published standards which indicate good business practices in governance, and raising, managing, and spending of its financial resources. It provides an easy way for a ministry to indicate that it is following accepted practices, voluntarily submitting itself to the oversight of another organization, and that it is reviewed annually to make certain that the ministry maintains compliance with the standards.

The ECFA standards help an organization understand what it should be doing and guide it in knowing how it should conduct its business. It also places emphasis on the fact that the business affairs of a ministry are important matters and must be attended to. Many organizations need help in understanding how to develop a board and how it should function. Some do not understand how to properly account for and report their finances. Others do not understand some of the most basic matters concerning the ethics of fund raising. The fact that there is an organization such as the ECFA that is able to call attention to these matters is a great benefit to many Christian ministries.

The religious broadcaster, like other Christian ministries, has been led by entrepreneurial charismatic leaders. These leaders often can instruct, lead, and inspire large groups of people, but are unaware of basic fundamentals of running a ministry (i.e., business). The existence of a standard setting and monitoring body that points out basic fundamentals in governance, accounting, and financial management is a help to charities of all kinds, including broadcast ministries. The donor benefits by being able to check with a third party about a Christian ministry. The donor is also guaranteed the right to get additional information from the ministry itself through the disclosure requirements of the ECFA.

Constitutional issues limit the ability of the government to require reporting and disclosure of information by religious organizations. In most cases, the government must determine that there is fraud involved before it can use its investigative powers to get information from a religious group. The government cannot require all religious groups to report. A self-regulating group, such as the ECFA, is one way to promote proper practices and disclosure among religious organizations.

Q. *Has there been any government regulation or intervention that has influenced the function of the ECFA or the size and composition of its membership? Has there been any action by the Religious Broadcasting Association to influence the function of ECFA?*

A. Government influence has had little or no effect on the ECFA constituency. However, the National Religious Broadcasters (NRB) voted in 1988 to make mandatory the adoption of a code of ethics for all its members and established the Ethics and Financial Integrity Commission (EFICOM). The ECFA has agreed to administer the program for the NRB. In November, 1988, there were 80 members of the NRB that already met the ECFA standards. There are approximately 400 other nonprofit members of the NRB. These must meet the EFICOM standards by the end of 1989. As of November, 1989, there are 196 NRB members certified by EFICOM; 50 members have requested extensions, 64 have cancelled NRB membership, 28 are foreign organizations and need not apply, and 140 are for-profit, and need not apply (see "EFICOM modified," 1989).

Q. *What trends do you see in the finances of religious broadcasters that belong to your organization? Have they prospered? Are they having difficulty, financially, in this very competitive market and in the shadow of the recent scandals?*

A. A significant number of the larger television ministries have refused to disclose vital information about their operations and finances. Otherwise, most all broadcasters and other religious charities have reported difficulty during certain months in raising money during the past 24 months. The large majority of ministries experienced this difficulty for only a month or 2. A few religious broadcasters have indicated that they have had difficulty raising money for extended periods during 1987 and 1988. In most cases it has been those organizations that were featured prominently in the media that have had the most difficulty.

Nonetheless, it appears that giving to religious broadcasters across the board has continued to grow. Donors that have given in the past have continued to give. Some may have redirected their giving from one ministry to another. The mail received by the ECFA indicates that donors want to contribute to support Christian ministries. Donors are requesting guidance and direction. They want assurance that their funds are going to be used for the purposes for which they were raised.

Q. *Has the ECFA been the target of any left-wing organizations as have several other organizations and agencies that are affiliated with religious broadcasters? For example, there has been a long-running and on-going battle between the Moral Majority and People For The American Way. If the ECFA has been a target of criticism or concern, what is the basis for this?*

A. The ECFA has received praise and support from many circles. Christian ministries have joined the ECFA in unprecedented numbers during the past 24 months. The media has reacted very favorably to the existence of the ECFA. The ECFA has proved to be a source of information about good practices and about ministries that are following these good practices.

Organizations that frequently criticize the "religious right" have also reacted positively toward the ECFA. Even though many of the leaders of ECFA member organizations are identified with the "religious right" and all ECFA members are conservative in their theology, not all ECFA members are identified with this segment of our society. The ECFA does not endorse the program or ministry of any organization; it only deals with certain governance, fiduciary, and financial matters. Nearly everyone appreciates and supports those who are trying to highlight good business practices and ethics of any sector of the community, including religious broadcasters.

There have been a few criticisms of the ECFA by some in the Christian community. They have criticized the Council because PTL was a member of the ECFA. The ECFA was accused of not being effective because it did not stop the PTL from carrying out the alleged wrong doing.

Q. *Is the PTL still a member of the ECFA?*

A. No. PTL was a member from April 1981 until December 1986. PTL resigned from ECFA on December 23, 1986. At that time PTL gave 2 reasons for its resignation: (a) PTL was an Assemblies of God church and no other AG church was a member of ECFA. PTL stated that it "submitted to the stringent code of ethics" of the denomination, and (b) PTL also indicated that it was in compliance with the ethical and financial integrity criteria of the National Religious Broadcasters. PTL stated that "having met the criteria of the National Religious Broadcasters and the Assemblies of God, we have more than fulfilled our responsibility." Subsequently, ECFA was informed that PTL had decided not to provide its audited financial statements upon request. This obvious violation of one of the ECFA standards requires that an organization either resign or its membership be terminated. Further, ECFA has been informed by The General Council of the Assemblies of God that "contrary to PTL's representations, the Assemblies of God has no 'code of ethics' to which PTL has ever 'submitted' itself."

Q. *Why did ECFA permit PTL to continue as a member with all the things that were going on?*

A. ECFA, like other national financial accrediting organizations, relies on the accuracy of the certified audits as well as other information provided by the applicants. In extending membership to PTL, ECFA relied heavily on the unqualified audit opinion of one of the Big-8 national auditing firms which PTL had engaged through May 31, 1984. For the last fiscal year ending May 31, 1985, which ECFA reviewed, PTL switched auditors but also received a clean opinion except for a routine qualification regarding federal income and state sales tax examinations. Neither auditing firm gave any indication in issuing their opinion from 1978 to 1985 that proper financial controls were not maintained.

Since the revelations of serious conduct have come to light, ECFA obtained the services of a senior tax-exempt specialist in a Big-8 accounting firm to reexamine all the PTL's certified audits during its term of membership in ECFA. His examination confirmed that none of those opinions gave any indication whatsoever of the serious problems we now know existed. In spite of the clean audit opinions, ECFA did probe with PTL a number of compliance issues which were brought to the Council's attention through other channels.

ECFA raised questions regarding the size of the board of directors, the frequency of board meetings, the responsibility that the board was taking in approving major capital expenditures, budgets, and major policy decisions. ECFA raised questions about high management costs and too little money going directly to the ministries, proper allocation of expenses, and the way in which fund-raising costs were allocated. ECFA raised questions about prompt response to requests for audited financial statements. ECFA raised questions about overdue accounts payable and the total indebtedness, conflict of interest by doing business with board members, purchase of expensive homes, automobiles, and so on, the use of funds for the purposes for which they were raised, and elaborate furnishings. ECFA also raised questions about tax issues and audits with the IRS, litigation, and the use of premiums and incentives.

From July of 1983 to January of 1986, there were 7 face-to-face meetings between representatives of PTL and ECFA to discuss these concerns. ECFA was assured by PTL staff, members of the PTL board, the PTL auditor, and their attorney that all of the issues raised by ECFA had been resolved or were soon to be resolved.

Q. *How would your organization address the general criticism that the body of religious broadcasters is hurting local churches by absorbing more than its share of a limited collection/contribution pool?*

A. In 1986, over $87 billion was given to all charitable causes. Religious causes received $41 billion or 47 percent of that amount. Television ministries received in excess of $1 billion annually, but considerably less than $2 billion, and no television ministry has reported receiving more than $150 million in contributions in one year. A number of universities receive more than that. Several relief agencies receive more than that. These organizations are not criticized for the amount of money that they receive and their leaders, who often receive generous salaries, are not criticized. If the amount of money was the root of the problem, there would be criticism of many types of charities. This is not the case. No, the controversy regarding television ministries seems to lie not in the amount of money, but somewhere else. It seems to be related to how contributions are solicited, how money is used, and the visibility that these ministries have through television.

Q. *Then let's examine how the money is used. Does the ECFA have access to information regarding where contributions go once they are given to the television ministry?*

A. For many of the religious broadcasters, the program *is* the ministry. Therefore, it is proper that the funds raised go to pay for programming, airtime, and to cover legitimate expenses in raising and administering that money. Many in the secular media have criticized religious broadcasting for raising millions of dollars and spending this money on more television time. This is a misunderstanding, possibly intentional, of the reason for which most broadcasters are on the air. This is the same as accusing a publisher of spending money on newsprint rather than on some other project. The mixture of the program with the means of paying for the program is unusual for contemporary commercial television, but not unusual for religious television since the receiving of the offering or collection in the church is usually an integral part of Christian worship. In secular television the commercial break is seen as something distinctive from the program. In most cases there is little relationship between the content of the program and the commercial. Public television has also separated the appeal for funds from the program with special fund raising weeks and by being funded by grants from corporations and foundations. Television ministries do not.

Q. *If visibility is a source of the criticism, as you suggest, what advice would you give religious broadcasters to remedy this situation?*

A. Very few sectors of the philanthropic community put the same emphasis on the individual that religious television does. There is much more emphasis on their program, service, and ministry. Who is the head of World Vision? Who is the president of the American Red Cross? These important and influential individuals are not household names. Now if one were to ask what these organizations do, most donors could rapidly respond with accurate answers.

If television ministries were to move away from the "star system" and find that the program brings in insufficient financial support, there are several alternatives. Restructure the program to better meet the needs of those being served so that sufficient income can be raised; scale back the program so that it serves the smaller constituency that is able to support it; cancel the program altogether and put the time, energy, and finances into something else. The worse thing would be to resort to regular crisis appeals, that intimidate the audience, and that raise funds for one purpose and spend them for another. But I hope that we have reached a day when no major television ministry will be able to do this for an extended period of time on a national scale. Oral Roberts recently illustrated this in a dramatic way.

Q. *What is your forecast on the financial status of religious broadcasters? Will they be more accountable and why? Will changes in the mass communication industry (e.g., cable saturation, satellite) help or hurt them financially?*

A. Many of the broadcasters have become more accountable since the recent scandals. However, a significant number will refuse to be accountable to anyone. Some Christian broadcasters believe that they are accountable only to God. Others have never disclosed their finances and do not see any reason to begin now just because a few have been involved in scandals. I believe that contributions to television ministries will continue to grow. The growth during the next decade will probably not be as fast as during the 1980s. Growth may be limited to the growth in the population and the growth in income. A donor's allegiance may change from one broadcaster to another, but the donor will likely continue to support religious broadcasting.

REFERENCES

EFICOM modified for smaller non-profits. (1989, September). *Religious Broadcasting*, p. 19.

VI

The Lack of Division Between Electronic Church and State

Pollster George Gallup declared 1976 the "Year of the Evangelical." This was in response to Jimmy Carter's public profession that he was a "born again" Christian and the fact that his electoral margin of victory may well have been provided by evangelical Christians. Interestingly, however, most analysts either missed or underplayed the importance of this group as a potentially powerful voting bloc in future elections. According to Hadden and Swann (1981, p. 126), "there was a tendency to see Carter's candidacy and victory as an aberration. He ran primarily against Washington in the fallout of Watergate. . . . Thus, there was no real need to assess seriously the significance of the 'evangelical vote'."

Clearly, this is no longer the case. The emergence of the "new Christian right," headed by Jerry Falwell's political arm the Moral Majority (now the Liberty Foundation), has served to minimize the division between church and state in the past decade and, subsequently, has received its share of national exposure. On September 15, 1980, for instance, Falwell and his organization were the coverstory in *Newsweek* (Mayer, 1980) and "Preachers and Politics" was the lead feature story in *U.S. News and World Report* (Mann & Petersen, 1980). That the religious community was "amassing a base of potential (political) power that dwarfed every other competing interest in American society" (Rifkin & Howard, 1979, p. 30), with the evangelical movement becoming the most active of all religious groups (Bromley & Schupe, 1984; Carey, 1985; Castelli, 1988a, 1988b; Pierand, 1985), was made most apparent in the 1984 election. Evangelicals made up roughly 20 percent of Reagan's vote in 1984 (Wills, 1988), obtained largely through his close affiliation with the Moral Majority and religious broadcasters. Reagan's statement that "religion and politics are necessarily related" (Johnson & Tamney, 1985, p. 124), made during the 1984 convention, and his regular participation in national religious broadcaster conferences typifies the concerned efforts of Republican conservatives to enlist the aid of evangelicals and their followers. According to Horsfield (1984, p. xiii):

For some fearful observers, the growth of evangelical broadcasting represented a massive takeover by the political and moral right and a plot to establish a religious republic with the evangelical and fundamentalist broad-casters as the major spokespersons. More moderately, some journalists ob-served that the television preachers, by unifying and motivating otherwise inactive voters, could hold the key to [elections].

The 1988 media campaign coverage had focused on evangelicals almost entirely within the context of televangelist Pat Robertson's presidential campaign—with due justification. Hal Quinley of the polling firm Yankelovich Clancy Shulman believes that "there is a core group of about 20 percent of those eligible to vote that is highly receptive to Robertson's evangelical message and can be mobilized" (Wills, 1988, p. 28). Indeed, it has been suggested that Robertson's success as candidate and demise as nominee was largely contingent on the mobilization of this core group (Abelman, 1990; Detwiller, 1988; Frankl, 1987).

Whether or not it is true that the "idea that religion and politics don't mix was invented by the devil to keep Christians from running their own coun-try," as Jerry Falwell has suggested (Lear, 1988, p. ix), the lack of division between the electronic church and state has been most apparent in recent years and is the subject of this section. Here, communication scientists Gary Pettey and Larry Gross both offer a historical view of the marriage between media, politics, and the "Christian right," from quite different perspectives, while a chapter by Anthony Podesta and James Kurtzke critically analyze the "Christian right's" political activities and ambitions.

In his chapter, Pettey applies Stewart, Smith, and Denton's (1984) framework of 5 stages of social movements to religious activism to best explain the contemporary scene. Tracing religious-political activism in this country to its roots in the abolitionist movements of the 1820s and 1840s, Pettey suggests that the most recent and high-profile wave of activity is coming to an end. Marked by Robertson's inability to win even 1 state on Super Tuesday during the 1988 presidential election, Falwell's abrupt de-parture from the Liberty Foundation, and the recent scandals within the religious broadcasting community, the "Christian right's" energies may be waning. However, if social movements evolve through 5 distinctive stages, as Pettey reports, than the next cycle of activism is already on the horizon.

Gross, on the other hand, notes that religious broadcasting has not only been a part of the contemporary sociopolitical landscape, but has given it form and is an integral, omnipresent part of the political process. Grounding his observations in cultivation theory, he suggests that "the media now compete with and even replace religious and social institutions as sources of information and knowledge." Thus, while Pettey identifies patterns in the course of social movements, Gross believes that patterns in media por-trayals have the power to create or destroy social movements. And, while Pettey foresees the termination of the "Christian right's" political activism, Gross believes that the "left" has been unable to match their success in harnessing the available resources of media technology, thereby reinforcing the longevity of the "Christian right's" activity within the political arena.

The "left," represented in the third chapter by Anthony Podesta and James Kurtzke for People For the American Way—a constitutional liberties organization—analyzes and criticizes the "right's" use and abuse of mass media. Its longtime battle with Jerry Falwell and his organization sets the stage for this chapter, as the authors conclude that "the only redeeming silver lining in the cloud called the "religious right" that we see is that the movement's radical agenda and practices have forced Americans to search more vigorously for answers to their social dilemmas, albeit dilemmas made even more difficult by "religious right" activities."

REFERENCES

Abelman, R. (1990). Pat Robertson's fall from grace: Viewer processing of PTL scandal information. In S. Kraus (Ed.), *Mass communication and political information processing* (pp. 113–129). Hillsdale, NJ: Lawrence Erlbaum.

Bromley, D., & Schupe, A. (1984). *New Christian politics.* Macon, GA: Mercer University Press.

Carey, J. (1985). Christian right aims votes at new targets. *U.S. News & World Report,* pp. 99, 70.

Castelli, J. (1988a). *A plea for common sense: Resolving the clash between religion & politics.* New York: Harper & Row.

Castelli, J. (1988b, Spring). The evangelical vote. *Forum: The Newsletter of People For The American Way Action Fund,* p. 8.

Detwiller, T. (1988). Viewing Robertson's rhetoric in an Augustinian mirror. *Journal of Communication and Religion, 11*(1), 22–31.

Frankl, R. (1987). *Televangelism: The marketing of popular religion.* Carbondale, IL: Southern Illinois University Press.

Hadden, J., & Swann, C.E. (1981). *Prime time preachers.* Reading, MA: Addison-Wesley.

Horsfield, P.G. (1984). *Religious television: The American experience.* New York: Longman.

Johnson, S.D., & Tamney, J.B. (1985). The Christian right and the 1984 presidential election. *Review of Religious Research, 27*(2), 124–133.

Lear, N. (1988). Forward. In J. Castelli (Ed.), *A plea for common sense: Resolving the clash between religion & politics* (pp. vii–xiii). New York: Harper & Row.

Mann, J., & Petersen, S. (1980, September 15). Preachers in politics: Decisive force in 1980? *U.S. News and World Report,* pp. 24–26.

Mayer, A. (1980, September 15). A tide of born again politics? *Newsweek,* pp. 28–36.

Pierand, R.V. (1985). Religion and the 1984 election campaign. *Review of Religious Research, 27*(2), 98–114.

Rifkin, J., & Howard, T. (1979). *The emerging order.* New York: G. P. Putnam's Sons.

Stewart, C., Smith, C., & Denton, R. (1984). *Persuasion and social movements.* Prospect Heights, IL: Waveland Press.

Wills, G. (1988, February 22). Robertson and the Reagan gap. *Time,* pp. 27–28.

17

Bibles, Ballots, and Beatific Vision: The Cycle of Religious Activism in the 1980s

Gary R. Pettey

Our collective memory as a nation is often very short. Perhaps egocentrically, we believe events that occur during our lifetimes are the first such events in U.S. history, or at least the biggest, best, or worst in our past. Usually, even a quick look back over our relatively brief history will reveal events of uncanny similarity.

The religious activism of the late 1970s and early 1980s can be seen as an example of this. The so-called "new right" came into the public domain as a coalition between the various evangelicals and the conservative wing of the Republican party. Fundamentalist and television minister Jerry Falwell and conservative political activist Richard Viguerie were the core of the movement. Their organization, The Moral Majority, became a lightning rod for supporters and critics alike. While the growth of religious television broadcasting may give some of the particulars of the movement a 1980s twist, the joining of religious fundamentalism and the political right is not particularly new. In fact, there appear to have been previous cycles of religious activism in this country. This chapter will examine the cycle of the evangelical right's role in politics in the 1980s.

THE CYCLES OF SOCIAL MOVEMENTS

The current religious activism can be seen as having a natural cycle not unlike other social movements. Stewart, Smith, and Denton (1984) offer a framework to help understand social movements, which they define as:

> an organized, uninstitutionalized, and significantly large collectivity that is created to bring about or to resist a program for change in societal norms and values, operates primarily through persuasive strategies, and is countered by an established order. (p. 14)

They describe such movements as having 6 stages: Genesis, Social Unrest, Enthusiasm, Mobilization, Maintenance, and Termination. By understanding how the "religious right" fits within a framework of social movements in general, it may be easier to understand how this particular movement emerged, enjoyed a certain popularity, and now appears to be retiring from the political scene.

Genesis. At first, there are scattered individuals who perceive a problem or set of issues, but the general public's attention is focused on other concerns. Early leaders may emerge. They will attempt to inform others around them, but this is largely a latency period. To make the move to the next stage, Stewart, Smith, and Denton argue that:

> A triggering event is usually required to move the generally unorganized and invisible social movement from the genesis stage to the social unrest stage. The trigger may be a Supreme Court decision, a nuclear accident, an insensitive reaction . . . a new law, an economic downturn, a military action, or the appearance of a movement-oriented book on the best seller list. (p. 39)

Social Unrest. The triggering event often precipitates some "manifesto that serves 3 important functions: (1) to describe the problem; (2) to identify the devils, scapegoats, and faulty principles that have caused and maintained the problem; and (3) to prescribe the solutions and the gods, principles and procedures that will bring it about" (p. 40). It is at this stage that the mass media can have a large impact on the groups, according to Todd Gitlin (1980). He argues that as the media seek to report on the issue and give some context to the "triggering event," they can ordain leaders and define the movement for the general population. These are leaders and issues, Gitlin suggests, that may not represent the fledgling organization's own view of itself.

Enthusiasm and Mobilization. With the public exposure that the media provide, the scattered organizations find a rallying point. Stewart, Smith, and Denton argue that:

> The converted see the social movement as the *only* way to bring about urgently needed change, and they are imbued with the belief that the movement's time has come. Optimism is rampant. Important legitimizers—actors, senators, clergy, physicians, labor leaders, educators—lend an air of excitement and inevitability to the cause. (p. 41)

At this point, an "us v. them" distinction crystallizes. The leaders of the movement may actually become the movement as their destiny and the movement's become inseparable. The attainment of some goals or the death of a leader may propel the movement to the fourth phase.

Maintenance. Both victories and defeats can have impact on the now-relatively popular organization. Its victories can both placate large numbers of supporters and push the movement more into the mainstream where it must become a self-perpetuating institution to survive. Leaders who excel at "revolution" may find it hard to govern a less vibrant and less spontaneous bureaucracy. The single attainable goal that initially served as the philosophical fire may be the movement's undoing when other hopes and dreams cannot reignite the spark dampened by the fatigue of confrontation.

Termination. The movement ceases to be a movement. It seldom disappears totally, but public attention has moved on to other issues. Leaders go in other directions. Fractures, perhaps always present, splinter the movement as various groups seek to direct the movement and in the end doom its popular existence.

EARLIER RELIGIOUS ACTIVISM: ABOLITION, ALCOHOL, APES, AND ANTI-COMMUNISM

Before examining the cycle of religious-political activism of the 1980s, it should be noted that the heritage of religious activism in this country should not be considered synonymous with right-wing politics. Mainstream religions in the 1820s and 1840s provided much of the basis for the abolitionist movements, but it was some nonmainstream groups, such as the Quakers, who took more active roles. While the Women's Christian Temperance Union was a more middle-class movement and was not specifically formed to advocate prohibition, the Anti-Saloon League, made up primarily of Methodists, lobbied specifically for prohibition and even constructed "hit lists" of state and national legislators who favored remaining "wet."[1]

Evangelicals became involved in 2 issues around the turn of the 20th century. The first was the Gold Standard. William Jennings Bryan embodied the evangelical stance when he found a Biblical sanction against programs designed to bring on inflation. This attempt at public policy making failed, as did the second issue also involving Bryan. The Scopes trial was to be the test of evolution (recent discussions of Creationist Science show that some issues never completely die). For evangelicals, evolution and Christianity were mutually exclusive, and several southern states outlawed its teaching in the public schools (note that the courts recently overturned statutes in two states requiring the teaching of Creationist Science whenever Darwinism was taught).

EVANGELICALS AND THE NEW RIGHT

Evangelicals had not been too involved politically in the post-World War II era, according to Reichley (1985).[2] After the Scopes "monkey trial" of the

---

[1] See Gusfield (1963) for a complete discussion.

[2] According to Reichley (1985), "Evangelism is best defined as a branch of Christianity,

1920s and the repeal of prohibition in the 1930s, "Evangelicals concentrated on conversion, and, except for occasional efforts to outlaw what they deem[ed] as person vices, evangelical Protestant groups largely ignore[d] social and political efforts for reform" (Wuthnow, 1983, p. 168).

Evangelicals and especially fundamentalists have been perpetually concerned with the general spread of "modernism" throughout American society. In the early part of the 20th century, Billy Sunday attacked liberal protestants for their acceptance of such "modern" ideas as Darwinism, psychology, and behavioral sciences (McLoughlin, 1978). More recently, increases in the rate of divorce, in the number of unwed mothers, in the openness of homosexuality, in the amount of drug use, and in violent- and sexually-oriented media content have incurred the wrath of evangelical protest (Schaffer, 1981). By the early 1960s, many groups were bothered by the increase in divorce as well as the spread of rock'n'roll. Billy Graham had become a national institution, who both political parties courted. Except for Graham, much of the country wasn't aware of evangelicals. But while Graham's televised sermons were largely free of political content, he reflected his own general political stance in the 1949 rhetorical question: "Will we turn to the leftwingers and atheists or will we turn to the right and embrace the cross?" (Hunter, 1983, pp. 44–45).

The *Genesis* period was in full swing by 1961 when the U.S. Supreme Court prohibited prayer in public schools. The evangelicals were outraged. But other concerns such as Civil Rights, Vietnam, and—eventually—Watergate caught the general public's attention. As Watergate and runaway inflation in the 1970s made all Americans reevaluate the current state of the nation, evangelicals were reaching the boiling point as the problems of modernism seemed to be escaping from "humanist" centers such as New York City and Los Angeles, only to invade their own communities and threaten their families and lifestyles. Further, the tax-exempt status of many church-sponsored schools was called into scrutiny under the argument that many of them were all-white and should not be federally subsidized. While the Civil Rights movement and Vietnam had cleared the way for liberal churches to become activist during the 1960s, the Roe v. Wade decision, which allowed abortion on demand, was a rallying point for more conservative groups. For evangelicals it was perhaps the final signal that the U.S. Supreme Court and perhaps the government itself was in need of Christian reform.

---

descended from the pietist movement of the Reformation by way of the Great Awakening, that emphasizes direct experience by the individual of the Holy Spirit (being "born again") and that regards the Bible as an infallible source of religious and moral authority. Fundamentalism is an extreme form of evangelicalism. All fundamentalists are evangelicals, but not all evangelicals are fundamentalists." For histories of evangelicalism and fundamentalism see Marsden (1980) and McLoughlin (1978).

The *Genesis* period was drawing to an end by the early 1970s; by 1975 it seemed the trigger had been pulled and the movement had been propelled into the *Social Unrest* phase. That trigger was Jimmy Carter. Much as John F. Kennedy had to deal with the question of his Roman Catholicism in the 1960 campaign, Carter would need to explain in 1976 what it meant to be "born again." He was a Southerner, and his sister was a minister. Initially, evangelicals saw him as the hope of their movement and the sign that the country was turning the corner on modernism. But by 1978, although the notion of being born again had been well popularized in the mass media, for many evangelicals Carter had turned out to be a betrayer rather than a savior. They perceived Carter as soft on communism, and they perceived his notion of human rights as damaging many international friends. Carter's increased tightening of the tax-exempt status of church-operated schools proved that more action was needed. Carter's election had proved to be a misfire. A second trigger would be required.

The 1978 congressional elections proved to be the spark. Antiabortionist groups, many made-up primarily of Roman Catholics, targeted several U.S. representatives because of their stand supporting abortion. Many, including Dick Clark of Iowa, were defeated. This time 2 evangelical groups were prepared.

The Christian Voice had been founded in California to encourage the passing of a referendum to ban admitted homosexuals from state school rooms. After 1978, the *Voice* broadened its concerns. While issues such as school prayer topped its national agenda, it was also concerned with the perceived threat of the Soviet Union as well as the Panama Canal treaties that would eventually return the canal to Panamanian control. By the 1980 elections, *The Voice* had constructed a "morality" index to rate office seekers and target those who scored too low. Benson and Williams (1982, p. 172) reported *The Voice* leader Gary Jarmin's strategy:

> We have targeted about 35 members of Congress and the Senate who have scored low on our voting record and whom we think we can successfully retire from Congress in November. We're going to do up a little flyer showing exactly how the targeted Congressmen or Senators voted on these issues . . . print up thousands of these and distribute these to Christians as they leave their churches on Sunday Morning.

The other group founded in 1979 was, of course, the Moral Majority. Pat Robertson's boast on his televised *700 Club* that "We have enough votes to run the country" and "We're going to take over" now had a young, but monied, organization with Jerry Falwell at the helm. By the end of the first month of Moral Majority money appeals, Falwell had collected one-third of his $3 million goal. His 250,000 person mailing list from *The Old Time Gospel Hour* combined with Richard Viguerie's virtual creation of mass direct mailing brought to life a powerful organization almost over-night. With no small support from the use of television, a new right-wing coalition had been formed. This "new right" was still concerned with the economy and foreign affairs, but it was also determined to rectify the problems created by busing, abortion, pornography, and removal of prayer from the public schools.

Stewart, Smith, and Denton's (1984) model calls for a manifesto, and between 1980 and 1981 several emerged. Tim LaHaye published *The Battle for the Mind* in 1980. In it he crystallizes the true enemy—secular humanism. He argues that the promulgators of evolution had brought us amorality and atheism, writing:

> There can be no question that the humanists control our government and have for many years. . . . [Those people] who control our national destiny represent sufficient humanistic philosophy or lack of true Christian consensus to have brought us to the threshold of fulfilling the humanist dreams of a secular, amoral society. (p. 17)

The next year Francis Schaffer's book *A Christian Manifesto* (1981) de-clared secular humanism a religion that "the government and courts of the United States favor over all others," saying:

> [Christians] have very gradually become disturbed over permissiveness, por-nography, the public schools, the breakdown of the family, and finally abor-tion. But they have not seen this as a totality—each thing being a part, a symptom of a much larger problem. They have failed to see that all of this has come about due to a shift in world view. (p. 17)

Falwell's own book *Listen America!* (1980) expands the plea linking a host of right-wing issues to basic moral and Christian concerns. For example, he writes that:

> The free enterprise system is clearly outlined in the Book of Proverbs in the Bible. Jesus Christ made it clear that the work ethic was part of his plan for man. Ownership of property is Biblical. Competition in business is Biblical. Ambitious and successful business management is clearly outlined as part of God's plan for His people. (p. 6)

To consider the movement's shift into the *Enthusiasm* and *Mobilization* stages, we must ask why the media and the public were willing to devote time, space, and attention to the evangelical message in the early 1980s. Reichley (1985) explains that part of the reason was Falwell's own visibility and his push in 1980 to get the name of the Moral Majority well known as quickly as possible. Falwell also had a well-publicized appeal for evangelicals to register to vote.[3] The nation's media noticed, and many media concluded—often incorrectly—that Moral Majority Inc. had a mass following. Reichley (1985, p. 323) reports:

> The *Washington Star* placed Falwell's weekly television audience at 25 million, making him the "second most watched TV personality in the country, surpassed only by Johnny Carson." *Newsweek* guessed that his televised appeals were reaching 18 million every week (. . . Nielson and Arbitron ratings [were] about 1.4 million.) The *New York Times* surmised that Falwell had "created something very similar to a political party." *U.S. News and World Report* found "a political holy war without precedent . . . in full swing in this country."

Televangelists added to the public's and the media's perceptions of the magnitude of the movement by claiming upwards of tens of millions of viewers and by claiming they could raise large sums of money in relatively short periods of time.

Still another reason may lie in the role religion was playing in other parts of the world. The Roman Catholic church had become a political actor in several nations. Pope John Paul II often spoke against communism, and in his native Poland he was a political figure. Roman Catholic leaders were active in Nicaragua and the Philippines. An Anglican leader in South Africa was becoming a nonviolent rallying point against apartheid, and a religious revolution in Iran had created major problems here in the United States and in the Middle East. Patricia Harris, who was secretary of Health and Social Services under President Carter, linked the Iranian situation directly: "I'm beginning to believe that we could have an Ayatollah Khomeini in this country, but he will not have a beard . . . he will have a television program" (Reichley, 1985, p. 323).

In many ways, the election of Ronald Reagan in 1980 and his reelection in 1984 were both the victory and the death knell for this revival of religious activism. The 1986 elections returned the Senate to the Democrats, and saw much of the general public begin its swing back toward center. This post-1984 period was crucial for the evangelicals. It was this period that could see either the movement's institutionalization and *Maintenance* or, in Stewart, Smith, and Denton's (1984) terms, the rapid movement into *Termination*. Though the "new right" may not be gone, it does seem that the very forces that would maintain the evangelical's political cause have

---

[3] The demographics of most evangelicals place them firmly among groups who are less likely to be politically active or to vote, but even by 1980 Gallup reported that members of the "religious right" were more likely to be registered to vote than were similar people who were not members of the evangelical movement.

mostly splintered. Falwell's Moral Majority is now the Liberty Foundation sans Falwell. It should probably have come as no surprise that Pentecostal and fundamentalist elements could not, for very long, remain allies. Both sides were suspicious of the other, and, by the time of the Jim Bakker scandal, the struggle had become public. Before the Jimmy Swaggart scandal, Gallup polls already were reporting that even people who classified themselves as "born again" were becoming cynical about televangelists and were sending less money (Ostling, 1987).

Two final signals that the "new right" coalition was in trouble could be found in the 1988 presidential race, where two possible standard bearers did not fare well. The early withdrawal of Jack Kemp and Pat Robertson's attempt to distance himself from his religious broadcasting past probably dashed the "new right's" hopes of further national political success. Robertson's failure to win even 1 state on Super Tuesday, when 20 states—mostly in the conservative South—held caucuses or primaries, probably spelled the end of the current religious-political activism. Robertson has since returned to his broadcasting network.

The current phase of religious activism may be over. But given the history of religious and social movements, both on the left and the right, it is probable that the next cycle of activism is already on the horizon. History shows that the conservative, business-oriented 1920s and 1950s were followed by a more liberal, social issue-oriented 1930s and 1960s. The 1990s may see a return of liberal religious activism. The *Genesis* phase might already be marked by the Nuclear Freeze Movement and antiapartheid concerns. A backlash to the Reagan years may well produce the sort of trigger that will allow a congelation of various groups on the left into a single identifiable movement.

REFERENCES

Benson, P., & Williams, D. (1982). *Religion on capitol hill: Myth and realities*. San Francisco, CA: Harper & Row.

Falwell, J. (1980). *Listen America!* New York: Doubleday.

Gitlin, T. (1980). *The whole world is watching*. Berkeley, CA: University of California Press.

Gusfield, J. (1963). *The symbolic crusade*. Urbana, IL: University of Illinois.

Hunter, J. (1983). *American evangelicalism: Conservative religion and the quandary of modernity*. New Brunswick, NJ: Rutgers University Press.

LaHaye, T. (1980). *The battle for the mind*. Old Tappan, NJ: Revell.

Marsden, G. (1980). *Fundamentalism and American culture*. New York: Oxford University Press.

McLoughlin, W. (1978). *Revivals, awakenings, and reform*. Chicago, IL: University of Chicago Press.

Ostling, R. (1987, June 8). Of God and greed. *Time*, pp. 70–74.

Reichley, A. (1985). *Religion in American public life*. Washington, DC: The Brookings Institution.

Schaffer, F. (1981). *A Christian manifesto*. Westchester, IL: Crossway.

Stewart, C., Smith, C., & Denton, R., Jr. (1984). *Persuasion and social movements*. Prospect Heights, IL: Waveland Press, Inc.

Wuthnow, R. (1983). Political rebirth of American evangelicalism. In R. Liebman & R. Wuthnow (Eds.), *The new Christian right* (pp. 168–182). New York: Aldine.

18

Conflict Between the Electronic Church and State: The Religious Right's Crusade Against Pluralism

Anthony T. Podesta
James S. Kurtzke

Since the 1960s America has experienced a troubled societal transformation less quiet but no less dramatic than the well-known upheavals of that turbulent decade. Our education system is beset by poorer student performance; young Americans are vulnerable to a drug epidemic and an AIDS plague both sweeping the nation; one of every 2 marriages ends in divorce; and every year 1 in 10 teenage girls, on average, becomes pregnant.

In 1980 many evangelical and fundamentalist Christians believed that these and other transformations indicated a disturbing decline in social values. They offered the nation an alternative through a new political movement, almost exclusively led by televangelists, with the objective of fostering, in the words of Christian Broadcasting Network founder Pat Robertson, "a common ethical standard that will bring us back to traditional conceptions of morality" (Robertson, 1984). This new morality would strengthen the nation's collective resolve to properly cope with societal problems where individual values had failed.

These conservative Christians, collectively known as the "religious right," worked to affect society's decision makers so that they would reform the nation's legal and educational systems according to this new public morality. The "religious right" formed large, national political organizations, actively campaigned for candidates for public office, and turned the electronic pulpit into a forum on public morality and political renewal. In fact, television played an important, perhaps central, role in the "religious right's" political involvement. More than 50 million television viewers watched the top 6 televangelists during the height of their popularity.[1]

---

[1] In an A. C. Nielsen survey conducted for the Christian Broadcasting Network in 1985, Pat Robertson's daily *700 Club* program reached 16.3 million viewers each month. Others

The "religious right" found a natural home in the Republican Party. By advocating a conservative cultural lifestyle governed by "traditional values," the evangelical and fundamentalist movement complemented the new conservative power base within the Republican Party, headed by the nostalgic Ronald Reagan, who yearned for simpler times. As time progressed, however, it soon became evident that the "religious right's" political involvement masked a religious crusade: To "Christianize" America by electing "Godly" candidates who shared their "Biblical" positions on public policy issues and to turn the nation's public schools into fundamentalist and evangelical Christian Sunday schools. The new public morality was to be their own.

These evangelicals and fundamentalists, who preached a literal reading of the Bible whose messages could not be challenged, first fought a sectarian battle with other conservative Christians who applied Biblical teachings in a nonliteralist fashion and, for example, accepted the scientific evidence supporting evolution rather than the Biblically-based theory of creationism.[2] After capturing control of the Southern Baptist Convention, evangelical and fundamentalist leaders attempted to forge the tens of millions of their fellow believers into a single voting bloc that would similarly control the U.S. political agenda through Biblical literalism.

Thus, "religious right" televangelists made their political appeal in religious terms. They proclaimed that all Americans had to join them in being "saved" or "born again" (i.e., believing in a literal, conservative interpretation of the Bible) or lead "inferior" lives. Public officials who agreed with the "religious right" that "our form of government came (sic) from the Bible" were embraced as "Godly," "pro-moral," and "pro-Biblical," and those who disagreed were assailed as "satanic," "anti-God," "immoral," and "anti-Biblical."

"Religious right" televangelists combined this religious intolerance with political intolerance. They claimed that they alone held the power to correctly interpret the Bible in both the sectarian and political arenas and that no one could challenge the infallibility of God's political prophets.

The televangelists' claims of political inerrancy raised tremendous difficulties, for refusal to debate any group's political agenda is obviously antidemocratic and does not allow for political compromise. But the "religious right" was not interested in political compromise. Public debate threatened "unity" by allowing other groups to promote their views. "If God came on television today," Pat Robertson once lamented, "you'd have to give equal time to the devil" (People for the American Way, 1987a).

---

who scored well included: Jimmy Swaggart, 9.3 million; Robert Schuller, 7.6 million; Jim Bakker, 5.8 million; Oral Roberts, 5.8 million; and Jerry Falwell, 5.6 million (Ostling, 1986, p. 67).

[2] Fundamentalists do not believe that man evolved, but that God created man exactly in His own image in one day.

The political agenda that "religious right" leaders commanded Americans to accept, however, suggested that they were far from inerrant on public policy matters. Robertson, for instance, stood more often outside of the political mainstream than within it by claiming that the Constitution does not provide for a separation of church and state, that states do not have to follow the Bill of Rights, that women must be subservient to their husbands, that the national debt can be wiped out by declaring a Year of the Jubilee, and that nuclear Armageddon is inevitable (see Abelman, in press; Castelli, 1988, pp. 141–171).

Thus, the "religious right" presented the American people with an alternative value system that appeared extremist, but one they could not debate because it rested in a Biblical literalism that only "religious right" televangelists could correctly interpret.

In the "religious right's" attempts to pressure the political branches of government to adopt their own religious views, the televangelists sought to redefine the constitutional separation of church and state in a manner in which they could gain political superiority over other religions; they judged political candidates for their belief in Jerry Falwell's God and perceived alliances with the devil; and they undermined religiously-neutral public education by engaging in a widespread censorship campaign against school textbooks, literary classics, and whole curricula.

The content and style of the "religious right's" moral agenda contained 2 fundamental flaws: The nation's would-be moral code excluded more people than it sought to protect; and the "religious right" justified this code through a harsh combination of religion and politics which prohibited public debate and conflicted with most Americans' strong opposition to extensive interaction between preachers and politicians.[3] Consequently, most Americans view "religious right" televangelist leaders with disdain[4], disagree with many of the "religious right's" positions on important public policy issues[5], and disapprove of the manner in which the "religious right" confuses matters of church and state[6] (see Harris, 1987). The sex and fraud

---

[3] An August, 1981 NBC/Associated Press poll asked, "Do you think churches and members of the clergy should be involved in politics, like backing a candidate for public office, or don't you think so?" Sixty-nine percent opposed such involvement; 31 percent approved.

[4] Seventy percent disagree with the statement that Jerry Falwell is "a religious leader who is a real moral force in his country and the world" (Harris, 1987, pp. 252–253).

[5] Only 16 percent, for example, agree with the "religious right's" position that eliminating sex education in schools would result in fewer teenage pregnancies; 55 percent oppose the "religious right's" support for a constitutional amendment to ban abortion; and 67 percent disagree with the "religious right's" opposition to economic sanctions against South Africa (Harris, 1987, pp. 84, 182, 252).

[6] When the "religious right" first targeted their political opponents for defeat in 1980, a Gallup poll asked, "Certain religious groups are actively working for the defeat of political candidates who don't agree with their positions on certain issues. Do you think they are right or wrong to do this?" Sixty percent objected while only 28 responded favorably (Castelli, 1988, p. 29).

scandals of televangelists Jimmy Swaggart and PTL founder Jim Bakker provide further confirmation of the public's suspicion that televangelists are filled more with self-righteousness than righteousness.[7]

In spite of its pretentions, we believe that the "religious right's" unusual claim to a Biblical mandate for (at times extremist) public policy views prevents the alliance from extending beyond the right wing of the Republican Party, where it has, nevertheless, exerted great influence.

The "religious right" today finds itself in a "catch-22" situation: In order to gain broader public support the movement's leaders would have to fundamentally alter their view of the separation of church and state, but their special mission—to communicate God's political message—rests on church-state integration. The Republican Party, too, has a difficult dilemma. Party officials must recognize and accommodate the strong emergence of the "religious right" within their ranks, but embracing the "religious right's" moral agenda too closely could offend moderate Republicans, independents, and conservative Democrats, all of whom Republicans need to win national office.

RELIGIOUS RIGHT V. FOUNDERS

When Thomas Jefferson first used the phrase "wall of separation between church and state," he stood on firm moral ground no less than the Bible: Jesus Christ told believers that they should "render unto Caesar the things that are Caesar's, and unto God's the things that are God's." The establishment and free exercise clauses of the First Amendment[8], along with the prohibition of religious tests for public office contained in Article VI of the Constitution[9], were designed to prevent the United States federal government from conducting the sort of religious persecution from which many early Americans had fled in Europe. The adoption of the Fourteenth Amendment, which applied the Bill of Rights directly to state action, prohibited individual states from engaging in similar discriminatory behavior.

Thus, the American government cannot establish an official church, favor any religious viewpoint above others, coerce church attendance or

---

[7] Bakker was indicted for wire and mail fraud in December, 1988. That same month, the Internal Revenue Service confirmed that it was investigating the ministries of 34 televangelists, including Falwell and Roberts for a variety of allegations, including diversion of ministry funds for personal use and political activities, receipt of salaries and benefits that exceeded the limits for tax-exempt organizations, and other unspecified charges. Robertson's presidential campaign organization was also being probed for any possible illegal diversion of funds from the Christian Broadcasting Network to his 1988 presidential campaign (IRS Probes Evangelists' Operations, 1988).

[8] "Congress shall make no law respecting an establishment of religion, or prohibiting the free exercise thereof. . ." (*Constitution of the United States of America*, Amendment I).

[9] "[N]o religious tests shall ever be required as a qualification to an office or public trust of the United States" (*Constitution of the United States of America*, Article VI).

nonattendance, encourage "a belief or a disbelief in any religion," punish citizens for their church attendance or beliefs, or participate in the affairs of religious organizations (Everson v. Board of Education, 1987, 330 US). These prohibitions, which constitute individual bricks in Jefferson's church-state wall, insure that all Americans remain free from religious tyranny.

Jefferson and other American founders did not intend the constitutional separation of church and state to mandate secular superiority over, or regulation of, sectarian life however. Jefferson's wall does not prohibit religious officials from participating in the affairs of government (such an interpretation would surely violate the First Amendment's free speech and free exercise clauses). The Constitution merely places religion beyond the reach of government so that purity of religious beliefs may never be poisoned by partisan politics.

Jim Castelli (1988, p. 3), an author who studies church-state issues, best explains Jefferson's idea of religious liberty:

> The separation of church and state is not the same thing as the separation of religion and politics. Church and state, as institutions, must be kept separate; religion and politics, as processes of thought and action, cannot be kept separate.

But the "religious right" has had a different view: All matters of religion and government are inextricable and all constitutional interpretations to the contrary are incorrect. To Pat Robertson (1982a) "the Constitution is a marvelous document for self-government by Christian people. But the minute you turn it into the hands of non-Christian people and atheistic people, they can use it to destroy the very foundation of our society." The Moral Majority's Jerry Falwell has rejected Castelli's differentiation between separating sectarian and secular institutions but not their ideas: "The idea that religion and politics don't mix was invented by the devil to keep Christians from running their own country" (People for the American Way, 1985a, p. 3).

Robertson, who believes that the roots for the separation of church and state rest in Soviet ideology, has an absolutely literal view of the Constitution: Since the actual text of the Constitution contains "nothing about a wall of separation, nothing about separation of church and state," the doctrine therefore does not exist. Indeed, the "religious right" has claimed that the Constitution only prohibits attempts by the federal government to adopt a particular denomination as our established national religion (People for the American Way, 1985a).

When the "religious right's" constitutional interpretations transform themselves into specific public policy positions, they present a vision of America as tyrannical as the societies from which the founders fled: Individual states are free to establish their own religions; state legislatures may coerce prayer from children; public school board officials may ban books that do not promote the community's dominant religious views; and failure to pass a religious litmus test provides a proper basis for exclusion from public office (see Castelli, 1988; People for the American Way, 1986a, 1986b, 1988).

THE BIBLICAL ROOTS OF THE MORAL AGENDA

These unusual interpretations of the separation of church and state are best explained by the fact that the "religious right" has seen itself in a battle between God and Satan over the moral soul of America. "We're fighting against all the systems of Satan that are destroying our nation today," Jerry Falwell (1981) has said, "The real conflict is between light and darkness, the kingdom of Satan and the kingdom of the Lord Jesus Christ." As a result, Falwell and his political allies have perceived all social problems as a reflection of Satan's immoral will at work, weakening societal values and diluting the importance of religion and morality in American life.

To combat the "immoral," "satanic" strategies, many televangelists and evangelical and fundamentalist ministers have seen themselves as modern-day disciples who reveal God's moral "truth" from the electronic pulpit to a nation in need of stronger values. Revealed religious "truth" rests in the ministers' literal interpretations of the Bible; congregations must accept the infallibility of the minister-as-disciple and cannot debate his Biblical pronouncements.[10] If other Americans are to escape Satan's domain, they, too, must embrace God's morality, as told by "religious right" ministers, and thereby become "saved" or "born again."

Since the "religious right's" moral war allows no room for church-state boundaries, the movement's ministers have demanded the same unswerving belief, from their congregations and from the American people, in their role as the inerrant messengers of revealed political truth as in their role as the inerrant messengers of revealed religious truth, both of which reject debate. Whether they have engaged in political speech making or preached the Gospel from the pulpit, the clarity of the ministers' moral message has been the same: That the ultimate choice in life is between good (God Himself) and evil (the devil). By identifying their views with the choice for good, the ministers and televangelists of the "religious right" have assigned those who disagree with their political views as choosing evil and Satan over God.

Robertson again embodies the "religious right's" peculiar combination of religious and political intolerance to the sectarian and secular views of other

---

[10] Individual preachers add nothing to the substance of the "truth;" they only communicate what God tells them. For both the preacher and the congregation the "truth" by its nature is not subject to debate.

people. In 1982, for example, People for the American Way asked television stations that broadcast the Robertson-hosted *700 Club* program to provide response time for people who disagreed with some of the televangelist's inflammatory political statements. Robertson learned of the request and, in a May 13, correspondence to group co-founder Norman Lear, wrote this reply:

> You are trying to silence a prophet of God. The Bible says this, 'He (God) removed kings for their sake, saying *touch not my anointed and do my prophets no harm.*' . . . I warn you, with all solemnity in the words of the Negro spiritual, 'Your arms are too short to box with God.' The suppression of the voice of God's servant is a terrible thing! God Himself will fight for me against you—and He will win! (emphasis in original)

A POLITICAL FORCE IN ACTION

A sophisticated political structure has executed the "religious right's" strategy to recast American society in its own religious mold. As a political alliance the religious right has contained 3 main tiers of activist evangelicals, fundamentalists, and televangelists. In the first tier have been the nationally prominent televangelists, who have defined and advocated the "religious right's" religious agenda in the national political forum.

Through their respective nationally syndicated television programs that have been broadcast daily or weekly, Pat Robertson (*700 Club*), Jerry Falwell (*Old Time Gospel Hour*), Jimmy Swaggart (*Jimmy Swaggart*), and dozens of other televangelists have spread the moral gospel to tens of millions of viewers who represent television congregations. Although Robertson took a sabbatical from the *700 Club* in 1987 and 1988, he did gain an additional audience through a forum not shared by either Falwell or Swaggart, the 1988 presidential campaign. As a result of Robertson's 2-year quest for the Republican Party's 1988 presidential nomination, Falwell's intentions to deemphasize politics, and Swaggart's sex scandal, Robertson became the "religious right's" chief national spokesman.

Aside from Robertson's political ambitions, the televangelists have concentrated their efforts on political campaigns for federal and state offices, public preaching, and organization efforts. Through the electronic media they have laid the intellectual groundwork for "religious right" interest groups and grass-roots activists to defeat public policy makers critical of the "religious right" and pressure education officials to indoctrinate children according to the "religious right's" religious principles.

The second tier, large national special interest groups, have constituted the heart of the "religious right's" political strength. Here, organizations such as Falwell's Moral Majority, Robertson's National Legal Foundation, televangelist Tim LaHaye's American Coalition for Traditional Values, the

Rev. Robert Grant's Christian Voice, and Beverly LaHaye's Concerned Women for America (self-proclaimed as the nation's largest women's organization), have executed political strategies at the grass-roots level as conduits between the "religious right's" national leaders and grass-roots supporters.

Hundreds of thousands local activists have comprised the third tier of the "religious right," in which pastors and congregation members have actively engaged in political campaigns and protest efforts. Together, the televangelists, special interest groups, and grass-roots activists have pressured politicians, school board officials, book publishers, and other community leaders to exclusively promote evangelical and fundamentalist Christianity in secular life.

CAMPAIGNING FOR "GODLY" CANDIDATES

The "religious right" has been very clear about its mission in U.S. politics: To convince the voters that Christians, "born-again" Christians, "feel more strongly than others do" about "love of country and support for the traditional family" (Castelli, 1988, p.141). Rob Scribner, a 1984 and 1986 Republican congressional nominee from California, was typical of many "religious right" candidates. In one campaign, Scribner said that he ran for Congress to "take territory for our Lord Jesus Christ" and charged that his opponent, Democratic Representative Mel Levine, was "opposed to nearly everything the Lord's church stands for in this nation" (People for the American Way, 1986a, p. 2).

With this kind of rhetoric, the "religious right" has exploited religious bigotry for political gain in campaigns where such appeals could make the difference, particularly in races between Christian Republicans and Jewish Democrats. Introducing religion as a political campaign issue has recast the fundamental equation for fundamentalist and evangelical Christians: Rather than voting for the candidate who is in greatest agreement on key issues, which can only be determined through public debate, the task was made simpler: Are you one of us or not? Falwell's national network of 90,000 pastors, for instance, has supported those candidates who have passed his religious litmus tests by alerting 40 million congregation members of the "dishonest" opponents of "pro-moral candidates."

The most controversial "religious right" political tactic has been the nationwide distribution of 20 million "Biblical scoreboards" by Christian Voice to voters just before each election (see People for the American Way, 1986a, pp. 28–30). These scoreboards, which Christian Voice has described as the "report cards" of members of Congress on a variety of "moral/family issues," have been typically used in congressional races where the "religious right" targeted an incumbent (usually, but not always, a Democrat) for defeat. In the scoreboards, candidates' positions on selected issues have been represented as either "pro-Biblical" (a passing grade), or "anti-

Biblical" (a failing grade). For instance, members of Congress were "pro-Biblical" in 1986 if they had supported Star Wars or aid to the Nicaraguan contras and "anti-Biblical" if they had opposed these policies (p. 29). Christian Voice displayed enormous religious arrogance in 1986 by awarding failing grades on "moral/family issues" to all the ordained religious ministers in Congress, Republican and Democrat.[11]

Local "religious right" activists have conducted more in-depth religious interrogations. One North Carolina pastor distributed a questionnaire to all candidates for public office in the state in 1986 and demanded to know "What is the name of your pastor and church?"; "If a regular church-goer, how many times each month are you in attendance for regular church services?"; "In your opinion, is the Bible (a) a good book; (b) a collection of religious writings; or (c) [the] literal inerrant word of God?"; and "Can you honestly say that you have a personal relationship with Christ? How well do you know Him?" (People for the American Way, 1986a, pp. 14–15).

That same year Republican candidates for public office in Texas were instructed to sign a statement of "adherence to the Christian faith" or risk losing political support from the self-appointed political foot soldiers of God. Yet another questionnaire asked, "Have you ever been or are you now a member of any group considered . . . anti-God?" (see People for the American Way, 1986a, pp. 11–20). Did anyone answer yes?

These tactics assisted in the election of "godly" public officials in 1980 and 1984, but success proved elusive in 1986. While observers credited the "religious right's" registration efforts with the defeat of several Democratic senators in 1980, the "religious right" was most memorable for introducing an intolerant style of public debate. Many office holders, including Republicans, were simply caught by surprise at the fact that ministers would claim, for example, that support for the federal Department of Education was "un-Christian" and then instruct their congregations to vote against candidates who disagreed.

Armed with millions of "moral/family issues" report cards, hundreds of hours on syndicated and cable television, and the newly formed American Coalition for Traditional Values—the political umbrella group of the "religious right"—the "religious right" in 1984 targeted moderate and conservative Democrats and defeated many of them. At least 9 Republican congressional candidates in California, Georgia, North Carolina, and Texas owed their victories to "religious right" support.[12] The Republican Party

---

[11] Sen. John Danforth (R-MO), an Episcopalian priest, received a score of 58; Rep. Bob Edger (D-PA), a methodist minister, and Rep. William Gray (D-PA), a Baptist minister, both received a zero (People for the American Way, 1986a, p. 30).

[12] "In 1984 . . . most political observers credit the "religious right" with helping elect (sic) Republican congressmen in Georgia (Pat Swindall); North Carolina (Bill Hedon, Bill Cobey, and Howard Coble); Texas (Joe Barton, Mac Sweeney, Richard Armey, and Beau Boulter); and California (Robert Dornan)" (People for the American Way, 1986a, p. 1).

openly embraced the "religious right's" leading televangelists; Falwell and James Robison were invited to preach at the 1984 Republican National Convention and devoted many of their television broadcasts to the reelection of President Reagan. Indeed, Falwell posed the voters' choice between President Reagan and former Vice President Walter F. Mondale in dramatic terms, "[W]e're either going to stand up for the principles that God can honor and bless . . . [and] stand up against every moral cancer in our society, . . . or we are going to lose the freedoms and privileges that we have known for so long in this country" (Falwell, 1984).

The 1986 midterm elections witnessed a significant decline in "religious right" victories, as only 31 percent (11 of 36) of the congressional candidates with substantial "religious right" support and endorsement won election. Among the defeated were Representative William Cobey (R-NC), who had once described himself as "an ambassador for Christ;" Representative Mark Siljander (R-MI), who had lost a Republican primary election after saying that his reelection was necessary "to break the back of Satan;" and Senator James Broyhill (R-NC), whose campaign had associated the Democratic challenger with the Antichrist (see People for the American Way, 1988). Further signs of decay in political strength were evident in 1988 as celebrated "religious right" figures, such as Representative Patrick Swindall (R-GA), indicted on drug money laundering charges just days after the election, were defeated.

But 1988 also witnessed Robertson's presidential candidacy, then-Vice President Bush's appeals to Jerry Falwell, and mainstream Republicans' objections to the "religious right."

THE GOP AND THE RELIGIOUS RIGHT

Pat Robertson told the nation very early in the 1988 presidential campaign that he was God's personal choice for president. In an interview with his own Christian Broadcasting Network in 1986, he said that his candidacy was "a direct call and leading of God; it was something He told me I had to do." Robertson explained that God had communicated His desire for Robertson to run for office by repelling through Robertson a hurricane from the Virginia coast. "I felt, interestingly enough, that if I couldn't move a hurricane, I could hardly move a nation," he said (People for the American Way, 1987a).

As "religious right" leaders often have done, Robertson attempted to stifle public debate over his candidacy through his representation of himself as God's political prophet. He had hoped that other candidates fearful of appearing antireligious would resist criticizing a minister who preaches God's word. But Robertson's strategy did not account for the possibility that his own past statements—such as his suggestion that God's solution to the national debt was to forgive all loans every 50 years[13]—would be used against him, and would cause the public to view him as too far outside the political mainstream and too unstable for the presidency, which was precisely what occurred.

Robertson's greatest asset, television, in fact turned out to be his greatest liability. His candidacy was based on the fact that he had visited tens of millions of homes over the years through his *700 Club* television program, often with a warm appearance. But as he discussed virtually every major public policy issue during this time, groups such as People for the American Way were recording his extremist views on videotape. These tapes were played repeatedly on network television during Robertson's campaign. As *Newsweek* ("The Inside Story . . . ," 1988, p. 93) reported, "[H]e remained lashed to his past, those not-long-ago days when he had healed the sick, prayed away hurricanes, and prophesied nuclear war as a prelude to the Second Coming, and in the age of audio and videotape, he was not allowed to forget it."

Despite Robertson's political self-destruction in 1988, the "religious right" has remained a powerful force within the Republican Party and presents a dilemma to GOP officials. On the one hand, the "religious right" has brought millions of evangelical and fundamentalist Christians who had previously voted for Democrats into the Republican Party, strengthened the Party's conservative base, and used effective political and media organizations in the Party's behalf. On the other hand, the "religious right" has also brought religious intolerance and bigotry into the Party of Lincoln. Nevertheless, the 2 have exploited each other's strengths to prosper.

The Republican Party has appropriated the "religious right's" tactics in attempts to win critical campaigns. For instance, the National Republican Senatorial Committee broadcast a radio commercial on fundamentalist radio stations in the final weeks of the 1986 campaigns in Alabama, Florida, and North Carolina that asked, "Ever wonder what's important to you? It's probably simple—a steady job, a healthy family, and a personal relationship with Christ" (People for the American Way, 1986a, p. 5).

That same year, the Republican Congressional Campaign Committee subsidized a fund-raising letter in which GOP candidate Jackie McGregor, a Christian, maligned her Jewish Democrat opponent, Representative Howard Wolpe, for raising money from Jews. McGregor called the funds "hate money," and demanded that Wolpe give them back. Asked about the letter, McGregor's campaign manager said, "We thought that people should know where the money is coming from" (Podesta, 1986).

The same committee subsidized another fund-raising letter on behalf of

---

[13] "God's way is every 50 years to have a Jubilee and cancel all the debts . . . that is the only way to solve the recession and national debt" (Castelli, 1988, p. 151; Robertson, 1982b).

a successful Christian Republican candidate in Georgia, Patrick Swindall; the letter asked local ministers and the general public to support Swindall, running against a Jewish Democrat, Representative Elliott Levitas, because he "is one of us" (Buchanan, 1985).

Perhaps the best indicators of the "religious right's" strength have been found in the opinions of national GOP leaders, who have been schizophrenic about the "religious right." President Bush's 1988 presidential campaign serves as an especially useful example. He learned first-hand of the "religious right's" influence in 1980; Falwell's opposition to him then contributed his unsuccessful effort to gain the Republican presidential nomination. In 1988, Bush was determined not to allow history to repeat itself. Very early in the campaign, he courted support from the "religious right," especially from Falwell, in order to reduce the possibility of a successful conservative alternative to the more moderate Bush.

At a Liberty Federation conference in January 1986, Bush praised the "great goals" of Falwell's new political organization and said of Falwell that "America is in crying need of the moral vision you have brought to our political life" ("Bush woos followers . . . ," 1986, p. A4). Such praise won Falwell's early endorsement for Bush.

But Bush, like many Republican leaders, knew that close relations with the "religious right" tested the outer limits of political support from moderate Republicans and independents. Therefore, one year after embracing the "religious right's" "moral vision," Bush attempted to distance himself.

In a speech before the National Association of Religious Broadcasters in February 1987, Bush, speaking as a "friend," warned of a "small minority" within the "religious right" "who would seek to impose their will and dictate their interpretation of morality on the rest of society" and "who would forget the need for tolerance." He specifically addressed the topic of censorship, "There is no reason *Huckleberry Finn* should be banned from the schools of this country. There is no reason *The Diary of Anne Frank* should not be read" (Bush, 1987).

As we shall discuss in the next section, the intolerance that President Bush deplored did not come from a "small minority" within the "religious right;" it came from the movement's leadership. Two major public education censorship lawsuits earlier in the decade were argued by Beverly LaHaye's Concerned Women for America and Robertson's National Legal Foundation. Indeed, Falwell's Moral Majority was the first in court attempting to ban a book (Gordon Parks's novel, *The Learning Tree*) on "secular humanism" grounds in 1982 (see People for the American Way, 1987b).

By describing censorship as the work of a fringe element, Bush distanced himself somewhat from the increasingly unpopular televangelists while holding the "religious right's" support for his candidacy through another vehicle, a comprehensive attack against liberalism. The social issues that dominated the fall campaign against the Democratic presidential nominee, Massachusetts Governor Michael Dukakis, provided the common ground on which the "religious right" and the Republican presidential candidate could hold their alliance together. Bush wisely seized upon the public's broad dissatisfaction with many social problems, such as crime, drug addiction, and teenage pregnancy, and rather than emphasizing his solutions he, like the "religious right," blamed those problems on liberal practices.

But, earlier in the primary season after Robertson had finished ahead of Bush in the important Iowa causes, mainstream Republican leaders displayed contempt for Robertson and the "religious right." In Michigan and Hawaii, Republican officials changed their caucus's rules to prevent Robertson victories (Robertson won in Hawaii, anyway), and in Michigan, Bush delegates distributed flyers that read, "Keep Religion out of Politics." During the critical South Carolina primary (which Bush won), Neil Bush, the President's son, called Robertson's workers "cockroaches from the Bible belt" (Podesta, 1988).

The alliance between the "religious right" and the Republican Party would appear to be a difficult one. Republicans are very willing to accept the evangelical and fundamentalist Christian votes but not the "religious right's" religious intolerance. But President Bush, who has sought to create at least some distance from the unpopular "religious right" televangelists, has proved very popular indeed with evangelical and fundamentalist Christians. In the 1988 race against Dukakis, 81 percent of the evangelical and fundamentalist Christians in the United States voted for Bush, exceeding former President Ronald Reagan's vote shares among the same group in 1980 and 1984 of 63 percent and 78 percent, respectively (Portrait of the Electorate, 1988, p. A16).

These remarkable figures do have a negative aspect to them; namely, if a majority of the American people conclude that the Republican embrace of the "religious right" also constitutes an embrace of religious intolerance, the GOP could suffer political consequences. But where is the line that separates the success that the "religious right" and the Republican Party have experienced with the selective use of intolerance and the American people's general disapproval for intolerant groups? Unfortunately for Republicans, in politics "lines" are almost always detected only after they have been crossed. Thus, Republicans have to decide for themselves how long this flammable substance called religious bigotry will help them before it explodes in their face, for it appears very much like they are playing with fire.

THE DESTRUCTION OF PUBLIC EDUCATION

Electing "Godly" federal public officials has been just one aim of the "religious right's" moral agenda. Of the remaining components, perhaps the most disturbing has been the definitive belief that public schools as we know them must cease to exist. "If the educational system in America . . . went totally, absolutely bankrupt tomorrow," Jimmy Swaggart has said, "it would be the finest thing that ever happened to this country" (see Podesta, 1987).

Why? Because by following a policy of strict neutrality toward all religions in the content of subject matters taught in public schools, as the First Amendment commands, the "religious right" has claimed that widely used textbooks have promoted a nonreligious life, "the religion of secular humanism." Pat Robertson (1984) has explained that through this public neutrality toward religion "the state is attempting to do something that few states other than the Nazis and the Soviets have attempted to do; namely, to . . . educate [children] in a philosophy that is amoral, anti-Christian, humanistic."

The "religious right's" special interest groups have engineered a national effort to convince school board officials and federal courts that fundamentalist and evangelical children should not have to read any material in public school that either ignores their religion or treats it on an equal footing with other religions. Their ultimate objective: "Biblically-sound textbooks must be written for every school child in every course of study" (Falwell, 1984b).

Unfortunately, in their zest to provide all children with greater moral instruction, the "religious right" has pursued a campaign to, as Jerry Falwell once commanded them, "rise up in arms and throw out every textbook!" (People for the American Way, 1985a). In other words the "religious right" has engaged in censorship, surely one of the most immoral acts known to free-thinking people, in an effort to strengthen public morality.

Indeed, "religious right" groups including Phyllis Schlafly's Eagle Forum, the National Association of Christian Educators/Citizens for Excellence in Education, and Educational Research Analysts, have been responsible for almost one-half of the public education censorship efforts in the United States. As reprinted in the People for the American Way publication *Attacks: 1985–86* (1986b), public education censorship increased by 117 percent in the United States from 1981 to 1986. Among those censored literary classics have been Alice Walker's *The Color Purple* and Arthur Miller's *Death of a Salesman*. "Religious right" groups have also objected to Shakespeare's *MacBeth* as "satanic," *Romeo and Juliet* as "pornographic," and John Steinbeck's *Of Mice and Men*, the most frequently challenged book in 1987–88, as "objectionable." Because the *Merriam-Webster College Dictionary* defined objectionable words, it, too, was banned from South Carolina schools. Overall, 2 of every 5 censorship efforts have resulted in a book being removed from classes or libraries or curricula being altered or ended.

"Religious right" groups have also pressured local school boards to censor sex education to exclude information about sexuality, including contraception; they have forced drug prevention counseling centers to close; and they have sued school boards for using textbooks that do not promote their religious beliefs. Two cases merit special attention.

In Hawkins County, Tennessee, Concerned Women for American provided legal counsel and financial support for a lawsuit filed in 1983 by a group of local fundamentalist parents who charged that the official reading materials in the local public schools offended their religious beliefs. The parents demanded a separate set of textbooks for their children. The case, *Mozert v. Hawkins County Public Schools,* achieved national publicity as "Scopes II" for its slightly imperfect parallel to its 1925 predecessor which also took place in a small east Tennessee courtroom and posed a similar question: Should sectarian beliefs override educational excellence in public schools?

According to the fundamentalist parents and Concerned Women for America, the textbooks used in reading classes, including *The Wizard of Oz* and *The Diary of Anne Frank,* taught "humanism," "one-worldism," and "witchcraft" ("A Reprise of Scopes," 1986). Unfortunately the school board could not rebut the charges and convince the parents differently because the parental objections were grounded in religious thought. For instance, the parents complained that educating their children about world pollution represented an indoctrination in a one-world government which Revelation foretells as the beginning of the Antichrist. Further, a first-grade reading book in which a boy cooks while a girl reads was said to have violated the sex roles as determined by God. Indeed, Vicki Frost, one of the parents who testified at trial, suggested that her fundamentalist religion should prevail over other religions in the public schools, "We cannot be tolerant in that we accept other religious views on an equal basis as ours" ("See Jim and Pat . . . ," 1986, pp. 21–23).

During the Scopes II litigation (1983–86), Pat Robertson initiated another major education lawsuit in Alabama. Desiring more than special books for fundamentalist children in 1 county, Robertson sought to ban dozens of textbooks used throughout the state and replace them with books that promoted only his religious dogma. Robertson's National Legal Foundation subsidized a lawsuit, *Smith v. Board of School Commissioners,* alleging that Alabama's public education promoted the "religion of secular humanism," which the group claimed was a violation of the First Amendment's establishment clause.

While Scopes II posed a threat to public education, Robertson's lawsuit was potentially far more dangerous. The issue went beyond whether public schools could provide only fundamentalist children with special textbooks. In Robertson's case fundamentalist parents demanded that a federal district court ban reading textbooks used by all schoolchildren throughout the state under their claim that the absence of, or neutrality toward, religion represented a religion itself, the "Godless" religion of secular humanism, and therefore violated the establishment clause of the First Amendment. The parents further asked that the court review all new textbooks for secular humanistic content, thus establishing a religious litmus test for public education.

The "religious right's" plaintiffs in both *Mozert* and *Smith* won at the trial court level. United States District Court Judge Thomas G. Hull ruled that the fundamentalist children in Hawkins County could "opt out" of reading classes, that their parents could teach their children reading at home, and ordered the local school board to pay more than $50,000 in damages to the fundamentalist parents. At the same time U.S. District Court Judge W. Brevard Hand agreed that secular humanism was in fact a religion and that 44 books in Alabama's schools promoted this religion. As a consequence he ordered the books removed from schools. However, federal appeals courts reversed both of the trial judges' decisions.

Even though they eventually lost in court, "religious right" groups have convinced textbook publishers to censor themselves on controversial topics. Fearing challenges from parents, political groups, and "religious right" lawyers in court, textbook publishers have decided to avoid many controversial topics including the role of religion in American life, evolution, and the Holocaust (see Americans United for the Separation of Church and State Foundation, 1985; People for the American Way, 1986b, 1987c). Some American history textbooks avoid an accurate account of religion to such a degree that Pilgrims are described as "people who make long trips," evangelical Christians are rural people "who follow the values and traditions of an earlier period," and Dr. Martin Luther King, Jr. is merely "a black leader" (People for the American Way, 1986c).

Former Reagan Administration Education Secretary Terrell Bell has called the publishers' practice of avoiding controversies in their books "dumbing down." The "religious right's" attacks on evolution have had their effect: One-half of the nation's textbooks do not discuss evolution adequately and one-sixth do not even mention the word (Johnson & Macy, 1986; People for the American Way, 1985b). Further, no textbook contains a full, unabridged version of *Romeo and Juliet* and many dictionaries refrain from including the words objectionable to the "religious right." The "religious right" truly has intimidated textbook publishers to do what they could not accomplish in federal court, to censor themselves.

CONCLUSION

Throughout this chapter we have concentrated on our opinion that claiming a Biblical mandate to preach a unitary view on every public issue raises 2 difficulties: It stifles public and academic debate (who can debate a Biblical literalist?) and it invites religious and political intolerance. By integrating the agendas of church and state to such a degree that they cannot be logically segregated, the "religious right's" ministers and televangelists have failed to communicate their moral message based on their own sectarian beliefs in a nonsectarian manner, which we believe is an essential ingredient for success in the U.S. political arena.

Roman Catholic Joseph Cardinal Bernadin of Chicago said in 1983 that Catholics "face the challenge of stating our case, which is shaped in terms of our faith and our religious convictions, in nonreligious terms which others of different faith convictions might find morally persuasive" (Castelli, 1988, p. 22). The "religious right" has failed the Cardinal's test.

From the earliest drafts of the Constitution to the latest Gallup polls, Americans have repeatedly stated their belief that the nation functions best when the affairs of religion and politics are separated. Spiritual inspiration may require submission to a particular religious leader, but the American tradition of true political dialogue rejects any form of suppression of ideas. While the Constitution protects the right of individuals to believe and practice religious truths without government interference, its own mechanism for "revealing" political truths is free and open debate. The "religious right's" platform, presented as the infallible political views of God, directly challenge the essence of democracy and pose a danger, should the "religious right" gain greater power, to groups who do not share the "religious right's" religious beliefs.

In their religious teachings the main spokesmen for the "religious right" preach that the road to salvation and redemption is narrow unless a person is "saved" by Jesus Christ. As Falwell puts it, "If a person is not a Christian, he is inherently a failure" (People for the American Way, 1985a, p. 2). This places a special burden on Jews, of course, who the "religious right" sees as "spiritually blind" and "under Satan's domain" (Podesta, 1987). But even many Christians do not gain acceptance from the "religious right;" people who do not identify themselves as "saved" or "born again" lead failed lives as well. Thus, according to Jimmy Swaggart, who is truly an equal opportunity bigot, Baptists "specialize in not worshipping God" and Roman Catholics practice a "false doctrine" replete with "superstition" and the "doctrine of devils" (the sacraments) (Podesta, 1987). Unless even Mother Theresa embraces Swaggart's religion, he has said that she will go to hell.

Once this kind of intolerance is introduced into public debate, whether it be for "Godly" candidates or against humanistic textbooks, there are frequently no limits. One "religious right" candidate said that non-Christians "have a right to do what they want, but they shouldn't live in the United States. Maybe they should live in another country." And of the thousands of "religious right" ministers, some have either suggested or openly declared that their political opponents should die (People for the American Way, 1986a).

The "religious right" is an extremist political movement that attempts to justify its positions with ministerial credentials. As we have argued, the American people are not inclined to follow the dictates of religious officials whose political positions are not subject to debate. But even if "religious right" leaders were to refrain from engaging in the politics of religious division and admit that there is more than one path to God in religion and to justice in politics, their political extremism would doom any opportunities for widespread public approval. Without the moral explanation that their answers come from the Bible, the "religious right's" positions on separation of church and state, public education, women's role in our society, among others, would have no coherent, supporting ideology, religious or political, that could be shared by large segments of the public.

Further, "religious right" televangelists would most likely appear hypocritical if they were to substantially alter their religious-political course since, we presume, God would not communicate His true moral wishes on religion and politics through the televangelists only to later say that He was mistaken.

What propelled the "religious right" to political heights we believe will prove to be its downfall: That it represents God in the political arena. We foresee no reasonable solution to the impasse created by the American people's strong belief in the separation of church and state and the importance of church-state integration to the "religious right." But without broad public support, the "religious right" has already proved that it can accomplish many goals, as reflected in the increased rate of censorship in our society.

Indeed, it appears that the "religious right" has actually exacerbated the social decline which initially motivated the movement's political activities. In their moral majoritarian zeal the "religious right" has added greater degrees of religious intolerance, censorship, and poorly educated schoolchildren to our nation's list of social dilemmas. Schoolchildren have less access to important information to avoid pregnancy and drug addiction as a result of the "religious right's" political pressures brought against sex education classes and drug prevention counseling. Textbook publishers, fearful of the "religious right's" scourge, appear more likely to educate our children from the lowest common denominator rather than the highest standards of academic excellence. The rich diversity of our nation for our children to inherit has therefore been eroded by narrow-minded censors and timid publishers.

The only redeeming silver lining in the cloud called the "religious right" that we see is that the movement's radical agenda and practices have forced Americans to search more vigorously for answers to their social dilemmas, albeit dilemmas made even more difficult by "religious right" activities. Throughout history there have been political movements that make us question and political movements that answer our questions. The "religious right" falls only into the former category, for the flames of intolerance for people who have different moral guideposts consumed the movement long before it could have entered into the latter. We, however, are left with the humbling assignment of answering the questions that the "religious right" could not answer for us.

REFERENCES

Abelman, R. (in press). Religious television news after the fall. *Journalism Quarterly, 67*(2).

Americans United for the Separation of Church and State Foundation. (1985). *Teaching about religious freedom in American secondary schools.* Washington, DC: Author.

Buchanan, J.H. (1985, April 4). Religious name-calling: No place in politics. *Paxton Daily Record,* op ed section.

Bush, G. (1987, February). Presentation to the National Association of Religious Broadcasters, Washington, DC.

Bush woos followers of Falwell. (1986, January 25). *The Washington Post,* p. A4.

Castelli, J. (1988). *A plea for common sense: Resolving the clash between religion and politics.* San Francisco, CA: Harper & Row.

Everson v. Board of Education 330 US (1987).

Falwell, J. (1981, November 8). "Old time gospel hour." Praise The Lord Network telecast: PTL.

Falwell, J. (1984a, November 4), "Old time gospel hour." Praise The Lord Network telecast: PTL.

Falwell, J. (1984b, August 29). "Old time gospel hour." Praise The Lord Network telecast: PTL.

Harris, L. (1987). *Inside America.* New York: Vintage Books.

The inside story of campaign '88. (1988, November 21). *Newsweek,* p. 93.

IRS probes evangelists' operations. (1988, December 10). *The Washington Post,* pp. A1, A16.

Johnson, M., & Macy, C. (1986, November 25). Scopes issue still alive. *Oceanside Blade-Tribune,* op ed section.

Ostling, R. (1986, February 17). Power, glory—and politics. *Time,* p. 67.

People for the American Way. (1985a). *Jerry Falwell: Intolerance in defense of intolerance.* Washington, DC: Author.

People for the American Way. (1985b). *A consumer's guide to biology textbooks.* Washington, DC: Author.

People for the American Way. (1986a). *Election 1986: Religion and politics.* Washington, DC: Author.

People for the American Way. (1986b). *Attacks on the freedom to learn: A 1985–86 report.* Washington, DC: Author.

People for the American Way. (1986c). *Looking at history: A review of major U.S. history textbooks.* Washington, DC: Author.

People for the American Way. (1987a). *Pat Robertson: Extremist.* Washington, DC: Author.

People for the American Way. (1987b). *Secular humanism attacks on public schools, 1982–1987*. Washington, DC: Author.

People for the American Way. (1987c). *Values, pluralism, and public education*. Washington, DC: Author.

People for the American Way. (1988). *Attacks on the freedom to learn: A 1987–88 report*. Washington, DC: Author.

Podesta, A.T. (1986, November 5). *"In the Public Interest."* Nationally syndicated broadcast: National Public Radio.

Podesta, A.T. (1987, January 14). *"In the Public Interest."* Nationally syndicated broadcast: National Public Radio.

Podesta, A.T. (1988, March 1). *"In the Public Interest."* Nationally syndicated broadcast: National Public Radio.

Portrait of the electorate. (1988, November 10). *The New York Times*, p. A16.

A reprise of scopes. (1986, July 28). *Newsweek*, pp. 21–23.

Robertson, P. (1982a, July 15). *"700 Club."* Christian Broadcast Network telecast: CBN.

Robertson, P. (1982b, December 30). *"700 Club."* Christian Broadcast Network telecast: CBN.

Robertson, P. (1984, May 13). *"700 Club."* Christian Broadcast Network telecast: CBN.

See Jim and Pat Cook. Jim cooks first. (1986, March 13). *The New York Times*, editorial.

19

Religion, Television, and Politics: The Right Bank of the Mainstream

Larry Gross

Theologically conservative Christians were the largest tract of virgin timber on the political landscape. (Morton Blackwell)[1]

Direct mail and religious broadcasting have been our means of making an end run to the minds of the American people. (Tim La Haye)

It may have been Jimmy Carter's election in 1976, as Richard Viguerie claims (1980), that first demonstrated the political potential of fundamentalist Christianity. Whatever the exact moment and the precise example, it does appear that religious broadcasting came together with conservative politics in the late 1970s at the birth rites of the "new right." Building on foundations laid in previous years by George Wallace and Spiro Agnew, the leaders of the "new right" offered a populist alternative to the Wall Street establishment of traditional conservative Republicanism. While not abandoning for a moment the rabid anticommunism which offers an earthly variant of the hellfire and brimstone preaching of old time religion, the "new right" founded its church on the solid ideological rock of a "social agenda:" Reclaiming old-fashioned family values from the debasement and corruption of liberalism, permissiveness, and secular humanism.

The insurgent people's movements of the 1950s and 1960s had put a core of social issues on the nation's agenda, as the civil rights movement, the antiwar movement, the women's movement, and the lesbian/gay movement, insisted on the rights of their members to challenge the authority of traditional values. The integration of schools, lunch counters, workplaces, and neighborhoods showed the power of the government to reach into the lives of people and force them to change their ways (though not their

---

[1] All unreferenced quotations in this essay come from interviews included in the documentary film "Thy Kingdom Come" (Fall, 1986) by Antony Thomas.

227

minds). The demands of women for independence and equality; the refusal of thousands of young men to go willingly to fight against Communism; the unapologetic visibility of lesbian women and gay men who would no longer hide in their closets—all of these represented dramatic evidence that traditional authority was everywhere under attack.

The sources of these attacks are everywhere around them, but nowhere more critical than those supposedly mounted by the state against the family or, more precisely, against the patriarchal family: "The progression of big government is amazing. A father's authority was lost first to the village, then to the city, next to the state, and finally to the empire" (Falwell, 1980, p. 26). Even after the election of Ronald Reagan, who represented in many ways the success of the movement begun by the "new right" in the late 1970s, the "right's" attack on the state as the enemy of the family continued (often made by the President himself). As Pat Robertson put it, before declaring his own candidacy for president:

> The state is steadily attempting to do something that few states other than the Nazis and the Soviets have attempted to do; namely to take the children away from the parents and to educate them in a philosophy which is amoral, anti-Christian, humanistic. And to show them a collectivist philosophy which will ultimately lead towards Marxist, socialist, communist type of ideology.

In this view of the corruption of America by liberalism, secular humanism, and permissiveness, the role of the media is absolutely central. More than any other institution in modern society, the media, and television in particular, represent the intrusion of alien values right into the homes and even the hearts and minds of Americans, especially young Americans.

THE MEDIATED MAINSTREAM

The leaders of the "new right" were not the first to call attention to, nor the first to denounce, the increasingly dominant role of the mass media in the contemporary world. Indeed, the appearance of each successive mass medium in the past century or so has been greeted by outcries bemoaning the new medium's inevitable contribution to the corruption of those—women, children, the lower classes—least able to resist its siren song.

The role of the mass media in modern industrial nations is unprecedented in its scope and power but not in its basic functions. The media, with television at the heart of an integrated complex, have become the central channel through which we learn what exists, what is important, and what is right in the world. The media now compete with and even replace religious and social institutions as sources of information and knowledge; they provide the arena for most political discussion and debate, and, in terms of both exposure time and impact, they are fast superseding educational institutions. And the power of the media can readily be perceived and felt as a coercive force of ideological pressure and domination.

Critics on the "left" and the "right" have shared a common perspective on the growing dominance of the mass media, each seeing a force beyond their control and indifferent if not hostile to their values. Their common analysis begins with the omnipresence of the media, the fact that the economic, political, and social integration of modern industrial society allows few communities or individuals to maintain an independent integrity. We are parts of a Leviathan, like it or not, and its nervous system is telecommunications. Our knowledge of the "wide world" is what this nervous system transmits to us. The mass media provide the chief common ground among the different groups that make up a heterogeneous national community. Never before have all classes and groups (as well as ages) shared so much of the same culture and the same perspectives while having so little to do with their creation.

Critics also recognize that representation in the mediated "reality" of our mass culture is in itself power; certainly it is the case that nonrepresentation maintains the powerless status of groups that do not possess significant material or political power bases. That is, while the holders of real power— the ruling class—do not require (or seek) mediated visibility, those who are at the bottom of the various power hierarchies will be kept in their places in part through their relative invisibility. This is a form of what Gerbner and I have termed symbolic annihilation (Gerbner & Gross, 1976, p. 182). Not all interests or points of view are equal; judgments are made constantly about exclusions and inclusions and these judgments broaden or narrow (mostly narrow) the spectrum of views presented.

A third criticism is when groups or perspectives do attain visibility, the manner of that representation will itself reflect the biases and interests of those elites who define the public agenda. And these elites are (mostly) white, (mostly) middle-aged, (mostly) male, (mostly) middle and upper-middle class and, from the right's perspective, committed to the permissive philosophy of secular humanism. The world according to television, then, may not accord with the world as adherents of various views and beliefs would wish it to be seen. These critics can take no comfort from the findings of much academic research on the patterns of media consumption and its probable consequences.

The average American adult spends several hours each day in this television world; children spend even more of their lives immersed in its "fictional reality." As I have already suggested, the mass media, and television foremost among them, have become the primary sources of common information and images that create and maintain a world view and a value system. In a word, the mass media have become central agents of enculturation. In the Cultural Indicators Project (cf. Gerbner, Gross, Morgan,

& Signorielli, 1986) we have used the concept of "cultivation" to describe the influence of television on viewers' conceptions of social reality.

On issue after issue we find that assumptions, beliefs, and values of heavy viewers of television differ systematically from those of light viewers in the same demographic groups. Sometimes these differences appear as overall, main effects, whereby those who watch more television are more likely—in all groups—to give what we call "television answers" to our questions. But in many cases the patterns are more complex. We have found that television viewing, not surprisingly, serves as a stable factor differentially integrated into and interacting with different groups' life situations and world views. In our recent work we have isolated a consistent pattern which we have termed "mainstreaming" (Gerbner, Gross, Morgan, & Signorielli, 1980, 1982, 1986).

The mainstream can be thought of as a relative commonality of outlooks and values that television tends to cultivate in viewers. By mainstreaming we mean the sharing of that commonality among heavy viewers in those demographic groups whose light viewers hold divergent positions. In other words, differences deriving from other factors and social forces—differences that may appear in the responses of light viewers in various groups—may be diminished or even absent when the heavy viewers in these same groups are compared. Overall, television viewing appears to signal a convergence of outlooks rather than absolute, across-the-board increments in all groups.

From the perspective of the "new right," the mainstream represented by secular television is the mainstream of secular humanism, of permissiveness, of challenges to the authority of the Father. In this light it is not surprising to detect an ambivalence among the legions of the "right" concerning the deregulation of the media which has been one of the notable accomplishments of the Reagan administration. While any effort to get the government "off the backs" of the people may be admirable as an abstract principle, it becomes somewhat more complex when put into practice, and how you feel about deregulation may depend on whose back you think the government should get off.

The issue of government deregulation has served to highlight some of the cracks in the conservative ranks, as leaders of the "new right" have fingered capitalism as a carrier of the seeds of moral breakdown. Paul Weyrich, an architect of the "new right," has noted the "direct tension between cultural conservatives and some economic conservatives" (1986, p. 1). As Barbara Ehrenreich put it:

> While traditional conservatism sought only to limit government, Weyrich's new "cultural conservatism" would use government to enforce the traditional values of family stability, hard work, and sexual puritanism. (1987, p. 183)

In the case of the media, deregulation carried out "religiously" by the FCC under the chairmanship of Mark Fowler, may have opened the door to even more of the permissiveness Reagan was supposed to abhor and combat. By the mid-1980s the "right's" ambivalence towards deregulation had focused around the issue of pornography and the demand for government intervention to combat sexual permissiveness, culminating in the appointment of Attorney General Meese's Commission on Pornography.

A typical example of this movement is the Washington Prayer Breakfast on June 5, 1986, organized by the National Decency Forum ("a coalition of national, state and local decency and pro-family organizations"), and chaired by Barbara Hattemer of the Florida Coalition for Clean Cable and Brad Curl of the National Christian Association. The Prayer Breakfast, which was to be addressed by the U.S. Senate Chaplain among others, was to focus on "the failure of the FCC to uphold decency standards for broadcasting" (Hattemer, 1986).

A CHOICE, NOT AN ECHO

The old saying was, find a need and fill it, and you'll be successful. I think the church today is filling a great void and a great need in people. (Jim Bakker)

The mainstream perspectives of mass culture, cultivated through the repetition of patterns and assumptions across the boundaries of media and genres, and absorbed by otherwise diverse segments of the population, nevertheless has to contend with the possibility of oppositional perspectives and values. As Raymond Williams has pointed out, hegemony "is never either total or exclusive. At any time, forms of alternative or directly oppositional politics and culture exist as significant elements in the society" (1977, p. 111).

What options and opportunities are available to those groups whose concerns, values, and even very existence are belittled, subverted, and denied by the dominant world view? Can one avoid being swept into the mainstream? The answer depends in large part on which group or segment we are considering; while many minorities are similarly ignored or distorted by the mass media, not all have the same options for resistance and the development of alternative channels.

In general the opportunities for organized opposition are greatest when there is a visible and even organized group which can provide solidarity and institutional means for creating and disseminating alternative messages. There are numerous examples of groupings that have sprung up, as it were, along the right bank of the mainstream. Most organized and visible among these are the Christian fundamentalist syndicated television programs which are the focus of this volume. These programs provide their (generally older and less educated) viewers with an array of programs, from news to talk shows to soap operas to church services and sermons, all reflecting perspectives and values that they quite correctly feel are not represented in mainstream, prime-time television or in the movies (cf. Gerbner et al., 1984; Hoover, 1982). As one of Hoover's conservative, religious respondents put it, in discussing network television:

> I think a good deal of it is written by very liberal, immoral people. . . . Some of the comedies, the weekly things that go on every week, they make extra-marital affairs, and sex before marriage an everyday thing like everybody should accept it . . . and they present it in a comic situation, a situation that looks like it could be fun and a good deal of these weekly shows I don't like go for that. (Hoover, 1985, p. 382f)

The religious sponsoring and producing organizations are not merely engaged in meeting their audiences' previously unmet needs for a symbolic environment in which they feel at home; they are also attempting to translate the (usually exaggerated) numbers of their audiences and their (constantly solicited) financial contributions into a power base from which they can exert pressure to alter the channel of the mainstream and bring it even closer to where they now reside, up on the right bank.

At the moment, and for the foreseeable future in the United States, at least, there is no comparable settlement on the left bank of the mainstream. There are many reasons why the "left" has been unable to match the "right's" success in harnessing the available resources of media technology. It is not hard to see that some minority perspectives are in fact ultimately supportive of the dominant ideology, however much the media's need for massive audiences might sacrifice or offend their interests, while other minority values are truly incompatible with the basic power relationships embodied in that mainstream.

Minority positions and interests which present radical challenges to the established order will not only be ignored, they will be discredited. Those who benefit from the status quo present their position as the moderate center, balanced between equal and opposing "extremes"—thus the American news media's cult of "objectivity," achieved through a "balance" which reflects an invisible, taken-for-granted ideology. As a CBS spokesman explained, when dismissing attempts by Jesse Helms and Ted Turner to take over the network:

> Anyone . . . who buys a media company for ideological reasons must be prepared to pay dearly for that conviction. The right-wingers and the left-wingers in this country are vociferous but small in number compared to the ordinary citizen, who, when it comes down to it, is a centrist. (Roth, 1985, p. 163)

The hidden truth in the credo of centrism and moderation is that how one defines the "responsible" extremes will determine where the center will fall.

In the United States the mass media-legitimated spectrum runs a lot further "right" than it does "left," which puts the "objectively balanced" mainstream clearly to the right of center. Jesse Helms can be elected and reelected to the Senate and can embark on a public campaign to take over CBS; his opposite number on the "left," whoever that might be, couldn't conceivably claim or receive that degree of visibility, power, and legitimacy.

Yet, in the final analysis, neither flank can avoid serving in one way or another to buttress the ramparts of the status quo, and to keep the truly oppositional from being taken seriously. American presidential politics recently sported a matched pair of Christian candidates, and neither the minister of the left, Jesse Jackson, nor the minister of the "right," Pat Robertson, could hope to do more than exert some small pressure on their respective branches of the Property party, whose 2 official divisions—the Democrats and the Republicans—offer an illusion of choice within the political mainstream.

ON THE RIGHT TRACK

We take the blame. We were told religion and politics don't mix and we swallowed it. We must penetrate every area of our society—yes, even the political area. (Jerry Falwell)

In 1983 a committee of more than 30 mainline and independent church groups commissioned a research team made up of the Cultural Indicators research group at the Annenberg School of Communications of the University of Pennsylvania and the Gallup Organization to conduct a research project on religion and television—what has subsequently become known as the Annenberg/Gallup study. Part of the focus of that study was relevant to the concerns of the present discussion, as we addressed questions relating to "social agenda" items to members of the religious television audience. We also attempted to compare the impact of religious television viewing and the viewing of "general" television fare—what we have termed the television mainstream.

Among the issues we focused on in our survey of audience groups were 4 questions pertaining to sexual behavior, asking respondents to express their attitudes towards premarital sex, extramarital sex, homosexuality, and legalized abortion. In part of our analysis and presentation we combined the responses to these 4 questions into an index of "traditional sexual values." As we would expect, there is a clear and significant relationship between scores on this index and viewing of religious television programs, even when simultaneously controlling for age, sex, race, education, income, political views, church attendance, denomination, region, and general television viewing (Gerbner et al., 1984, p. 125).

Two questions on the Annenberg/Gallup study survey assessed audience members' views on what might be considered the traditional role of women in our society. We asked to what extent respondents agreed or disagreed with the following statements: "Most women are happiest when they are making a home and caring for children," and "A woman should not work outside the home if her husband can support her." When these questions were combined into an index we found a similar pattern of relationship with religious television viewing, controlling for age, sex, education, political views, and church attendance.

These patterns are not all that different, it should be noted, from those associated with viewing of "general" television programs, but there are differences worth attending to. In brief, the pattern we find in relation to general television viewing is the "mainstreaming" pattern of convergence on a middle position, whereas among the heavy viewers of religious television viewing the convergence we observe is more one-sided—towards the "right." Of course, the appropriate conclusion to be reached would not simply be that these programs are influencing their viewers to adopt more conservative views. It is precisely the argument I am making that these programs are appealing to their audiences in large part because of their existent attitudinal compatibility. What they may most notably achieve, therefore, is not conversion but mobilization.

One of the familiar concerns voiced about the impact of the broadcast media on modern society is that the public will be made apathetic, choosing to sit on the sidelines and watch rather than participate actively in the public sphere. In no area of society is this concern sharper than in the political arena, where television in particular has been blamed for helping turn politics into a spectator sport, and contributing to the steadily declining voter turnout in recent elections. This claim is bolstered by the fact that viewing "general" television is consistently and strongly correlated with *not* voting—as shown by national surveys as well as by the Annenberg/Gallup study. In striking contrast, those in our sample who are heavy viewers of religious programs are significantly more likely than their light viewing counterparts to say that they *did* vote in the 1980 presidential elections.

Of course, as is well known, the religious programs themselves are only the tip of the organizational iceberg which audience members encounter. The frequent exhortations to call in lead to one's enrollment among the "new right's" computerized legions: The mailing list. It is the mailing list which provides the "new right" with its most cherished form of access to the constituency it needs to mobilize. In Richard Viguerie's (1980) words, "through direct mail we were able to bypass the monopoly that the left had on the microphones of this country, and go into America's homes by the millions and talk about our candidates and our causes."

The 75 million letters a year which Viguerie estimates have been sent by the various "new right" organizations are the vehicles through which they are attempting, as Gary Jarman of the Christian Voice put it, "to push the agenda beyond theology into straight politics." The religious programs, Jarman notes, provide a "ready made audience that is highly ideological— you can just plug into it."

The size of the audience for religious television may not be as large as once thought—the Annenberg/Gallup study arrived at an estimate of 13.3 million—but the political impact of an ideologically coherent, financially generous, and emotionally charged group can far outweigh mere numbers. Money and commitment produce powerful multiplier effects in politics. In the midst of the first post-Reagan electoral contest, the once thriving settlement established on the right bank of the mainstream was shaken by quakes in its moral substratum brought about by the exposure and downfall of several founding pioneers. It is too early to tell whether the right bank will recover its firm footing of moral self-satisfaction and patriarchal rectitude. But as long as the mainstream of the mass-mediated culture continues to follow the course of pursuing the largest possible audience, it can safely be assumed that the interests and values of millions will be ignored and insulted, and that those who offer an ideologically compatible alternative will have devoted customers.

REFERENCES

Ehrenreich, B. (1987). The new right attack on social welfare. In F. Block, B. Ehrenreich, R. Cloward, & F.F. Piven (Eds.), *The mean season*. New York: Pantheon Books.

Falwell, J. (1980). *Listen America!* New York: Doubleday and Co.

Gerbner, G., & Gross, L. (1976). Living with television. *Journal of Communication, 26*(2), 173–199.

Gerbner, G., Gross, L., Morgan, M., & Signorielli, N. (1980). The mainstreaming of America. *Journal of Communication, 30*(3), 10–29.

Gerbner, G., Gross, L., Morgan, M., & Signorielli, N. (1982). Charting the mainstream: Television's contributions to political orientations. *Journal of Communication, 32*(2), 100–127.

Gerbner, G., Gross, L., Morgan, M., & Signorielli, N. (1986). Living with television: The dynamics of the cultivation process. In J. Bryant & D. Zillmann (Eds.), *Perspectives on media effects* (pp. 17–40). Hillsdale, NJ: Lawrence Erlbaum.

Gerbner, G., Gross, L., Hoover, S., Morgan, M., Signorielli, N., Cotugno, H., & Wuthnow, R. (1984). *Religion and television*. New York: Committee on Electronic Church Research.

Hattemer, B. (1986). Form letter on "National move toward rebuilding decency standards—Washington prayer breakfast, June 5, 1986." Florida Coalition for Clean Cable. Miami, FL.

Hoover, S. (1985). *The "700 Club" as religion and as television*. Unpublished doctoral dissertation, University of Pennsylvania, Philadelphia, PA.

Roth, M. (1985, April 24). CBS evaluates Turner takeover: 'Not a snowball's chance . . .'. *Variety*, p. 1.

Viguerie, R. (1980). *The new right: We're ready to lead*. Falls Church, VA: The Viguerie Company.

Weyrich, P. (1986, May 4). The cultural right's hot new agenda. *Washington Post*, p. 1.

Williams, R. (1977). *Marxism and literature*. New York: Oxford University Press.

VII

The Portrayal of Religion on Secular Television

Religious television is, at its base, a kind of television. For most Americans, television is the dominant leisure activity of their lives. Even viewers who primarily identify with "religious TV" are also viewers of "regular" television. Their familiarity with television overall is, in fact, vital to their experience of the more specialized religious genre.

Most accounts of religious television describe it with specific reference to television in general. It can be said that the contrast between these 2 types of television helps to define modern religious broadcasting, both for its viewers and for the experts who evaluate it from scientific, theological, political, or policy viewpoints.

How, then, do religious and "conventional" television relate to one another? First, conventional television is the definitive context for the religious variety. It sets the context in terms of its *form*. It is national, public, and a central social ritual. Its *formats*—the "talk show," "variety show," "news," "commentary," "documentary," and so on, provide a descriptive language through which religious television is created and interpreted by its producers and viewers.

Second, the content, the "message" of conventional television, provides standards of what is dominant, appropriate, and possible in the medium. The values, norms, and relationships conveyed lay out a certain structure against which religious television can either set a consistent *or* a contrasting worldview.

Third, the orientation of conventional television form and content is one which has often been accused of being at odds with the basic claims and affirmations of Judaism and Christianity (Fore, 1987). Its materialism, violence, and sexual messages have frequently been the object of criticism by religious groups and spokespeople. Television is even considered an inherently "profane" medium by certain religious groups.

The chapters in this section look at these issues in more depth. Communication professor Quentin Schultze presents a systematic and theologically informed analysis of the central myths and meanings of conventional television. There is a sense in which all of television is "religious," and Schultze's essay suggests a way in which this might be so.

Journalism researcher and professor Judith Buddenbaum provides an enlightening analysis of the way religion, as a topic, is covered by television journalism. If, in fact, the religious and secular media environments are in a struggle for authenticity, the assumption that secular media treat religious issues in an idiosyncratic or critical way deserves analysis. Buddenbaum provides a systematic assessment of these issues and raises questions concerning gate-keeping practices and media ethics.

This section ends with a sharp controversy—a comparison of the positions of 2 well-known observers of the values and social impacts of conventional television. Humanities professor Robert Alley presents a detailed discussion of the religiously based critique of conventional television's supposed "humanism" and "anti-Christian bias." By focusing on one of the most prominent religious critics of television's values, the Rev. Donald Wildmon of Tupelo, Mississippi, the head of the American Family Association, Alley presents a reasoned and logical defense of television, proposing that its values are, in fact, positive ones.

Rev. Donald Wildmon is profiled in an interview conducted by one of the editors of this volume. As the object of Alley's criticism, Wildmon is allowed to speak for himself. This colloquy should provide readers with an opportunity to evaluate the competing claims made by these very different perspectives.

The essays presented here illuminate the points at which the "religious" and the "secular" meet on the mass media stage. They are not a comprehensive view, but instead provide specific coherent perspectives. The subject of the interaction between religious and secular television, or of the religious meanings of secular television itself, justifies an entire volume of its own. This section outlines some of the dimensions such a work might encompass.

REFERENCES

Fore, W.F. (1987). *Television and religion*. Minneapolis, MN: Augsburg Press.

20

Secular Television as Popular Religion

Quentin J. Schultze

In the modern world religion is usually associated with religious institutions and organizations rather than with faith and belief. The religious person is said to attend church or synagogue, participate in the sacraments, and generally live a pious life. Religion is the compartment of life that contains the duties and obligations required for true membership in a religious organization. To be religious is to act religiously.

Of course this is a relatively new way of understanding religion. In the Western world the Judeo-Christian tradition historically integrated religious faith and institutions into all of life. Religion formed the identities of individuals and communities by providing values and beliefs that permeated culture. Work, for example, was defined religiously as vocation or "calling." Marriages were more importantly religious celebrations than civil ceremonies or legal contracts. True piety was not Sunday worship or Sabbath observance, but living the life of faith. Religion was a way of life with its own worldview and culture.

This premodern conception of religion suggests that all of the contemporary discussion about religious broadcasting may be seriously misguided. Even if broadcasts are not made for specifically religious purposes, they might serve the historic religious function of organizing life around shared beliefs. Perhaps broadcasting need not reflect the beliefs or doctrines of an organized religious group or movement for it to be religious. This essay argues that any attempt to identify "religious" broadcasting must look beyond the modern compartmentalization of religion for evidence of how the prevailing values and beliefs of society are embodied even in "secular" programming. It suggests that popular television programs serve a religious function even though they are not produced by particular religious organizations or for the purpose of religious proselytism. More importantly, it suggests that a program need not even address the religious "compartment" of modern life for it to be religious.

THE COMPARTMENTALIZED VIEW

The implied purpose of "religious television" is obvious in the various ways that popular writers and scholars have used the term in recent years. The narrowest view defines religious television in terms of persuasive intent. "Christian television," for example, is frequently used to describe programs whose clear purpose is to win converts to a particular expression of the Christian faith. Among evangelicals this view is the clearest: Christian television proclaims the good news of salvation from sin and the promise of eternal life. Religious broadcasts, as opposed to secular programs, are meant to convert people to a religious faith and perhaps to join a religious organization. The problem with this concept of religious broadcasting is that persuasive intent is often a slippery activity to define. Is singing a gospel song necessarily evangelistic? What about a talk show, such as *John Ankerberg,* where members of a religious group debate with skeptics the veracity of their faith? If we accept a broad concept of persuasive intent, it becomes clear that virtually all television programming is evangelistic. Game shows indoctrinate Americans in the tenets of a capitalistic economy and consumer society with their emphasis on competition and product consumption. Some situation comedies sell the traditional family as the moral center of society. Both nonreligious and religious broadcasts persuade and educate; they proclaim their own "good news," even if the faith is not associated with religious organizations and their doctrines.

In recent years a growing number of broadcasters have expanded the definition of "religious" to include any programming reflecting the values or beliefs of a religious group. From this perspective religious programs can include far more than evangelistic intentions. A religious program could be produced in order to entertain and inform as much as to persuade. Once again, the term "Christian television" is highly instructive as an example of this approach to defining religious broadcasting. Christian television stations air many national and local preachers, but they also carry Bible game shows, variety programs, talk shows, and magazine formats. The Seventh-Day Adventists produce *Christian Life Style Magazine,* a rather unique approach for any denomination. Organized around the ways that various individuals and groups are working at improving the quality of life for others, the program only indirectly suggests the beliefs of that church. This type of show is considered "Christian television" even though it probably attracts more non-Christian viewers than do the evangelistic programs. Moreover, many of these types of Christian broadcasts depict the values and life styles of North American, not merely of the church or a denomination.

The problem with this definition of religious broadcasting is that it is not easy to determine when a program reflects the values and beliefs of a religious group. In fact, organizations such as the Christian Broadcasting Network (CBN) and some Christian television stations have turned the definition into a negative statement: Christian broadcasts are those which do not contradict the values and beliefs of Christians. On this basis CBN Cable has loaded its program schedule with commercial network reruns, including domestic situation comedies from the 1950s and westerns from the 1960s (Traub, 1985). Even fundamentalist Christians use "Christian TV" and "pro-family programming" synonymously (LaHaye, 1984).

Both of these views of religious broadcasting have some merit and are useful concepts for discussing and analyzing the phenomenon. However, both definitions wrongly assume that it is easy to distinguish between the religious and the nonreligious, between the secular and sacred. Invariably these definitions will be challenged not just by scholars, but also by other religious broadcasters who disagree with how the definitions have compartmentalized religion. Indeed, we may ask whether or not the programming standards of a religious station or network are more informed by the tenets of a religious faith or by the values of a secular culture.

THE SECULARIZATION OF RELIGIOUS BROADCASTS

Contemporary religious broadcasting, as the term is commonly used, is a hodgepodge of formats and theologies. In the United States it is difficult to link many of the highest-rated religious programs to particular church organizations or traditions. Individual preachers or program hosts may be members of a specific church or denomination, but their broadcasts are the product mostly of independent planning and production. Since they are dependent upon viewer contributions for survival, their programming must attract a faithful audience of supporters. As a result, contemporary religious broadcasting has become increasingly nonreligious—if by "religious" we mean the religious compartment of life.

Bruce Barron (1987) has addressed the secularization of religious broadcasting in his analysis of the writings and programs of the "health-and-wealth" preachers. According to Barron, this gospel proclaims that Christ's death and resurrection have enabled all believers to claim health and prosperity. The only real obstacle is the lack of personal faith; all who truly believe will be healed and prospered. As Barron shows, the strongest versions of the health-and-wealth gospel, advanced by preachers such as Kenneth Copeland and Kenneth Hagin, are clearly at odds with the historic Christian faith. Moreover, this gospel can best be explained not as the doctrine of particular churches or denominations, but as the product of various media evangelists whose success depends on their ability to tell people what they want to hear. These television preachers have created a new dogma founded on the demands of their own ministries. They have not organized a new religion as much as they have grafted American culture onto particular expressions of American Pentecostalism.

The lesson to be learned from the health-and-wealth preachers is that secular culture influences religion, especially when religion takes to the airways. Religion is probably even less compartmentalized on television than in the local congregation because of the requirements for media popularity and success. Television audiences are often fickle and unpredictable. Independent religious broadcasters, lacking a steady source of denominational or church support, must appeal to their audiences both religiously and culturally. This was the genius in part behind the remarkable success of the *Jim and Tammy Show* in the last few years before the resignation of Bakker amid a sex scandal. The Bakkers created a show in tune with the social aspirations of Southern Pentecostals who wanted to be freed from the cultural restrictions of their religious tradition. As Edith Blumhoefer (1987) has argued, this was the major difference between Bakker and Swaggart, who represented the more ascetic and restrictive old-style Pentecostalism.

NARRATIVE AND CULTURE

Religious broadcasting shows how culture and religion are always related. It makes little sense to speak of religious faith or action without also speaking of how religion is expressed in and through culture. Even belief in God is shaped by the secular values and nonreligious beliefs of a people. This is not to relativize religious faith, but only to assert that human beings are cultural creatures who decide when and how God shall be worshipped or ignored, petitioned or condemned. Humankind's "religious" nature—its drive for meaning and *shalom*—always takes specific form in culture. As a result, the world is filled with conflicting concepts of God and modes of worship.

Nevertheless, cultures share an appeal to narrative as a structure for meaning and significance. For thousands of years humankind has lived by mythic stories which link the past and present to the future. Like the Bible and the Torah, these narratives are far more than lists of religious dogmas or enumerations of moral commandments. Myths are general and thematic, not merely idiosyncratic and legalistic. They do not only chronicle events; they account for human origins, responsibilities, and destinations. As Johann Baptist Metz has written, religious faith is necessarily communicated as a story because "the beginning and the end can only be discussed in narrative form" (1973, p. 86). The faithful Jew today lives in the story of the survival of her people during the Passover. She plays a role in the narrative, waiting for the prophet Elijah. The Christian lives in the saving grace of the Father in heaven who sacrificed His only Son on the cross. He exists in the New Testament story, waiting for Christ to return. Religious narratives, like mythic tales of all kinds, share this sacramental quality. Martin Buber even claims that a "story is itself an event and has the quality of a sacred action. . . . It is more than a reflection—the sacred essence to which it bears witness continues to live in it" (quoted in Metz, 1973, p. 86).

Secular television is religious because popular storytelling is necessarily the foundation for culture. All societies, from the tribal to the most industrialized, spin meaningful webs of culture which are held together partly by shared narratives. Culture, which T.S. Eliot defined as the *"whole way of life* of a people," exists in and through narrative (1949, p. 49). Certainly this is the easiest to see in preindustrial societies, which produced only a few surviving *Illiads* and *Odysseys* for the eventual perusal of anthropologists. But it's just as true of modern society, where the mass media assume the major storytelling role. If we limit our concept of religious broadcasting to the programs of churches and evangelists, or to the expression of religious values and beliefs, we overlook the universal function of narrative in human culture.

TELEVISION MYTHOPOETICS

Television programming is religious because its stories are the shared narratives of American culture (Fore, 1987; Nelson, 1976; Schultze, 1986). People do not actually worship television drama, but they indeed capture a shared understanding of their world through the news, commercials, and entertainment. Few Americans experience many of the events in the world and the nation firsthand. They rely on the media, especially television, to provide a picture of that outside world. This picture, or pseudo-environment as Walter Lippmann (1922) called it, orients the individual to public life in modern democratic societies. News reporters, for example, eventually replaced the early American pastors as New Englanders' primary conduits to information and perspectives about distant happenings (Hatch, 1989). Believing the pastors was a matter of faith and credibility, but so is trusting contemporary news reporters or advertisers.

One key to understanding television is the way that it packages almost everything in the form of a story. On television "the news" is a collection of entertaining stories organized around the conflicts of public figures and nations or around the tragic and joyful lives of common folk (Henry, 1981). Commercials are typically packaged as visual vignettes about the benefits of particular product brands. We see and hear the tales of lonely hearts who found romance after using the right toothpaste or mouthwash; depressed wives who won the attentions of their husbands with spaghetti sauce; youthful men who corralled an adorable woman with the scent of aftershave lotion. And in television dramas the characters, settings, and especially the plots tell us much about the culture in which we live. British drama critic Martin Esslin (1982) puts it this way:

> Though it may well be true that our present-day archetypal heroes cut pale figures when set aside by side with those of earlier cultures, the *genesis* of today's archetypes is by no means as different as it might appear at first

glance. . . . The pantheon of archetypal characters in ever-recurring situations on present-day American television does, I believe, accurately reflect the collective psyche, the collective fears and aspirations, neuroses and nightmares of the average American, as distinct from the factual reality of the state of the nation. Does not the prominence of hospitals and disease in story lines indicate a national preoccupation with health, even a certain hypochondria? Do not the sex kittens of the evening series actually represent current ideals of beauty? Are not the mix-ups, the grotesqueries of family situation comedies an accurate, if exaggerated, scenario of the embarrassments and triumphs of family life, real or fantasized. . . . These then are the collective daydreams of this culture. (p. 44)

As Esslin's observations suggest, television programs are mythopoetic. Television does not merely entertain or inform; it is a storyteller that spins mythic tales. These tales provide a national identity, personal self-images, and especially a public faith. The viewer of secular programs does not tune in to learn of God, to pay, or to confess her sins. But like the religious congregant, she does reap meaning and significance from the broadcasts. She finds stories to call her own and to share with millions of others.

SECULAR LITURGIES

Religious worship is organized by proscribed forms of symbolic ritual. So is television viewing. In the communion service the congregation shares in the story of Jesus' death and resurrection as told at the Last Supper. In the domestic comedy the viewers share in the hope that all confusion and complication will be resolved and families will live happily ever after. The various television genres organize secular narratives on the tube, rendering the stories predictable and enjoyable. Just as the local congregant needs liturgical structure, the television viewer requires dramatic form. Consequently, few religious liturgists or television producers have the freedom to create their own private stories. Television narratives are meant to be understandable public tales for the entire community of followers. They are mass religion expressed in popular forms.

On television the many liturgies are defined by program types or genres. There are action programs, detective shows, westerns, soap operas, ensemble programs, and so forth. New genres appear now and then, such as the evening soap operas of the late 1970s and the ensemble programs such as *Hill Street Blues* and *L.A. Law*. However, TV liturgies are amazingly stable and predictable. New types of situation comedies have appeared in recent years, but the old formula of building complication and confusion and then resolving it is still the mainstay of the genre. Even the very popular *Cosby Show* is far from innovative; it reflects much of the family life and simple moral universe of the early domestic comedies, like *Leave It to Beaver* and *My Three Sons*.

These simple dramatic genres help make secular television mythopoetic. Viewers don't watch most popular dramas to be challenged or to gain new perspectives on the world. They view them precisely because of their pre- dictability—because they meet expectations. If Cliff Huxtable of the *Cosby Show* is unfairly mean and insulting to his wife, viewers would be greatly offended. If the characters on a typical soap opera suddenly all acted as loving and forgiving as Cliff Huxtable, viewers would be shocked—and probably displeased. When television drama meets viewer expectations it functions well at reaffirming the basic myths and values that animate the programs. At the same time such drama affirms broader beliefs which exist in the culture of viewers. Television genres and religious liturgies are the meaningful formulas that enable viewers and congregants to communicate their faith publicly. Both are the rituals of communities of believers. In this sense, too, secular drama serves the same social function of most religious art over the centuries—confirming the values and beliefs of the community (Wolterstorff, 1980, p. 144). To put it differently, the arts often function like religion, giving an apparent meaning to life, providing the framework for a culture, and protecting humanity from boredom and despair.

TELEVISION MYTHS

The television viewing public shares a few basic myths formulated repeat- edly in secular dramas. These myths are the doctrines of the believing culture that regularly views and enjoys popular television fare. Among the myths are the following:

1. *Good triumphs over evil.* Who can doubt this belief given the tube's insatiable thirst for happy endings and resolved conflicts? Americans have never enjoyed a lot of tragedy in their television programming. Even the news is often capped with a light story reaffirming that life goes on in spite of all of the dire circumstances and wide-ranging calamities reported during the previous 25 minutes. From situation comedies to westerns and detec- tive programs, this myth permeates the televised narrative. It is the true statement of hope for the modern believer. In spite of all of the evidence from the world and the viewer's own life to the contrary, he hopes and believes that things will work out for good. On commercial TV, only soap operas regularly challenge this myth as they bring together villains of all kinds bent on repeatedly challenging the goodness and hope of other char- acters. But even in the soap opera the faith is maintained as hopeful view- ers watch expectantly for villains to fall and good people to triumph. "Next time," exclaims the viewer, "everything will work together for good." Such anticipation never completely bears fruit with the soap opera, but viewers carry on the vigil, like prayerful petitioners wait expectantly for the answer to divine petitions.

2. *Evil people cause evil.* Every religion must account for the existence

of evil in a world supposedly governed by God and His goodness. From whence does evil come on the tube? From the sinful actions of evil people. Evil is not universal to humankind, but the product of the evil desires and works of evil individuals. It is not part of the human condition, but particular to specific character types, such as animalistic gangsters, savage Indians, greedy corporate executives, hardened criminals, and for-hire thugs. Lacking such characters, situation comedies usually reduce evil to mere misunderstanding and confusion, which are easily treated by the doctors of plot. On television, evil is not natural to the world, but an aberration caused by evil people. Evil actions are the sins of people in the television world.

3. *Evil can be eliminated by eliminating evil people.* Religions typically offer ways to battle evil and to ensure the maintenance of a moral and just society. Secular television drama is no exception. By objectifying evil in the lives and actions of particular individuals, television claims that evil can be rounded up like gunslingers or criminals and removed from our streets and communities. Because evil is limited to the actions of evil people, it can be kept under control and eventually eliminated. The goal of society should be to keep evil people from working out their evil plans. Jails can be used for this purpose, but the most effective action is simply to extirpate evil people from society. In action shows, detective programs and westerns, evil characters are snuffed out and harmony reigns—until the next episode, when evil once again rears its ugly head. Thus, television evil is rarely institutional and almost always personal. J.R. and the oil barons of *Dallas* personally cause the wickedness in the industry; there is no corporate evil. The tube personifies evil, thereby identifying it and rendering it manageable.

4. *Society can be redeemed by the good and effective works of moral individuals.* Religions have their carriers of God's grace who combat evil. So do secular television stories. On television the agents of good works are righteous individuals committed to wiping out evil. They include private and public detectives, sheriffs, former military specialists, and a wide array of other fighters of evil. They also include the gentle inhabitants of situation comedies who bring about understanding and reconciliation among confused characters. In addition, the saints of television extend to the virtuous individuals who surface now and then on the soap operas in the midst of wickedness, depravity, and selfishness. These characters are the gods of television, which in its mythic formulas largely rejects the existence of an omnipotent or omniscient deity. The tube has traded a mysterious and unexplainable concept of God for a more humanly understandable one: God is in us and works through us. He is immanent, not transcendent. Our good works are His good works. Our justice is His justice.

TELEVISION'S PROPHETIC ROLE

In the contemporary world there are 2 types of prophets. The traditional religious prophet speaks the unpopular truth critically and candidly. Like the Old Testament prophet, he claims divine insight and chastises the people for their idolatry and evil ways. His message offers hope contingent upon the repentance of all who have ears to hear. The modern prophet, on the other hand, derives his authority from the people. He speaks what the people wish to hear and is given authority by the congregation of faithful believers. Secular television drama is such a prophet.

Since the advent of television over 4 decades ago, the tube has been one of the major prophets in the United States. Television has spoken repeatedly for the people in the form of popular narratives that formulate the culture's basic beliefs. As the mythological giant of the late 20th century, the medium has spun its tales of hope and faith for millions of congregants gathering in their family rooms every day. The message of this prophet has been tailored for the hopeful throng: All things will work together for good for those who believe in themselves and their society. This myth has been formulated and reformulated in thousands of programs, hundreds of series, and all of the major genres. Television prophets offer comfort and hope.

The mythology of the tube is driven by the audience ratings system which largely guarantees that narratives on commercial television will play their prophetic role. Television writers and producers cannot speak for themselves or for a divine authority, like the traditional religious prophet, because the message must be shaped for the consuming masses. For this reason commercial television has rarely offered tragic drama; no one likes to see unhappy endings for anyone but the evil characters. Under a system of advertiser-supported broadcasting, television networks and producers conspire to provide the most myth-affirming stories possible. Writers, directors, and many technicians are acolytes for the narratives brought to us every day through the liturgical forms of prime time.

RELIGIOUS BROADCASTING RECONSIDERED

If anthropologists uncover the remains of North America in several hundred years, what will they most likely identify as the icons and idols of the culture? Will they find that churches and synagogues are the most productive sites for archeological digs? Or will they conclude that the storage vaults of advertising agencies and television networks were the most fertile repositories of our nation's cultural heritage? In a short story entitled "The Lost Civilization of Deli," Jean Shepherd (1981) concludes the latter. Archeologists who stumble upon the archives of an advertising agency decide that the find was far "more revealing than any of the poor fables and tepid myths these people had left behind, what they called Arts and Literature." We might further conclude that the find was more revealing than the dusty scriptures and unread theological tomes unearthed in the cobwebby basements of churches and seminaries.

The term "religious broadcasting" suggests that other programs are nonreligious. As this essay has argued, such a distinction between prime-time drama and Sunday morning religious broadcasts overlooks the historical role that narrative has played in culture. Of course religious broadcasts are more obvious extensions of the beliefs and activities of organized religious groups in the United States. However, these religious programs and the doctrines they espouse have been greatly influenced by the "secular" culture. Religious programs are secular just as secular programs are religious. Programs can still be compartmentalized as "religious" and "nonreligious," but such categories are gross oversimplifications of the ways that both types of broadcasts function in the lives of their respective communities. Secular television narratives are prophetic voices for the wider culture; they interpret the world around us and ritualize experience for us. For thousands of years Jews have gathered around the Passover table to share the story of their salvation from Egyptians. Today we all gather around the television set to comfort each other that all things will work together for good in the lives of the viewing elect.

REFERENCES

Barron, B. (1987). *The health and wealth gospel.* Downers Grove, IL: InterVaristy Press.

Blumhoefer, E.L. (1987, May 6). Divided Pentecostals: Bakker vs. Swaggart. *Christian Century,* pp. 323–324.

Eliot, T.S. (1949). *Notes toward the definition of culture.* New York: Harcourt, Brace and Company.

Esslin, M. (1982). *Age of television.* San Francisco, CA: Freeman Press.

Fore, W.F. (1987). *Television and religion.* Minneapolis, MN: Augusburg Publishing House.

Hatch, N.O. (1989). *The democratization of American Christianity.* New Haven, CT: Yale University Press.

Henry, W.A., III. (1981). News as entertainment: The search for dramatic unity. In E. Abel (Ed.), *What's news* (pp. 133–158). San Francisco, CA: Institute for Contemporary Studies.

LaHaye, T. (1984). *The hidden censors.* Old Tappan, NJ: Fleming H. Revell Company.

Lippmann, W. (1922). *Public opinion.* New York: Macmillan.

Metz, J.B. (1973). A short apology of narrative. In J.B. Metz & J. Jassua (Eds.), *The crisis of religious language* (pp. 84–96). New York: Herder & Herder.

Nelson, J.W. (1976). *Your God is alive and well and appearing in popular culture.* Philadelphia, PA: The Westminster Press.

Schultze, Q. (1986). *Television: Manna from Hollywood.* Grand Rapids, MI: Zondervan Publishing House.

Shepherd, J. (1981). *A fistful of fig newtons.* New York: Doubleday.

Traub, J. (1985, May/June). CBN counts its blessings. *Channels,* pp. 28–32.

Wolterstorff, N. (1980). *Art in action.* Grand Rapids, MI: William B. Eerdmans Publishing Company.

21
Religion News Coverage in Commercial Network Newscasts

Judith M. Buddenbaum

The "new Christian right." The political campaigns of the Revs. Pat Robertson and Jesse Jackson. The rise of the electronic church and the downfall of televangelists Jim and Tammy Bakker and Jimmy Swaggart. Religion, long ignored by the mass media or considered a second-class beat to be shunned by talented reporters, is now news. During the first 10-1/2 months of 1987 alone, *The Charlotte Observer* published 1661 stories about religion, more than one-third of them chronicling the latest findings concerning scandals involving Jim and Tammy Bakker and their PTL ministry (Oppel, 1988, p. 5).

The Charlotte Observer is not alone. Recent research indicates that many newspapers now take religion news seriously. Not only have many increased and improved their hard news coverage of religion during the past decade (Buddenbaum, 1988; Hynds, 1987), but they have also begun to pay attention to the kind of journalist who covers the beat. About 90 percent of religion journalists today identify with a particular religion and take it seriously. Most also try to be sensitive to other peoples' religious beliefs. Even at smaller papers, they are generally better educated in both religion and journalism and more experienced than their counterparts at the largest newspapers a decade ago (Buddenbaum, 1988).

But the attention to religion news has also spawned criticism. *The Charlotte Observer* received nearly 2000 critical letters and 189 cancellations traceable to their coverage of the PTL scandal (Oppel, 1988, p. 6). While those complaints were undoubtedly heartfelt reactions to a particular story, the underlying criticisms echo those that have been raised ever since James Gordon Bennett began systematically covering religion in the 1830s (Buddenbaum, 1987a).

One group of critics complains that there isn't enough coverage. What there is, they say, is shallow and doesn't cover the full range of religions or issues. While these critics also complain about particular stories that they feel were poorly done, they rarely detect deliberate bias. They simply want more and better hard news coverage of religion (Ferré, 1980; Kraps, 1986; Rockefeller Foundation, 1981; Seigenthaler, 1988; Shaw, 1983). Calling religion news "the best-kept secret," they agree there should be scrutiny of all aspects of religion because:

> If we allow church bureaucracies to hold closed meetings or tell us what we can report, we're false prophets. We shouldn't be blind boosters for our cause. ("No News," 1986, p. 14F)

But "boosterism" is what other critics seem to want. Equating hard news about religion with sensationalism and bias, they often call for softer features designed to promote and defend their own religion (Duggan, 1981; Guzda, 1985; Hitchcock, 1986; Thomas, 1986; Wildmon, 1982). According to Fodiak (1986), only 19 percent of the Catholic priests surveyed said the press is "fair, honest, or objective" in handling religion news. They complained that journalists are:

> interested only in the sensational, the shocking, the scandalous and not necessarily in the more staid and less dramatic. This assessment is far more true in respect to television people. (p. 40)

While recent research indicates the complains about the kinds of stories, the total amount of coverage, its allocation among subject matter and religions, and about the thoroughness and fairness of the reporting are now taken seriously at many newspapers (Buddenbaum, 1988; Hynds, 1987), the same may not be true for television. This may be due to television's severely limited news hole which allows for only about 22 minutes of actual news during a 30-minute program, the general absence of specialty reporters, and the story-telling conventions used in newscasts.

Indeed, early content analyses typically report that fewer than 2 percent of television news stories are about religion (e.g., Liroff, 1971), but that may seriously underestimate the proportion that at least mentions the subject. In a more recent study of television news coverage of international affairs, for example, Larson (1984) does not use religion as a category, but his work indicates that approximately 1 percent of the stories between 1972 and 1981 covered the Vatican, while about one-third came from other trouble spots associated with religion such as Northern Ireland, Iran, and the Middle East. However, the only available analysis specifically of religion news (Kalder, 1985) confirms that it is not only neglected but also distorted through an overemphasis on the power of Christian fundamentalists and the drama surrounding papal tours.

It should be noted that, while Kalder (1985) suggests inequities in the subject matter and religions covered, her analysis offers little insight into why critics may complain about fairness. However, on the basis of a qualitative study of press coverage, including that by the 3 commercial television networks, Fields (1985) concluded that the "new Christian right" is presented as effective on technical grounds but its concerns and proposals are portrayed as violations of societal norms concerning freedom of religion, speech, and press. This interpretation is consistent with the criticisms by various partisan religious groups.

Similarly, in their analysis of crisis coverage that happens to include 2 religion-related crises (the Peoples' Temple massacre in Jonestown, Guyana, and the Iranian hostage crisis), Nimmo and Combs (1985) found that each of the 3 networks had developed a distinctive news style which, to the extent that it is used in noncrisis reporting about religion, could lead some viewers to react negatively. ABC, they say, used a "good grief" style which portrayed religion as just an irrational and out-of-control force. CBS supported Walter Cronkite's traditional "that's the way it is" sign-off with facts and expert opinions to create an official version of reality that may not correspond closely to the religious experience of viewers. NBC coverage suggested events were embedded in a social, political, economic, religious, and human context, but the connections usually were made only through juxtaposed sources, information, and images that may confuse viewers.

Taken together, these studies suggest that there may be more television news stories mentioning religion than critics imagine, but that many complaints may be well-taken. However, critics usually voice their concerns in connection with coverage of a particular story such as the televangelist scandals or the presidential campaigns of clergy candidates Pat Robertson and Jesse Jackson, but rarely provide solid documentation for their assertions. The purpose of this chapter is to offer such documentation.

Because coverage can be quite variable among stories (Buddenbaum, 1985, 1987b), this chapter addresses the common complaints about the nature, amount, allocation, thoroughness, and fairness of religion news by reporting the findings from a study of coverage during a constructed month in 1976, 1981, and 1986. The investigation used a content analysis scheme with reliability checks developed for other studies of religion news (see Buddenbaum, 1985, pp. 41–60, pp. 283–327, 1986) to analyze videotapes of the 240 religion news stories broadcast by ABC, CBS, and NBC on their regularly scheduled nightly newscasts. The scheme calls for coding each story according to network and date, classifying it by the focus and significance of the information, by religion, topic, news value, and type of information, and by noting stylistic features that create general impressions about religion. A religion news story is defined as one that mentions a religion, religious institution, or religious person, or that uses religious language (e.g., "holy") or shows a religious person, institution, or symbol (e.g., a cross) in a way that suggests the story would tell the average viewer something about religion.

RELIGION NEWS COVERAGE

What is religion news?

This analysis confirms accusations that the dominant feature of religion news on secular network newscasts is that it is not primarily about religion. Except for ABC during 1981, only about 30 percent of the stories focused on religion by mentioning it prominently in the lead or the introduction to an internal segment of the story.

Even fewer were solely about religion. Consistent with the networks' emphasis on national and international public affairs reporting, at least half of the stories on each network each year were really political ones about disputes and violent confrontations between religious factions abroad, about church-state conflict in Poland and the United States, or about religion in American political elections. Fully half the stories mentioned religion in connection with foreign news. Most of that coverage came from traditional religious trouble spots: The Middle East and Northern Ireland, but also Poland (in 1981) and the Philippines and South Africa (in 1986). No more than one-fifth of the stories, mostly from within the United States, were about interactions between religious people or institutions and non-political aspects of society (see Table 21.1).

Consistent with the topics covered, conflict and violence were the 2 most common news values (see Table 21.2). Nonviolent conflict appeared in both foreign and U.S. news. However, violent conflict and consensus/conflict resolution showed up primarily in stories from the Middle East and Northern Ireland. Human interest as a news value was more common in 1981 and 1986 than in 1976 because of heavy coverage of Pope John Paul II's travels and because of stories with a holiday theme during those years.

Most information in the stories was about one-time events or issues that only tangentially involved religion. In fact, fewer than one-fourth of the stories on any network in any year provided information about religious beliefs and practices, about social ministry or missionary projects, or about demographics and trends.

The definition of religion news the networks use is much more in tune with the interests of those who call for religion to be treated as hard news. Therefore, those critics who expect religion news to promote and defend their faith are likely to be quite disappointed. Not only are there very few stories that address beliefs and behaviors, show people worshipping, or describe missionary and social ministry projects, but the limited attention to

Table 21.1. Topic of Religion News Stories by Year and Network

Topic	1976			1981			1986		
	ABC (n=18) (7.5%)	CBS (n=23) (9.6%)	NBC (n=15) (6.3%)	ABC (n=25) (10.4%)	CBS (n=27) (11.3%)	NBC (n=42) (17.5%)	ABC (n=23) (9.6%)	CBS (n=29) (12.1%)	NBC (n=38) (15.8%)
Religion Only	—	—	6.7%	20.0%	14.8%	7.1%	8.7%	13.8%	15.8%
Religion and:									
Military/Guerilla/Terrorism	38.9	26.1	26.7	8.0	7.4	11.9	—	6.9	13.2
Politics/Government	27.8	56.5	46.7	28.0	40.7	40.5	47.8	37.9	34.2
Law/Crime/Courts	16.7	8.7	6.7	20.0	14.8	14.3	13.0	17.2	13.2
Business/Labor/Economics	—	—	6.7	4.0	—	7.2	4.3	3.4	7.9
Social Services	5.6	—	6.7	—	—	—	—	—	—
Science/Medicine	—	4.3	—	—	—	4.8	—	—	—
Education	—	—	—	—	—	2.4	—	—	—
Media	5.6	4.3	—	—	—	4.8	—	—	—
Culture/Entertainment	—	—	—	8.0	3.7	4.8	—	—	—
Lifestyle/Behavior	—	—	—	—	3.7	2.4	—	6.9	—
Important People	5.6	—	—	12.0	11.1	4.8	26.1	13.8	15.8

Differences among networks: 1976, 1981, 1986 p = n.s.
Differences within networks: ABC p < .01; CBS, NBC p = n.s.
NOTE: Totals do not equal 100 percent because of rounding.

Table 21.2. Main News Value in Religion News Stories by Year and Network

News Value	1976			1981			1986		
	ABC (n=18) (7.5%)	CBS (n=23) (9.6%)	NBC (n=15) (6.3%)	ABC (n=25) (10.4%)	CBS (n=27) (11.3%)	NBC (n=42) (17.5%)	ABC (n=23) (9.6%)	CBS (n=29) (12.1%)	NBC (n=38) (15.8%)
Novelty	11.1%	4.3%	6.7%	8.0%	—	2.4%	—	—	5.3%
Change	5.6	4.3	6.7	—	—	2.4	—	3.4	5.3
Conflict	38.9	34.8	46.7	44.0	40.7	54.7	60.9	55.2	47.3
Consensus/Conflict Resolution	5.6	13.0	20.0	4.0	3.7	9.5	—	—	5.3
Violence	22.2	26.1	6.7	8.0	18.5	14.3	4.3	6.9	10.5
Human Interest	16.7	8.7	6.7	20.0	14.8	16.7	30.4	34.5	23.7
Other[a]	—	8.7	6.7	16.0	22.2	—	4.3	—	2.6

[a]This category includes routine stories for which the probably news values are impact and/or timeliness. These news values were not included in the coding scheme because of the difficulty in making the appropriate subjective judgment; impact and/or timeliness are assumed to apply to all news stories.

Differences among networks: 1976, 1981, 1986 p = n.s.

Differences within networks: ABC p = n.s.; CBS $p \leq .01$; NBC p = n.s.

NOTE: Totals do not equal 100 percent because of rounding.

those concerns is primarily confined to seemingly obligatory holiday features. Harder news relating religion to political and social issues, however, is more evenly scattered throughout the year. For the most part, this kind of news determines the amount of coverage.

How much religion news is there?

The networks typically carried more stories mentioning religion than the 2 percent suggested by the more general content analyses of network news previously discussed. The attention may even be comparable to that afforded other specialized subjects such as business or science but, as the topics suggest, there really is rather little information about religion. Except in 1976, NBC provided a slightly higher proportion of religion news stories (about 10% of all stories) than the other networks, but only CBS in 1976 devoted more than 6 percent of the news hole to actual mentions or discussions of religion.

While a total of 240 religion news stories suggests that, on the average, there will be 1 religion news story every second or third day, in reality there were many days with no religion news because each of the 3 networks tended to group religion news stories together on some days. Stories with a holiday theme account for the apparent increase over time because the networks carried newscasts on Christmas Day in 1981 and 1986 but not in 1976. In addition, Good Friday coincided with a sample day in 1981. However, if holiday features are excluded, the coverage was quite stable. For the most part, variations in the quantity of stories and in the religions covered can best be explained by political events at home and abroad.

Is that coverage distributed equitably among religions?

Besides providing very little time for actual news about religion, the networks paid little attention to most religions. With the possible exception of coverage of Catholicism, there is little to suggest that the networks attempt to create a representative picture of religion in the United States by allocating coverage according to a religion's strength among viewers as was the networks' practice for providing free time for religious programming until the mid-1970s.

In all years, Catholicism was mentioned in at least one-fifth of the stories on all networks. While Moslems were mentioned in a similar proportion of stories in 1976 because of conflict between Moslems and Christians in Lebanon, occasional heavy attention to Protestants is divided among various groups. Therefore, even the largest denominations (Baptist, Methodist, and Lutheran) receive very little attention relative to their strength within the United States.

Mainline Protestants were nearly invisible. During 1986 the coverage was heavier, amounting to about one-fifth of all stories, but most of those were divided between ones relying on Anglican Bishop Desmond Tutu as an antiapartheid spokesperson in news from South Africa and ones mentioning Anglican envoy Terry Waite and the Rev. Benjamin Weir, a Presbyterian, in stories about Weir and the Rev. Lawrence Jenco, a Roman Catholic, who were held hostage in Lebanon and then released. Lutherans, Methodists, and Presbyterians were each mentioned in several news stories from within the United States during the entire period of this study, but most attention to mainline Protestants simply showed a choir singing as part of a holiday feature.

Coverage of evangelicals was even more limited than that given mainline Protestants. Not only were evangelicals never mentioned in even one-fifth of the stories, but the coverage was entirely from within the United States. It was also divided among stories mentioning or covering organizations and religious leaders associated with the "new Christian right" and others more closely aligned with civil rights issues. While no organization or leader of the "new Christian right" was the focus of more than 1 story, large black Baptist congregations in Georgia received coverage in several stories in 1981 and the Rev. Jesse Jackson was quoted or featured in stories each year. However, that coverage never identified Jackson by denominational affiliation; at least 3 times as many stories about him were excluded from the sample because they failed even to identify him by his clerical title.

Pentecostals showed up only in 1 story from the Soviet Union; Latter-day Saints were mentioned only during 1976 in one story on each network about William Dummar and the Howard Hughes "Mormon Will." If reports from the Middle East mentioning Moslems and Jews are excluded, fewer than 10 percent of the stories on any network in any year mentioned a non-Christian religion. Even that limited attention was fragmented among stories about Hindus, Native Americans, and several cults.

While the attention to the Pope and to Catholicism, both in foreign news and holiday features, generally supports Kalder's (1985) contention that the networks overemphasize Catholicism, the pattern of coverage suggests no similar fascination with other religions. Temporarily heavy coverage of other religions, as occurred for mainline Protestants in 1981 and more recently for presidential candidates and televangelists, probably is not a singling out of certain religions for unfavorable scrutiny. It more likely is a response to a definition of religion news that emphasizes public affairs reporting with violence and conflict as news values. Coverage of non-Christian religions and Protestant denominations tended to occur only when those groups were caught up in events or somehow "making news" that corresponds to a hard-news definition. Therefore, the package as a whole failed to create a representative picture of religion both within the United States and in foreign countries.

How thorough is the coverage?

As the lack of attention to individual religions suggests, the networks do not seem to make an effort to cover the varieties of religious beliefs systematically and thoroughly or go out of their way to find news involving religion. Although between one-fifth and two-fifths of the individual stories on each network each year provided some significant information about religion, in many cases the significant information accounted for fewer than 30 seconds of a much longer news story. The coverage was least thorough in 1976 and most thorough in 1981, but a few individual reports each year were very good, both addressing a substantive issue involving religion and providing enough information about the religion to explain its involvement in the issue or show its appeal to believers.

During 1981, for example, all 3 networks provided extensive coverage of international Catholicism. Some of the stories seemed designed primarily to take advantage of the Pope as an easily identifiable and charismatic leader or of the dramaturgical elements of Catholic worship. Coverage of church-state conflict in Poland was somewhat excessive—about 10 percent of all stories—but quite thorough. In that coverage, the 3 networks effectively used a mixture of clips of people worshipping, clear excerpts from statements by church, government, and Solidarity leaders, and reactions from Polish Catholics in the United States to show both the power of the Catholic Church and its appeal to church members.

Stories devoted to cults and other nontraditional religions were also generally well done, combining scenes of worship and other religion-related activities with comments from both members and their opponents. Coverage by both ABC and NBC during June 1981 of the Rev. Sun Myung Moon's immigration and tax problems, for example, included more direct commentary by Unification Church leaders than occurred in *The New York Times* reports during the same period (Buddenbaum, 1985, pp. 227–234).

However, most coverage consisted only of scattered references and unexplained labels. These problems were quite common in foreign news during 1976 and 1986. In 17 stories from Lebanon during 1976, for example, the networks used the labels "Christian" and "Moslem" along with political terms such as "right wing," "leftist," "Phalangist," "Palestinian," and "Arab" in a way that made it hard to tell who was fighting whom. Most did not explain reasons for the war or why sides were drawn along quasireligious lines. Similarly, stories from Northern Ireland in all 3 years mentioned fighting between Catholics and Protestants but never explained the roots of the conflict or reasons for religious involvement.

While unexplained mentions were most common in foreign news, they also occurred in stories from within the United States. Most stories mentioning religion during the 1976 election and most involving Protestants included only unexplained labels or relied on inadequately identified religious sources. In stories about prominent American religious leaders including the Revs. Jerry Falwell, Jesse Jackson, Pat Robertson, Donald Wildmon, and Benjamin Weir, as well as lesser-known clergy who were used as sources in only a single story, the networks never reported the religious basis for their comments on social and political issues. Nor did they provide even a simple denominational label as a clue for viewers.

Although the networks generally treat religion as hard news, the stories almost certainly cannot satisfy those critics who complain of shallow coverage. Not only is there little systematic attention to the varieties of religious experience, beliefs that inspire behaviors, and stories that have not already blossomed into easily identified and reported events or controversies, but the coverage often mentions religion in a way that is more likely to confuse than inform. In foreign news unexplained labels and inadequate identification of sources may be merely baffling, but in national political news they are more troublesome. In cases such as the 1988 election campaign involving 2 clergy candidates for the presidential nomination, omitting information about the denominational affiliation and specific religious beliefs of the Revs. Jackson and Robertson can at best make it difficult for voters to make an informed decision about the candidates. At worst, it can mislead them into assuming that all clergy candidates are alike. Indeed, the presentation style of stories about Robertson noted in this study supports Martz's (1988) contention that Robertson was found guilty by association as a result of imprecise media coverage. This helped terminate his campaign for the presidency.

How fair is the coverage?

In a general sense, the coverage is fair. No religion that was the subject of more than 3 stories received exclusively favorable or unfavorable coverage. Even Moslems in the Middle East, who were most often portrayed as irrational fanatics, got some favorable attention. During 1976 coverage of fighting in Lebanon, for example, most stories emphasized attacks by Moslems on Christian communities, but NBC's January 27 and February 2 stories emphasized that both Christians and Moslems seek a democratic and essentially secular Lebanon with religious freedom for all. NBC also frequently included the Moslem perspective, as in an October 21 story that showed scenes of devastation in the Moslem community and profiled a Moslem businessman struggling to survive in a community under continual fire from Christian troops.

However, there are aspects of the coverage as a whole that could easily lead viewers to believe that the networks are biased against religion in general or against particular religions. For the most part, the networks treat religion like other kinds of news, covering it most heavily only when it meets traditional journalistic standards of newsworthiness. However, reliance on violence and conflict as news values produced stories that almost certainly missed the reality of religion as most people experience it. Scenes of people worshipping and information about beliefs and practices were rare except on holidays. Therefore, the coverage invites charges of sensationalism.

The coverage as a whole also invites charges that the networks treat individual religious traditions unfairly. Because the networks covered primarily groups such as Roman Catholics or black Baptists whose worship lends itself to strong visual coverage, or those that were "making news" according to the traditional news values of violence and conflict, in any given time period some traditions will be covered much more extensively than others. This sporadic attention can appear as deliberate bias for or against a religion.

While the criteria for selecting stories created some distortion in the image of religion conveyed by the newscasts, the common story-telling techniques the networks used in individual stories frequently produced individual reports that seemed biased and misleading. Occasionally the problem came from something as subtle as the visuals the networks chose to illustrate the story. On other occasions, it came from the juxtaposition of images and information, charges, and countercharges. During September 1981, for example, all 3 networks gave extensive coverage to allegations that Cardinal John Cody of Chicago was involved in a diversion of church money to his cousin, Helen Dolan Wilson. In those stories, the networks reported charges and countercharges against video closeups of banner headlines from newspapers in a way that in a September 28 story on NBC led Cody to say, much as the Bakkers and Jimmy Swaggart might:

> The press is trying to destroy the civil rights of the church. . . . An accusation is deemed condemnation. . . . Allegations are evidence and innuendos, wherever they may be, are considered proof.

Although issue-oriented stories almost always included multiple perspectives, bias seemed overt in about one-fourth of the reports when the story structure let a secular spokesperson or even the reporter get the last word. Perhaps the most egregious examples of this problem came when ABC used its "good grief" style to develop a story angle, then let the reporter give a simplistic conclusion. on May 19, 1986, for example, in coverage of a proposal to eliminate militant songs from the Methodist hymnal, the ABC reporter developed the theme that "people attend church for the music," but never offered evidence for that assertion, and then concluded with his own opinion:

> In this 20th century world of war and hunger and nuclear accidents and terrorism, to sing or not to sing is clearly not the question. But in a world of so few answers, it was bound to be asked.

Although both the coverage as a whole and most individual stories adhered to traditional journalistic standards, the coverage undoubtedly failed to satisfy both groups of critics. The networks' preference for stories about violence and conflict tended to prevent coverage of many religious traditions and exclude significant stories that are not easily illustrated with colorful video clips or that do not conform to a limited definition of news. As a result, those who complain about the lack of variety and the shallowness of the coverage are not getting the marketplace of ideas or the in-depth information they want.

At the same time, the emphasis on violence and conflict and the tendency to let either a secular spokesperson or the reporter get the last word may appear as sensationalism and bias to those who prefer religion news that promotes and defends religion. Those who identify with a particular religion, but do not see it covered in the news, may too easily assume they have been excluded because journalists are biased against them. Others, like supporters of the ministries of Jim and Tammy Bakker and Jimmy Swaggart, may feel themselves unfairly under attack when events temporarily make their religion newsworthy.

CONCLUSION

Overall, religion news is a rather stable commodity. Although all networks except ABC decreased their news hole by at least 1 minute between 1976 and 1986, all consistently mentioned religion in between 6 and 11 percent of their stories and devoted between 7 and 15 percent of their available time to them. While that is probably as much religion news as one can reasonably expect, the networks did not seem to go out of their way to cover religion news. Instead, they sometimes found it while routinely reporting public affairs. The coverage focused on events and political conflict rather than on religion itself. As a result the networks consistently produced religion coverage that is an easy target for media critics.

That religion news is generally treated as hard news should satisfy those critics who complain mostly about shallow coverage. Nonetheless, this coverage failed to produce a marketplace of significant information about religion. Many religious traditions and many potentially significant stories undoubtedly went unreported because they did not have violence or conflict as news values or lend themselves to visual coverage. Because the networks frequently relied on simple labels instead of including relevant background information to link beliefs to behaviors and issues or set controversies into some kind of broader perspective, the coverage often created the illusion of informing about religion. However, most stories probably produced little real understanding. As a result of the way the stories were reported, the occasional heavy attention to particular religions may invite inflated estimates of the importance of the issue and of religion's influence on its outcome.

If stories emphasizing conflict and violence can be equated with sensational coverage, then the critics who want religion news to be religious may also be correct in their assertion that the coverage creates an unfair image of religion. The emphasis on violence and conflict as news values led to few stories explaining beliefs and practices, showing people worshipping, or describing social ministry or missionary activities. As a result the coverage more often portrayed religion mired in conflict or causing problems than as a socially beneficial, meaningful part of many peoples' lives. Moreover, in these conflict-oriented stories, the storytelling style that favored simplistic explanations and labels often seemed to lump all religions together, and create guilt by association. Similarly, the absence of stories on many religions and sporadic, heavy attention to others could easily lead religious leaders and their flock to believe their faith is being unfairly ignored or singled out for unwarranted scrutiny.

Television journalists, committed to upholding the First Amendment which guarantees freedom of religion as well as freedom of speech and press, probably cannot fully satisfy those critics who want religion news to uphold and defend their own brand of religiosity. Nor should they be expected to, given the multiplicity of religions within the United States. News about religion reported from a particular religion's perspective is readily available through denominational publications and the Christian broadcasting networks. However, the commercial networks could easily address many of this group's complaints about unfairness and also go a long way toward satisfying those who complain primarily about shallow coverage without devoting significantly more time to religion and without abandoning their traditional emphasis on international and national public affairs.

To alleviate many of the most common complaints, the networks probably would have to sacrifice some of the coverage they lavish on the Catholic Church abroad in holiday and feature coverage in order to devote more systematic attention to the diverse religious traditions within the United States. They would also have to devote more off-camera reporting time to come up with substantive information about beliefs, patterns, and trends that could replace reliance on simple event- and conflict-oriented stories and prevent the meaningless labels that may baffle or mislead viewers. In their storytelling they would also have to take more care in their selection of graphics and in the arrangement of information within the stories so that casual juxtapositions do not create the illusion of bias.

REFERENCES

Buddenbaum, J.M. (1985). *Religion in the news: Factors associated with the selection of stories from an international denominational news service.* Unpublished doctoral dissertation, Indiana University. *Dissertation Abstracts International, 45,* 2682A.

Buddenbaum, J.M. (1986). Analysis of religion news coverage in three major newspapers. *Journalism Quarterly, 63,* 600–606.

Buddenbaum, J.M. (1987a). "Judge . . . what their acts will justify": The religion journalism of James Gordon Bennett. *Journalism History, 14,* 54–68.

Buddenbaum, J.M. (1987b, November). *Religion news coverage in network newscasts.* Paper presented at the meeting of the Speech Communication Association, Boston, MA.

Buddenbaum, J.M. (1988). The religion beat at daily newspapers. *Newspaper Research Journal, 9*(4), 57–69.

Duggan, J.P. (1981, August 1). Is the media's language a "Marxist bulgate?" *Vital Speeches of the Day, 47,* 635–637.

Ferre, J.P. (1980). Denominational biases in the American press. *Review of Religious Research, 21,* 276–283.

Fields, E.E. (1985). *Preachers, press, and politics: The media career of a conservative social movement.* Unpublished doctoral dissertation, University of Oregon, Eugene, OR.

Fodiak, W. (1986, December 27). How the Catholic clergy in Pennsylvania views the media. *Editor and Publisher,* pp. 25, 40.

Guzda, M.K. (1985, May 11). Billy Graham to newspapers: Cover religion news better. *Editor and Publisher,* pp. 30, 48.

Hitchcock, J. (1986, July–August). Most journalists fail to understand how religion fits into readers' lives. *ASNE Bulletin,* p. 35.

Hynds, E.C. (1987). Large daily newspapers have improved coverage of religion. *Journalism Quarterly, 64,* 444–448.

Kalder, J. (1985, November 16). The greatest story never told . . . right. *TV Guide,* pp. 14–16, 18, 20, 22.

Kraps, J.M. (1986, November 5). Press coverage of religion: Better, but not good enough. *The Christian Century,* pp. 978–979.

Larson, J.F. (1984). *Television's window on the world: International affairs coverage on the U.S. networks.* Norwood, NJ: Ablex.

Liroff, D.B. (1971). *A comparative content analysis of network television evening news programs and other national news media in the United States.* Unpublished doctoral dissertation, Northwestern University. *Dissertation Abstracts International, 31,* 5556A.

Martz, L. (1988, July 11). TV preachers on the rocks. *Newsweek,* pp. 26–28.

Nimmo, D. & Combs, J.E. (1985). *Nightly horrors: Crisis coverage by television network news.* Knoxville, TN: University of Tennessee Press.

No news is bad news. (1986, March 15). *The Denver Post*, p. 14F.

Oppel, R.A. (1988, January). We don't need a scandal to make religion an important beat. *ASNE Bulletin*, pp. 4–11.

Rockefeller Foundation. (1981). *The religion beat: The reporting of religion in the media.* New York: Author.

Seigenthaler, J. (1988, January). Here's how one minister views media coverage of televangelism. *ASNE Bulletin*, pp. 12–13.

Shaw, D. (1983, December 28). Coverage increases: Media view religion in a news light. *Los Angeles Times*, p. 12.

Thomas, C. (1986, September). Not ready for prime-time prayers. *The Quill, 74,* 15–19.

Wildmon, D.E. (1982, February 19). Let's get religion in the picture. *Christianity Today*, p. 11.

22

Television, Religion, and Fundamentalist Distortions

Robert S. Alley

Direct attention to religion in commercial television series has been fairly restricted over the 50 years of its history. A brief experiment with Bishop Sheen in the 1950s marks the one and only specifically religious prime-time effort on the networks. Similarly, efforts to explicitly discuss or focus on religion in fiction have been scarce. To be sure, *The Family Holvak* was a failed effort to portray a Protestant minister in a weekly drama, and from time to time Catholic priests have emerged as stars of short-lived efforts. *Helltown* is probably the most memorable of that genre. At present *Amen* focuses upon a church deacon and highlights the minister in a seriocomic format, while *Highway to Heaven* has created a theistic fantasy out of Michael Landon's personal beliefs. Along the same lines Norman Lear was particularly successful in introducing realistic Protestant clergy into his series such as *Maude* and *All in the Family*.

A more recent example of explicit use of religious material is *Designing Women* which, in 1988, offered a remarkable episode concentrating upon current conflict over female ordination in the Southern Baptist Convention. This treatment of the role of women in Christian churches was a brilliant example of contemporary events folded into a comedic series form. In this episode, Bernice joined Charlene to challenge the latter's minister in his opposition to women receiving ordination. With the skill born of long years of Bible study, Bernice jousted with the preacher, trading Bible quotes verse for verse. Along the way Bernice found occasion to chide Roman Catholic priests who, she suggested, were in violation of the Scriptures [by remaining unmarried]. Charlene informed her minister that she could no longer attend his church because he would deny young girls the dream of receiving ordination in an institution so influential in their childhood. He argued, "we should not question God's wisdom." Charlene responded, "I'm not, I'm questioning yours!"

Beyond these overt representations of and references to religion, television has been making general moral statements since its inception. There have been few series which have not provided moral lessons on honesty, fairness, justice, decency, and humaneness. In short, the religion of commercial television has been and is in the form of an enlightened, liberal-spirited humanism colored with a broad brush of tolerance and acceptance of human differences. The espoused humanism presumes a certain optimistic vision of humanity, in direct conflict with the rigid adherence to original sin firmly asserted by orthodox Christianity.

Certainly, it is important to remember that, in the beginning, television programming was designed exclusively by male, white producers whose limited humanism incorporated discrimination against minorities as well as a basic sexism. The 1988 network schedule probably demonstrates "deliberate speed" in changing that aspect of programming content. Bob Wood, former CBS President, commented to me on one occasion that television "is not like a speed boat, you can't turn its direction quickly. Television is more like an ocean liner with tug boats analogous to pressures, bringing the ship ever so slowly to a new direction." The tugs, Wood observed, represent "hundreds of discreet publics."

Media scholar and critic Horace Newcomb (Newcomb & Alley, 1983) describes commercial television as "the most popular art." As such, it is inappropriate for it to promote particular ideological religious bias as a policy. But this suggested restriction does not prevent the individual writer or producer from offering viewers a glimpse of their own insights respecting religious ethics and values. Whether one thinks of Jack Webb (*Dragnet*), Quinn Martin (*The FBI, The Streets of San Francisco*), Normal Lear (*Maude*), Loretta Young (*The Loretta Young Show*), Larry Gelbart (*M*A*S*H*), or Linda Bloodworth-Thomason (*Designing Women*), it is clear enough that ideas about social behavior and ethics emerge in direct relation to the persons in charge. It is also evident that a pervasive humanism is at the base of most of the writing.

The history of broadcasting offers overwhelming evidence that networks and producers alike have been concerned to reflect this basic humanism as a means to portray reality. *M*A*S*H*'s Alan Alda often spoke of pursuing "good values" in his work, including the thought "that people come first."

The 1980s, in particular, have presented an interesting variety of series in which the broad strokes of humanism are in evidence. The success over the past 5 years of *Family Ties* makes it a natural source for examining television "values." The series is a remarkable blend of outrageous comedy and sensitive human relationships. Over its broadcast history it has established a warmth among family members that rivals the gentleness of *Leave it to Beaver,* but unlike that earlier series, *Family Ties* ventures into the world of politics, social inequity, varient life styles, vocation, and sexual mores. The key to its character lies in its tolerance for differences. This, in turn, reflects the serious social concerns of its producer, Gary Goldberg. He and his wife, professor Diana Meehan, products of the socially sensitive 1960s, incorporate those attitudes into script ideas.

The premise of *Family Ties,* that the parents are products of the protest days of the 1960s, generates the believable tensions between traditional parental expectations and the commitment to freedom. The resolution is typically the triumph of freedom within the context of deeper appreciation for "family ties." These are decent people bound together by love and mutual respect. It is the stuff of family solidarity in modern America.

Nonetheless, the breadth of this perspective has often brought networks under heavy pressure from special religious interest groups whose ideologies are, from time to time, in their minds offended or not taken seriously.

THE DEMISE OF SELF-MONITORING

In the early days the internal checkpoint for complaints was usually the sponsor, who regularly produced programming for use by the networks. From 1960, with the removal of advertiser control, through the mid-1980s objections to program content were referred to powerful network divisions concerned with broadcast standards. The vice-presidents of network standards held the position of internal censor. In their capacity of "watchdogs" they did daily battle with the more commercially oriented programming executives. They also responded to external pressure groups that regularly identified "offending material."

Since the election of President Reagan there has surfaced a new and strident community bent upon imposing certain ideological guidelines upon network programming. It has its own blacklist of series and sponsors. The interests of these religiously motivated groups is most often directed toward ideas inherent in dialogue rather than in visual images of violence and sex. Much attention has been directed toward the Hollywood representation of the family (see Chapter 24), resulting in serious objections to such seemingly wholesome series as *Family Ties.* The key to this conflict is the rejection by the new breed of critics of the presupposition that moral decisions are dependent upon human understanding and free choice. For them the source of ethics is an unchanging law of God, usually believed to be found in an infallible Bible.

The irony is that, as these pressures grew, the networks appear to have decided that the very existence of internally administered standards created a flashpoint for controversy. That fact, coupled with budgetary cutbacks, has now effectively silenced self-monitoring. The financial bottom line has become the single controlling influence. Beginning with a CBS decision in 1987 to slash the staff of its Standards and Practices Department, the demise of the internal censor seems imminent. Questions of taste and social responsibilities have devolved upon a new, quite young, group of programming executives who seldom reflect any great awareness of history or of the various sensibilities of the discreet publics they serve. This change, at least in part, may be the inevitable response to an ever-increasing pressure from interest groups constantly threatening economic boycotts.

It is to be hoped that as these changes take place in the network hierarchy—changes that place programming in greater proximity to financial considerations—executives will refuse to bend to specific agendas by interest groups intent on forcing their own particular brand of American values as a litmus test in program content. Certainly television writers and producers should remain free to poke fun at religious foibles, arrogance, and indiscretions. More important, those responsible for writing and production should be expected to express their own visions through their art without becoming victims of censorship.

My own support for freedom in television's creative community is, I believe, consistent with our democratic ideals and promises to provide that wide variety of perspectives in network series and films so essential to the free exchange of ideas in a diverse community of citizens. A democracy implies risks and clearly the enormous power of persuasion and promotion associated with television highlights those risks. Yet the free market of ideas is surely as precious as a free market economy. Pressure group efforts to control television content endanger far more than creative freedom. No matter how well-intentioned, organized efforts to impose a single code of values upon television's dramatic and comedic content threatens the genius of our secular Republic.

We are a pluralistic, multicultural nation with hundreds of institutions claiming to possess moral truth, each at odds with all the others on important points. Religious institutions, asserting divine revelation, often propound values totally different from my own. When a single organization seeks to impose its vision of truth upon a popular art form, the result of success is a diminution of the free flow of opinion. The arrogance of righteousness is a threat as old as the colonial experiment itself. Roger Williams, founder of Rhode Island and early advocate of absolute separation between church and state, made it clear to the self-proclaimed Saints of Massachusetts that righteousness gave them no right to impose upon others their own definitions.

THE FUNDAMENTALIST HUE AND CRY

Today on dozens of cable and broadcast channels, often 24 hours a day, a vigorous message of condemnation against the programming of network television coupled with a call for imposition of "Christian standards" is heard in the land. But widespread as is the evidence of such concerns, the source appears to be a narrow band of extremely conservative Christians crusading for a clearly defined agenda. Representative of this movement is the National Federation for Decency (NFD)—a self-proclaimed "Christian organization promoting the Biblical ethic of decency in the American society with primary emphasis on television and other media" (see National

Federation for Decency, 1985c). It is important to highlight the activities of this movement because it has become the single most effective voice in developing a fundamentalist critique of religious content on commercial television.

The primary complaint of this movement, as expressed by the NFD, is that television is not only humanist but anti-Christian. In the *NFD Journal* for December, 1983, an editorial claimed networks were broadcasting "anti-Christian programs." The *Journal* often displays banner headlines using "anti-Christian." In Vail, Colorado on November 12, 1981 Donald Wildmon, director and founder of the NFD, charged all 3 networks with promotion of the secular, of excluding religion, and discriminating against Christians. Wildmon, a Biblical literalist like his fellow fundamentalists, does employ the phrase *"Judeo-*Christian heritage," but it is clear that by using it he seeks only to counter critics while, in fact, he asserts that Jewish ethics and values are only valid when filtered through belief in Jesus as God. On March 9, 1982 I appeared with Wildmon on Richard Hogue's talk show, *Weekdays,* broadcast from Oklahoma City where he admitted that he had, on a televised talk show, told a rabbi that the problem with television is that it is run by a group that is 90 percent Jewish, while the nation is 90 percent Christian.

This proclivity to denigrate Jewish members of the industry and by extension, the entire Jewish population, was made clear in an editorial in March, 1985 (National Federation for Decency, 1985b), where he quoted a study done by Lichter, Lichter, and Rothman (1982). The study examined 104 leaders in the television industry, and determined that 59 percent of television's top people were reared in Jewish homes, 25 percent in Protestant homes, and 12 percent in Catholic homes. In selectively addressing the results, the NFD chose only to include the line "raised in Jewish religion . . . 59 percent" and attributed what it called the networks' "anti-Christian" bias to that 59 percent Jewish community. Wildmon asserted that if Christians made up 59 percent of the network/Hollywood community, such Christians would certainly not be anti-Semitic. The implication is clear: Jews are innately anti-Christian.

Clearly, there is not one iota of evidence that Jewish television producers and other executives have some demonic scheme to undermine Christianity. Based upon my own thorough personal survey of dozens of television industry executives (see Newcomb & Alley, 1983) spanning 15 years, I would categorically deny that the meager poll data that the NFD flaunts prove anything like what they claim. In personally taped conversations Normal Lear, Garry Marshall, Marian Rees, James Brooks, Richard Levinson, Virginia Carter, William Link, Gene Roddenberry, Georgia Jeffries, Quinn Martin, Blue Andre, and John Mantley have all expressed pride in striving for racial and religious equality, laws to protect abused children and wives, better education, mental health, and the rights of women and the elderly. As far as I can tell these issues are not the private preserve of secular humanists nor is espousal of them proof of anti-Christian bias.

There is ample evidence from history, however, that it is the fundamentalists who are ethnocentric by condemning all Jews to hell who do not accept Jesus as God (see National Federation for Decency, 1985a). By that definition, then, Jews are anti-Christian in their rejection of Jesus' divinity. Falwell (1980, p. 8) continued this line of thought in the name of the Moral Majority when he wrote, "Only those who have been born-again by placing their faith in Jesus Christ can effectively call upon God to bless our nation." This is a longstanding position for Christian exclusivists, one that the NFD makes explicit in its continual reference to Jews in Hollywood.

Along the same lines, the term "Biblical ethics" is the linchpin of the religious right's attack against television. The presumption is that there is one, understood and accepted, ethic from the Bible or, according to Charles Colson quoted in the NFD's *Journal* "the Bible is absolutely authoritative—God's inerrant revelation (National Federation for Decency, 1984). This is the key to any absolutist view of ethics and theology. First, establish the source as God ordained. Second, claim the power from God to explain what the source means. Using that style Martin Luther admonished "loyal" citizens to "hew, stab, and slay" the obstinate peasants because the Bible says, "It is better to cut off one member without mercy than to have the whole body perish by fire, or by disease" (Matthew 5:29–30). When the "religious right" employs this tactic it is espousing a view of the Bible rejected by millions of persons in America who call themselves Christians. A claim that there is a single clear inerrant Biblical ethic on complex human problems related to government, religious diversity, sexuality, education, and popular art merely demonstrates an inability to comprehend the range of human potential in a free society.

Sadly, it is against this backdrop that popular attitudes about the television industry are frequently developed. It must be asked, in a diverse and pluralistic democracy consisting of dozens of discreet publics, which self-styled group of "true believers" has the right to impose on others their own definitions? In the real world the NFD and similar groups merely express the views of one minority when they speak of their "Biblical ethic." They cannot in good conscience claim, for they know better, that the Christian population in this country is of one mind on the television programming they address.

The NFD is symtomatic of a widespread effort in the political arena today to discredit "humanism," a philosophy that, in point of fact, has a richly textured fabric, including theists as well as nontheists. Indeed, it is the beauty of humanism that it provides a common meeting ground for Christian and non-Christian in a pluralistic society. The bitter attacks on humanism fail to comprehend that richness, as well as its history which demonstrates a natural affinity with many interpretations of the Christian faith. Thomas Jefferson understood this relationship.

Roger Shinn (1968, p. 166) properly defines humanism as "the appreciation of man and of the values, real and potential, in human life." And the Christian humanist martyr, Dietrich Bonhoeffer, suggested shortly before his execution by the Nazis: "people are more important in life than anything else. . . . One can of course speak like that only if one has found others in one's life" (1966, p. 116). It was Bonhoeffer who offered the picture of the humanistic Jesus, the "man for others." Sir Thomas More gave perhaps the classic definition of the Christian humanist when he wrote: "There are some who through knowledge of things natural construct a ladder by which to rise to the contemplation of things supernatural; they build a path to Theology through Philosophy and the Liberal Arts" (1947, pp. 112–120).

It is the tradition of these persons, and others like them, that enlivens current theistic humanism. The "religious right," led by Jerry Falwell and Pat Robertson, insists that all humanists are atheists or secular humanists. This is an outright falsehood. The dishonest claim that all humanists are, by definition, secular humanists is an affront to both traditions (see Kurtz's essay, Chapter 12, of this volume).

IN FAIRNESS TO THE INDUSTRY

Television is a special type of economic venture. The very nature of popular art requires a particular kind of vision. In order to be competitive network programming must achieve a balance in its offerings that avoids appealing exclusively to any narrow-taste public. Ethnic and cultural diversity are necessary considerations in order that one avoid fracturing that mass audience. No single group is going to be satisfied consistently. Television programming seeks to be diverse and broad in popular appeal, thereby earning its label as the most popular art. When any single large faction becomes dissatisfied with this format trouble is likely. For most of its history commercial television has been accepted on this premise by the vast majority of citizens, albeit with grumbling on occasion from advocates of self-styled "high culture."

It is my view that, traditionally, the networks have been responsive to intelligent, reasoned criticism of their programming. The most dangerous effect of unreasoned attacks would be the loss of rational discourse concerning television's role in society. The questions of sex and violence are legitimate ones to be discussed by fair-minded persons who may differ from industry standards. We dare not lose this option to the hate and suspicion created by those with a single dogmatic agenda. Creators of television series must resist the urge to allow episodes to become small battlegrounds against interest group crusades where an occasional profanity may be celebrated as a victory against the fundamentalists. Such nonsense could destroy creativity, defeat the best interests of the networks, and play directly into the hands of theological terrorists.

In point of fact, family solidarity and traditional values of integrity and honesty are regularly reinforced in the vast majority of commercial programming. My position is that, far more than art, literature, music, radio, theatre, recordings, books, magazines and film, television conserves traditional mores. Certainly such values are perceived quite differently today than in the era of *Father Knows Best,* but the current crop of family-oriented series have the same basic thrust. At no point do the network programs qualify as "anti-Christian."

Indeed, there are numerous examples of programs reinforcing Christian ethics. In a 1986 episode of *Family Ties,* young Jennifer's boyfriend was accosted by bullies. He confronted the chief bully, urged him to use his fists. He reminded him that he would probably be caught if he did so, might be dismissed from school, lose an education, and possibly end his adult days in prison. The bully was totally outclassed by this verbal barrage and backed away muttering nasty thoughts. The boyfriend returned to Jennifer and presumed that she was disappointed in him for not fighting. She corrected him instantly, asserting that his gentleness and pacific nature were precisely what she liked best about him. It was a fine statement about nonviolent alternatives, a sharp rebuke to the notion that the solution to physical bullies is to become one yourself. It also reflected an intelligent examination of traditional sex roles.

Another example is *Night Court,* a series critiqued by the *NFD Journal* in July of 1985. Here we find a series with a high priority on values and moral lessons. With the exception of Dan, or perhaps in comparison to him, these people are exceptional human beings. And even Dan seems almost redeemable when one sees him finally respond to his parents who have cared so much for him. He struggles with his past, as many people do. The figures in this comedy care a great deal about their work and their responsibilities. This was demonstrated in shows concerned with mental illness, racial prejudice, and economic deprivation. There were episodes addressing death and the social dilemma of deprived children. The judge took custody of a homeless boy. Through all these problems there ran the thread of caring one for another that characterizes this series. Judge Stone exhibits a passion for the law based on compassion for those brought before him for trial. Traditional values of integrity, honor, justice, and freedom run through all the plots. The series accepts variant life styles without being judgmental. It may be this characteristic that makes such shows anathema to fundamentalist Christians who construe their faith as a narrow revelation of absolute truth on all issues.

Also Norman Lear's more recent series are exemplary. *Palmerstown, USA* was a story about a black child and a white child growing up friends in the South during the Depression. *A.K.A. Pablo* was a series devoted to the life of a Mexican-American family that expressed the values of family life.

In closing, some remarks about the 1987–88 television season seem an appropriate way to affirm the positive humanism and profamily sensitivities of large numbers of television producers. The effective work of Marian Rees in *Foxfire* and *Love is Never Silent* is testimony to the deep passionate concern for human values existing today among dozens of women in the business. From Dianne English (*My Sister Sam*) to Georgia Jeffries, Shelley List, and P. K. Knelman (*Cagney and Lacey*) to Linda Bloodworth-Thomason (*Designing Women*), the careful crafting of scripts has reflected genuine "religious" concerns.

Television is not a church, but it is a pulpit of ideas, freely available in multiple forms. It is only the dogmatic and self-righteous purveyors of fear and orthodoxy who retreat from its open forum. To repeat, the medium of commercial television remains today the most conserving and traditional of the media, a fair sample of parts of our multicultures. That it remains largely closed to minorities and the poor is an indictment of the society it reflects, including the most segregated institutions in the nation, the Christian churches.

REFERENCES

Bonhoeffer, D. (1966). *Letters and papers from prison*. New York: Macmillan.

Falwell, J. (1980). *Listen America!* New York: Doubleday.

Lichter, L., Lichter, R., & Rothman, S. (1982, October/November). How show business shows business. *Public Opinion, 5,* 10–12.

More, T. (1947). *Correspondence of Sir Thomas More*. New York: Princeton University Press.

National Federation for Decency. (1983, December). *NFD Journal*. Tupelo, MS: Author.

National Federation for Decency. (1984, April). *NFD Journal*. Tupelo, MS: Author.

National Federation for Decency. (1985a, May/June). *NFD Journal*. Tupelo, MS: Author.

National Federation for Decency. (1985b, March). *NFD Journal*. Tupelo, MS: Author.

National Federation for Decency. (1985c, January). *NFD Journal*. Tupelo, MS: Author.

Newcomb, H., and Alley, R.S. (1983). *The producer's medium: Conversations with creators of American TV*. New York: Oxford University Press.

Shinn, R. (1968). *New directions in theology today, Vol. VI, Man: The new humanism*. New York: Westminster.

23

In Conversation: Donald E. Wildmon, American Family Association

with Robert Abelman

Q. *Briefly describe the primary goals and functions of the American Family Association (AFA). Have your goals changed since the organization's inception as the National Federation for Decency in 1977?*

A. The AFA is a Christian organization promoting the Biblical ethic of decency in the American society, with primary emphasis on television and other media. Our goal has not changed since we originally started; rather we have learned that we need to address a broader base of issues than when we initially started. The change in title reflects the fact that the one point where all these issues come together is the family.

Q. *In your book* Home Invaders *(Wildmon, 1985, p. 5), you suggest that "the organized church in America faces the greatest threat to its existence since our country was founded. . . . There is an intentional effort among many of the leaders of our media to reshape our society, to replace the Christian view of man as our foundation with the humanist view of man." Please elaborate on your concern.*

A. If you had expressed this concern back in 1977, I would have laughed at you because I did not believe this. But after monitoring television for 11 years, and after reading the Lichter, Lichter, and Rothman Report (1982)[1]—which said that the most striking finding in their study was that the people who controlled television want to reshape society in their own image—that confirmed every conclusion I reached but was hesitant to say because it sounded so extreme.

The church is basically responsible for a lot of this. In fact, I put the blame of the current moral situation totally at the Church's door. It has refused to address these moral issues. The Church could have been a witness and a force. What has happened in the Church, and I say this

---

[1] Also, see Lichter, Lichter, and Rothman (1986).

out of love and not bitterness, is that it began to withdraw from society and focus on just keeping the machinery running. Only the "liberal" element got involved in politics and society beyond the 4 walls of the institution. Other elements withdrew. They said "don't even buy a television, don't go to the movies . . . withdraw from the world and create a separate society." Interestingly, it is now the fundamentalists who are concerned with society and the mainline church which is withdrawing; it used to be the other way around.

Q. *From your vantage point, how would you rate the current commercial television lineup? Does it show any improvement in terms of its portrayal of morality, family, and Christianity from previous seasons? Are there specific programs, or episodes of programs, that meet with your approval?*

A. From all accounts in the secular media—*USA Today, Newsweek, TV Guide,* and secular television columnists around the country—they are all saying that television is going farther, being more graphic, more explicit. No, morally speaking, network television is the worst that it has ever been. Now the AFA does not recommend programs, per se, but probably the only program that we could give unqualified recommendation for would be *The Cosby Show.* This show does a good job, week in and week out, of portraying family and moral values. But that is the exception to the rule. Cable is a mixed bag. It offers options for nonoffensive quality programs, but you also have Playboy, HBO, Showtime.

Q. *Is the impact of secular humanism more prevalent or explicit in commercial prime-time programming or children's daytime programming? Which form of programming offers the greatest "dangers" to its viewership?*

A. Well, is cancer worse for a person that is 65 years of age or 6 years of age? You have to say that it is bad in either case. By the way, children's television is not relegated to Saturday morning. In fact, CBS found that there are over a million kids watching television after midnight. Furthermore, in a recent interview with the creator of "Mighty Mouse," he was quoted as saying that he is going after the adult audience as much as the child audience. If you watch this program, you are aware of this. There are words used that a child would have no conception of what the character is speaking about.

Q. *In an earlier chapter in this section, Judith Buddenbaum addresses the coverage of religion on network newscasts. Her comparison of the 3 commercial networks reveals a paucity of coverage of religion. When religion or religious figures are covered, it is usually in the context of* some nonreligious event or a holiday celebration. Are these observations consistent with your own? Is this an example of a humanistic philosophy and practice pervading our news media? Referring back to an earlier question, is the impact of secular humanism any more profound in network newscasts than in prime-time fare or children's programming?

A. It has also been found that religion is covered when it is something negative in the Christian community or it is an unusual event like the Pope's visit to America. This is and isn't an intentional thing. The people responsible for news do not count religion as newsworthy, and as Ben Stein says in *The View From Sunset Boulevard* (1979), what you see on television is reflective of the lifestyles, morals, values of the people responsible for it being there. Now I don't think that most of these people say "Hey, we're humanists and we're not going to show religion." They just don't think that religion is important, it just doesn't exist.

Q. Does religious television programming—that is, programming produced, sponsored, and distributed by religious organizations—offer a viable alternative to commercial fare? Does it meet your standards in terms of its promotion of Christianity and family?

A. The amount and variety of Christian television is seriously hampered by a lack of funds, so its true potential is limited. Existing programming itself is a mixed bag. No 2 people are going to agree entirely on everything, although Pat Robertson and CBN (which has changed its name to the CBN Family Network) does a good job. And there are many religious stations that run religious programming 24 hours a day. Unfortunately, there is not a wealth of programs that people can draw on. While the nature of this programming is weak and in its walking or crawling stage, it is certainly going in the right direction. It is certainly better than having none out there . . . absolutely.

Q. Have the recent scandals influenced your view of the purpose or impact of religious television programming? Which represents the greatest threat to the organized church in America, the secular humanism found in commercial television or the version of Christianity found in Bakker's "PTL Club" and "The Jimmy Swaggart Ministry?"

A. Again, is it better to have cancer at 65 years of age or 6? Both hurt Christianity. The networks hurt by their exclusion or negative stereotypes of Christian characters. And there is no doubt that the Bakker and Swaggart controversies have hurt tremendously, and perhaps the religious scandals have hurt most. What is most interesting is the way the secular media have treated Jim Bakker and Jimmy Swaggart, in relationship to how they treated Gary Hart. A year later, Gary Hart has disappeared, he is not in the news, not a news item. But yet the media keep referring to and bringing back the Bakker and Swaggart controversies. The only difference between these people is that Bakker and Swaggart were recognized as Christians and Hart was not. Neither lived by what they preached. This has hurt the image of the Christian community. All along, the secular media have been saying that television evangelists are con men and rip-off artists. They finally found one and now they are saying, "we told you, here they are." It is very wrong to say that all evangelists are like this.

Q. *In an earlier chapter, Robert Alley suggests that your belief in an intentional effort among leaders of our media to reshape society is unfounded. He claims that taped conversations with Norman Lear, Garry Marshall, Quinn Martin, and others (see Newcomb & Alley, 1983) reveal an "expressed pride in striving for racial and religious equality" and an accurate portrayal of family and community. Your response?*

A. Go back to the Lichter, Lichter, and Rothman report which says that these people are intentionally trying to reshape society. For Dr. Alley to say that this is not true reflects ignorance on his part or an intentional effort to distort what was said. Why did Norman Lear found People For The American Way? Because he has a political agenda and a particular perspective. And there is nothing wrong with that. But it is wrong for him to say he doesn't have a political agenda.

Q. *And you believe this infiltrates his programming?*

A. You can't separate the two. People say that the leading evangelists in the country are Billy Graham or Oral Roberts or Jerry Falwell. Well, they're wrong. They are absolutely wrong. The leading evangelists on television are the faceless people who produce programming every night. Watch programming on the networks and with some rare exceptions, every program is pushing a particular moral, political, value agenda. This is not wrong. This is America. But they have denied that they are doing this, and that is wrong. And people that are overt Christians or anyone that says upfront that they are coming from a distinctive religious perspective, they have to pay for programming. The faceless producers are paid for their sermons.

Q. *Aren't there any true Christian producers of popular commercial programming to rectify this situation?*

A. I can't say for a fact. But I assume that birds of a feather flock together. If you come from that particular perspective you don't get far in the industry. It is a closed door. If you are not of a like mind with the media elite who control television, and they are trying to change society, they are not going to open doors to people with a different moral and political viewpoint. That's the way the game's played. Now we have to change it.

Q. *Dr. Alley charges that your organization supports the view that television is not only humanist but anti-Christian. Your response?*

A. He is correct. I can count on one hand, certainly on two, the number of programs that have depicted Christians in a modern-day setting in a positive manner. However, regularly, there are programs where Christians are negatively portrayed. It is 99.5 percent negative. I have not seen any other religion treated in that manner. They have a hostility toward Christians.

Q. *Dr. Alley states that the networks have been responsive to intelligent, reasoned criticism of its programming. Have your efforts and those of other organizations (e.g., "Morality in Media, Inc.") found this to be the case?*

A. No. In a February 2, 1985 *New York Post* article, it was noted that a woman complaining about the content of a particular program was told by an industry representative that people who are members of decency organizations are not listened to by the industry and were dismissed as fanatics. I agree with this. The most powerful group effecting television is the homosexual lobby. Our influence has yet to be seen.

The greatest influence is just around the corner through CLeaR-TV—Christian Leaders for Responsible Television—a coalition of 1600 Christian leaders, over 100 Catholic Bishops, and the heads of 70 denominations. We will soon be sending out a letter from this office to network advertisers saying that CLeaR-TV will monitor programs and have a one-year boycott of one or more sponsors of programs with sex, violence, profanity, and anti-Christian stereotyping. If you want to change, change up front. The interesting thing is that I have spent years trying to get Christian leaders involved in our efforts. This has changed. I am now getting tremendous support from mainline Christian leadership. Now these people will listen to me. They see that what I have been saying is coming true and television is getting worse. The best thing going for us now is the sorry state of television.

REFERENCES

Lichter, L., Lichter, R., & Rothman, S. (1982, October/November). How show business shows business. *Public Opinion, 5,* 10–12.

Lichter, L., Lichter, R., & Rothman, S. (1986, August). Hollywood and America: The odd couple. *NFD Journal*, pp. 4–17.

Newcomb, H., & Alley, R.S. (1983). *The Producer's medium: Conversations with creators of American TV*. New York: Oxford University Press.

Stein, B. (1979). *The view from Sunset Boulevard*. New York: Basic Books.

Wildmon, D.E. (1985). *The home invaders*. Wheaton, IL: Victor Books.

VIII

The Portrayal of Family on Religious Television

Two decades ago, *New York Times* columnist Russell Baker (1970) wrote an essay entitled "The State of the Family Message." It began:

> The family being all assembled in the parlor for the annual occasion, Great Morgaged Father entered the chamber, took his place at the hearth and spoke as follows: "Madam Wife, Minister Grandfather, members of the younger generation, distinguished cats and tropical fish. Occasionally there comes a time when profound and far-reaching events command a break with tradition in the style of the State of the Family Address. This is such a time. I say this not only because 1970 marks the beginning of a decade in which the entire family may well die of its own environment unless visionary measures are taken. I say it because the most casual glance about the house as well as hard experience argue persuasively that both our programs and our habits need to be reformed. Quiet air, clean bathrooms, uncluttered hallways, neatly packed garbage cans, these should once again be the birthright of every member of the family. Accordingly, the program I propose today is the most comprehensive design for improving family environment that I have ever put before you."

The essay goes on to call for an end to household disturbances that have become the norm for the average family. These include clusters of dog hair on clothes, hotdogs in the glove compartment, mashed bananas and peanut butter on the television screen, and aging grease behind the stove.

Interesting though this essay might be, there are obviously more complicated issues than a congested environment facing today's family. Changing social patterns prompted by industrialization, urbanization, increased mobility, inflationary economics, new work habits and ethics, and media-induced popular culture have deeply affected the size, structure, and function of the American family. According to many learned observers (e.g., Gelman, 1985; Lometti, 1987), traditional roles and values that previously undergirded family life are currently in a state of turmoil. Recent U. S. Bureau of Census statistics (1989) suggest that the rate of divorce continues to increase, illegitimacy has more than doubled in the past 3 decades, 1 out of every 6 children lives with a single parent, and family violence is more than just a minor occurrence in the American household.

Living in a family has never been easy; one need only read the Bible to discover that marital deceit, sibling rivalry, incest, abusive husbands and parents, and family violence are not inventions of the late-20th century. The family has always been an institution under stress (Anderson, 1982; McAdoo, 1981), and the church has often been a vehicle to bring the family together. In its promotion of family roles and values, the church has sought to preserve the family unit and teach our youth about the strength in family unity. Lessons from the Bible are often perceived as lessons in family cohesion and parsimony (D'Antonio & Aldous, 1983; Pipes, 1981).

It has been suggested, however, that the church's impact on the family has been usurped by a more contemporary and powerful institution. Over forty years ago, social scientist Harold Laswell (1948) noted that mass media have replaced yesterday's cathedrals and parish churches as teachers of the young. This was due to the media's incomparable potential to reflect our social heritage, preserve it, and dynamically transmit it from one generation to the next. Laswell's observation is even more in tune today, given the astronomical prevalence and popularity of television. Recent Nielsen ratings suggest that 2- to 5-year-old children watch an average of 25:43 hours of television per week; 6- to 11-year-olds watch an average of 23:17 hours per week (Nielsen, 1989).

In recent years, clergy have come to not only recognize the impact of commercial television as an educator of youth, but have employed the medium for their own purposes. One need only watch commercial television during the early morning or late night hours or randomly turn the television dial through the plethora of cable channels to find programming sponsored by religious organizations, focusing on religious issues, and grounded in religious theology and morality. Over 212 stations across the country carry large amounts of religious fare offered by as many as 5 religious networks via statellite and cable. According to televangelist Billy Graham (1983, p. 5), "I can preach to more people in one night on TV than perhaps Christ did in his entire lifetime."

Consequently, one needs to wonder whether this popular and wide-reaching fare is meeting Laswell's expectations as a replacement of or supplement to parish churches as teachers of the young. In particular, what is this form of programming telling our children about the role and function of the family unit? Is it offering a more optimistic or pessimistic message about family than that which exists in reality? Although their first experience with families are with their own and those of their playmates, young children soon begin to observe and vicariously experience the families presented on television. The same social learning theories that have yielded testable propositions about the learning of aggression, prosocial behaviors, and sex-role expectations from television (e.g., Bandura, 1977; Baran, Chase, & Courtright, 1979; Berkowitz, 1962; Liebert, Sprafkin, &

Davidson, 1982; Miller & Reeves, 1976) would also be applicable to the learning of family roles, interaction patterns, and behaviors.

In addition, how does the portrayal of family on religious television compare to that of secular television? According to Schultze (1986), "television stories serve the same purpose for American viewers that the Bible does for the Christian community . . . and the images and sounds emanating from the television set reflect some of the most basic beliefs of the people who watch them." Many televangelists propose that religious television's real converts are coming "from commercial TV, whose diets of secular programming leaves viewers starved for spiritual nourishment" (Graham, 1983, p. 8). Donald Wildmon (1985) has gone so far as to suggest that secular television is a "mind-polluting tide seeking to submerge us all . . . and overthrow our faith and our families." Is the portrayal of family on religious television complementing or contradicting the portrayal of family on its secular counterpart?

The following 2 chapters address these questions. The first, written by religious studies professor Julie Mitchell Corbett, examines the portrait of the family as a reflection of the new religious-political "right." She suggests that Christian television is the "media arm" of this coalition of groups and that its programming represents and reinforces its collective vision of the ideal family. According to Corbett, there are serious problems regarding validity and pragmatic utility associated with the family style advocated by and depicted on Christian television. She argues that there are serious inconsistencies between the portrayal of family in these programs and as depicted in the Bible, thereby rendering religious broadcasting irrelavant and potentially dysfunctional.

Communication scientist Robert Abelman addresses these criticisms by reporting the results of various content analyses of popular secular and religious programming. This chapter compares research findings to Census Bureau statistics on contemporary family composition and research on family interaction patterns. Abelman examines the accuracy of these portrayals and the extent of their possible impact on viewers' perceptions of their own families.

REFERENCES

Anderson, H. (1982). The purpose of family. *Television & Children, 5*(2), 21–26.

Baker, R. (1970, January 25). The state of the family message. *The New York Times,* Editorial.

Bandura, A. (1977). *Social learning theory.* Englewood Cliffs, NJ: Prentice-Hall.

Baran, S.J., Chase, L.J., & Courtright, J.A. (1979). Television drama as a facilitator of prosocial behavior: "The Waltons." *Journal of Broadcasting, 23*(3), 277–284.

Berkowitz, L. (1962). *Aggression: A special psychological analysis*. New York: McGraw-Hall.

D'Antonio, W.V., & Aldous, J. (1983). *Families and religions*. Beverly Hills, CA: Sage Publications.

Gelman, D. (1985, July 15). Playing both mother and father. *Newsweek*, pp. 42–50.

Graham, B. (1983). The future of TV evangelism. *TV Guide, 31*(10), 4–8.

Laswell, H. (1948). The structure and function of communication in society. In L. Bryson (Ed.), *The communication of ideas* (pp. 37–51). New York: Harper Brothers.

Liebert, R.M., Sprafkin, J.N., & Davidson, E.S. (1982). *The early window*. New York: Pergamon Press.

Lometti, G. (1987). Address at the Sixth Annual Conference of the National Council for Families and Television. *Television & Families, 9*(4), 45–47.

McAdoo, H.P. (1981). *Black families*. Beverly Hills, CA: Sage Publications.

Miller, M.M., & Reeves, B. (1976). TV content and children's sex-role stereotypes. *Journal of Broadcasting, 20*(1), 35–50.

Nielsen, A.C. (1989). *Year end report*. Chicago, IL: Author.

Pipes, W.H. (1981). Old-time religion: Benches can't say "amen." In H. Pipes McAdoo (Ed.), *Black families* (pp. 54–76). Beverly Hills, CA: Sage Publications.

Schultze, Q. (1986). *Television: Manna from Hollywood?* Grand Rapids, MI: Zondervan Publishing.

U.S. Bureau of Census. (1989). *Household and family characteristics*. Washington, DC: U.S. Government Printing Office.

Wildmon, D.E. (1985). *The home invaders*. Weaton, IL: Victor Press.

24

The Family As Seen Through the Eyes of the New Religious-Political Right

Julia Mitchell Corbett

Christian television is, in effect, the media arm of the new religious-political "right." It is its main public relations tool. The "religious right's" loose coalition of groups and individuals share a strong conviction that the United States is in the midst of a severe spiritual and moral decline, a decline that will ultimately lead to its defeat at the hands of atheistic Communism, if it is not reversed. They believe that a return to traditional American values, of which fundamentalist Christianity is the guardian, will again make America a strong and righteous nation. They believe that laws should be passed to enforce these values. The movement has been described as "a blend of old-time religion and far-right politics coordinated with Madison Avenue sophistication" (Benson & Williams, 1986, p. 173).

Several of the key spokesmen for this movement are also heavily involved in Christian broadcasting. Jerry Falwell, founder of the Moral Majority (now Liberty Foundation), is also the founder and star of the popular *Old Time Gospel Hour*. Another key figure is Pat Robertson, who founded CBN (the Christian Broadcasting Network), the nation's first Christian network. Jimmy Swaggart broadcasts his views from a large and sophisticated television studio.

The religious dimension of the "religious right's" self-definition makes its participation in politics more than simply political. Its supporters believe that America is "becoming a new Sodom and Gomorrah—a land where the pornographers, atheists, and socialists [hold] sway, threatening to destroy all that [is] virtuous. Therefore, their participation in electoral politics [is] not that of just another pressure group but [is] a holy cause" (Plotkin, 1985, p. 49).

The family is a central, if not *the* central unit of the "religious right's" agenda. Their general influence over political decisions has lacked both the breadth and the power that they had originally hoped (Erikson, Luttbeg, & Tedin, 1988). The world remains sadly under the influence of Satan. However, the family unit allows for the creation of a microcosm arranged according to their beliefs and values. It is not only the key factor in the salvation of the world, but it is a refuge from the yet-unsaved world:

> The New Christian Right finds in the family a means to recover a lost meaning as well as a lost past. It has become a primary symbol of the worldview, and the story they offer as a countermythology. The family is both a symbol for that mythology and necessary socializer . . . . Restructuring or redefining the family is a powerful means of creating alternative myths. To gain control of definitions is to gain the power to stabilize or de-stabilize the myth for which the New Christian Right is contending. (Heinz, 1983, p. 142)

The family that is portrayed on Christian television is then the ideal family. As with the messages of Christian programming in general, there is only 1 correct *family* style. The traditional, intact family consisting of 2 parents and children, in which the mother stays home to care for her family's needs and the father is the sole wage earner is the only arrangement that this point of view recognizes as acceptable. Falwell (1980, pp. 121, 128) elaborates on this viewpoint:

> The family is the God-ordained institution of the marriage of one man and one women together for a lifetime with their biological or adopted children. [This] is the fundamental building block and the basic unit of our society. . . . The answer to stable families with children who grow up to be great leaders in our society and who themselves have stable homes will not come from . . . more part-time work for fathers and mothers, or parental leaves of absence, or thirty-hour weeks, or parental co-operatives and other forms of sharing childraising responsibilities. It will come only as men and women in America get in a right relationship to God and His principles for the home.

Christenson (1970, pp. 32, 33, 39, 44) also confirms this perception of the family:

> God has given wives the opportunity to choose freely the submissive role. . . . To be submissive means to yield humble and intelligent obedience to an ordained power or authority. . . . There is a firm, unalterable decree of God in the position of men and women. . . . The Bible teaches a *subordination* of the wife to her husband. . . . Not that there's anything wrong with a father occasionally giving a baby a bottle, if the situation requires it or he enjoys it. What's wrong is thinking that it adds to his parenthood. When a man tries to be a "better" father by acting like a mother, he is not only less fulfilled as a father, but as a man, too.

The only family style that is portrayed in a positive light on Christian television is that of the traditional family. While this is not necessarily a criticism, it does control virtually everything else that is done with the family there. When other family styles are shown in religious fare, it is as a foil against which to portray the ideal. Nontraditional families are those of the unconverted or the not-yet-converted, or they are the "before" in a "before and after" contrast (Mitchell, 1985, pp. 65–66).

Even a cursory reading of "religious right" documents reveals that its ethic is one of absolutes. There is little or no room for compromise, no consideration of what might be "better" or "best" (as compared with simply right or wrong) in a particular situation (Corbett, 1988, p. 21; Mitchell, 1985, p. 64). This may account for the large number of reruns of old Westerns on the CBN "family" network. In programs such as *Gunsmoke, Bat Masterson,* and *Wagon Train,* the good guys are totally good, the bad guys are utterly bad, and it is completely clear which is which.

An ethic that allows only one "right answer" cannot consider that it might be better for a seriously mismatched couple who has sincerely tried to work out their differences to divorce than to remain in a marriage which is in all likelihood hopeless, for example. The ethic is obedience and compulsion, not love and freedom. In that situation, people remain married because their interpretation of the Bible says they must, not out of love and free choice. The question must at least be asked whether or not love can be coerced in this way. To hold that love cannot be coerced is not to suggest that people ought not to remain in marriages when they simply do not *feel* like it; feelings are ephemeral, and many times what is called for is to "hang in there" until things seem brighter.

Other interpretations of the love spoken of in the Bible hold that it is a love that is free, not coerced. To remain in a loveless marriage may well be a poison which will finally corrode what they are trying so hard to preserve.

A passage from Christenson (1970, pp. 25–26), a movement writer, illustrates how far the "religious right" is willing to take its interpretation:

> [Remaining in a loveless marriage] is an evil of inexpressible magnitude. Yes, so it is; and so it ought to be. Let it not be said that such a punishment is too hard for the youthful levity which has determined the choice. That levity ought to undergo the hardest possible punishment, because it has made the most solemn and holy of all human relationships a matter of sport, of carelessness, and of sensual gratification.

When this is applied to how Christian television portrays the family, 2 features stand out. Families that are portrayed in a positive light are intact and traditional. Examples include reruns of older family shows such as *Father Knows Best, Leave It To Beaver, Green Acres,* and *Lassie.* These reruns are a staple of Christian network broadcasting. Second, when marital conflicts are portrayed, as they sometimes were in the Christian Broadcasting Network soap opera *Another Life,* divorce is never pictured as a potential solution. That the couple will remain together is simply assumed.

Two additional "religious right" themes have a direct bearing on the portrayal of the family on Christian television. The first theme is that of order, cast very starkly as the conflict between authoritarianism on the one hand and chaos on the other, with no middle ground in between. This is a recasting of the age-old scenario in which the world is a huge stage upon which a battle to the death between God and Satan is being enacted. The second theme—again not a new one in the history of Christianity—is purity. Images of disease, corruption, and filth are standard in descriptions of both individuals and society (Hill & Owen, 1982). This is reflected in both the literature of the "religious right" and the sermons preached on Christian television.

Much of the overall style of this variety of Christianity can be traced back to the frontier revivalists of the 1800s. They knew of no middle ground; it was Heaven or Hell, holiness or sin, morality or immorality. Living a morally upright life became a sign of one's assured salvation, especially in contrast to the rough-and-ready lifestyle of the frontier. Interestingly enough for the present discussion, a morally upright life came to be defined as *not* doing the evil things done by the unconverted—an interpretation with a remarkable resemblance to how such a life is pictured by Christian broadcasters (Corbett, 1989). For example, the main evidence of someone's conversion is often that they no longer do the sinful things they did prior to their conversion.

The family as conceived by the "religious right," and as portrayed on Christian television, is part of a coherent worldview that admits of no exceptions or variations. Salvation means accepting *all* of the picture, including the family style portrayed. If one wants to be the kind of joyful, exuberant, and attractive person presented, then one must be a part of the traditional family in which such persons are seen. Kater (1982, p. 8) highlights this view:

Most of all, the vision of the New Right is a *complete world-view*. It is a coherent whole, providing an all-encompassing set of moral values, a political philosophy, a religious perspective, and a prescribed social structure—a complete culture—which hangs together, and from which nothing can be removed or altered without causing the whole to collapse.

There are obviously serious problems with this family style as it is pictured on Christian television. These problems relate to both its validity and its pragmatic usefulness.

First, there are problems with its *validity*. Significant inconsistencies seriously compromise what Christian television has to say on the subject of the family. Its preachers and teachers fervently proclaim that God loves *all* people, without regard for their state or condition. Jesus died and rose again because "God so loved the world . . ." (John 3:16). However, another note in their message strongly suggests that God's approval is reserved for those people who are part of structures that fit the traditional model. This conflict between the message of grace and the demand for works runs throughout Protestant fundamentalism as a whole. Where the family is concerned, it exacts a very high price. Spouses are described as "saved" or "unsaved," and if the latter, a tremendous strain is placed on the marriage. Such a home may be described a "half-Christian" by the saved spouse. Those who find that they no longer fit the 1 model, perhaps following a divorce that they neither wanted nor sought, may be made to feel that there is no possibility of their continuing to have a Christian home, even when to do so is very important to them (Ammerman, 1987, p. 132). If a believer is married to an unbeliever, they are often said to be "unequally yoked," and such marriages do not have the "correct" status of marriages between 2 Christians. Again, religious questions about God's approval and acceptance are added to the strains already there.

Another problem not unrelated to the first is that of God's power, and the seeming limits placed upon that power by the emphasis on the traditional family. The "religious right" holds that power is one of God's primary attributes (Corbett, 1988, 1989; Mitchell, 1985). The sermons of its preachers abound with images of God's almightiness. When people testify about God's work in their lives, it is described at least as often in terms of power as it is in terms of love. It is, then, quite inconsistent to maintain that there is but one family structure through which society can be upheld and salvation secured. It would seem more consistent, or at least no *less* so, to demonstrate God's power at work in a whole host of lifestyles.

A third problem concerns the use that the movement makes of the Bible, particularly the New Testament, to support its view of the family. It takes the Bible as absolutely and literally authoritative (Corbett, 1988, 1989). Texts such as Ephesians 5:22–25 and I Peter 3:1–7 are often cited in support of the traditional family style characterized by male dominance. However, there are other Biblical passages that support the equality of women. According to John 4:25–26, one of the earliest times that Jesus acknowledged himself to be the Messiah was to a woman. According to Luke's gospel, Jesus appeared first to Mary Magdalene and other women after the resurrection (Luke 24). The Ephesians 5:23 passage advocating women's submissiveness is in the context of the mutual submission of husbands and wives to each other (Corbett, 1989; Russell, 1985). The Bible as a whole does not present a unified message where gender roles are concerned. Elements from the prevailing patriarchal culture of its time are mixed with support for equality that is derived from its view that all persons are equally children of God.

This is an especially telling problem, since the "religious right" grounds its authority in the Bible. Since that authority does not speak with an unequivocal voice, can the movement limit itself to but 1 point of view? On its own terms, it cannot.

There is a fourth issue that stems from the view of human nature held by most proponents of the "religious right" point of view. According to their teaching, human nature is thoroughly corrupted by sin. Sin encompasses many things, but there is a tendency to pay much more attention to the traditional "sins of the flesh" than to the sins against social justice that the prophets of the Hebrew Scriptures spoke out against so eloquently. They believe that the family is the principal force for order in the society. Strong traditional families are the main check on the passions of a sinful human race (Mitchell, 1985). That the family is the basic unit of American culture and that the moral and social health of the nation as a whole is ultimately linked to the fate of the family is an assertion with which it is difficult to disagree, and certainly one with which the present author has no desire to quarrel.

However, something is lost amidst this talk about the controlling function of the family. The family also has positive functions. It is the primary place in which people find unconditional acceptance, love, and their most intimate human contacts. Hadden (1983, p. 251) has also noted this point:

> But what about the family itself? What about the positive roles of nurture, love, and support? . . . [R]elatively little space is devoted to elaboration of these positive dimensions of the family.

It is this positive function that gets lost, or at least seriously hidden. Among the religiously motivated and supported functions of the family is certainly the reflecting in human form of God's love and care for God's human family. Where else can people learn about God's unconditional love so well? Christianity has always emphasized the love of God, shown in Christ especially, but reflected in the love and compassion that human beings have for each other. The style of Christianity that lies behind much of what is seen on religious television talks about the love of God; it would serve well to show that love in families. The perspective of love finds at least as much support in the Bible, taken as a whole, as does the theme of control.

Another problematic theme is that of a return to the type of society, including the family structure, that comes from a remembered past. The movement seeks to "preserve American society as we have always known it" (Viguerie, 1981, p. 159). There are at least 2 problems with this. This remembered "traditional family" is a fairly recent development, one that came about with the industrialization and concommitant urbanization of America. Men left the home in droves to work, work being defined as something for which wages were paid. Previously, women and men had been much more co-workers in the unified task of maintaining a home, a farm, and raising a family. So this remembered family is *not* the way it always has been (Rapp, 1982). Second, the solutions that worked in the culture of the Industrial Revolution (if they did then) are very likely not the best for a much larger, more complex postindustrial society.

The profamily stance of the religious right and the image of the family constructed by Christian television, turns out to be more a rejection than an affirmation in the end. The affirmation of the traditional, nuclear family is made at the expense of a rejection of all other forms of households and family life. Divorce, cohabitation, and homosexuality are rejected. Situations which involve more than 2 adults with their children fall outside the pale. Voluntary childlessness is rejected, as are most of the newer medical attempts to remedy involuntary childlessness. Women employed outside the home fail to meet the one criterion held up as God-ordained. Anything, in fact, which suggests that the "ideal" family structure may not be the only way, or even in some cases, the best way, is rejected.

Another problem has to do with the amount of guilt generated by the point of view we have been describing. The goal is to make the family an environment in which certain values are taken for granted and embodied on a day-to-day basis. The prescribed rules, however, "come up against hard realities that demand compromise" (Ammerman, 1987, p. 134). The situation of an unsaved spouse mentioned earlier is one such example; a fully Christian home cannot be created under those circumstances, no matter how hard the other spouse may try. Economic necessities that dictate that a woman join the workforce, a factor in the lives of an increasing number of women, is another such instance. If a man is laid off and cannot be the sole breadwinner for his family, the inevitable blow to his self-esteem is made harder to bear by the knowledge that he is not following God's plan. Any of these situations is hard enough in and of itself, without the added burden of a person's feeling that he or she has failed God as well.

These weaknesses create problems of another sort, limitations on the *pragmatic* usefulness of the way in which Christian television portrays the family. The intention of Christian television is the conversion of as many people as possible, of the nation as a whole, to its version of Christianity. The fact that most viewers are already believers (Corbett, 1989; Hoover, 1988; Mitchell, 1985), while crucial in evaluating televangelism's proclaimed aim, is not crucial for the point to be made here. Demographic data clearly show that a substantial number of people do not fit the family pattern being presented as the only one acceptable in God's sight (National Opinion Research Center, 1987). Forecasts for the next 50 years indicate that little change can be expected in this situation. Of those persons between the ages of 23 and 41 now, a third will marry at least twice and half will divorce once. One in 5 will divorce twice. Less than 10 percent will achieve the ideal family, a lifetime marriage with 2 children, 1 of either gender. Eighty percent of the women in this group will be in the workforce

workforce by 1995, and most children will be raised in homes in which both parents work outside the home (Russell, 1987). We do not have to credit these predictions with total accuracy to see that future demographic trends are such that a lot of people will receive at best a "double message" from Christian television. On the one hand, they are invited to participate in something which is described as a great good, which will bring earthly happiness and ultimately life eternal with God. On the other hand, it is linked to a lifestyle of which many of them will not be a part. This cannot help but decrease the relevance of televangelism's message.

If, on the other hand, Christian television has become, as noted in previous essays, a type of viewer-supported broadcasting, then a similar point can be made. One image of the family is being beamed to a viewing audience which includes an increasing plurality of family structures. It is interesting that there are among the supporters of a platform that mandates marriage and the nuclear family a substantial percentage of those who fail to meet that mandate. Might not Christian television do a greater service to its viewers, and as a secondary effect increase its viewing public as well, if a greater range of lifestyles were portrayed, and living by God's Word in whatever family setting one finds oneself were given greater emphasis?

A final pragmatic consideration is that the means by which the "religious right" and Christian television seek to preserve the family may in fact be counterproductive. They may be defeating their own fondest hopes. It seems clear at this point in our social and cultural history that we truly cannot go home again. A vast variety of family structures and alternatives is here to stay. While we *must* support and strengthen the family if we are to solve some of the most pressing problems of our time and place, the most effective strategy for doing so is probably *not* to insist that the only way is a return to something that in all likelihood cannot be (if in fact it ever was). A far more promising method is to find new and creative ways to support those family structures and households that *do* evolve. What is needed instead of clinging to the old is help in developing new models, patterns, and support networks for nontraditional households. If this is done, then these households, too, will become more able to provide what is necessary to become whole and healthy and thus to contribute to a whole, healthy, and sane society.

The larger value of the family is not to be found in a specific structure as such, but in the constancy, love, intimacy, and relatedness which that structure has come to symbolize. And surely we can develop these same qualities in other structures as well. Just as surely, for those who want to, support for doing so can be found in the message of the Bible. According to the Christian story itself, there was an individual who embodied these qualities to such as extent that he became known as the Christ, the bringer of salvation. That individual was an unmarried man who went about the countryside with a scraggly band of other unmarried men, never established a permanent home, and had the audacity to say that a woman of thoroughly questionable reputation was also the daughter of God. Can anyone of Christian faith strive for less than such a vision?

REFERENCES

Ammerman, N.T. (1987). *Bible believers: Fundamentalists in the modern world.* New Brunswick, NJ: Rutgers University Press.

Benson, P.L., & Williams, D.L. (1986). *Religion on capitol hill: Myths and realities.* New York: Oxford University Press.

Christenson, L. (1970). *The Christian family.* Minneapolis, MN: Bethany Fellowship.

Corbett, J.M. (1988, September/October). The new Puritanism: We must say "no" again. *The Humanist, 48*(5), 19–23, 38.

Corbett, J.M. (1989). *Religion in America: An academic approach.* Englewood Cliffs, NJ: Prentice-Hall.

Erikson, R.S., Luttbeg, N.R., & Tedin, K.L. (1988). *American public opinion: Its origins, content, and impact* (3rd ed.). New York: Macmillan.

Falwell, J. (1980). *Listen, America!* Garden City, NY: Doubleday and Company.

Hadden, J.K. (1983). Televangelism and the mobilization of a new Christian right family policy. In W.V. D'Antonio & J. Aldous (Eds.), *Families and religions: Conflict and change in modern society* (pp. 247–266). Beverly Hills, CA: Sage Publications.

Heinz, D. (1983). The struggle to define America. In R.C. Liebman & R. Wuthnow (Eds.), *The new Christian right: Mobilization and legitimation* (pp. 133–148). New York: Aldine.

Hill, S.S., & Owen, D.E. (1982). *The new religious political right in America.* Nashville, TN: Abingdon Press.

Hoover, S.M. (1988). *Mass media religion: The social sources of the electronic church.* Beverly Hills, CA: Sage.

Kater, J.L. (1982). *Christians on the right: The moral majority in perspective.* New York: The Seabury Press.

Mitchell (Corbett), J. (1985). Images of the family in commercial and religious television. In E. Lange (Ed.), *Using media to promote knowledge and skills in family dynamics* (pp. 55-71). Dayton, OH: University of Dayton Center for Religious Telecommunications.

National Opinion Research Center. (1987). *General social surveys, 1987.* Chicago, IL: National Opinion Research Center.

Plotkin, H.A. (1985). Issues in the campaign. In G.M. Pomper (Ed.), *The election of 1984: Reports and interpretations* (pp. 35–59). Chatham, NJ: Chatham House Publishers, Incorporated.

Rapp, R. (1982). Family and class in contemporary America: Notes toward an understanding of ideology. In B. Thorne & M. Yalom (Eds.), *Rethinking the family: some feminist questions* (pp. 168–187). New York: Longman.

Russell, C. (1987). *100 predictions for the baby boom: The next fifty years*. New York: Plenum.

Russell, L.M. (1985). *Feminist interpretation of the Bible*. Philadelphia, PA: Westminster Press.

Viguerie, R.A. (1981). *The new right: We're ready to lead*. Falls Church, VA: The Richard A. Viguerie Company.

25

The Religious Television Family Portrait

Robert Abelman

According to recent Census Bureau statistics (U.S. Bureau of Census, 1989) and academic reports (e.g., Hanson & Sporakowski, 1986; Lometti, 1987; Norton & Glick, 1986; Stanley, Hunt, & Hunt, 1986), things look fairly grim for the American family, particularly in terms of size and stability. With nearly half of new marriages ending in divorce, single parents currently head over 25 percent of the families with young children in the United States. Experts predict that 1 of every 3 families, possibly even 1 out of 2, will be headed by a single parent by 1990. They further estimate that a quarter of the now married mothers and fathers with children will be single parents sometime in this decade. As a consequence of the breakup of the nuclear family, the occurrence of extended families has dramatically declined over the years. Currently, less than 13 percent of all elderly individuals live with other relatives.

In addition, recent *Newsweek* articles have suggested that the percentage of couples without children has doubled in the last few decades. In 1960 only about 13 percent of married women between 25 and 29 were childless; last year 29 percent were childless. Today, 1 out of every 4 women between the ages of 25 and 34 has never had a child—a total of nearly 3.3 million women—compared to 1 out of 10 women in 1960. The current overall rates of childlessness are the highest since the end of the Great Depression. In the 1930s, it was the lack of a reliable income that kept families from starting. In the 1980s, according to these articles, a good salary may be the main reason to delay or forgo parenthood; childlessness has increased as women have moved into well-paying careers in record numbers (Kantrowitz, 1986b). Lometti (1987, p. 47) confirms this observation, suggesting that "in the mid-1980s, 55 percent of women in the U.S. are employed . . . but those numbers are significantly higher—72 percent and 70 percent—for women in the prime childbearing years of 20–24 and childbearing years of 25–54."

Along the same lines, young couples with children are having less children than in previous years. Last year there were 13 million "only children" in this country—about 50 percent more than 20 years ago. Currently, the average number of children per household stands at 1.85. Considering the increasing rate of divorce, childlessness, and "only children" and the demise of the extended family, the overall size and stability of the American family has decreased significantly (Kantrowitz, 1986a, 1986b) and shows signs of continuing in this direction.

A FAMILY PORTRAIT: SECULAR
TELEVISION PROGRAMMING

Based on reports of prime-time portrayals of family over the past decade (see Dreielbis, 1987; Greenberg, Buerkel-Rothfuss, Neuendorf, & Atkin, 1980; Greenberg, Hines, Buerkel-Rothfuss, & Atkin, 1980; Larson, 1987; Thomas & Callahan, 1982), it is clear that television cannot be accused of contributing to the recent decay of the American family. Indeed, things look a bit brighter for the American family on commercial television than in real life. For the most part, commercial television reinforces the illusion of the intact, extended, and interacting family unit. This is especially the case in the contemporary prime-time lineup.

In the 1986–87 television season, for example, the family was in the forefront of network prime-time programming with over 60 percent of the new shows featuring or focusing on a family—that is, 2 or more people portrayed as blood or marital kin. Approximately 42 percent of the 1985–86 season's new programs and 56 percent of the programs from the previous year revolved around a family or family life. Within all these television families, the traditional family structure is the norm; the majority of all families are nuclear (2 parents with 1 or more children), followed by families consisting of 1 parent plus children, assorted relatives living together, and husbands and wives without children (Abelman, 1989). According to Zoglin (1986, p. 73), "under the Cosby spell, family shows have reverted to classic form . . . the old-fashioned 2-parent model has staged a comeback." Indeed, John Marcus—coexecutive producer and head writer of *The Cosby Show*—suggests that his program offers "a fresh and honest approach to the family. It shows a desire to move back to more traditional structure, with strong parental figures" (Abelman, 1985, p. 16).

In the 1986–87 season in particular, television offered a great diversity of family composition and lifestyle. Of the nuclear families portrayed, we were offered a family consisting of 2 parents, 2 children, and an alien, and a family consisting of 2 parents, 1 child by birth, and 3 children by adoption (1 white, 1 Asian, 1 black). A close examination of the evening lineup also offered 2 cousins living together, 2 sisters living together, a grandfather sharing his roof with his daughter-in-law and her children, and a niece and uncle (plus friend) sharing rent. Most of the single-parent families portrayed on television were headed by widows and widowers; incidences of divorce were not found with the frequency of previous years' programming (Dreibelbis, 1987; Greenberg, Hines, Buerkel-Rothfuss, & Atkin, 1980).

Although extended families are infrequent on television, the representation of the elderly as family members is much more accurate than in previous years (Greenberg, Korzenny, & Atkin, 1980). "The circle of kinfolk is expanding," observes Zoglin (1986, p. 73), "grandparents are central figures in several of TV's newest households," both dramatic and comical, and many others offer the elderly in significant cameo appearances. This trend continues in more contemporary programming.[1]

In addition to families being more diverse and stable on commercial television than in reality, Larson (1987) found that there is more interaction between televised family members than among their real world counterparts. Similarly, Abelman and Ross (1986, pp. 48–49) suggested that:

> Children appear to be the center of most action and interaction in TV programming; conversations between TV husbands and wives, alone, constitute only 29 percent of all family interactions and it is the child that typically initiates and dominates conversations with adults. The lack of communication between family members, particularly between parents and children, is regularly identified as the primary problem facing today's families. While much of the interaction between TV families can be labeled as "going toward" behavior—that is, approaching the other person in a positive, constructive fashion—all too much real family interaction has been found to include "going against" or conflict-producing behavior.

Clearly, then, a significant amount of programs on prime-time television is family oriented and, within these programs, much of the interaction is child-oriented.

A FAMILY PORTRAIT: RELIGIOUS TELEVISION PROGRAMMING

Two extensive content analyses of religious television—a joint effort between the Annenberg School of Communications and the Gallup Organization (see Gerbner, Gross, Hoover, Morgan, Signorilli, Cotugno, & Wuthnow, 1984; Hoover, 1987, 1988) and the Religion in Broadcasting (RIB) project at Cleveland State University (see, for example, Abelman & Neuendorf, 1985, 1987, in press; Neuendorf & Abelman, 1987a, 1987b)—have been recently conducted. Both specifically examined the portrayal of family and family interaction on religious programming—that is, regularly appearing programming that has religion or religious issues and topics as a major theme or focus.

---

[1]A.C. Nielsen (1989) reports indicate that programs featuring the life and times of a nuclear family comprise 8 of the 15 top-rated programs of the 1988 season.

Findings from the Annenberg/Gallup project were based on the analysis of a sample of programs from 2 weeks of nationally syndicated and 1 week of local religious programming broadcast in Philadelphia or Atlanta. A total of 101 programs (75 hours) constituted the final sample of content. The RIB project at Cleveland State University analyzed 3 randomly selected episodes each of the 30 most popular nationally syndicated programs. Popularity was based on an index composed of: (a) the frequency with which the show was aired in a stratified random sample of 40 U.S. towns and cities. The sample was stratified by size of the town and city, and included 10 towns/cities each with populations of less than 20,000, 20,000–100,000, 100,000–1,000,000, and the 10 most populated cities in the U.S.; (b) the number of different markets in which the show was available; (c) the length of the average episode; (d) the number of different cable and broadcast stations on which the show was available; and (e) the total number of households, both broadcast and narrowcast, capable of receiving the show.

Regarding the actual frequency with which families are portrayed or featured on television, both investigations concluded that it appears as if "family and family life is presented as important for proportionately more secular TV characters than participants on religious programs" (Gerbner et al., 1984, p. 53). In religious television programming there is more talk about domestic and family issues than the actual presentation or portrayal of family life. For example, the marital status of most adults in religious programs is rarely (30%) explicitly stated or obviously implied; by comparison, this information was available for two-thirds of the men and nine-tens of the women in commercial, prime-time programming.

When the family is portrayed in religious fare, it is primarily limited to a nuclear structure with very few relatives playing major roles. Both investigations found that the elderly were highly underrepresented, with Abelman and Neuendorf (in press) reporting that the elderly comprise only 5 percent of all characters in religious fare and only 8 percent of the characters in programs that would be classified as "family dramas," while Gerbner et al. (1984, p. 49) reported that the elderly, "who comprise 12 percent of the U.S. population, make up little more than 3 percent of the sample."

Actually, those at either end of the life cycle are strikingly underrepresented, for children are also relatively limited in number. Although most religious television families appear to have approximately 2 children, the children are rarely seen. According to the Annenberg/Gallup report, children and adolescents, who comprise about a third of the U.S. population, "account for only 4 percent of the people in the religious television world" (Gerbner et al., 1984, p. 49). As can be seen in Table 25.1, results from the RIB investigation were a bit more optimistic, reporting, among other things, that "7 percent of all coded individuals were children and 4 percent were adolescents" (Abelman & Neuendorf, in press, p. 13), and were most likely featured in child-oriented programming (e.g., *Davey & Goliath, Storybook Club*).

Table 25.1.   Frequency of Selected Demographic Characteristics By Individual Program Type.

		Program Type			
	Total Shows	Preaching/ Revival	Talk	Drama	Music/ Variety
Social Age					
Child	7%	7%	4%	2%	14%
Adolescent	4	2	2	4	5
Young Adult	37	33	34	39	28
Mature Adult	47	54	57	47	48
Elderly	5	5	3	8	5
Occupation					
Blue Collar	3	—	—	7	—
White Collar	4	2	4	8	—
Professional	17	12	17	17	9
Farm	1	—	—	1	—
Church	18	31	20	9	25
Student	11	12	3	2	3
Housewife	1	—	—	2	—
Other	12	11	26	7	10
Don't Know	33	31	29	48	53
Marital Status					
Married	30	34	44	23	34
Single	11	7	8	10	15
Divorced	1	—	—	1	—
Widowed	1	—	—	3	—
Don't Know	58	59	49	63	50
Gender					
Male	67	70	66	69	59
Female	33	30	34	31	41
Socioeconomic Status					
Upper	13	22	15	8	16
Middle	78	78	83	79	83
Lower	2	—	—	6	—
Don't Know	6	—	3	7	1
Race					
White	86	82	91	90	82
Black	6	7	4	4	5
Hispanic	2	1	—	4	—
Other	6	9	5	2	12
Role					
Reg/Major	24	28	25	29	27
Reg/Minor	13	10	11	9	12
Guest/Major	22	15	34	26	22
Guest/Minor	41	47	29	36	40
Audience	1	—	1	—	—

*percentages should be read down each column
From Abelman & Neuendorf, in press.

Despite this relatively sparse representation of family members, it is still likely that an important class of information about family life exists for viewers. Observations of family interaction patterns—who interacts with whom, with what frequency, for what reasons, and to what end—offer information regarding: The power associated with particular family roles; security concerning family stability; expectations concerning parent and sibling behavior; and sources of particular types of information within the family unit.

By and large, children interact with other children in religious programming. When children are with adults, they are seen but rarely heard; approximately 87.4 percent of all verbal exchanges in the most popular and nationally prevalent religious programs were between adults. Parents, particularly the father, dominate information exchange among family members and frequently serve to direct the behavior of others. There is more interaction between male heads of the household than between the women or between men and women. "Mothers and wives are quite submissive," suggests Neuendorf and Abelman (1987b, p. 190), "typically seeking moral support from the men." When interacting with others, children are most often seen accepting direction. Furthermore, there is little conflict between children on religious programming, perhaps because of the little interaction between children in general.

In addition, there appears to be a hierarchy of interaction that dictates who initiates conversations with whom. According to the sample of programs examined in the RIB research effort (see Table 25.2), children never initiated conversations with adolescents, and adolescents never initiated conversation with adults. There were also very few exchanges between the elderly and children. Based on these interaction patterns, "neither children nor the elderly appear to play an important role in the conduct or functioning of the Christian family" (Neuendorf & Abelman, 1987b, p. 192).

SOCIAL LEARNING IMPLICATIONS

What are children learning from watching family life as portrayed on secular and religious television? The relationship between children's exposure to secular and religious television content and their subsequent beliefs about their own family communication was examined by Buerkel-Rothfuss, Greenberg, Atkin, and Neuendorf (1982) and Abelman (1987a), respectively.

Interviewing 648 children in the fourth, sixth, and eighth grades, Buerkel-Rothfuss et al. first devised a list of "most watched" family shows. Abelman's sample included 285 children in the third through fourth grade whose religious television consumption comprised 50 percent or more of their total television viewing and, through a questionnaire, devised a list of "most watched" religious programs. The content of these programs were

Table 25.2. Interaction Patterns of Individuals By Selected Demographic Characteristics.

	Frequency	Percentage
Social Age		
Child to:		
Child	198	2.4%
Adolescent	—	—
Young Adult	181	2.2
Mature Adult	427	5.1
Elderly	—	—
Adolescent to:		
Child	2	<0.1
Adolescent	46	0.1
Young Adult	—	—
Mature Adult	89	1.1
Elderly	—	—
Young Adult to:		
Child	235	2.8
Adolescent	1	<0.1
Young Adult	918	10.9
Mature Adult	1214	14.4
Elderly	20	0.2
Mature Adult to:		
Child	473	5.6
Adolescent	124	1.5
Young Adult	1181	14.0
Mature Adult	2787	33.2
Elderly	114	1.4
Elderly to:		
Child	—	—
Adolescent	—	—
Young Adult	20	0.2
Mature Adult	97	1.2
Elderly	280	3.3
Gender		
Male to:		
Male	3992	46.2
Female	2149	24.9
Female to:		
Male	2148	24.8
Female	360	4.2

From Neuendorf & Abelman, 1987b, p. 182.

analyzed and family interaction was coded by both investigations as follows: "going toward"—offering and seeking information, supporting and showing concern for others, directing others and accepting support and direction; and "going against"—ignoring, opposing, and attacking verbally.

Table 25.3.   Correlations between Viewing Indices for Secular Television
Shows and Children's Beliefs about Real-life Families,
Controlling for Demographic Variables and Total Viewing.

Family Viewing Indices	Support	Compliance	Oppose	Ignore
High affiliation				
Zero-order	.20***	.14***	−.01	.03
First-order	.18***	.10**	−.01	−.03
Sixth-order	.15***	.11**	−.02	−.03
Low affilitation				
Zero-order	.10*	.16***	.06	.08*
First-order	.07*	.13**	.05	.02
Sixth-order	.10*	.13**	.02	.00
Conflict				
Zero-order	.10*	.16***	.06	.11**
First-order	.07	.12**	.05	.05
Sixth-order	.09*	.11**	.03	.03
All Family				
Zero-order	.12**	.13**	.09*	.11**
First-order	.09*	.08*	.09*	.05
Sixth-order	.10**	.08*	.06	.03

* $p < .05$
** $p < .01$
*** $p < .001$
From Buerkel-Rothfuss et al., 1982, p. 197.

Shows highest in "going toward" behavior were labeled as containing
"high affilation," shows lowest in this type of behavior were identified as
"low affiliation." Shows highest in "going against" behavior were identified
as containing "conflict." Indices were then created which weighted children's television exposure with information pertaining to the nature of
family interaction contained in those programs.

Both investigations also constructed indices to measure children's perceptions of affiliative and conflictual behavior in real-life families. Two
affiliative indices—support and compliance—assessed the amount of perceived helping, seeking help and sharing information (the Support index)
and the amount of perceived direction-following (the Compliance index).
The 2 conflict indices measured the amount of ignoring and opposing children perceived in real-life families. Correlations between the viewing indices and children's beliefs about real-life families were then performed.

Tables 25.3 and 25.4, from Buerkel-Rothfuss et al. and Abelman, respectively, indicate that children's exposure to secular family shows or
religious programming high in affiliative behavior is related solely to their
belief about the occurrence of affiliative behavior in real-life families. Children's exposure to secular or religious shows low in affiliative behavior and
high in conflictual behavior is related to their beliefs about the occurrence

Table 25.4. Correlations between Viewing Indices for Religious Television Shows and Children's Beliefs about Real-life Families, Controlling for Demographic Variables and Total Viewing.

Family Viewing Indices	Support	Compliance	Oppose	Ignore
High affiliation				
Zero-order	.18***	.21***	−.03	.01
First-order	.14**	.16***	−.03	−.02
Sixth-order	.14**	.15***	−.03	.00
Low affilitation				
Zero-order	.12**	.17***	.07	.08*
First-order	.09*	.16***	.06	.03
Sixth-order	.10*	.15***	.02	.01
Conflict				
Zero-order	.08	.19***	.05	.09*
First-order	.07	.15***	.04	.04
Sixth-order	.06	.13**	.03	.02
All Family				
Zero-order	.12**	.14**	.07	.18*
First-order	.08*	.14**	.04	.05
Sixth-order	.09*	.11**	.04	.03

* $p < .05$
** $p < .01$
***$p < .001$
From Abelman, 1987a, p. 20.

of affiliative and ignoring behavior among real-life family members. After effects of viewing and demographic variables have been removed, the strongest relationships appear to be between all the viewing indices and the 2 indices of affiliative behavior, support, and compliance. In general, then, both investigations found that children's viewing of secular family programs and religious programming is significantly related to their belief about the occurrence of affiliative behavior in real-life families, even when indices have been created to discriminate between the most and least affiliative of family shows.

Noting that this relationship does not operate in isolation, due to the complex nature of the system in which social learning takes place, both investigations sought to examine variables that might intervene or mediate children's perceptions of affiliative (i.e., supportive, compliant) and conflictual (i.e., ignoring, opposing) behavior in real-life families. Each will be examined in turn (see Tables 25.5 and 25.6).

Perceived Reality and Learning

It has been suggested that accounting for children's belief in the true-to-life nature of television content will increase the prediction of television effects

(Reeves, 1979). The most general expectation about the role of perceived reality is that, to the extent television content is perceived to be real, children's attitudes and behaviors will be consistent with the content of their television experiences.

Such was the case with these 2 investigations. Both found that the correlation between children's exposure to secular or religious programming featuring a family or family life and their beliefs about the occurrence of supporting and compliance behavior was enhanced when their perceived reality of television was high. It was further enhanced when children's perceptions of how much they learned from television about family life was high. Similarly, it was found that children's beliefs about the frequency of conflictual behavior occuring in real family interaction were highest when their perceived reality of television and their perceptions of how much they learned from television were low. This was particularly the case with young viewers of religious fare; religious programming contains significantly little conflictual behavior among interactants, especially when compared with secular fare.

Parental Influence

Because the family environment is an important source of social information for children, it follows that family attitudes and interaction patterns should impact on children's perceptions of family and what they learn from television's portrayals of family. A significant body of research indicates that parents have the potential to greatly influence their children's viewing patterns (Lyle & Hoffman, 1972; Wartella, 1979), interpretation of television content (Desmond, Singer, Singer, Calam, & Colimore, 1985; McLeod, Atkin, & Chaffee, 1972), and acceptance of television portrayals (Abelman, 1986; Greenberg, 1972).

Parental Mediation. When parents exhibited a high degree of control over their children's television viewing (e.g., rules regarding how much and what to watch), the correlation with children's beliefs about the occurrence of supporting behavior in real families was higher than when parents exhibited less control. When parents maintained a high level of guidance toward their children's viewing of family shows in particular, both investigations found that the relationship between children's viewing and beliefs about the occurrence of supportive behavior was enhanced. A low degree of parental guidance resulted in a stronger relationship between children's viewing and their beliefs about the real-life occurrence of opposing behavior among family members.

Coviewing. Children's viewing of television with parents as a mediating variable was examined by Buerkel-Rothfuss et al. only (see Table 25.5). It was found that a high level of coviewing resulted in a stronger relationship between children's viewing of secular television and their be-

Table 25.5. Partial Correlations Between Family Show Viewing and Beliefs at High and Low Levels of Mediating Variables, Controlling for Demographic Variables and Total Viewing (Secular Television).

	Support	Compliance	Oppose	Ignore
Perceived reality				
High	.16**	.07	.10*	.03
Low	.04	.11*	.01	.03
Perceived learning				
High	.13*	.12*	.03	−.03
Low	.06	.04	.09	.12*
Control				
High	.12	.10	.08	.09
Low	.04	.08	.12*	.05
Parental guidance				
High	.13*	.02	.02	.00
Low	.02	.04	.11*	.07
Coviewing				
High	.12*	.14*	.07	.04
Low	.09	.03	.07	.05
Positive comments				
High	.14**	.13**	.09	.06
Low	−.02	−.06	−.03	−.02
Negative comments				
High	.12*	.08	.06	.02
Low	.04	.07	.05	.05
Direct experience				
High	.14**	.11	.06	.01
Low	.04	.05	.09	.06
Communicated experience				
High	.09	.09	.01	.07
Low	.11*	.09	.12*	.02

* $p < .05$
**$p < .01$
From Buerkel Rothfuss et al., 1982, p. 199.

liefs about the real-life occurrence of compliance behavior than did a lower level of coviewing. In addition, parents comments about the television shows appeared to exert some influence as well. Their positive comments resulted in a stronger relationship between children's exposure to family shows and their beliefs about the occurrence of support and compliance in real families.

Parental disciplinary style. Research suggests that parental disciplinary style indirectly influences children's beliefs about televised portrayals and how they related to the real world (e.g., Abelman, 1986, 1987b; Singer, Singer, & Rapaczynski, 1984). The relationship between general parental disciplinary style and children's beliefs about family behavior ap-

Table 25.6.   Partial Correlations Between Family Show Viewing and
Beliefs at High and Low Levels of Mediating Variables,
Controlling for Demographic Variables and Total Viewing
(Religious Television).

	Support	Compliance	Oppose	Ignore
Perceived reality				
High	.15**	.17**	−.04	−.01
Low	.04	.12*	.02	.10*
Perceived learning				
High	.18*	.16**	.02	−.02
Low	.02	.10*	.01	−.04
Parental mediation				
High	.14**	.11*	.04	.09
Low	.02	.10*	−.02	−.03
Inductive style				
High	.16**	.06	−.06	−.03
Low	.06	.09	.04	.04
Sensitizing style				
High	.08	.17**	.11*	.05
Low	.05	−.01	−.08	−.06
Church attendance				
High	.13*	.12*	.06	−.08
Low	.08	.03	.06	.04
Importance of religion				
High	.12*	.08	.06	−.05
Low	.07	.07	.05	.02
Direct experience				
High	.10	.15**	.02	.01
Low	.05	.04	.06	.08
Communicated experience				
High	.07	.11*	.03	.04
Low	.09	.07	.06	.03

* $p < .05$
** $p < .01$
From Abelman, 1987a, p. 22.

pear to be more significant than parental rules and other direct forms of
control over their children's television viewing behavior. As can be seen in
Table 25.6, Abelman found that, when parents exhibited primarily induc-
tive disciplinary techniques (i.e., use of reasoning, explanation), the relationship between their children's religious television viewing and beliefs
about the occurrence of supportive behavior was enhanced; sensitizing
modes of parental discipline (i.e., physical punishment, deprivation of material objects or privileges) were highly correlated with children's beliefs
about the occurrence of compliance behavior and, to a lesser degree, opposition in real-life families.

Religiosity. Due to the religious nature of the television content under investigation, Abelman also included measures of family church attendance and parents' perceptions of the importance of religion in one's life—referred to as "religiosity" in the literature (e.g., Gaddy & Pritchard, 1985; Gerbner et al., 1984)—as possible intervening variables. As might be expected, he found that church attendance exerted some influence and resulted in a stronger relationship between children's exposure to religious programs and their beliefs about the occurrence of support and compliance behavior in real-life families than does the absence of avid church attendance. Similarly, for parents who hold the importance of religion in their children's lives to be high, the correlation with children's beliefs about the occurrence of supporting behavior in real families was higher than when parents believed in the importance of religion to a lesser extent.

SUMMARY & CONCLUSIONS

In general, research suggests that commercial prime-time programming offers a much more optimistic picture of the American family than census statistics. According to the portrait painted in this secular fare, the family is relatively strong, intact, and larger than life (the majority of television families have 2 or more children). Divorce is not as much a part of the family on television as it is in reality, nor are childless families as prevalent. Furthermore, family members talk with each other on television, albeit monopolized by the youngsters.

If children do learn and model relationships they observe in commercial television family interactions, as the previously cited social learning literature suggests, what they are likely to learn is information about how families *should* communicate. Indeed, Buerkel-Rothfuss et al. (1982, pp. 200–201) suggest that, with the impetus of parents who are actively involved in their children's television viewing, "children learn about affiliative behavior from viewing family television shows [which] makes a difference in the beliefs those children hold about how family members behave in the real world."

Interestingly, commercial programming is often identified by members of the clergy as offering inappropriate role models to our children (e.g., Falwell, 1984; Marty, 1961; Strober & Tomczak, 1979; Wildmon, 1985). Novelist and Roman Catholic priest Andrew Greeley once noted that television "is the modern equivalent of the medieval morality play, teaching important values about self, family and society they would not otherwise learn. Ministers of religion condemn television; and television does the work they are not doing. There are many ironies in the fire" (Eisner, 1987, pp. 16–17).

Among these ironies is that religious broadcasting offers less information about family than its secular counterpart. When religious programming does portray family and family life, it typically offers a highly formal, though traditional, portrayal. Like secular programming, religious fare depicts a more optimistic picture of the size and stability of family life than real-world statistics and reports. However, children are much more a part of family activities and interactions in popular programming. Open avenues of communication between parent and child appear to be more available in the variety of commercial network programming than in the body of television programming produced and distributed by the predominately Christian organizations that dominate religious broadcasting.

Yet another irony can be found in the fact that religious television programmers have explicitly proclaimed that it is their ascribed function to offer an "appropriate" portrayal of the American family (Fore, 1987; Harrell, 1985, 1987; Horsfield, 1984; Straub, 1988). This is quite unlike commercial program producers, who typically claim no intent or responsibility to teach its young audience about social roles, family interaction, or morality (Anderson, 1982; Newcomb & Alley, 1986). Regardless of the intent behind these television programs, learning about family does occur and, as Abelman (1987a) has indicated, the learning of affiliative family interaction from religious programming is acquired, and enhanced, by active parental mediation.

Although research supports the contention that prosocial learning does occur from television, the fact remains that an exceptionally large percentage of the "baby boomers," who were raised with the Andersons, the Cleavers, and other idealized television families of the 1950s, have marriages ending in divorce and are having fewer children than previous generations. This brings to question the resultant impact of social learning from television by today's children, who are being raised on the likes of the Huxables and Colbys via the commercial channels and/or the Humbards and Christophers through religious programs.

REFERENCES

Abelman, R. (1985). John Markus of "The Cosby Show" in conversation. *Television & Families, 8*(3), 13–16.

Abelman, R. (1986). Children's awareness of television's prosocial fare: Parental discipline as an antecedent. *Journal of Family Issues, 7*(1), 51–66.

Abelman, R. (1987a). Learning about family from religious television programming. *Journal of Communication and Religion, 10*(1), 15–25.

Abelman, R. (1987b). Child giftedness and its role in the parental mediation of television viewing. *Roeper Review, 9*(4), 217–220.

Abelman, R. (1989). A comparison of black and white families as portrayed on religious and secular TV programming. *Journal of Black Studies, 20*(1), 60–79.

Abelman, R., & Neuendorf, K. (1985). The cost of membership in the electronic church. *Religious Communication Today, 8*, 63–67.

Abelman, R., & Neuendorf, K. (1987). Themes and topics in religious television programming. *Review of Religious Research, 29*(2), 152–174.

Abelman, R., & Neuendorf, K. (in press). The demography of religious television programming. *Journal of Religious Studies.*

Abelman, R., & Ross, R. (1986). Children, television and families: An evolution in understanding. *Television & Families, 9*(1), 2–55.

Anderson, H. (1982). The purpose of family. *Television & Children, 5*(2), 21–26.

Buerkel-Rothfuss, N.L., Greenberg, B.S., Atkin, C.K., & Neuendorf, K. (1982). Learning about family from television. *Journal of Communication, 32*(3), 191–201.

Desmond, R.J., Singer, J.L., Singer, D.G., Calam, R., & Colimore, K. (1985). Family mediation patterns and television viewing: Young children's use and grasp of the medium. *Human Communication Research, 11*(4), 461–480.

Dreibelbis, G. (1987). *A value comparison of family sitcoms of the 1950s and 1980s.* Paper presented at the Speech Communication Association Conference, Boston, MA.

Eisner, M.D. (1987). Keynote address at the Sixth Annual Conference of the National Council for Families and Television. *Television & Families, 9*(4), 12–17.

Falwell, J. (1984). Let's be fair about fairness. *Journal of Broadcasting, 28*(3), 273–274.

Fore, W. (1987). *Television and religion: The shaping of faith, values and culture.* Minneapolis, MN: Augsburg.

Gaddy, G., & Pritchard, D. (1985). When watching religious TV is like attending church. *Journal of Communication, 35*(1), 123–131.

Gerbner, G., Gross, L., Hoover, S., Morgan, M., Signorilli, N., Cotugno, H., & Wuthnow, R. (1984). *Religion and television.* New York: Committee on Electronic Church Research.

Greenberg, B.S. (1972). Children's reaction's to television blacks. *Journalism Quarterly, 49*(1), 5–14.

Greenberg, B.S., Buerkel-Rothfuss, N., Neuendorf, K.A., & Atkin, C.K. (1980). Three seasons of television family role interactions. In B.S. Greenberg (Ed.), *Life on television* (pp. 161–172). Norwood, NJ: Ablex Publishing.

Greenberg, B.S., Hines, M., Buerkel-Rothfuss, N., & Atkin, C.K. (1980). Family role structures and interactions on commercial television. In B.S. Greenberg (Ed.), *Life on television* (pp. 149–160). Norwood, NJ: Ablex Publishing.

Greenberg, B.S., Korzenny, F., & Atkin, C.K. (1980). Trends in the portrayal of the elderly. In B.S. Greenberg (Ed.), *Life on television* (pp. 23–34). Norwood, NJ: Ablex Publishing.

Hanson, S.M.H., & Sporakowski, M.J. (1986). Single-parent families. *Family Relations, 35*(1), 3–8.

Harrell, D.E. (1985). *Oral Roberts: An American life.* New York: Harper & Row.

Harrell, D.E. (1987). *Pat Robertson: A personal, political and religious portrait.* New York: Harper & Row.

Hoover, S. (1987). The religious television audience. *Review of Religious Research, 29*(2), 135–151.

Hoover, S. (1988). Audience size: Some questions. *Critical Studies in Mass Communication, 5*(3), 265–271.

Horsfield, P. (1984). *Religious television: The American experience.* New York: Longman.

Hull, J.D. (1987, August 3). The rise and fall of "Holy Joe." *Time,* pp. 54–55.

Kantrowitz, B. (1986a, June 16). Only but not lonely. *Newsweek,* pp. 66–67.

Kantrowitz, B. (1986b, September 1). Three's a crowd. *Newsweek,* pp. 68–72.

Larson, M.S. (1987). *Interaction patterns in families with dependent children on prime time television.* Paper presented at the Speech Communication Association Conference, Boston, MA.

Lometti, G. (1987). Address at the Sixth Annual Conference of the National Council for Families and Television. *Television & Families, 9*(4), 45–47.

Lyle, J., & Hoffman, H.R. (1972). Children's use of television and other media. In G.A. Comstock & J.P. Murray (Eds.), *Television and social behavior.* Washington, DC: U.S. Government Printing Office.

Marty, M.E. (1961). *The improper opinion: Mass media and the Christian faith.* Philadelphia, PA: Westminster Press.

McLeod, J., Atkin, C., & Chaffee, S. (1972). Adolescents, parents, and television use. In G. Comstock & E. Rubenstein (Eds.), *Television and Social Behavior, Vol. III: Television and Adolescent Aggressiveness.* Washington, DC: U.S. Government Printing Office.

Nielsen, A.C. (1989). *Year end report—1988.* Chicago, IL: Author.

Neuendorf, K., & Abelman, R. (1987a). Televangelism: A look at communicator style. *Journal of Religious Studies, 13*(1), 41–59.

Neuendorf, K., & Abelman, R. (1987b). An interaction analysis of religious television programming. *Review of Religious Research, 29*(2), 175–198.

Newcomb, H., & Alley, R. (1986). *The producer's medium:* Conversations with creators of American TV. New York: Oxford University Press.

Norton, A.J., & Glick, P.C. (1986). One parent families: A social and economic profile. *Family Relations, 35*(1), 9–16.

Reeves, B. (1979). Children's understanding of television people. In E. Wartella (Ed.), *Children communicating: Media and Development of Thought, Speech, Understanding* (pp. 115–156). Beverly Hills, CA: Sage.

Singer, J.L., Singer, D.G., & Rapaczynski, W.S. (1984). Family patterns and television viewing as predictors of children's beliefs and aggression. *Journal of Communication, 34*(2), 73–89.

Stanley, S.C., Hunt, J.G., & Hunt, L.L. (1986). The relative deprivation of husbands in dual-earner households. *Journal of Family Issues, 7*(1), 3–20.

Straub, G.T. (1988). *Salvation for sale: An insider's view of Pat Robertson.* New York: Prometheus Books.

Strober, G., & Tomczak, R. (1979). *Jerry Falwell: Aflame for God.* Nashville, TN: Thomas Nelson Publishers.

Thomas, S., & Callahan, B.P. (1982). Allocating happiness: TV families and social class. *Journal of Communication, 32*(3), 184–190.

U.S. Bureau of Census. (1989). *Household and family characteristics.* Washington, DC: U.S. Government Printing Office.

Wartella, E. (Ed.). (1979). *Children communicating: Media and development of thought, speech, understanding.* Beverly Hills, CA: Sage.

Wildmon, D.E. (1985). *The home invaders.* Weaton, IL: Victor Press.

Zoglin, R. (1986, September 29). All in the family again. *Time,* pp. 73–75

IX

Issues in International Religious Broadcasting

A little known or considered fact about the electronic church is that it has increasingly become an *international* phenomenon. Many of the best-known of these programs have been on the air in foreign countries for years. In its heyday, the late PTL Network was on the air, with specially produced local versions of its format, in countries from Africa to Asia. Programs from PTL have also been widely available even in countries which do not have broadcast television, through syndication of cassette tapes (Conklin, 1988).

This worldwide mission of religious broadcasting is, of course consistent with the centuries-old missionary enterprises of American Protestantism. "Foreign missions" have long been one of the most important activities of the Christian church, and have often formed the justification for its most aggressive fund-raising efforts.

Simply put, it has always been easier to raise money (in some circles) to preach the word abroad than it has been to do some kinds of activities closer to home. This is not to say that these works are not authentic, or that their whole *raison d'etre* was to raise funds. Rather, it is to say that the idea of international outreach has always been a part of Protestant practice (in particular), and that the means and justifications for financial support of foreign missions are well-established modes of religious thought and activity.

In a sense, foreign distribution makes a great deal of sense for religious broadcasting. Commercial broadcasters have always known that foreign syndication is a market ripe for picking by American programming. The quality of American production makes it an attractive alternative on many third-world broadcasting systems. Often, such broadcasters are eager to fill air time that would otherwise have to go vacant. The marginal costs of foreign distribution are remarkably low.

For religious broadcasters, the challenge of extending their reach beyond American shores has a unique benefit, however. Since much of their income must come from people who support religious broadcasting in order that it might serve the needs of nonbelievers, and "lead them to Christ," the appeal of broadcasting abroad provides an additional justification for fund raising. To put it another way, the costs of foreign distribution are more than balanced by the additional income that it can generate from American financial supporters.

There are some obvious implications of this phenomenon, however. It has been observed that electronic church broadcasting represents a particular form of American cultural witness, one which is focused on some of the most basic (and, some might say, idiosyncratic) of American values (Conklin, 1988). Some part of electronic church broadcasting must, then, represent American culture as much as it represents a noncultural, "authentic" religious message. When, if ever, does American electronic church broadcasting cease to be purely religious, and begin to be just another arm of American "cultural imperialism?" To what extent might it be involved in destabilizing local customs and cultures, be they "religious" or "secular?"

The 2 chapters in this section address the issue of the electronic church abroad from listening posts on opposite sides of the world. Peter Horsfield, an Australian expert on American religious broadcasting who has authored a major book on the topic (1984), looks at these issues from the perspective of the Antipodes. The sophistication of his understanding of the American system of religious broadcasting gives him insight into the institutional and religious implications of these practices.

Eric Shegog is a British sociologist, an ordained minister, and a broadcasting executive based in London. He takes a special interest in the potential for European distribution of electronic church programming. His chapter describes the prospects of such broadcasting within Europe, and projects what some of the potential consequences might be.

REFERENCES

Conklin, G. (1988, May 20). Remarks to the Central Committee, World Association for Christian Communication, Larnaca, Cyprus.

Horsfield, P. (1984). *Religious broadcasting: The American experience*. New York: Longman.

26

American Religious Programs in Australia

Peter Horsfield

U.S. religious programs are not a new phenomenon on Australian radio and television. They have been broadcast on Australian radio stations for almost half a century, and on television for several decades. The implications of such intercultural communication for cultural autonomy, information control, and international power relationships has been the subject of a long debate. To understand some of the impact of the presence of these programs on Australian radio and television, one needs to understand something of the context in which such programs are broadcast.

The broadcasting of religious matter on radio and television has been a matter of ongoing tension and confrontation between different groups within the Australian situation, particularly on the commercial broadcasting system. Australia has basically a bipartite system of broadcast organization. The Australian Broadcasting Corporation (A.B.C.) and Special Broadcasting System (S.B.S.) are autonomous national bodies financed primarily by government funding. The A.B.C. provides a comprehensive service of noncommercial radio and television programming throughout the country, broadcasting a variety of religious programs produced or procured by its own religious programs department. The S.B.S. was established 10 years ago by the Australian government under similar terms to the A.B.C. to cater specifically to Australia's growing ethnic communities.

The noncommercial structure of the A.B.C. has given it a greater freedom to pursue a diversity of religious programming. It has been the mainstay of Australian religious media programming, producing not only regular worship services for radio and television, but also religious documentaries, news and news commentary, interview, music, and educational programming. Though it frequently broadcasts religious programs of overseas origin, these tend to be documentaries dealing with issues of religious significance. The A.B.C. does not accept any U.S. evangelical programming. While recent budget cutbacks and government discussion papers have threatened a significant reduction in the amount of religious programming on the A.B.C., for the time being it appears that it will continue.

The commercial broadcasting system is comprised of 51 television licenses and 139 radio licenses whose stations are either independent or related together by affiliation or networking. In the past 2 years, with changes in government regulation, there has been a flurry of buying and selling of broadcast licenses resulting in increased concentration of ownership within the broadcasting industry. The result in television has been the emergence of 3 highly centralized, corporately owned networks dominating the powerful capital city stations and thus most of the broadcast production in Australia.

The major regulation governing the broadcast of religious programs on commercial radio and television stations is Section 103 of the Broadcasting and Television Act, which states:

> A licensee shall broadcast or televise from his station Divine Worship or other matter of a religious nature during such periods as the Tribunal determines and, if the Tribunal so directs, shall do so without charge.

"The Tribunal," so named, is the Australian Broadcasting Tribunal (A.B.T.) which, with its predecessor the Australian Broadcasting Control Board (A.B.C.B.), is the government agency responsible for the allocation and renewal of broadcast licenses and the determination and supervision of program standards. The A.B.T. and the A.B.C.B. have consistently required, in terms of Section 103, that commercial stations broadcast a certain amount of religious programming each week free of charge. On radio this has been determined as at least 1 hour each week; on television at least 1 percent of normal weekly hours with a minimum of 30 minutes each week.

This requirement has ensured that, despite ongoing changes in broadcast programming and strategies, a certain amount of broadcast time each week has been given over to religious programming. In the determination and enaction of this requirement, however, there have been constant matters of contention between the station licensees, community bodies, and the Tribunal, such as:

- Is such a requirement legitimate?
- What is the aim of religious programming on commercial television?
- Who is to decide what kinds of programs these shall be?
- Who is responsible for the funding of such programs?
- When are such programs to be broadcast?
- What role are the churches to play in the production of these programs?

While these questions have frequently been discussed, they have never been satisfactorily resolved (Tasker, 1983). This contention has found expression in different ways. The station licensees, while maintaining the required level of statutory religious programming, have variously opposed the statute, resenting the need to provide free air time to community groups, the imposition of mandatory program requirements on the exercise of their licence, and the requirement to produce a form of programming which they largely consider to be unsuitable to the entertainment and commercial nature of the medium.

The churches have played a historical role as partners with the stations in the fulfilling of this regulation. In practice the stations have met their statutory obligations generally by allocating time to church media bodies on the basis of their denominational representativeness in the general population. However the churches have frequently been in conflict or tension with the stations over program goals and content, the financing of production, and program scheduling. The stations generally have made no financing and minimal production facilities available for the production of these statutory programs, with the result that many of the religious programs produced under the statutory time provision have been lackluster. The lack of financing for promotion has further reduced their competitiveness with other general programming and reinforced their broadcast as marginal time slots.

Other community groups have at times challenged the constitutionality of the statute governing religious programming, and have questioned the favored treatment enjoyed by religious bodies over other community groups. The Australian Humanists, for example, have on occasion lobbied for the right to be given time "similar to that of the churches free of charge to present secular ethics and morality and to provide programmes able to critically examine religion and religious teachings" (Australian Humanists, 1983b, p. 7).

In the midst of this, the regulatory bodies which have been responsible for the supervision of Section 103 were perceived by many as lacking power, resources, or determination to establish and supervise a relationship between the station owners and the churches which would give full expression to the intent of the regulation (Tasker, 1983). This situation has been steadily deteriorating over the past 15 years as television has become more economically competitive. Despite repeated efforts on both the national and local level to improve the quality of religious programming and relationships between the churches and the broadcasting industry, the marginalization of religious programming has worsened. Efforts to persuade station managers to see potential in religious programming as a station activity have generally been fruitless.

To a certain extent the attitude and practice of the churches have contributed to this deteriorating situation. Organization of church media agencies has tended to be on a state denominational basis. While a number of denominations have combined their resources and cooperated in program production, others have continued to "go it alone" by maintaining denominational and state divisions. This, in turn, has served to divide already meager resources, reduce their lobbying power, and in some cases force station managers to mediate between competing church groups with different views on the goals and content of broadcast programming.

Most churches have also failed, historically, to commit adequate resources to take advantage of the opportunities offered by the free-time provision. With some church agencies employing only a part-time staff person faced with the need at times to fill up to an hour or 2 of television air time each week, few statutory time programs have reached their potential and have failed to achieve any form of competitiveness with other secular programs.

The exception to this was the development of the concept of religious "spots" or "scatters" in the late 1960s. Where satisfactory negotiations could be made with station managements, several of the church agencies began reducing the number of longer programs and substituting 60-second spots which were scattered throughout all periods of the station's program schedule. By breaking out of the marginal time, this type of religious programming was able to reach a much wider audience. Research in 1984 in one television market indicated that almost all people questioned had seen a religious "spot" on local television, and many were able to recall the nature of the spot seen (McClune, 1984). While this programming device relieved the churches of some of the pressure of producing longer programs and presented a form of religious programming which blended with programming formats, the limited finances available for church media production has reduced even its effectiveness and acceptance. Further, differences in artistic tastes and theology between different church media agencies meant that duplication of effort, even in the production of spots, continued. To a certain extent, therefore, the statutory obligation has become a millstone around the churches' necks, forcing them to use their already meager broadcast media resources to keep up with the obligations of providing what became excessive program requirements for broadcast in statutory time at marginal time periods.

In the process many church people, unaware of the cost of effective production and the politics of religious programming in broadcasting, had become dissatisfied with what they saw of their church's media programming. What they saw of the church on television convinced many of the general ineffectiveness of their church's use of the broadcast media.

THE EXTENT OF U.S. RELIGIOUS PROGRAMMING

Data on television programming, presented in Table 26.1, indicate that U.S. religious programs increased markedly in Australia in the late 1970s. On metropolitan stations the average amount of overseas religious programming for each station rose from 30 minutes each week in 1976–77 to

Table 26.1. Religious Programs on Australian Commercial Television.

	Metropolitan Stations			Prov./Country Stations		
	Av. Hrs of Rel. Progs per stn per year	Av. Hrs of Rel. Progs of Aust origin per stn per year	Av. Hrs of Rel. Progs of O'seas origin per stn per year	Av. Hrs of Rel. Progs per stn per year	Av. Hrs of Rel. Progs of Aust origin per stn per year	Av. Hrs of Rel. Progs of O'seas origin per stn per year
1968–69	62.4	48.3	14.1	39.2	24.1	15.1
1969–70	61.6	48.0	13.6	44.3	32.5	11.8
1970–71	50.4	39.6	10.8	45.6	29.4	16.2
1971–72	58.3	50.6	7.7	48.1	39.6	8.5
1972–73	65.4	45.6	19.8	44.2	29.4	14.8
1973–74	54.6	41.6	12.9	40.8	32.0	8.8
1974–75	43.2	29.2	14.0	45.5	26.3	19.2
1975–76	47.2	26.6	20.6	40.2	20.3	19.9
1976–77	64.2	28.0	26.2	33.0	19.5	13.5
1977–78	94.3	21.0	73.3	51.7	14.0	37.7
1978–79	103.5	29.2	74.3	83.9	21.0	62.9
1979–80	92.8	30.8	62.0	80.0	24.5	55.5
1980–81	119.0	35.0	84.0	88.0	24.0	64.0
1981–82	105.4	34.2	71.2	95.6	22.0	73.6
1982–83	93.7	33.3	60.4	124.2	24.0	100.2
1983–84	100.8	34.2	66.6	126.9	24.5	102.4
1984–85	96.0	33.5	62.5	141.1	26.0	115.4
1985–86	83.8	29.5	54.3	132.0	31.5	100.5
1986–87	76.8	30.1	46.7	93.5	30.5	63.0

Source: Annual Reports of the Australian Broadcasting Control Board (1968–76) and the Australian Broadcasting Tribunal (1977–87).

97 minutes in 1980–81. On country and provincial stations it rose from an average of 15 minutes in 1976–77 to 133 minutes in 1984–85.

There are a number of contributing reasons for the growth in these programs in Australia at this time. On the one hand, this increase closely matches the years of their peak audience within the U.S. situation (Horsfield, 1984), and the time therefore of their greatest momentum and expansionism, both within the United States and overseas. The ability of the televangelists to operate a centralized organization with a sophisticated technological base provided them with a structure eminently suitable for international extension.

At the same time there existed in Australia fertile social subculture among which the televangelists would find support. Australian society in the 1960s and 1970s shared similar characteristics to U.S. society which spawned and supported the growth of the evangelical broadcasters over other forms of religious broadcasting. Australian society had experienced the changes and questioning of authority of the 1960s, the trauma of the Vietnam War, the declining impact of liberal religious bodies, the rise of a more vocal conservative strata within society, and a search in some quarters for more stable values (Hoge & Roozen, 1979; Horsfield, 1984).

There was in Australia also a growing charismatic and Pentecostal religious movement. Because of their low representation proportionally within the population they received little benefit from the statutory allocation of free air time for religious programs. They found a greater resonance with and were prepared to support the more explicitly dogmatic, professionally produced, up-tempo, technologically sophisticated U.S. evangelical programs.

A recent survey of church attenders in Australia shows that members of this expression of Christian faith indicate a higher use of religious programs than do members of the mainline denominations. While representing less than 20 percent of the survey respondents, the Pentecostals made up almost 45 percent of those who rated religious television as very encouraging for them in their faith. Members of other denominations show nowhere near that same enthusiasm (Blombery & Hughes, 1987).

The televangelists also found acceptance within that group of mainline church members who were disappointed with their own churches' media efforts, and who frequently disagreed with their church programs' theological outlook. These were frequently older members who found support in the programs' personal encouragement and reaffirmation of traditional values. Research indicates that religious programs on television take on a greater significance for the older age groups. Whereas under 18 percent of the 15- to 19-year olds rated television as helpful in encouraging their faith, 38 percent of 70- to 79-year-olds and 44 percent of the over-80s saw it as encouraging (Blombery & Hughes, 1987).

This growth ·in the programs' Australian distribution reached a peak early in the 1980s, and began to decline after that. The figures presented in Table 26.1 indicate that this occurred earlier in the metropolitan markets than in the country markets. Whereas the decrease began in 1980–81 in the metropolitan markets, it did not commence until 1984–86 in the provincial and country markets.

The reasons for this may be several. The decline coincides with decreases in audience for the programs in the United States, and may reflect organizational decisions to remove the programs from financially unviable markets. In at least one cast, it reflects a deliberate decision by one of the capital city networks to refuse overseas religious programming because of public criticism and controversy over the financial integrity of some of the U.S.-based religious broadcast organizations. The difference between metropolitan and country markets may be explained partly by the leadership role exercised by the larger metropolitan stations, and also by the more conservative approach towards programming taken by provincial and country stations.

Table 26.2. Total Hours of Religious Programs on Australian Commercial Radio Stations per week.

Year	No. of Stations	Hours of Free-time Programs	Hours of Sponsored Programs
1969–70	114	228	242
1972–73	118	215	224
1974–75	118	199	183
1975–76	120	193	161
1976–77	123	186	139
1977–78	125	206	130
1978–79	138	219	120
1979–80	128	223.5	132.5*

Source: Annual Reports of the Australian Broadcasting Control Board (1969–76) and the Australian Broadcasting Tribunal (1977–80)

Note: The A.B.T. stopped collating figures on free and sponsored religious radio programs in 1980.

*The increase in sponsored religious programs in 1979–80 ended what had been a continuous decrease since 1963.

The situation in radio, by the way, has been quite different. A.B.C.B. and A.B.T. data presented in Table 26.2 indicates that sponsored programs on Australian radio stations reached a peak in 1963, when there was a total of 320 hours of sponsored religious programs on Australian radio stations each week. After that sponsored religious programs on radio began a decline which continued until the late 1970s, dropping from an average of 2.12 hours per week per station in 1969–70, to 1.03 hours per week per station in 1979–80.

The number of stations carrying no sponsored religious programming increased during this period. In 1975–76, 23.3 percent of stations carried no sponsored religious material; this had increased to 45 percent in 1979–80. It is interesting to note that during this period the amount of statutory time programming on radio had remained relatively constant.

There are no specific indications of the reason for this continued decline, though it is likely that a major reason has been that the changing formats of radio stations have made the longer religious programs less compatible with new styles of station programming.

The specific U.S. programs which are broadcast on Australian television are presented in Table 26.3. The significant decreases in the 4-year period are: *Kenneth Copeland,* whose drop from 23 stations in 1983 to 3 in 1987 may be due to pecularities of the sample or a real decline in acceptance: *It Is Written,* which has been used by an Australian denomination for airing on statutory time; and several televangelists whose decline in Australia reflects their decline in the United States. The significant stayers are *Jimmy Swaggart,* (though it should be noted that these figures refer to the period before recent troubles within his organization); *The World Tomor-*

Table 26.3.   U.S. Religious Programs on Australian Commercial Television Stations, 1983 and 1987.

Program/Host	Number of Stations	
	1983	1987
Jimmy Swaggart	20	20
World Tomorrow	20	19
Robert Schuller	7	6
Kenneth Copeland	23	3
Insight	2	2
It is Written	13	3
This is the Life		2
Ever Increasing Faith		1
Rex Humbard	8	0
Day of Discovery	6	0
Oral Roberts	2	0
Jerry Falwell	1	0
Fred Price	1	0

Source: Australian Humanists' Submission to the Australian Broadcasting Tribunal in relation to the Review of Television Program Standards, June, 1983; Station Returns on Australian Content of Programs to the Australian Broadcasting Tribunal for the week of 8.11.1987 to 14.11.1987.

row, which has been broadcast in Australia now for several decades; and *Robert Schuller* who, in 1988, has increased the number of stations on which his program is broadcast to 10 (Robert Schuller Ministries, 1988).

Though the U.S. televangelists have been able to purchase their air time, a survey of the station returns to the Australian Broadcasting Tribunal on program content for the week of 8.11.1987 to 14.11.1987 indicates that the televangelists have not been able to break out of the ghetto periods in which the statutory programs also have become locked. In all but a few exceptions on country stations most religious programs, both statutory and sponsored, are broadcast between 6:00 and 8:00 a.m. or after 11:30 p.m. on Sundays. The evidence does not support the view that these programs in Australia have been able to break out of the ghetto in which other religious programs generally find themselves.

Survey data indicate also that these programs do not establish a large audience. Their rating in the capital city markets frequently is less than 1 and does not rise above 2 (McNair Anderson Media Research, 1987). In a number of cases statutory programs were rating better and in the case of religious spots they reach a much larger and more diverse audience than the U.S. ones. The evidence does not support the view that these programs are more popular or attract a larger audience than local statutory programs. Robert Schuller Ministries in Australia estimate their total Australian audience to be around 100,000 people (Eichenberger, 1988).

CONTROVERSY SURROUNDING U.S. RELIGIOUS PROGRAMMING

There have been occasional criticisms of U.S.-originated religious programs from time to time. First official mention of their presence on Australian television was made in the 1971–72 Report of the A.B.C.B., and the increase in their syndication was noted in the 1974–75 Report. Criticism and analysis of the programs and their hosts increased significantly with the rise in their syndication in Australia in the 1970s. Apart from isolated articles on the general topic of the presence of U.S. religious programs on Australian radio and television, major debate has centered around several hearings held by the A.B.T. for the purpose of review of broadcast regulations or standards, particularly The Inquiry into the Concept of Self-Regulation for Australian Broadcasters (Australian Broadcast Tribunal, 1977), the Review of Television Program Standards (Australian Broadcast Tribunal, 1983b), and the Discussion Paper on Religious Matter on Television (Australian Broadcast Tribunal, 1983a).

There are several major issues raised by the increased presence of U.S. religious programs on Australian broadcast stations. One of the major issues addressed has been that of cultural imperialism. Growing attention has been given in the past 2 decades to the broad issue of cultural autonomy, imperialism, and the role of mass communication in that process. Some of the implications relevant to the Australian issue are those expressed by Cees Hamelink:

> Cultural autonomy is fundamental to the independent and full development of every society. . . . Today, however, we see the rapid disappearance of the rich variety of techniques, symbols, and social patterns developed under conditions of relative autonomy . . . the impressive variety of the world's cultural systems is waning due to a process of "cultural synchronization" that is without historic precedent. (Hamelink, 1983, pp. 1–3)

Australia has had close ties to the United States for many decades and has long reflected a strong U.S. influence both economically, politically, and culturally. A significant questioning of this relationship occurred in 1972 when the Whitlam government, the first Labor government in 23 years, spearheaded a significant drive to redefine some of Australia's long-standing political ties, and identify and reestablish a more independent Australian national and cultural identity. This move was reflected in several areas of relevance to this study. In the mass communications area, it resulted in the rejuvenation of the Australian film industry whose effects have been noticed worldwide, and a restructuring of a points system to increase the use of material of Australian origin in Australian broadcasting. In the religious area, it coincided with and enhanced a search for a more distinctive Australian emphasis in theology and religious practice, one which broke from its European and American ties and took more seriously Australia's aboriginal spirituality and Asian-Pacific context.

Allied with this movement were changes to Australia's immigation policies and a growth in Australia's multiculturalism. As one of the most multicultural nations in the world, Australia in the past decade has had to grapple with the implications of this diversity in its national, social, and religious life. It is within this context that the proliferation of American religious programs on Australian television in the late 1970s came under scrutiny and criticism. Table 26.1 indicates the substantial basis for this scrutiny. Since 1977 the volume of American religious programs on television, which reflect not only a foreign perspective on religious faith but also a very specific subcultural one, have exceeded the volume of Australian religious programs. At their peak in 1980–81 American programs on metropolitan stations exceeded Australian programs by 2 and a half times. From 1982–85 the volume of American programs on country television stations exceeded Australian programs by more than 4 times. The intrusion of these programs was resented by various church members and leaders who considered that they had no appreciation for the characteristics, needs, and imperatives of the local or national situation. At a time when the Australian churches were grappling with addressing local issues relevantly, and in some cases coming into significant conflict with government authorities over particular social issues, the U.S. programs bypassed the contextual issues and presented what was considered by many to be a narrow pietistic social escapism.

The U.S. programs were not in a position to address at all some of the contemporary issues facing Australian society, such as the aboriginal issue, the challenge of multiculturalism, or the economic restructuring of Australia, issues which many of the Australian churches were addressing. The detached form of religious practice and proclamation as presented on the U.S. programs reinforced an opinion that religious faith had little to do with practical issues within the nation or society.

Opposition to the U.S. programs occurred because they also occasionally displaced Australian religious programs on television. This issue was represented during the A.B.T. Self-Regulation hearings:

> The New South Wales Council of Churches expressed regret that, on occasions, broadcasters seemed to give preference to sponsored religious programs over material broadcast free of charge. They argued that, in the case of sponsored programs produced overseas, this preferential treatment worked

against locally produced religious programming. (Australian Broadcast Tribunal, 1977, p. 115)

While this occurred partly because U.S. programs paid for their air time and stations were keen to maximize their income, it occurred also because station managers frequently took little time to distinguish between different types of religious programs, allowing the U.S. programs opportunity to broadcast their programs under regulations developed for the Australian religious community.

There was strong reaction also to the perception that the U.S. broadcasters brought not only a religious message but a strong economic and political one as well. In a submission to the A.B.T., the Australian Humanist Society lodged a strong objection to the presence of such programs on Australian television on the basis that they were a "guise:"

> We do not believe that programs broadcast on Australian television under the guise of religious programs should be used to support the fund raising and political campaigns of American right wing groups. (1983a, p. 14)

The Humanist submission argued that "U.S. televangelism is attempting to impose an alien culture onto Australia and affecting the promotion of Australian produced religious programming" (p. 14).[1]

The cost of maintaining a certain level of cultural integrity and autonomy in broadcast programming can be high. There is a high level of American programs on general Australian television because of its relative inexpensiveness. In 1980–81 Consolidated Press, the owners of one of the Australian television networks, spent $61.4 million on Australian programs and only $12.7 million on imported programs, though Australian programs accounted for only 35.6 percent of total program time (Bonney & Wilson, 1983). To ensure that broadcasters maintained a reasonable level of Australian content in spite of its cost, the Tribunal has consistently required a percentage of time given over for Australian programming, and receives weekly reports from stations in this regard.

The U.S. broadcasters were aware of these requirements and their implications. In an article in *Religious Broadcasting* magazine, Douglas Mills (1983), general manager of an Australian public relations company, warned that religious broadcasters were "under attack down under" because of the Australian content requirements. While recognizing that Australia had approximately 50 percent of its religious programming originating from foreign producers, Mills presented the challenges as obstacles to overcome

---

[1] It is not incidental that one of the leading figures in the Humanist Society at that time was also the head of the newly developed Australian Film Commission.

rather than as legitimate issues which may pose questions to the integrity of the televangelists' expansionism.

Robert Schuller, through his Australian organization, has pressed on further by making application to the A.B.T. to be recognized as an Australian body whose programs should be recognized as Australian programs for broadcast in the statutory time provided by stations. The reasons given for his application were that his program maintained an Australian office, supported the work of the local churches by encouraging church growth and being "transdenominational" in character, was supported by Australian churchmen, and included Australian content in the program (Robert Schuller Ministries, 1987). The Australian content which Schuller referred to were 5-minute talking head segments produced locally and inserted in the 1-hour program for the purpose of promoting Schuller products, seeking donations, and giving an Australian mailing address. A substantial proportion of the income received by the U.S. broadcasters Australian organizations goes out of the country for the purchase of the broadcast programs and promotional materials.

The financial affairs of the televangelists and their implications have also been strong points of criticism. Australia has been portrayed as a potentially lucrative market for religious broadcasters. In his article in 1983, Douglas Mills highlighted this potential:

> On the positive side, several international ministries have found that the average dollar gift per letter in Australia is significantly higher (sometimes 50% higher) than the average per letter in America. This happens despite the fact that Australian gifts to religious organisations are not—repeat not—tax-deductible. (p. 30)

Several of the broadcast organizations have obviously found it sufficiently lucrative to continue operations in Australia. The director of Kenneth Copeland's Australian and South Pacific operation was reported as saying in 1984 that the organization would take more than one million dollars from donations and the sale of Copeland's records, tapes, and books in that year. The organization at that time reported having 30,000 names on the Australian mailing list and was purchasing time for Copeland's program on 20 radio stations (Levinson, 1984). The Robert Schuller organization in 1981 had a total income of $563,910, which was $30,000 higher than the previous year. In addition a further $63,000 was raised in the 2 years as direct income for the purchase of balcony seats in the Crystal Cathedral (Robert Schuller Ministries, 1981). In 1987 their total income was a little under $900,000 (Eichenberger, 1988).

As indicated in other studies (Fore, 1987; Horsfield, 1984) it is unlikely that giving in this area would significantly reduce that being given to local churches. Nevertheless, the exploitative methods used for raising the mon-

ey, the motives behind it, and the broadcasters' lack of financial accountability have come under intense attack, the reverberations of which have
been felt by local religious bodies as well. The Humanist Society's submission to the A.B.T. (1983a) focused the issue:

> The biggest issue in televangelism is accountability. A crucial aspect is
> whether money raised in Australia from televangelism is spent in the commu-
> nity from which it is raised. . . . We believe one U.S. televangelist has misled
> the Tribunal as to the spending of money raised in Australia and details are
> given in the confidential section. (p. 12)

In response to these criticisms, the Tribunal in 1977 articulated its concern that "ability to purchase air time for religious programming is necessarily related to the financial resources of the particular religious organization and not to the spiritual or other needs of the community." It reaffirmed
its attitude that religious programming "should be provided only in accordance with the needs of each station's service community," and should be
provided free of charge (Australian Broadcast Tribunal, 1977, p. 115).

It was largely the financial aspects of the broadcasters' activities, along
with a reorganization of their Sunday morning schedule, which finally
caused the Nine Network, 1 of the 3 major commercial television networks
in Australia, in 1981 to discontinue broadcast of U.S. religious programs on
its network stations. The recent revelations of personal and financial scandals involving the broadcasters has further reinforced some of these concerns, and highlighted some of the exploitative aspects of their fund-raising
activities (Adams, 1983).

The other major issue which has arisen in the debate is the relationship
of these broadcasters and their activities to the work of the church in
Australia. While local programming on radio and television has the ability
to tap into the local ethos and support the work of the Australian church in a
complementary way, religious programs which are produced and packaged
in a foreign culture are not able to do this.

The extent to which this is an important issue depends to a large extent
on one's theology and understanding of the nature of the church. The
church in Australia is a diverse organization. Within the Uniting Church,
the third largest Australian denomination with a national membership of
around 220,000, there are over 30 ethnic congregations and greater than
34 Aboriginal congregations. On any Sunday, worship within the Uniting
Church alone takes place in 23 different languages and an unknown
number of Aboriginal dialects. U.S. religious programs cannot accomodate
nor reflect that diversity. They allow for no adaptation to local conditions,
yet by their major presence on television reinforce a stereotype of religion
which is no longer relevant to the Australian situation.

As with the other U.S. televangelists, the Robert Schuller organization in

Australia has become in effect a marketing arm for an American based industry. In 1980 and 1981, $246,900 was spent in the purchase of Robert Schuller material for distribution to viewers in Australia. In 1988 Robert Schuller Ministries in Australia organized a Glory of Easter tour which included a visit to the Crystal Cathedral and to Disneyland. Apart from occasional speaking tours by some of the broadcasters, in general they do not have close working relationships with local churches. Schuller Ministries' major relationship with churches has been in the form of promotion of their Californian church growth seminars amongst Australian church leaders. Though they receive between 700 and 800 letters each week (Eichenberger, 1988), Schuller Ministries, which is one of the few broadcast organizations to maintain a staffed Australian office, does not have any established means of systematic referral of responses to local churches. As indicated by other studies, contacts with viewers are maintained almost solely for the purpose of financial exploitation (Horsfield, 1985). The implications of this situation for the development of genuine religious community are exacerbated when the intercultural dimension is added. The U.S. televangelists are seen in many quarters as envoys of U.S. cultural imperialism.

THE FUTURE

The presence of Australian religious programs on Australian television has been safeguarded to this point because of the statutory requirement placed on station licencees of Section 103 of the Broadcast Act. Regardless of how much sponsored religious programming they broadcast, Australian broadcasters must still broadcast a specified amount of religious programming free of charge. This has prevented the situation of a total displacement of statutory religious programming by sponsored programming, as occurred in U.S. broadcasting in the 1960s, from happening in Australia. Table 26.1 indicates that despite fluctuations in sponsored religious programming, the amount of Australian religious programming has remained relatively constant. The local nature of station licensing and program control to date in Australia has also ensured that religious programming has retained a measure of local consultation, conflictual as it may be in some cases.

Changes which are taking place within Australian society and the Australian broadcasting system at present may alter some of those factors. Recent changes in media ownership, the development of Aussat (The Australian domestic satellite system), and the establishment of more centralized networks under sole ownership control may move Australia towards a more centralized system of television production and distribution. This may challenge the former local nature of television under which the churches have tended to operate in their media liaison.

There is also a significant movement toward greater deregulation by the present Hawke Labor Government. This, together with some serious questioning of the privileged position in relation to religious programming held by Christian organizations in an increasingly multicultural and secular society, may create significant changes in the nature of religious programming in Australia in the coming years.

REFERENCES

Adams, P. (1983, August 30). What in God's name is going on? *The Bulletin*, pp. 45–46.

Australian Broadcasting Control Board. (1977). *Annual reports, 1969–76*. Canberra: Australian Government Publishing Service.

Australian Broadcasting Tribunal. (1983a). *Discussion paper - religious matter on television*. North Sydney: Australian Broadcasting Tribunal.

Australian Broadcasting Tribunal. (1983b). *Discussion paper - review of television programme standards*. North Sydney: Australian Broadcasting Tribunal.

Australian Broadcasting Tribunal. (1977). *Self-Regulation for broadcasters: A report on the public inquiry into the concept of self-regulation for Australian broadcasters*. Canberra: Australian Government Publishing Service.

Australian Broadcasting Tribunal. (1988). *Annual reports, 1977–87*. Canberra: Australian Government Publishing Service.

Australian Humanists. (1983a). *Submission to Australian Broadcasting Tribunal's inquiry into the Australian content on commercial television*. Melbourne: Australian Humanists.

Australian Humanists. (1983b). *Submission to Australian Broadcasting Tribunal's review of television programme standards*. Melbourne: Australian Humanists.

Blombery, T., & Hughes, P. (1987). *Combined churches survey for faith and mission: Preliminary report*. Newtown: Christian Research Association.

Bonney, B., & Wilson, H. (1983). *Australia's commercial media*. South Melbourne: Macmillan.

Eichenberger, W.B. (1988, February 4). Letter to the author from Robert Schuller Ministries, Sydney, Australia.

Fore, W.F. (1987). *Television and religion: The shaping of faith, values, and culture*. Minneapolis, MN: Augsburg.

Hamelink, C.J. (1983). *Cultural autonomy in global communications: Planning national information policy*. New York: Longman.

Hoge, D., & Roozen, D. (1979). *Understanding church growth and decline, 1950–78*. New York: Pilgrim Press.

Horsfield, P.G. (1984). *Religious television: The American experience*. New York: Longman.

Horsfield, P.G. (1985). Evangelism by mail: Letters from the broadcasters. *Journal of Communication, 35*, 89–97.

Levinson, A. (1984, February 11). Abide with Him, and send me $100 a month. *Sydney Morning Herald*, p. 37.

McClune, D. (1984). The role of religious broadcasting within Brisbane television. Unpublished paper, Queensland Institute of Technology, Brisbane, Australia.

McNair Anderson Media Research. (1987). Television audience survey, survey period 4, 1987: 31st May to 27th June. Melbourne: McNair Anderson.

Mills, D. (1983, December). Religious broadcasters under attack "down under." *Religious Broadcasting,* pp. 30–31.

Robert Schuller Ministries. (1981). Return submitted to the Corporate Affairs Commission, Sydney, Australia.

Robert Schuller Ministries. (1987). Submission to the Australian Broadcasting Tribunal re Discussion Paper - Religious Matter on Television. Sydney: Robert Schuller Ministries.

Robert Schuller Ministries. (1988, December/January). *Move ahead: Newsletter for Friends of Hour of Power.* North Sydney: Robert Schuller Ministries.

Tasker, D. (1983). *The place of religion in commercial television in Australia from 1956 to 1978.* Unpublished doctoral dissertation, University of Melbourne, Australia.

27
Religion and Media Imperialism: A European Perspective

Eric Shegog

So far, Europe has not been subjected to the importation of religious television programs on any significant scale. The growth of cable and satellite channels will, however, create an enormous appetite for programming. The rate and scale of religious media imperialism in Europe will, though, be dependent on national government regulatory policy, finance, and above all imported American religious programs' appeal to the European viewer.

Media imperialism, or to use its alternative, "cultural dependency," has been a talking point for over 60 years (Smith, 1980). In that time, Europe has been both an exporter of press and broadcasting to its colonies and also an importer. As Britain exported systems based on *The Times* newspaper, the British Broadcasting Corporation (BBC), or Reuters news agency, for example, so it imported films for the cinema and then television programs like *Dallas*. Britain has, therefore, been guilty of promoting media imperialism but also at the same time, been a victim of it. Even now, 40 percent of all films registered in the United Kingdom originate in the United States, and up to 90 percent of capital invested in British films in some years is American (Smith, 1980, p. 41).

The cartel that developed around the feature film subsequently spread to the print and electronic media. Associated Press and United Press International, together with Reuters and Agence France-Presse, dominate the flow of international news. Since 1945, American agencies have also dominated the world of advertising. In Britain, West Germany, and France, for example, 50 percent of the major advertising agencies are American. Almost as much revenue is generated by these agencies outside the United States as inside it (Smith, 1980, p. 46).

In the field of television, Europe has been very dependent on U.S. imports to fill its schedules. In the study conducted for UNESCO by Tapio Varis (1985), tracing the flow of television programs, Western Europe imported 27 percent of its television output. Most of the imported programs

Table 27.1.   Distribution of the Total Import in the Western European Region by Program Categories and the Main Countries of Origin.

| Category | Total Import | | Countries of origin | | |
| | Minutes | in percent of the overall output of the region in the category | with at least a 5 per cent share of the import in the category | | |
				Minutes	%
News	91	0	—		
Other informa-tive programs	1,250	5	UK	477	38
			Sweden	288	23
			USA	149	12
			FRG	75	6
Documentaries	2,189	18	USA	415	19
			FRG	294	13
			Canada	290	13
			France	133.5	6
Educational programs re-lated to a spe-cific curriculum	544	4	UK	167	30
			FRG	125	23
			Sweden	97	18
			USA	58	10
Educational programs for rural develop-ment	20	3	UK	20	100
Other educa-tional pro-grams	1,490	27	UK	789	53
			USA	409	27
			Sweden	100	7
Cultural pro-grams	1,701	12	France	491	29
			FRG	439	26
			UK	295	17
			Switzerland	105	6
Religious pro-grams	326	11	Italy	194	60
			USA	80	25
			France	52	16
Children's pro-grams	7,653	36	USA	3,550	46
			UK	629	8
			FRG	420	5
			(Czechosl.	256	3)
Cinema films	18,238	72	USA	11,323	62
			France	1,540	8
			FRG	1,225	7
			UK	1,210	7
			(DDR	217	1)
TV-plays	21,121	70	USA	10,822	51
			UK	4,042	19
			FRG	1,724	8
Sports pro-grams	6,940	36	UK	795.5	12
			USA	329.5	5

Table 27.1.   *(Continued)*

| Category | Total Import | | Countries of origin | | |
| | Minutes | in percent of the overall output of the region in the category | with at least a 5 per cent share of the import in the category | | |
				Minutes	%
Other entertainment programs	2,359	17	France	311.5	5
			(Eurov.	3,781	55)
			UK	860	37
			USA	766	33
			FRG	365	16
			Canada	105	5

From "International Flow of Television Programmes," by Tapio Varis. Copyright © 1985 by Unesco. Reproduced with permission of Unesco.

came from the United States (44%). At least 10 percent of total program time in Europe is allotted to American programs. Most of these are entertainment but there are also significant numbers of information and children's programs (see Table 27.1).

So far, however, religion has not been a significant part of this cultural invasion from the North American continent. The percentage of religious programs imported by European countries, either from each other or from the U.S., is extremely low. Belgium imported the highest percentage of its religious output (French speaking 47% and Flemish speaking 62%) followed by Finland (23%). Most countries with a public service tradition imported none—Austria, Denmark, France, Ireland, Italy, Sweden, and the United Kingdom. Overall 11 percent of religious television in Europe was imported. This added up to 326 minutes per year (see Table 27.2), an average of a mere 6 minutes a week. What is more, most of the imported religious programs originated from Europe. Italy exported most (194 minutes), the United States provided 80 minutes, and France 52 minutes. So although the proportion of religious output on European public service systems is small (2% maximum), most of it is made in-house. By comparison with the percentage of acquired material in other program categories like film, entertainment, and children, religion has been less at risk from cultural domination.

One of the reasons for the low level of penetration by American religious material of public service channels is the longstanding domination by national churches. In general the place of religious television in the different national broadcasting services has varied from country to country, and the nature of the relationship of the churches to religious broadcasting has been equally varied. In France, Spain, and Italy—traditionally strong Roman

Table 27.2. The Structure of Programs in Western Europe (The percentage of imported programs within each category is shown in parenthesis).

Program Categories	Austria %	Belgium		Denmark %	Federal Republic of Germany		
		BRT %	RTBF %		ARD %	ZDF %	Regional %
Informational	29 (8)	27 (4)	26 (6)	17 (—)	30 (2)	29 (2)	30 (8)
Educational	6 (20)	22 (—)	13 (—)	8 (14)	—*	4 (14)	—
Cultural	6 (26)	6 (27)	6 (30)	10 (15)	3 (—)	3 (13)	—
Religious	1 (—)	2 (47)	2 (62)	0 (—)	1 (—)	2 (14)	—
Children's	7 (35)	4 (33)	4 (30)	14 (43)	9 (20)	10 (38)	3 (—)
Entertainment	47 (77)	38 (63)	48 (49)	49 (68)	37 (22)	50 (37)	39 (42)
Unclassified	3 (—)	1 (—)	1 (—)	2 (—)	18** (—)	—	5 (—)
Advertisements	2 (—)	—	—	—	3*** (—)	2 (—)	23 (—)
TOTAL %	100	100	100	100	100	100	100
Total minutes	14,543	8,969	10,378	6,366	8,216	10,443	9,545
Import %	(43)	(28)	(29)	(43)	(13)	(23)	(24)

Program Categories	Finland %	France %	Iceland %	Ireland %	Italy %	Netherlands %
Informational	33 (16)	40 (0)	31 (38)	18 (11)	30 (2)	27 [15]
Educational	9 (30)	2 (—)	2 (100)	1 (38)	2 [36]	15 [—]
Cultural	1 (—)	7 (—)	1 (—)	4 (28)	16 (14)	5 [2]
Religious	2 (23)	1 (—)	1 (—)	1 (—)	1 (—)	2 [12]
Children's	8 (30)	8 (34)	6 (36)	14 [52]	7 [38]	11 [55]
Entertainment	45 [56]	34 (40)	55 [91]	59 [78]	40 [31]	35 [42]
Unclassified	0 [—]	3 [—]	—	2 [—]	1 [—]	1 [—]
Advertisements	3 [—]	4 [—]	4 (17)	—	4 [—]	4 [—]
TOTAL %	100	100	100	100	100	100
Total minutes	10,746	25,170	3,311	13,585	26,923	12,710
Import %	(37)	(17)	(66)	(57)	(12)	(25)

* Educational programs transmitted via 3rd channel
** Includes regional programs
***Only during regional programs

Table 27.2. (*Continued*)

Program Categories	Norway %	Spain %	Spain EIT.B(Regional) %	Sweden %	Turkey %
Informational	20 (5)	31 (14)	34 (24)	35 (14)	19 (5)
Educational	16 (16)	3 (7)	—	—y	15 (3)
Cultural	7 (25)	6 (20)	—	—yy	3 (—)
Religious	2 (2)	1 (—)	—	1 (—)	1 (—)
Children's	10 (43)	7 (51)	36 (100)	12 (32)	3 (9)
Entertainment	44 (46)	44 (57)	30 (100)	47 (53)	54 (65)
Unclassified	0 (—)	5 (—)	—	5 (51)	2 (—)
Advertisements	—	3 (—)	—	—	3 (—)
TOTAL %	100	100	100	100	100
Total minutes	6,401	14,638	1,634	11,140	4,864
Import %	(30)	(33)	(74)	(35)	(36)

y Educational programs by a separate institution
yyImpossible to give figures

Program Categories	BBC %	United Kingdom ITV %	Channel 4 %	Yugoslavia %
Informational	30 (—)	33 (—)	30 (—)	23 (2)
Educational	18 (—)	11 (—)	1 (—)	19 (31)
Cultural	4 (6)	1 (—)	4 (—)	10 (5)
Religious	1 (—)	2 (—)	—	—
Children's	9 (9)	10 (10)	3 (—)	10 (39)
Entertainment	37 [37]	42 [30]	52 [48]	35 [50]
Unclassified	2 (—)	0 (—)	4 (—)	1 (—)
Advertisements	—	—[z]	7 (—)	1 (—)
TOTAL %	100	100	100	100
Total minutes	23,723	14,975	7,913	16,203
Import %	(15)	(14)	(26)	(29)

[z]Advertisements are included in other categories

From "International Flow of Television Programmes," by Tapio Varis. Copyright © 1985 by Unesco. Reproduced with permission of Unesco.

(continued)

Catholic countries—religious television has on the whole been allotted time on Sunday morning. In the Republic of Ireland and in Austria, religious programs have been much more integrated into the network schedules. In the Scandinavian countries of Norway, Sweden, and Finland, religion has always been accorded favorable treatment on television. In Holland, Switzerland, and the Federal Republic of Germany, religious broadcasting has enjoyed considerable prestige and been strongly integrated into the broadcasting systems.

The degree of involvement by the churches has also varied from country to country. On the whole, though clergy are frequently employed by state broadcasting systems, editorial control has remained firmly with the broadcasters. In France, however, the Roman Catholic group which provides "Le Jour de Seigneur" for Antenne 2, the second state channel, is controlled and funded by the Church. In West Germany, the Evangelical Protestant Churches Group supplies programs for ARD and ZDF, the network and regional systems. Holland, with its democratic approach to the allocation of television time on the basis of the membership of interest groups, has given access to religious groups since 1945. The Catholic KRO and the Protestant NCRV have major places in the system and the latest arrival, Evangelische Omroep (EO), represents the more fundamentalist and charismatic Christian.

In the United Kingdom the churches have never had direct access to television. They have, however, advised the BBC and the Independent Broadcasting Authority (IBA), through the Central Religious Advisory Committee, on policy for religious broadcasting. In this way they have been influential in determining the type of religious television in Britain. Though some would have preferred religious television to have a sharper cutting edge, the *quid pro quo* has been that religious groups have been able, within a policy that prohibits proselytizing, to advocate their cause with passion, and at no cost to themselves.

THE CHANGING TIDE

The ecology of broadcasting in Europe is, however, changing. Public service systems are under threat and could be undermined by technology which brings increased competition and by government policy to deregulate. There are a number of possible developments. All of them revolve around the twin focii of regulatory policy and finance. If the British government decides, for example, to dismantle public service broadcasting on independent television and allow market forces to determine the future pattern of programming, then the only religious television available on terrestrial channels is likely to be provided by the BBC as the last bastion of public service broadcasting. The latter was defined recently in a government discussion document (British Home Office, 1987) on the future of non-BBC radio as "something for the public good, rather than for the benefit of particular groups."

Changes in British broadcasting policy are usually preceded by a committee of inquiry set up by the government of the day. In 1960 the Pilkington Committee (1960) led to the setting up of the second BBC channel and in 1976, the Annan Committee (1977) led to Channel 4, the second commercial channel being launched. These committees are usually made up of a cross-section of people representing the good and the great in British society. They meet usually for 18 months or so. They invite evidence from individuals and interest groups and then produce a substantial report recommending a course of action to the government of the day.

In line with this practice, the Peacock Committee chaired by Sir Alan Peacock, an economist, recommended that the BBC should receive grant in aid from central government funds to provide such programming not likely to be available on cable systems and satellite broadcasting in a deregulated commercial environment (Peacock, 1986). The ensuing vacuum could in theory be filled by religious groups on cable and satellite channels, provided they have the financial support necessary.

So far, even on cable systems, government policy has prohibited soliciting of funds on air. Over the years, appeals for money for charitable purposes have been carefully controlled by the IBA and the BBC on the advice of a Central Appeals Committee. This has effectively prevented any particular group from scooping the pool. In 1988, the IBA has relaxed the regulations governing advertisements by charities, so that they may now buy advertising time. They may still, however, only advertise their aims and activities and may not ask for money. In the 1984 Cable and Broadcasting Act there is no requirement for cable systems to provide particular programs (though they must carry existing BBC and IBA channels) and it is still not possible to ask for any donations on or off air (Peacock Committee, 1984). If this policy was continued, any religious body wanting to air its programs on cable or satellite would need to have the ability not only to fund the production costs, but also to pay for air time. Or, it could adopt the Pat Robertson CBN model by providing a variety of programs on a leased channel.

The third scenario would be to continue in Britain with a public service policy for terrestrial broadcasting and to have little regulation for cable and satellite other than that for standards of taste and decency. In this case, BBC, ITV, and Channel 4 would continue to provide religious television. Religious groups would have opportunities to broadcast on developing cable and satellite channels. The ban on fund raising might or might not be relaxed. Either way some groups are so well funded for this not to be of any great concern. This system would favor the economically well off.

Ray Wilson, advertising agent for the European Broadcasting Network (an evangelical broadcasting organization) has said of Europe, "I have never seen a missionary opportunity of this magnitude . . . it is a miracle . . . the second 'Great Reformation.' Truly a new era has begun" (Elvy, 1986, p. 148). Whether this vision will be realized will be influenced by 4 factors: (a) the availability of an extensive network of cable and satellite systems throughout Europe to deliver their programs and the financial wherewithal to support them; (b) the strength of national government policies to protect cultural sovereignty as a whole throughout Europe and to safeguard indige- nous film and television industries; (c) the competition American tele- vangelists would face from European religious bodies including mainstream churches, some of whom have considerable financial potential (the Lutheran Church, for example); and (d) probably most telling—the likely appeal of American religious television.

Broader and Narrowcast Systems

Over the last 5 years most West European Governments have been con- cerned to maximize the economic benefits from the growing revolution in information technology. The British Government was no different. It saw information technology as an engine to pull the country out of economic recession. Following the white hot technology of the Labour Government, the Tories elected in 1979 saw information technology as a way of expand- ing jobs in the newly privatized aerospace industry. The first of several attempts to develop a direct broadcasting satellite by the BBC failed, not least because using a British satellite was mandatory even though cheaper options were available in the United States.

The government also determined to develop cable systems for interac- tive services such as home banking, shopping, and home security using television programs as a catalyst. The spread of cable in Britain and Europe as whole, has however been sporadic (Table 27.3). Belgium and the Netherlands closely followed by Luxembourg are the most densely cabled with 86 percent, 67 percent, and 66 percent of homes passed, respectively. At present the United Kingdom, France, and the German Federal Republic have only 1 percent, 1 percent, and 8 percent respectively. It is estimated by the Manchester European Institute for Media Studies that there will be significant development of cable systems in France and Germany (see Ta- bles 27.3 and 27.4). Although only 11 of the 22 licences issued by the British Government are operating, with only 250,000 homes on cable, 1988 saw increasing interest from American finance houses.

At the same time as cable is developing, satellite broadcasts will in- crease. So far, low-powered satellites have been used for distributing off-air services to homes via cable systems. It is a high risk venture at the moment with film channels being most popular. The attraction for producers of cable channels via satellite is the potentially lucrative European market

Table 27.3. Cable Penetration in Europe.

Country	POP/HH's (in m)	HH's cabled in 1987[1]		Growth 1985–87		HH's receiving satellite distributed TV programs	
		in '000	% of HH	in '000	% of HH	in '000	% of HH
Austria	7.6/2.7	290	11%	+40	+1.5%	290	11%
Belgium	9.8/3.5	3,000	86%	±0	±0%	1,000	28%
Denmark	5.1/2.1	900	40%	+100	+4.9%	95	4%
Finland	4.8/1.8	275	15%	+125	+7%	275	15%
France	54.0/20.0	200	1%	±0	±0%	40	<1%
FRG	61.4/25.5	2,100	8%	+800	+3%	2,000	8%
Greece	9.7/3.0	0.9	<1%	+0.9	—	0.9	<1%
Ireland	3.4/1.0	260	26%	+35	+3.5%	235	23%
Italy	56.2/18.5	NONE	—	NONE		²	—
Luxembourg	0.4/0.12	80	66%	±0	±0%	75	62%
Netherlands	14.3/5.5	3,700	67%	±0	±0%	3,100	56%
Norway	4.1/1.6	390	24%	±0	±0%	270	17%
Portugal	9.3/3.0	0.8	<1%	+0.8	—	1³	<1%
Spain	37.7/9.8	7	<1%	+7	—	10³	<1%
Sweden	8.3/3.4	250	7%	+100	+3%	250	7%
Switzerland	6.4/2.5	1,200	48%	+240	+10%	1,200	48%
United Kingdom	55.9/20.1	185	1%	+55	—	185	<1%
Europe	348.4/123.8	12,838.7	10%	+1,503	+1.2%	9,026.9	7%
E.C.	317.2/111.8	10,433.7	9%	+998	<1%	6,741.9	6%

HH = Households,   POP = population
[1] excluding SMATV
² RAI UNO is transmitted by EUTELSAT but received terrestrially in Italy
³ including estimated unauthorised direct ECS reception
Source: European Institute for the Media Research, compiled from Cable & Satellite Europe, de visu, DGT-SPES, Kabel und Satellit, Neue Medien, Deutsch Bundespost, Ogilvy & Mather TV Guide 1986, WEDELL/LUYKEN: Media in Competition.

Table 27.4. Cable Penetration Forecast 1987–1995.

	Cabled Households in					
	1987		1990		1995	
	in '000	in % of HH's	in '000	in % of HH's	in '000	in % of HH's
France	200	1%	1,400	7%	5,800	29%
Fed. Rep. of Germany	2,100	8%	4,500	18%	12,000	47%

Source: European Institute for the Media Research.

when in 1992 all trade and tariff barriers between the European countries will be relaxed. However, so far cable channels have not attracted sufficient revenue and their development has been complicated by national regulations on copyright and the problems of language. Even though there is a diversity of special interest channels available, European viewers still prefer national channels. Two British channels, Sky, owned by Murdoch, and Super Channel, owned by a consortium of ITV companies, are in great financial trouble. Sky, in spite of being on the air for 10 years, lost $10 million in 1987.

In 1989, the first European Direct Broadcast Satellites became operational. Astra, a Luxembourg-based medium power satellite, provides 16 channels accessible to most of Western Europe. British Satellite Broadcasting regulated by the IBA offers 4 services on 3 channels. The West Germans, whose satellite was launched in 1987 but due to technical reasons has been written off, will probably share the new French satellite. The European satellite organization, Eutelsat, is also planning 4 new medium-powered satellites for television and telecommunications.

There will also be the possibility of more terrestrial channels. In the United Kingdom it is now technically feasible to provide a fifth channel for up to 70 percent of the population and a sixth channel, MMD, using microwave links could be available for local television. Europe will therefore experience over the next 5 years an explosion in the number of television channels. It is calculated that 1.5 billion hours of television programming will be needed by the year 2000 to fill cable and satellite channels in Europe.

Government Policy

At the same time as technology is making more channels available, national governments are also pursuing an active policy to deregulate. This has serious consequences for religious television which has always been regarded as an essential part of a balanced schedule. Total deregulation would effectively leave the field to religious groups willing and able to buy time as in the United States. In France, deregulation is already a fact. In 1986, the French Government privatized TF1, the State channel. Religious broadcasting was moved to Antenne 2 in 1987. The Catholic segment known as *Le Jour de Seigneur* lasts for 90 minutes and is divided into 3 parts: A religious magazine, a Mass, and a 7-minute reflection. Protestants have 30 minutes per week. The Jews and Muslims have 15 minutes each.

In Italy, private local broadcasting was deregulated in 1976. There are now 3 national television channels provided by the State broadcasting company R.A.I. and 23 private local channels. In a country which also contains Vatican City, it is not surprising that most religious television is Catholic, though the Protestants have 30 minutes per fortnight on RAI. The Order of St. Paul also runs a channel on the local network in Milan. It is mixed programming with some religion.

Britain's public service broadcasting is at a crossroads. The BBC and IBA, though funded by license fees and advertising respectively, have both been required to provide balanced programming which educates, informs, and entertains. This is the price they have paid for a duopoly. Religious programs have been provided as part of this public service commitment. The present Conservative government wishes to deregulate broadcasting. The trend began with the 1984 Cable and Broadcasting Act and will continue with a deregulated independent radio system. The Peacock Committee of Enquiry in 1986 recommended advertising on BBC radio and the auctioning of the ITV franchises when they fall due for renewal in 1992. To encourage competition they also suggested ITV and BBC Television should commission 25 percent of their programing from independent producers as Channel 4 has done since its inception. Both the BBC and ITV have responded. The stranglehold of the major 5 ITV companies on network programing is gradually being relaxed as their guaranteed air time is reduced in favor of an open competitive approach.

The crucial decision for independent television is how the ITV franchises are decided. In its 1988 policy document "Television in the 1990s," the IBA argued strongly that the ability to deliver quality programs should be a prime requirement, while not excluding outright the possibility of auctioning or tendering. If the franchises are auctioned off to the highest bidder there is likely to be little serious programming, including religion, as schedules go down market to attract good ratings to attract advertising revenue. The stage would be set for an invasion by American televangelists. They would not, however, have things all their own way. They would face competition from previously marginalized European Protestant groups and from mainstream churches.

In Britain—although as has been indicated, cable television has been a slow developer—religious groups have responded to these new, if limited, opportunities. The Worldwide Church of God founded by Herbert Armstrong has been available on cable since 1986, first on Sky Channel at midnight on Saturday evening, now also on Super Channel at noon. On the Arabic channel, so far only available in London, there are daily readings of the Koran followed by a sermon. Vision Broadcasting International has a channel, *Vision on Sunday* on 2 cable systems only. It recycles some North American religious programming, *100 Huntly St,* and *700 Club,* as well as showing videos from British sources like the Salvation Army and Assemblies of God.

Probably the most successful group is the Churches Television and Radio Center, started by Methodist J. Arthur Rank and supported by the

Rank Foundation. Between 1982 and 1986 it sold 410 programs to ITV companies, Channel 4, and the Home Video Channel. Most religious groups are, however, biding their time until cable systems are more developed and able to deliver more substantial audiences.

Crucial to the development of religious programing in a deregulated environment will be government policy. Legislators in the United Kingdom have been cautious about the place of religion in broadcasting. Successive Acts of Parliament which govern independent broadcasting have always included checks and balances for religion. The Broadcasting Act (1981) requires the IBA's "previous approval for any religious service or any propaganda relating to matters of a religious nature." This clause has always been interpreted to include all religious programming. The IBA is also required by the Act to arrange for the assistance of "a committee representative of the main streams of religious thought in the United Kingdom" to advise on religious programs "and on any other matters of a religious nature included in programs broadcast by the Authority." The Act also prohibits advertisements "by or on behalf of any body whose objects are wholly or mainly of a religious nature, and no advertisement shall be permitted which is directed towards any religious end."

The Cable and Broadcasting Act (1984), authorizing the development of cable systems, relaxed some of these prohibitions, but even in a less tightly regulated industry, religion was still circumscribed. Bodies or individuals whose aims are wholly or mainly religious may not hold a cable license. Those providing the cable services may not use them to express their own views and opinions on religious matters and undue prominence may not be given in the programs "to the views and opinions of particular persons or bodies on religious matters." In other words, there must be a balance of religious views. Religious programs are required to state at the beginning and end of a program who provides it. If viewers are interested to write in for literature, the announcement on air required by cable television's regulatory body, the Cable Authority, is: "There will be no follow up, no one will call on you." The indications are that similar restrictions will be contained in new legislation for deregulated independent radio. So even where there has been considerable relaxation by government on general program provision, this relaxation has not been reflected to the same degree as far as religious programs are concerned.

Another aspect of government policy in Britain and other European countries used to protect indigenous film and television industries, has been the quota system. Both the BBC and the IBA operate a self-imposed quota for foreign programs of 14 percent, though programs originating from within the European Economic Community are exempt. ITV companies may only permit 4 hours per week of foreign material at peak time (6:30–10:30 p.m. on weekdays and 7:15–10:30 p.m. on Sundays). The Cable and Broadcasting Act of 1984 requires the Cable Authority to take account when deciding to allocate a license of whether the applicant intends including material originating from Europe and performed by Europeans. It is also envisioned that the proportion of European material should increase.

As well as national quotas on foreign material, there is an increasing move within Europe as a whole to promote an exchange of programs as part of an European Economic Community (EEC) broadcasting market. A draft directive in March 1986 following discussion of the EEC Green Paper, "Television without Frontiers" (1984), set out proposals to remove potential obstacles to cross frontier broadcasting. These covered advertising and sponsorship, protection of children and young people, copyright, and the origin of programs. It is suggested that member states reserve at least 30 percent of television output (apart from news, sport, game shows, advertising, and teletext services) for European programs. This quota should rise to 60 percent within 3 years after the directive becomes operational. At the same time, the Council of Europe's Committee of Foreign Ministers met to produce a convention on transfrontier broadcasting which is only binding on those countries signing it. One of the concerns expressed is to increase production and screening of European programs.

So far, there has been no agreement on either the EEC Directive of the Council of Europe's Convention. There is strong opposition from most governments for broadcasting to be considered as part of the EEC's remit under the Treaty of Rome which establishes relationships in broader economic areas. Even so, there is no doubt about European resolve to abide by quotas to protect and foster its television industry as much for economic as for cultural reasons. In Holland, a third television channel was set up in April 1988 to promote Dutch culture through religious, art, and drama programs and as a means of combating American media imperialism.

This is fine, but there will be many hours of cable and satellite to be filled and for the first time religious groups in Europe, previously denied access to public service systems, will have the opportunity to buy time. Some, as indicated above, have already put their toe in the water. what success are they likely to have? How will the televangelist fare on European shores?

The Appeal of American Religious Fare in Britain

A comparison of the results of the Annenberg/Gallup investigation (1984) on audience ratings, profile, and declared interests and attitudes with similar findings about British audience reactions to religion and religious television shows a marked divergence. Ratings for British religious programs on the whole are higher than for their American counterparts, though this is in part due to differences in scheduling.

British audience attitudes to religion in particular are much more liberal and broader in scope than those for the televangelists. What is more, the aims of religious broadcasting in Britain have tended to reflect these declared attitudes.

Over the last 20 years, program policy for religious television has shifted. In 1960 the Pilkington Committee stated that the objectives of religious broadcasting are: First, to reflect the worship, thought, and actions of those Churches that represent the mainstream of the Christian tradition in Britain; second, to stress that which is most relevant in the Christian faith for the modern world; finally, to try to reach those outside the Churches. In 1977, the Central Religious Advisory Committee recommended to the Annan Committee that religious broadcasting's objectives were:

1. To seek to reflect the worship thought and action of the principal religious traditions represented in Britain, recognizing that those traditions are mainly, though not exclusively, Christian.
2. To seek to present viewers and listeners those beliefs, ideas, issues, and experiences in the contemporary world which are evidently related to a religious interpretation or dimension of life.
3. To seek also to meet the religious interests, concerns and needs of those on the fringe of, or outside, the organized life of the Churches.

So, within 20 years, the main thrust of religious broadcasting shifted. Churches became "traditions;" trying to reach those outside the Churches with its evangelistic overtones became "meeting religious interests." The Annan Committee was quite specific in its outlawing of those who are keen to use religion programs to proselytize: "If their religion lays a duty upon believers to proselytise, they must not use broadcasting to fulfil that duty. Religious broadcasting should not be the religious equivalent of party political broadcasts" (1977).

In practice, religious programs have tended to adopt a phenomenological approach. They try to show how religious belief is celebrated and affirmed, to explain its fundamental tenets, to show what its consequences are for the individual, and to indicate how the world and its problems appear when viewed through a religious lens. Unlike the American paid-time religious programs, therefore, religious programs in the United Kingdom have taken account of the liberal tradition and been reluctant to preach. It has nonetheless always been possible to have passionate advocacy of religious views and to propagate religious belief provided it is accepted that other denominations or faiths have the same right, and provided that there are opportunities for these beliefs to be challenged. On the whole, church services apart, the main thrust has been to provide religious programs of equal value to churchgoer and nonchurchgoer alike.

Historically, religious programs on ITV and BBC1 have always been scheduled on Sunday. This has to some extent determined the audience response. Each Sunday morning an act of worship is televised; the BBC tries to involve the viewer with a television liturgy designed to draw him or her in. ITV still provides a live transmission of a church service. An average audience for *Morning Worship* at 11 a.m. on ITV in the month of March 1988 was 926,000 viewers, the BBC1s *This is the Day* at 9:30 a.m., had an average of 318,000.

Each Sunday there is a serious religious program, usually a documentary. At 2 p.m. on ITV, *Encounter* transmitted in March against a soap opera *Eastenders* on BBC1, had an average audience of 961,000 viewers. The BBC's *Everyman* program at 10:30 p.m. on Sunday evening achieved a much better audience—averaging 2.5 million viewers.

The most popular religious television programs are both music-based and transmitted simultaneously on BBC1 and ITV at 6:40 p.m. on Sunday evening. ITV's *Highway* had an average audience on the Sundays in March 1988 of almost 8 million. BBC's *Songs of Praise* at the same time achieved an average audience of just over 6 million. Between them these 2 programs attract over 33 percent of the audience available at the time they are transmitted.

Channel 4, the independent second channel also provides an average of 1 hour of religious programs a week. The Channel's policy for religious programs has to take account of editorial policy for the Channel as a whole.

This is determined by the Broadcasting Act 1981 which requires Channel 4, a wholly owned subsidiary of the IBA, "to ensure that the programs contain a suitable proportion of matter calculated to appeal to tastes and interests not generally catered for by ITV," and "to encourage innovation and experiment in the form and content of programs, and generally to give the Fourth Channel a distinctive character of its own." As a result, some religious programs challenge the basis for religious belief, very often in the form of a personal view. Programs are devoted to the needs of some of the non-Christian faiths or the black Christian community. The staple diet of 5 years has been a "current affairs" style program examining the previous week's news from an ethical or spiritual angle. This is being replaced by a religious magazine format. There has also been a strong emphasis on the use of music and drama to communicate religious belief.

On the whole, Channel 4's religious programs are not transmitted on Sundays but Monday through Saturday and in accordance with overall scheduling policy for programs. Audiences for Channel 4 are considerably less than for ITV or BBC1 because it is catering for minority interests in many of the programs. In the period surveyed, religious programs attracted an average of 684,000 viewers.

Now what are the preferences of audiences for existing religious programs and what is the general attitude of the public to religious matters? Approximately every 5 years, research has been carried out by the IBA into audiences for religious programs. In 1963, a survey was carried out for the BBC by Gallup (The Gallup Organization, 1963). It showed that women watched more services of worship than men, older people watched more than young people, and regular church goers were more interested than others.

In 1968 and 1978 two surveys were carried out by the IBA to investigate audience attitudes to religious television in relation to people's religious beliefs, worries, and problems (see Haldane, 1978). More recently, Gunter and Fazal (1984) and Gunter (1984) analyzed audiences for religious programs on BBC1 and ITV. The most recent research was carried out in 1987 for the IBA by Insight Social Research providing data about audience reactions to religious programs and their views about religious belief.

The 1968 survey showed that 40 percent of respondents deliberately turned on to watch a religious program and over half said they paid attention when a religious program was on. In the 1987 survey this had changed, only 7 percent had deliberately turned on. When questioned on the goals of religious programs, respondents' three most popular opinions were: to provide services for people who are unable to attend Church (47%), to make people stop and think (34%), and to link religion with everyday life (31%). The first two were endorsed in equal numbers by religious and nonreligious alike and the third mostly by religious people.

In 1978 a further survey was carried out for the IBA by Opinion Research Center (Gunter, 1978). It confirmed that religious programs appealed more to people with strong religious beliefs and that worship programs were used more often by lonely people.

In 1984 work by Gunter and Fazal from the IBA's research department showed that overall the audience for religious programs was more or less evenly balanced between men and women. The largest age group watching *Songs of Praise* and *Highway* was 55+. The latter attracted 40 percent of working class people whereas *Songs of Praise* audience was 40 percent professionals. One of the main findings was that viewers felt religious programs should show the church or religion being involved in tackling potential problems affecting ordinary people in their everyday lives. Gunter's survey in December 1984 revealed that religious programs were seen as likely to be most popular with churchgoers, the lonely, and those needing comfort. The 3 aims for religious programs endorsed by 90 percent of those surveyed were:

1. To help people understand the problems of those less fortunate than themselves.
2. To link religion with every day life.
3. To show how the Church today is actively tackling life's problems.

At a secondary level of importance, 80 percent endorsed as important aims: "To make people more understanding;" "to bring the Church to those who cannot get to church themselves;" "to make people stop and think about religious matters;" and "to bring God into the home."

In Svennevig's research, conducted in June 1987 (Svennevig, Haldane, Spiers, & Gunter, 1988) to establish attitudes to religion and religious programs, almost all the people interviewed were sympathetic to religion. They were prepared to consider its claims and accepted it had a possible role in society, particularly in coping with life's problems. Surprisingly a large number of the population (87%) believed in a supernatural being, and as people got older they appeared to become more religious, particularly those in the higher better-paid professions. Most British people still felt that religion had shaped their attitudes and behavior, even though this was not generally reflected in attendance at a place of worship. In their attitude to different religious groups people were extremely tolerant and felt they should all be reflected on television. They rated behavior to others higher than what you believed, in a list criteria defining what it meant to be religious. It is clear from this research that the British public still has implicit faith, still sees a role for religion in society, is tolerant and liberal in its attitudes to religion, but will have little to do with organized religion on Sunday!

When these characteristics and attitudes are compared with those for audiences who watch the paid-time religious television in the United States there are some similarities but marked differences. On the whole audiences for both tend to be older and female, though the ratio of men to women is higher than in the United States. In both cases, programs are likely to appeal to churchgoers. There, however, the similarities end.

Audiences for United Kingdom religious television are nearer the general television audience than are those for their American counterparts. In the latter, viewers are predominantly skilled or unskilled workers and below the average American in terms of education, intelligence, and income. English audiences contain a higher proportion of professional people normally because of the range of religious programs available. This is particularly the case with Channel 4's religious programs. In religious terms, the difference between the 2 audiences are striking. Whereas the U.S. paid-time religious program audiences are 92 percent Protestant and a narrow section of Protestantism at that, mainly from the South, Midwest, and rural areas, British religious television audiences are drawn from all religious groups and most geographical areas.

When the attitudes and expectations of viewers for both sets of religious programs are compared, the differences are almost as striking. The American audience does not think the Church should be concerned with social goals, only with evangelism and missionary activity. In contrast British audience wishes to be made to think about religion, to be shown how religious belief helps people to cope with life's difficulties and to make people more understanding of others. At a secondary level they accept that religious programs may be a substitute for church attendance, particularly for the elderly and housebound. In its religious beliefs the U.K. audience reflects a liberal tradition. Behavior to one's neighbor is rated higher than belief in God as a criterion for being religious. Church attendance is way down the list. Though people accept the Bible as true they are not literalists nor have they had a deep religious experience. In short the profile is of a tolerant, utilitarian, and liberal group. They expect religious television to reflect all religions, not just Christianity.

It is clear, then, when comparing audiences for paid-time religious television in the United States and for British religious programs that there are some parallels, but these are far outweighed by the differences in terms of the kind of people who watch and in their attitudes and expectations of religion and religious programs. The difference is due in part to the religious climate of the U.S. and Britain. In the former, churchgoing is practiced by 52 percent of the population whereas in the U.K. it is only 12 percent, although over the last 10 years Britain has moved progressively right in religion and politics. The fastest-growing religious groups are the house churches or Restoration Church and the black Pentecostal community. Denominational boundaries become increasingly irrelevant however, as the dividing lines are drawn more on theological criteria which cut across old boundaries.

Although Britain has become increasingly secular there are many survivals of folk religion. People on the whole still wish to have their babies baptized and be married and buried in church. Religion is still protected in state schools where it is required to be undenominational.

It must also be remembered that over the last 40 years, immigrants from former British colonies have brought their religion with them. There are now a million Hindus and a million Muslims in the U.K., 300,000 Jews, and 60,000 Sikhs. This is less than 5 percent of the total population, but over 30 percent of those claiming church membership. Hindus and Muslims are more numerous than nonconformists in Britain.

In summary, the prospects for British and European religion being subject to media imperialism seem remote. It is true that there is the possibility of a massive expansion in the number of channels available in Europe on cable and satellite, though indications are that it will not be significant before 1992. It is still regarded as a high risk venture. So, even if public service television as Europe has experienced it is deregulated, as in the U.S., it will be some time before the means of delivering programs is fully developed. A crucial factor influencing the growth of American and British religious groups' use of television will be whether government permits them to solicit funds on or off the air. The likelihood of this being permitted in Britain is extremely doubtful if policy for cable and the future commercial radio system is a guide. This means those religious groups with financial muscle will have the advantage. With the number of direct broadcast channels becoming available in the next 10 years it would not be impossible for a channel based on the CBN model to be established with general programming including religious television. So far, however, existing channels like Sky and Super Channel have not been able to attract sufficient advertising revenue to make a profit. And research by the IBA to establish audience preferences for DBS showed religion had very little appeal to a general audience.

On the basis of audience preferences, American-style religion is unlikely to appeal to a European audience culturally very different, and one which certainly in Britain is liberal in its outlook and averse to being preached at in any shape or form. When the last word is said it is program appeal that counts. Some words of Klaus van Hendrick from the Dutch television company NOS are instructive: "You have to accept and understand that your beliefs, your religious world, can only be spread to a larger audience when you understand their world as well" (Elvy, 1986).

REFERENCES

Annan Committee. (1977). *Report of the Committee on the Future of Broadcasting*. London: Her Majesty's Stationers Office (Official British Government publication).

British Home Office. (1987). *Radio: Choice & opportunity* (Government White Paper). London: Her Majesty's Stationers Office.

Elvy, P. (1986). *Buying time: The foundations of the electronic church*. Great Wakering, Essex: McCrimmons.

The Gallup Organization, Inc. (1963). *BBC audience survey*. London: The Gallup Organization, Inc.

Gunter, B. (1978). *Lonely people in the media (IBA Report)*. London: The Independent Broadcasting Authority.

Gunter, B. (1984). *Attitudes to Sunday evening religious broadcasts on television* (IBA Research Paper). London: The Independent Broadcasting Authority.

Gunter, B., & Fazal, K. (1984). *The audience and religious television* (IBA Research Paper). London: The Independent Broadcasting Authority.

Haldane, I. (1978). *Who and what is religious broadcasting for?* (IBA Report). London: The Independent Broadcasting Authority.

Independent Broadcasting Authority. (1988). *Television in the 1990s*. London: The Independent Broadcasting Authority.

Peacock, A. (1986). *Report on financing of the BBC*. London: Her Majesty's Stationers Office (Official British Government publication).

Peacock Committee. (1984). *The cable and broadcasting act*. London: Her Majesty's Stationers Office (Official British Government publication).

Pilkington Committee. (1960). *Report of the committee on broadcasting.* London: Her Majesty's Stationers Office (Official British Government publication).

Smith, A. (1980). *The geopolitics of information.* London: Faber and Faber.

Svennevig, M., Haldane, I., Spiers, S., & Gunter, B. (1988). *Attitudes to religion in the 1980s.* London: John Libby.

Varis, T. (1985). *The international flow of television programs.* Paris: UNESCO.

List of Contributors

Robert Abelman is associate professor of communication at Cleveland State University and board member of the National Council for Families and Television. In addition to being widely published in social and behavioral science journals, his research on religious broadcasting for Unda-USA, a Catholic-based organization interested in media issues, has been featured in such popular periodicals as *Newsweek, Psychology Today, Variety, Channels of Communication,* and *Playboy* as well as national radio and television.

Bruce Abrams is rabbi at the Temple Ner Tamid, Euclid, Ohio. He is the recipient of the Jack C. Skirball Award for Homiletics, the 1986 Cleveland Mayor's Award for Volunteerism for work with Project Hunger, and he has been recognized as one of "Cleveland's Most Interesting Persons" by *Cleveland Magazine.* He also serves on the board of contributing editors of the Cleveland *Plain Dealer* and writes regular columns on politics and religion.

Robert S. Alley is professor of humanities at the University of Richmond and chairperson of Area Studies. He has produced the PBS documentary "Television: For Better or Worse" (1976) and is the author of numerous books including *So Help Me God: Religion and The Presidency* (John Knox, 1972), *Television: Ethics For Hire* (Abingdon, 1977), and *The Supreme Court on Church and State* (Oxford University Press, 1988). He is coauthor with Horace Newcomb on *The Producer's Medium* (Oxford University Press, 1983).

Joe E. Barnhart, past president of the Southwest Division of the American Academy of Religion, is professor of philosophy at the University of North Texas in Denton. He has written numerous articles and books on religion, including *The Billy Graham Religion* (United Church Press, 1972), *The Study of Religion and Its Meaning,* (Mouton Publishers, 1977), *The Southern Baptist Holy War* (Texas Monthly Press, 1986) and, most recently, *Jim and Tammy: Charismatic Intrigue Inside PTL* (Prometheus Publishing, 1988).

Arthur C. Borden is president and chief executive officer of the Evangelical Council for Financial Accountability. He is a member of the Executive Committee of the National Association of Evangelicals. Mr. Borden has been awarded an Honorary Doctor of Laws from John Brown University, and was the 1988 recipient of Alumnus of the Year Award from the King's College.

Judith M. Buddenbaum is associate professor in the Department of Technical Journalism at Colorado State University. She has worked as a reporter-photographer covering lifestyles, religion, science, and education for *The Valley Times,* Beaverton, Oregon, written freelance magazine articles and conducted media research for The Lutheran World Federation, Geneva, Switzerland. Her research on religion and mass media has been published in *Journalism History, Journalism Quarterly,* and *Newspaper Research Journal.*

Julia Mitchell Corbett is associate professor of religious studies in the Philosophy Department at Ball State University. She is the author of *Through a Glass Darkly: Readings on the Concept of God* (Abingdon Press, 1989) and *Religion in America: An Academic Approach* (Prentice-Hall, 1989), as well as several articles and chapters on religion.

William F. Fore is visiting lecturer in communication at Yale University Divinity School, having served as executive director of the Communication Commission of the National Council of Churches for 25 years. He is president of the World Association for Christian Communication and cochair of the National Coalition Against Censorship. He is author of *Television and Religion: The Shaping of Faith, Values and Culture* (Augsburg Press, 1987) and, most recently, *Gospel, Culture and Media* (Friendship Press, 1990).

Razelle Frankl is associate professor of management in the School of Business Administration, Glassboro State College, where she teaches organizational behavior and human resources management. She is the author of *Televangelism: The Marketing of Popular Religion* (Southern Illinois University Press, 1987).

Larry Gross is professor of communication at the Annenberg School, University of Pennsylvania, where he conducts research on the content and effects of mass media, the structure and function of art worlds, and the communicative aspects of the arts. He is coeditor of *Image Ethics: The Moral Rights of Subjects of Photography, Film and Television* (Oxford University Press, 1988) and associate editor of the *International Encyclopedia of Communications* (Oxford University Press, 1989).

Jeffrey K. Hadden is professor of sociology at the University of Virginia and former president of the Society for the Scientific Study of Religion and the Association for the Sociology of Religion. He is the author of numerous books on religious broadcasting, including *Prime Time Preachers* (Addison-Wesley, 1981) and most recently, with Anson Shupe, *Televangelism: Power and Politics on God's Frontier* (Holt, 1988).

Carl F. H. Henry is recognized as a foremost author, educator, lecturer, and theologian. He has taught and lectured on college campuses throughout the United States and in countries on every continent, and has written or edited more than 40 books, including *Money For Ministry: Biblical Guidelines For Giving and Asking* (Victor Books, 1989).

Stewart M. Hoover is associate professor of communications at Temple University. He served on the research team of the Annenberg/Gallup Study of religious broadcasting, and was coauthor of the resultant report *Religion and Television* (1984). Dr. Hoover is also author of *Mass Media Religion: The Social Sources of the Electronic Church* (Sage, 1988). He has conducted research on religion and mass communication and the social and cultural impact of communication technology sponsored by the Lilly Endowment, UNESCO, and Intermedia.

Peter Horsfield is dean of the Uniting Church, Theological Hall and teaches in the United Faculty of Theology in Melbourne, Australia. He is a former chairperson of the Australian Churches Media Association. Dr. Horsfield is the author of *Religious television: The American Experience* (Longman, 1984) and *Taming of Television: A Parent's Guide to Children and Television* (Albatross, 1986), and editor of the quarterly journal *Australian Ministry*.

Paul Kurtz is professor of philosophy at the State University of New York at Buffalo. He is the editor of *Free Inquiry* magazine, which is published by the Council for Democratic and Secular Humanism, founding chairman of the Committee for the Scientific Investigation of the Paranormal, and copresident of the International Humanist and Ethical Union. Dr. Kurtz is author of *The Transcendental Temptation: A Critique of Religion and the Paranormal* (Prometheus, 1986), *Forbidden Fruit: The Ethics of Humanism* (Prometheus, 1988), *Eupraxophy: Living Without Religion* (Prometheus, 1989), among other books.

James S. Kurtzke is a writer and editor on legal, political, and social issues. He is currently director of public relations at Georgetown University Law Center, editor of *Res Ipsa Loquitur,* and a consultant to Podesta Associates. Mr. Kurtzke has previously worked as staff writer at People for the American Way and domestic policy issues advisor to former Vice President Walter F. Mondale.

William Martin is professor of sociology at Rice University and has written about religious radio and television for over 20 years. His articles have appeared in *Atlantic, Harper's, Esquire* and *Texas Monthly,* as well as in professional journals. His most recent work has been a study of the ministry of Billy Graham.

Kimberly A. Neuendorf is associate professor of communication at Cleveland State University. She was coprincipal investigator with Dr. Abelman on the Religion in Broadcasting (RIB) project, which conducted an extensive and widely published content analysis of religious broadcasting. Her other research interests include the uses of popular media (e.g., MTV, horror films, soaps) by consumers.

Gary R. Pettey is assistant professor of communication at Cleveland State University. His work on political communication has most recently been published in *Communication Research, Journalism Quarterly,* and as several chapters in Sidney Kraus' *Mass Communication and Political Informa-*

tion Processing (Erlbaum, 1990). Dr. Pettey is currently working on a mass media campaign as part of a multimillion dollar AIDS grant from NIDA. **Anthony T. Podesta** is president of Podesta Associates, Inc., a national policy consulting and public affairs firm, and founding president (1981–1987) of People For The American Way, a 275,000 member constitutional liberties organization. Mr. Podesta is a contributor to *Trust Your Children* (Neal-Schuman Publishers, 1988) and *Representative American Speeches, 1987–1989.* The authoritative *National Journal* featured him as the "New Right's Nemesis." He was also named to the 1987 Washington Power Elite List by *Dossier* magazine as "The Power Liberal" (Pat Buchanan was "The Power Conservative"). The Almanac of Presidential Politics lists him as one of the "Most Valuable Players" of the 1988 presidential campaign.

Quentin J. Schultze is professor of communication arts and sciences at Calvin College. He has published dozens of articles in religious periodicals and has authored over 30 scholarly articles in publications such as *Critical Studies in Mass Communication, Journal of Communication, Qualitative Sociology, Communication Research,* and *Journalism Quarterly.* His books include *Television: Manna From Hollywood?* (Zondervan Publishing, 1986) and *American Evangelicals and the Mass Media* (forthcoming).

Eric Shegog is chair of the BBC Regional Advisory for the North East, and is a member of its General Advisory Council. He oversees the religious broadcasting on ITV, Channel 4, and Independent Radio for Britain's Independent Broadcasting Authority.

Anson Shupe chairs the sociology-anthropology departments at Indiana University-Purdue University at Fort Wayne. He has authored and co-authored 15 books including *Moonies in America* (Sage, 1979), *The Mormon Corporate Empire* (Beacon, 1985), and *Televangelism: Power and Politics on God's Frontier* (Holt, 1988).

Donald E. Wildmon pastored in the United Methodist Church for 13 years before founding the National Federation for Decency (now the American Family Association) in 1977. He is a highly visible spokesperson for the religious right, having appeared on *Donahue, Nightline, The Today Show,* and *Good Morning America,* and has been featured in *TV Guide* and major news magazines. He is the author of *The Home Invaders* (Victor Books, 1985).

Robert Wuthnow is professor of sociology at Princeton University. He is the author of *The Consciousness Reformation* (University of California Press, 1976) and *The Restructuring of American Religion* (Princeton University Press, 1988), and has served on the research team of the Annenberg/Gallup Study of religious broadcasting.

Author Index

Subject Index

A

Abolitionist Movement, 199
Abortion, 200, 202
Activism, 131–132
Advertising, 80–81
Agnew, Spiro, 227
American Broadcasting Company, 251–257
American Family Association, *see* Wildmon
Ancillary ministries, 48–50
Ankerberg, John, 240
Annenberg-Gallup study of religious broadcasting, 26, 90, 94–96, 110ff, 135–136, 233–234, 297, 344
"Another Life," 46, 81, 122
Anti-War Movement, 227
Apartheid, 203
Arbitron Corporation, 110
Armstrong, Ben, 25, 47
Assemblies of God, 67, 189
Audience demographics, 27–29, 91–94, 99ff, 119–121
Audience saliencies, 67–69
Audience size, 24–25, 85, 320–321
  cable television and, 123–125
  ratings and, 110
  sources of error in measuring, 113ff
Audience, diversity of, 100
Audience, U.S.–U.K. comparisons, 344–350
Audiences in Britain, 344–348
Australian Broadcasting Control Board, 314
Australian Broadcasting Corporation, 313
Australian Broadcasting Tribunal, 314

B

Bakkers, The, 242, 249, 259
  Bakker, Jim, 15, 41, 99, 159–160, 162–164, 174, 178–179, 277
  Bakker, Tammy, 15, 159, 164, 174, 178
  "Heritage USA," 45, 179
  "Jim and Tammy Show," 242
  ministry, 159, 189–190, 249
  network, 163–164, 174

  "PTL Club," 45, 277
  scandal, 15, 17, 174, 178–181, 249
Bennett, James Gorden, 249
Bible
  Acts, 167, 170
  Corinthians, 167
  Deuteronomy, 161
  Ephesians, 289
  Ezra, 69
  Genesis, 147–148
  John, 160, 165, 289
  Luke, 167, 289
  Malachi, 166
  Mark, 167
  Matthew, 166, 167
  Peter, 181, 289
  Philippians, 161
  Proverbs, 161
  Revelation, 149
British Broadcasting Corporation, 336–337
British religious broadcasting, 345–347
Broadcasting Act of 1981 (U.K.), 346
Bryan, William Jennings, 199

C

Cable Act of 1984 (U.S.), 80
Cable and Broadcasting Act of 1984 (U.K.), 343
Cable Television, 29–30, 80–82, 173, 276, 342–344
Carson, Johnny, 203
Carter, Jimmy, 201, 227
Castelli, Jim, 211
Channel Four (U.K.), 346
Charismatic movement, 135, 159–162
Charlotte *Observer,* 45
Children's Television, 276
Children's viewing of religious television, 300–304
Christ, Jesus, 160, 165, 166, 202, 241–242, 244, 289
Christian Broadcasting Network (CBN), *see* Robertson, M.G.

362